Shakespeare Adaptations

Gravelot inv.   G. V.dr gucht Sculp

The Tempest; or, the Enchanted Island
Act 3

From the 12mo Dryden (vol. ii), 1735

Shakespeare Adaptations

The Tempest, The Mock Tempest, and King Lear. With an Introduction and Notes by Montague Summers

BENJAMIN BLOM

New York/London

First Published 1922, London, England
Reissued 1966, by Benjamin Blom, Inc., New York 10452
Library of Congress Catalog Card No. 65-27919

Printed in U.S.A. by
NOBLE OFFSET PRINTERS, INC.
NEW YORK 3, N. Y.

To

EDMUND GOSSE

A small and single recognition
of many and great kindnesses

Contents

Prefatory Note

THE three plays included in the present volume are here exactly given from the original editions: Davenant and Dryden's *The Tempest, or The Enchanted Island* from the quarto of 1670 (*The Term Catalogues,* Hilary (17 February) 1670); Duffett's *The Mock-Tempest: or The Enchanted Castle* (also termed *The New Tempest or The Enchanted Castle*) from the quarto of 1675 (*The Term Catalogues,* Hilary (15 February) 1675); and Nahum Tate's *The History of King Lear* from the quarto of 1681 (*The Term Catalogues,* Easter (May) 1681).

Of these, Davenant and Dryden's *The Tempest* has only once been reprinted, in the folio Dryden (Tonson, two volumes) of 1701. The version that appears in all the collected editions of Dryden, and which is given by Scott, and again by Saintsbury in his recension of Scott, is none other than the book of Thomas Shadwell's opera, *The Tempest, or The Inchanted Island,* first printed quarto 1674 (*The Term Catalogues,* Michaelmas (25 November) 1674). It must be particularly noted that in his Variorum *The Tempest,* Furness unwarily presents this libretto (in a mutilated state) for the Davenant and Dryden comedy, and, moreover, he most inaccurately heads this reprint (p. 389) " Dryden's Version." His unscholarly comments upon the text and banal treatment of the whole matter are entirely negligible, and, indeed, thoroughly mistaken and misleading. Shadwell's version was re-issued quarto 1676, 1690, 1695, 1701, and frequently during the eighteenth century. The edition of *The Tempest* (*price 8d.*) in the collection called " English Plays " (*Neatly & correctly printed, in small volumes fit for the pocket, & sold by* T. Johnson, *Bookseller in the* Hague), and advertised under Shakespeare's name, " altered by *Davenant & Dryden*," contains, it is true, more of the comedy than most editions supply, although even in this case Shadwell's elaborate scenic directions are freely interpolated throughout, and the text is very faulty, whole lines and speeches having been carelessly dropped.

Of the 1670 quarto of the Davenant and Dryden comedy there are two issues. The first can be distinguished by the following points, *viz.*, in the first issue the name at the end of the preface is spelt *Driden*, in the second issue *Dryden*. In the preface, *Davenant* in first issue, *D'avenant* in second. Page 2, line 32, *Vall's* in first issue, corrected to *Viall's* in second. Page 3, line 16, *sttar-board* in first issue, corrected to *star-board* in second. In the first issue the pagination of page 7 is mis-printed 5.

It would almost seem that the 1670 quarto can only have been most cursorily revised by Dryden, as many passages, which are manifestly blank verse, are printed as stark prose; *e.g.*, Prospero's speech " Dull thing, I say so ; " (p. 20 of this edition : 4to, p. 10) ; and again the beginning of Act III, " Excuse it not, *Miranda*," in which case the quarto (p. 21) haphazardly alternates, from speech to speech, between a pell-mell jumble of prose and verse. In these exceptional instances I have not hesitated to set as verse.

It is not impertinent here to notice a curious disposition of lines which may be found in other plays, *e.g.*, in Shadwell's *The Sullen Lovers*, 4to, 1668 ; and Etherege's *The Man of Mode ; or, Sir Fopling Flutter*, 4to, 1676 ; prose comedies, where the printed speeches are often cut up, as it were, into blank verse, although being pure prose they have neither the rhythm nor the scansion of poetry. This arrangement is varied, quite irregularly, with the normal setting of plain prose. So far as I know, no satisfactory explanation of these oddities has been yet suggested.

Thomas Duffett's burlesque *The Mock-Tempest ; or, The Enchanted Castle* has never been before reprinted. The quarto, 1675, is of excessive rarity.

It has not till now been recognized that of this quarto there are two issues which can be distinguished by the following points, *viz.*, in the first issue we have at the conclusion of Act IV a misprint (4to, p. 42, l. 5 ; of this edition, p. 158, l. 21), *The End of the Second Act,* corrected in the second issue to *The End of the Fourth Act.* In the first issue again, Act V, scene I (4to, p. 42, l. 26, and p. 43, l. 13 ; of this edition, p. 159, l. 12 and l. 34), Ariel's two echoes " Thou art the very Devil " and " Alas poor Codshead," are clean omitted ; whilst the last four words of Quakero's speech which begins, " Nay, but I will not . . ." are misprinted " as Poo Cod said," corrected in the second issue to " as Poor Cod said." In Act V, scene I (4to, p. 44, l. 15 ; of this edition, p. 161, l. 3), the first issue reads "followe'd," the second "follow'd " : in Act V, scene 2 (4to, p. 44, l. 27 ; of this edition, p. 161, l. 14), the first issue has " the sneer," the second " thee sneer " : in Act V, scene 2 (4to, p. 48, l. 11 ; of this edition, p. 165, l. 31), the first issue reads " that is to sayo be pacified," the second, " that is to say, be pacified." In " *The Scene of* Bridewell," Act V, 2, both issues read as speech-prefix (4to, p. 50, l. 17) to *As big as thy Thumb* (4to, p. 51, l. 1) " Foran," and to *By thy Beard and thy Wigg* " Faran." In Duffett's first draft of his burlesque Quakero was probably called by some name that closely resembled Ferdinand, the rôle in *The Tempest* which is parodied, and when our author rechristened the character he, no doubt, forgot to alter the speech-prefix in these two instances. Both issues of the quarto supply after the *Persons Represented* the list of nine errata.

Nahum Tate's *The History of King Lear* was reprinted quarto 1699 (price 1s.), and again in 1712. There are also a number of later eighteenth century reprints, but most of these must be described as worthless. Many verbal changes have crept in, and sometimes considerable passages (and these none of the least important) are found to have disappeared.

None of the pieces given in the present volume has before been edited. In each case very obvious misprints —*e.g.* of this edition, p. 212, 1. 32, "the poor old King bareheaded," where the quartos 1681 and 1699 read "the poor old King beheaded"—and turned letters are silently corrected. I have not, however, in any instance beyond these ventured to tamper with the spelling, although Duffett's vagaries in this direction will often seem unnecessarily erratic. Nevertheless, I am convinced that by accommodating authors to modern norms and fashions something even more valuable than old-time flavour and atmosphere is irretrievably lost.

It is once more my duty and my pleasure to express my most grateful thanks for the kindliest encouragement throughout, and continual help in dealing with many a difficult point to Mr. G. Thorn-Drury, K.C., our acknowledged authority on the Restoration period. He has again, with his wonted generosity, entrusted me with many a rare volume from his library. In particular did he lend me his fine copies of the Davenant and Dryden comedy *The Tempest*, quarto, 1670, and of that uncommonly scarce play *The Mock-Tempest*, quarto, 1675, a loan which materially facilitated my work upon these two difficult pieces.

As Mr. W. J. Lawrence was the first to elucidate in print the crux concerning *The Tempest* in its post-Restoration versions, so must all future workers, who have to discuss these alterations of Shakespeare, base their records upon his article *Did Thomas Shadwell write an Opera on "The Tempest"?* the scholarship of which is so ample and complete that it leaves nothing to be added thereto. In general with every writer on the theatre I am also deeply indebted to Mr. Lawrence's researches in many another direction, but I have yet further to make a personal and particular acknowledgement to our distinguished stage historian for much valuable information with which he has ungrudgingly furnished me.

The complicated story of the music to *The Tempest*, both as a comedy and as an opera, has been related in detail by Mr. W. Barclay Squire in " Purcell's Dramatic Music," *Sammelbände* of the International Music Society, vol. 5; and in his more recent article *The Music of Shadwell's " Tempest,"* " The Musical Quarterly," October, 1921.

The frontispiece to this edition has been taken from the Congreve collection of Dryden's Dramatic Works, six volumes with illustrations, 1735, re-issued in 1762. Although the text there given (volume II) is Shadwell's libretto, nevertheless the scene depicted, Act III, when Prospero charms Ferdinand from drawing his sword, is the same both in the comedy and in the opera.

It only remains to add that the portrait of Davenant upon the title-page is copied from the Frontispiece to the folio, 1673, which was kindly lent by Mr. G. Thorn-Drury for the purpose of reproduction.

Introduction

SHAKESPEARE, although he did not so exclusively dominate the Restoration stage with the same singular monopoly as he held the theatre of the nineteenth century—an exaggeration against which there are at the present moment notable signs of an intellectual reaction—was nevertheless well and amply represented in the reign of Charles II and the monarchs immediately succeeding.* For even if in order to demonstrate this we had not the Diary of Pepys supplemented by the record of Downes, *Roscius Anglicanus*, yet the intimate and judicious appreciation, the unbounded admiration of Shakespeare we find in the prefaces and essays of the greatest of all English critical writers, John Dryden, the constant allusions to, and apt quotations from, the plays, not merely *Hamlet, Macbeth, Othello*, but *The Merry Wives of Windsor, The Taming of the Shrew*, and *Love's Labour's Lost*, which we meet in the pages of such prolific authors as Edward Howard and D'Urfey, Winstanley and Ward, are sufficient evidence of the popularity of Shakespeare at that time and the close attention with which his works were generally being read.†

Indeed, it may be broadly affirmed that the reasonable and reasoning love of the seventeenth century for

* Cf. also at a little later date Pope's *Imitations of Horace* (1738), the First Epistle of the Second Book:
   " Shakespear (whom you and ev'ry Play-house bill
   Style the divine, the matchless, what you will.)"

† There has recently (1920) been published a work of wide research and great value, *Some Seventeenth Century Allusions to Shakespeare and his Works, Not Hitherto Collected*, compiled by G. Thorn-Drury, Esq., K.C.

Shakespeare hardly differed from the enthusiasm of the nineteenth century in degree, only the poets and play-goers of that day did not narrowly give their applause to Shakespeare alone, but were also equally familiar with the masterpieces of Ben Jonson, the great tragedies of Webster, the fifty brilliant dramas that conveniently go under the names of Beaumont and Fletcher.

Immediately upon the Restoration the remnant of the older actors who had survived the Commonwealth, Charles Hart, Michael Mohun, William Cartwright, John Lacy, Walter Clun, Nicholas Burt, Robert and William Shatterel, William Wintersell, Bateman, Baxter, and others of less note, joined themselves into a Company, and began to give public performances at the Red Bull, an unroofed Elizabethan playhouse, situated in John Street, Clerkenwell. Thus was formed the nucleus of the King's Company, which was definitely so con-stituted under the managership of Thomas Killigrew by an official document from the Lord Chamberlain dated 6 October 1660.* On Thursday, 8 November, the King's Company† opened at their new Vere Street theatre, which is described by Mr. W. J. Lawrence as " the last

---

* Charles II had two months previously given a Grant (21 August 1660) to Killigrew and Davenant, which empowered them to " Erect two Companies of Players," and by which they also enjoyed the fullest rights of censorship. This was contested by Sir Henry Herbert and considerable difficulty ensued.

† It would seem that for about a couple of months, September and October 1660, there was an amalgamation of Rhodes' Cockpit Company and the Red Bull actors. When Davenant formed his separate company (the agreement is dated 5 November 1660), Edward Kynaston, the young prentice who originally acted women's parts and was, according to Pepys, " the loveliest lady that ever I saw in my life," remained with Killigrew. On 7 January 1660-61, Kynaston was playing Epicoene at Vere Street.

constructed house of the Elizabethan order."* It was an oblong roofed building and stood in Gibbon's Tennis Court at Bear Yard, Vere Street, Clare Market. " There they continued for a year or two, and then removed to the Theatre Royal in Drury Lane, where they first made use of scenes, which had been a little before introduced upon the publick stage by Sir William D'Avenant, at the duke's old theatre in Lincoln's-inn-fields, but afterwards very much improved, with the addition of curious machines by Mr. Betterton at the New Theatre in Dorset Garden to the great expense and continual charge of the players."†

It should be noticed that, as Mr. W. J. Lawrence has pointed out in scholarly and exact detail, the first Drury Lane theatre which was burned down on Thursday, 25 January 1672, was never known as such during the nine years of its existence. It stood in Bridges Street and Russell Street, and both the first and second Theatre Royal are termed either The Theatre Royal in Covent Garden; or, mostly in legal nomenclature, the Theatre Royal in Bridges Street. In 1682 the second Theatre Royal is described in an official document as " in or neare Covent Garden commonly called the King's Playhouse." The term Drury Lane dates from about 1690, although for convenience theatrical historians often refer to the first Theatre Royal as the first Drury Lane theatre.

* Mr. Lawrence emphasizes the fact that " from first to last' scenery was never used at Vere Street " (*Elizabethan Playhouse*, II, p. 139). Indeed, the old Elizabethan title boards were still in use. In a revival of Daborne's *The Poor Man's Comfort*, 28 May 1661, the speaker of the Prologue is directed to " *Enter reading the Title*,
    " The *Poor Man's Comfort*, this Title some will say
    Is fitter for a *Pray'r-book* then a *Play*."
† J. Wright, *Historia Histrionica* (1699).

Among the repertory of the Red Bull were *Henry IV*, *The Merry Wives of Windsor*, and *Othello*. The last piece to be acted at this house on Wednesday, 7 November, was Fletcher's *Beggar's Bush*, and the following afternoon the new Vere Street theatre opened with *Henry IV*. No doubt the cast was that given by Downes: Henry IV, Wintersell;* Prince Hal, Burt; Hotspur, Hart; Falstaff, Cartwright; Poins, Shatterel. It proved a great favourite with Restoration audiences and is several times mentioned by Pepys, who judged it " a good play." On Monday, 31 December 1660, having bought the book in S. Paul's Churchyard he went to Vere Street, " the new Theatre," and saw it acted. " But my expectation being too great, it did not please me, as otherwise I believe it would; and my having a book, I believe did spoil it a little." On another occasion, seven years later (Saturday, 2 November 1667), he went to the Theatre Royal, Bridges Street, " and there saw ' Henry the Fourth ': and contrary to expectation was pleased in nothing more than in Cartwright's speaking of Falstaffe's † speech about ' What is Honour? ' "

On Friday, 9 November 1660, the second day of acting at Vere Street, *The Merry Wives of Windsor* was given. On Wednesday, 5 December following, Pepys, who saw

* Thirty years later the King was acted by Kynaston, who then excelled in this rôle. " There is a grave and rational majesty in Shakespeare's *Henry the Fourth*. . . . This true majesty Kynaston had so entire a command of, that when he whispered the following plain line to *Hotspur*
    ' Send us your prisoners, or you'll hear of it!'
he conveyed a more terrible menace in it than the loudest intemperance of voice could swell to" (Cibber, *Apology*, chap. V). Wintersall died in July 1679.

† Langbaine, speaking of Falstaff, tells us: " This part used to be played by Mr. Lacy, and never failed of applause."

this comedy, expresses himself as not at all satisfied with the acting: "the humours of the country gentleman and the French doctor very well done, but the rest very poorly, and Sir J. Falstaffe as bad as any." In all probability Cartwright was the Falstaff, but there is no record of the representatives of Shallow and Dr. Caius. On Wednesday, 25 September 1661, Pepys again saw *The Merry Wives* at Vere Street, "ill done"; whilst on Thursday, 15 August 1667, when it was acted at the Theatre Royal he notes it "did not please me at all, in no part of it."

Saturday, 8 December 1660, is a date of particular interest in the history of the English theatre, as on that day *The More of Venice* was acted at Vere Street, and it may well be that this was the occasion when the first English actress appeared. Unfortunately, although there is the strongest presumption, we are not able to speak with absolute certainty on this important point. However, it was at Vere Street on Thursday, 3 January 1661, that Pepys first "saw women come upon the stage" in *Beggar's Bush*. On Tuesday, the twentieth of the preceding November, he had witnessed a performance of the same comedy played entirely by a male cast. Within that six weeks then our first professional actress* made her appearance in the part of Desdemona. The rôle we know from Thomas Jordan's *A Prologue†‡ to introduce the first Woman that came to Act on the Stage in the Tragedy, call'd* The Moor of Venice:

* Mrs. Coleman, "a pleasant jolly woman," wife of Edward Coleman, sang in recitative Ianthe when the First Part of Davenant's *The Siege of Rhodes* was performed at Rutland House in 1656. She cannot, however, be claimed to have been the first English actress in any real sense of the term. In after years she was anxious to repudiate any connection with the theatre.

† First printed in *A Royal Arbor of Loyal Poesie Consisting of Poems and Songs. . . . Composed by Tho. J.* (1664).

" I come, unknown to any of the rest
To tell you news, I saw the Lady drest;
The Woman playes to day, mistake me not,
No Man in Gown, or Page in Petty-Coat;
A Woman to my knowledge, yet I cann't
(If I should dye) make Affidavit on't.
Do you not twitter Gentlemen? I know
You will be censuring, do't fairly though.
'Tis possible a vertuous woman may
Abhor all sorts of looseness, and yet play;
Play on the Stage, where all eyes are upon her,
Shall we count that a crime *France* calls an honour:
In other Kingdoms Husbands safely trust 'um,
The difference lies onely in the custom;
And let it be our custom I advise,
I'm sure this Custom's better then th'Excise,
And may procure us custom, hearts of flint
Will melt in passion when a woman's in't.
  But Gentlemen you that as judges sit
  In the Star-Chamber of the House the Pit;
Have modest thoughts of her; pray do not run
To give her visits when the Play is done,
With dam me, your most humble Servant Lady,
She knows these things as well as you it may be:
Not a bit there dear Gallants, she doth know
Her own deserts and your temptations too.
  But to the point, in this reforming age
  We have intents to civilize the Stage.
Our women are defective, and so siz'd
You'd think they were some of the Guard disguiz'd;
For (to speak truth) men act, that are between
Forty and fifty, Wenches of fifteen;
With bone so large, and nerve so incomplyant,
When you call *Desdemona*, enter Giant.
We shall purge every thing that is unclean,
Lascivious, scurrilous, impious or obscene;

And when we've put all things in this fair way
Barebones himself may come and see a Play."

The epilogue is equally pertinent.

> " *Epilogue.*
> And how d'ye like her, come what is't ye drive at,
> She's the same thing in publick as in private;
> As far from being what you call a Whore,
> As *Desdemona* injur'd by the Moor?
> Then he that censures her in such a case
> Hath a soul blacker than *Othello's* face:
>> But Ladies what think you, for if you tax
>> Her freedom with dishonour to your Sex,
> She means to act no more and this shall be
> No other Play but her own Tragedy;
> She will submit to none but your commands,
> And take Commission onely from your hands."

In his *Roscius Anglicanus* Downes supplies us with the following cast of *Othello* : Brabantio, Cartwright; Moor, Burt; Cassio, Hart; Iago, Mohun; Roderigo, Beeston; Desdemona, Mrs. Hughes; Emilia, Mrs. Rutter. Arguing from this it is often asserted that Mrs. Hughes was the actress for whom Jordan's prologue was written, and there is every probability such was the case. At the same time several points needing careful consideration arise in connection with the actors as here listed. It is demonstrably not in every particular the cast of *Othello* as first revived in the post-Restoration theatre. Walter Clun, who was murdered by footpads in a Tottenham Court lane on Tuesday night, 2 August 1664, originally played Iago, a rôle he made peculiarly his own. Clun, who in the reign of Charles I had been greatly applauded as a representative of female characters, in the summer of 1660 was acting at the Red Bull; and upon its formation he at once took a recognized position as a leading member of the King's

Company. It was not, of course, until after Clun's death that Michael Mohun succeeded to Iago. On Saturday, 6 February 1668-9, Pepys went to the Theatre Royal, and " did see ' The Moor of Venice ' : but ill acted in most parts; Mohun, which did a little surprise me, not acting Iago's part by much so well as Clun used to do ; nor another* Hart's, which was Cassio's ; nor, indeed, Burt doing the Moor's so well as I once thought he did." The writer of *An Egley Upon The Most Execrable Murther of Mr. Clun*† after praising his Bessus, Falstaff, Humorous Lieutenant, and other characters, exclaims as a climax :

"O! but *Iago*, when we think on thee,
Not to applaud thy vice of Flattery ;
Yet must that Part never in our thoughts dye,
Since thou didst Act, not mean that Subtilty."

Downes, moreover, informs us that Beeston did not come " into the Company 'till after they had begun in *Drury-Lane*," that is, the opening of the Theatre Royal, 7 May 1663 ; and there is some doubt whether Mrs. Rutter appeared on the stage until the same date. It must be borne in mind, however, that, as Mr. W. J. Lawrence has so usefully emphasized, " through sloven-

---

* This was Kynaston's understudy. On Saturday, 30 January, Kynaston appeared in *The Heiress*, a new play. The rôle, however, was " in abuse to Sir Charles Sedley," and on the following night the young actor was " exceedingly beaten with sticks by two or three that assaulted him, so as he is mightily bruised, and forced to keep his bed." Charles II was furious with Sedley, who denied in vain any complicity. Kynaston returned to the theatre on Monday, 8 February, when he acted the King of Tidore in *The Island Princess* " very well."

† Reprinted by Mr. Thorn-Drury in *A Little Ark containing Seventeenth-Century Verse* (1921).

liness of arrangement " the *Roscius Anglicanus*, which
was not published until 1708, " is positively honeycombed with error. It is the perspective of the thing
that is wholly wrong.   In other words, the events
related mostly took place, but seldom in the sequence
indicated."*   We know that Downes blundered badly
about so important a date as the opening of the Theatre
Royal, and we must not too confidently rely upon his
knowledge, which had to be obtained second hand,† of
the intimate workings of the King's Company, especially
in the earlier years of its existence.

It is not improbable that when Mrs. Hughes‡ played
Desdemona at Vere Street in December 1660, her
Emilia was a young actor. Something of an experiment
was being essayed, and however successful with the
town, for the first few weeks at any rate it would hardly
be possible to train and rehearse actresses for every
female rôle. As Cibber says: " Though . . . women
were not admitted to the stage till the return of King
Charles, yet it could not be so suddenly supplied with
them, but that there was still a necessity, for some
time, to put the handsomest young men into petticoats,

* *The Elizabethan Playhouse*, I, p. 193.

† " Having the Account from *Mr. Charles Booth*, sometimes
Book-keeper " at the Theatre Royal.

‡ Curll's assertion that Mrs. Norris was our first professional
actress is mere invention.   Davies, *Dramatic Miscellanies*, II,
p. 364, writes: " The first woman-actress was the grandmother
of Norris, commonly called Jubilee Dicky." There are two bad
errors here. Mrs. Norris was a member of Davenant's company,
and it was her son who was known as Jubilee Dicky from his
superlative performance in Farquhar's *The Constant Couple*
(1699). See the present editor's Mrs. Behn, I, p. 445. It has
been ineptly claimed that Mrs. Betterton was our first actress.
Bellchambers' suggestion of Mrs. Ann Marshall is also entirely
unwarranted.

which Kynaston* was then said to have worn with
success; particularly in the part of *Evadne,* in ' The
Maid's Tragedy,' which I have heard him speak of . . ."
(*Apology*, chapter v).

With reference to the fact that for a little while after
the appearance of actresses " heroines of the stage were
still occasionally impersonated by men," Dutton Cook
in his *A Book of the Play*, chapter xvi, " Her First
Appearance," gives so unfortunate and inapposite an
example that it must not stand without correction. He
cites the appearance of Kynaston as Epicœne in Ben
Jonson's comedy of that name. But the whole point of
the play turns upon the fact that Epicœne is a lad
disguised as a woman, and the climax is the discovery
of his real sex. Says Pepys, who saw the piece on
Monday, 7 January 1660-1: " It is an excellent play.
Among other things here, Kinaston, the boy, had the
good turn to appear in three shapes: first, as a poor
woman in ordinary clothes, to please Morose; then, in
fine clothes, as a gallant, and in them was clearly the
prettiest woman in the whole house, and lastly, as a
man; and then likewise did appear the handsomest man
in the house." It is true that Downes gives a cast of
Epicœne with Kynaston as Dauphine and Mrs. Knepp as
Epicœne. But it is incomprehensible why the title-rôle
should have been assigned to a woman. The *dénouement*
can but have fallen absolutely flat. Yet we find that
throughout the eighteenth century Mrs. Oldfield, Mrs.
Pritchard, and other actresses made the same silly
mistake of attempting this part. When, under Garrick's

* On Saturday, 18 August 1660, Pepys saw *The Loyal Subject.*
Kynaston acted Olympia, and " made the loveliest lady that
ever I saw in my life." It is interesting to notice that in this
drama a lad, young Archas, is until the Fifth Act disguised as
a girl, Alinda.

In *The Maid's Tragedy* the great Evadne of Restoration days
was Rebecca Marshall.

auspices, *Epicœne*, with some re-arrangement and a few alterations by Colman, was revived at Drury Lane, 13 January 1776, Mrs. Siddons was cast for the title-rôle, which she played thrice, 13, 15, and 17 January. On the twenty-third it was wisely given to Lamash, an elegant young actor of rising merit.* But the mischief had been done. As Gifford well writes: " This comedy . . . failed of success from a singular circumstance: the managers most injudiciously gave the part of Epicœne to a woman; so that when she threw off her female attire in the last act, and appeared as a boy, the whole cunning of the scene was lost, and the audience felt themselves rather trifled with than surprised. Garrick was immediately sensible of his error and attempted to remedy it by a different cast of the parts; but it was too late." It is incredible that in the face of this lesson when Jonson's play was acted at Covent Garden, 26 April 1784, for Edwin's benefit, Mrs. Bates undertook Epicœne. The result was as might have been foretold.

It would appear that some years before his retirement from the stage, which event took place early in 1678, Burt † resigned the part of Othello to Charles Hart. The following cast‡ is probably that of *Othello* as acted at the second Theatre Royal, which opened 26 March,

* Lamash was the original Trip in *The School for Scandal*, Drury Lane, 8 May 1777; and the Justice's Son in *The Critic*, 30 October 1779.

† Burt may have died in the spring of 1678. The last rôle in which his name can be traced is Maldrin in Edward Howard's *The Man of Newmarket* (4to, 1678), which was produced in February-March 1678, and licensed for printing, 13 April, though not in Term Catalogues until 6 December.

‡ In the British Museum copy of the 1695 quarto, a contemporary hand has recorded that *Othello* was acted at the Theatre Royal, " 21 May, Fryday, 1703." Othello, Batterton; Cassio, Powell; Iago, Verbruggen; Roderigo, Pack; Desdemona, Mrs. Bracegirdle; Emilia, Mrs. Lee.

1674: Duke of Venice, Lydal; Brabantio, Cartwright; Gratiano, Griffin; Lodovico, Will Harris; Othello, Hart; Iago, " Standard-bearer to the Moor; a Villain," Mohun; Cassio, Kynaston; Roderigo, " a foolish Gentleman that follows the Moor in hopes to Cuckold him," Beeston; Montano, Watson; Clown, Joe Haines; Desdemona, Mrs. Cox; Emilia, Mrs. Rutter; Bianca, Mrs. James; Downes, Cibber, and other writers extol the supreme greatness and grandeur of Hart as the Moor.

In *Julius Caesar*, which was produced at the first Theatre Royal, Hart won equal renown. Mohun played Cassius to his Brutus, in which rôles the two friends, " our Aesopus and Roscius," as Rymer calls them, were considered by the critics of the day to be inimitable, and have never, if we may believe theatrical annals, been approached, much less surpassed. Kynaston acted Mark Antony, Mrs. Marshall, Calphurnia, and Mrs. Corbet, Portia.

A Midsummer-Night's Dream was produced at Vere Street in September 1662, but although some good dancing was introduced as a special attraction it does not appear that the play drew the town. Downes chronicles an early revival of *Titus Andronicus* in which, as Genest suggests, Tamora was probably acted by Mrs. Marshall.

In November 1663, as we know from Sir Henry Herbert's accounts, *The Taming of the Shrew* was revived by Killigrew. It will be noticed that the King's Company played Shakespeare without adaptation, indeed the only Shakespearean alteration given at the Theatre Royal seems to have been Lacy's *Sauny the Scot*, a version of this comedy, which was produced Easter Tuesday, 9 April 1667. *Sauny the Scot* is a good bustling farce. The dialogue of the original is shortened and converted into prose throughout; the Induction is wholly omitted;* the fifth act, which is entirely new, has taken something more than a hint from that excellent comedy, *The Woman's Prize*; the scene is changed from Padua to London; and Sauny,† " Petruchio's Scotch Footman," makes a considerable character. Pepys, who was present at the first performance, remarks: " the best part ' Sawny,' done by Lacy,‡ hath not half its life, by reason of the words, I suppose, not being understood, at least by me." Maidment and Logan, who ought to speak with authority on the point, say that " the language of Sauny . . . is not Scotch in its idiom or apparent pronunciation, but savours strongly of the meridian of Doncaster, Lacy's birthplace."

It should be remarked that, so far as is recorded, during the twenty years which directly followed the Restoration the plays of Shakespeare performed at Vere Street and the Theatre Royal were, with the single exception of *Sauny the Scot*, given as originally written, whilst in that same period Davenant's company produced no fewer than nine known alterations and adaptations. Such a record cannot be the result of mere chance or accident, and the fact that the King's House

---

* In the Prologue to Ravenscroft's *The London Cuckolds*, produced at the Duke's Theatre in the winter of 1681, Christopher Sly is alluded to, a reference which must have been well-known to the audience. Perhaps the original *The Taming of the Shrew*, with the Induction, had again been recently performed.

† Perhaps suggested by Sander in *The Taming of A Shrew*.

‡ Wheatley, who is doubtless correct, says that Sauny is the Scotch figure in Michael Wright's picture of Lacy in three rôles, done upon one canvas. This painting is now at Hampton Court. Langbaine and Aubrey, who have been often followed, state that this figure is Teague in *The Committee*. But see Evelyn, 3 October 1662.

played Shakespeare without tamperings and trimmings I incline to attribute to the influence and judgement of Charles Hart,* who was (if one may hazard an opinion not unduly speculative) the greatest and most sublime actor who has ever graced any stage. My attention has been drawn by Mr. Thorn-Drury to certain lines in a lampoon " *To Mr.* Julian,"† whence it would appear that, temporarily, Shakespeare was not popular in the theatre :

> " None that come within the Verge of Sense,
> Have to Preferment now the least pretence.
> Nay Poets, guilty of that Treason prov'd,
> Are by a general Hiss from Court remov'd.
> *Shakespear* himself reviv'd, finds no success,
> And living Authors sure must hope for less."

This pasquil may be dated *circa* 1680, about which time Hart,‡ " by reason of his malady ; being afflicted with the Stone and Gravel," had already begun to make far less frequent appearances than formerly, whilst, as Cibber tells us, the younger actors, especially Cardell Goodman and Clark, were impatient to divide his characters between them, leaving inferior rôles to newcomers such as Saunders, Disney, Perin, and Coysh. Mohun also, cruelly crippled with gout, was on the eve of retirement.‖ It was not likely that audiences who

* Hart's relationship to Shakespeare is often asserted, but no proof is forthcoming.

† *Poems on Affairs of State*, vol. III (1704), p. 141.

‡ Hart died Thursday, 18 August 1683. See " An Elegy On that Worthy and Famous Actor, Mr. Charles Hart," reprinted in *A Little Ark*.

‖ Mohun's name does not appear after the Union in November 1682. He created Burleigh in Banks' *The Unhappy Favourite* at the Theatre Royal in the autumn of 1681, and his last recorded original part (perhaps his last appearance) was Ismael in Southerne's *The Loyal Brother*, produced in the spring of 1682.

had applauded Hart as Othello and Brutus would accept Clark in these parts. The stage languished, and for a while the Theatre Royal played even Shakespeare to empty houses.

When Sir William Davenant formed from Rhodes' Cockpit players his new company which began to act at Salisbury Court (a quasi-Elizabethan roofed theatre erected on the site of the old granary of Dorset House, near Fleet Street), on 15 November 1660, a curious regulation was shortly made by which certain plays were assigned to him as his own particular property. Amongst these the following by Shakespeare were named: *The Tempest, Measure for Measure, Much Ado about Nothing, Romeo and Juliet, Twelfth Night, Henry VIII, King Lear, Macbeth, Hamlet,* and for two months from the date of the permission, *Pericles.* These he proposed " to reform and make fitt for the Company of Actors appointed under his direction and command." With such material Davenant soon set to work and before long produced *The Law Against Lovers*, the sorriest amalgamation of *Measure for Measure* and *Much Ado about Nothing.* Benedick has become brother to Angelo, and Beatrice, a relative of Claudio's Juliet, owns a sister Viola, " very young " and very impertinent, who enters " dancing a saraband, awhile with castanietos." Pepys, who saw *The Law Against Lovers* on Tuesday, 18 February 1661-2, thought it "a good play and well performed, especially the little girl's (whom I never saw act before) dancing and singing."

Downes notes that Betterton was " highly applauded" as Pericles. This play had been produced at the Cockpit under Rhodes' management.

He died in the first week of October 1684. The register of S. Giles in the Fields records the burial of " Mr. Michael Moon of Brownlow Street, 11 October 1684."

Late in June* 1661, Davenant's company opened their newly-built theatre, the Duke's House, situated on Lisle's tennis-court, which extended from the back of Portugal Row, on the south side of Lincoln's Inn Fields, to Portugal Street. It was a small and inconvenient theatre, yet it was here that scenery first came into public and regular use. In the words of Mr. W. J. Lawrence: " The picture-stage era undoubtedly began with the opening of the new Duke's Theatre in Lincoln's Inn Fields late in June, 1661, when *The Siege of Rhodes* was revived."†

The first Shakespearean play to be given on the picture-stage was *Hamlet*. " The Tragedy of *Hamlet, Hamlet* being performed by Mr. *Betterton*: *Sir William* (having seen Mr. *Taylor*, of the *Black-Fryars* Company act it; who being instructed by the Author Mr. *Shakespear*) taught Mr. *Betterton* in every particle of it, gain'd him esteem and reputation superlative to all other plays. *Horatio* by Mr. *Harris*; the *King* by Mr. *Lilliston*; the *Ghost* by Mr. *Richards*; (after by Mr. *Medburn*.) *Polonius* by Mr. *Lovel*; *Rosencrans* by Mr. *Dixon*; *Guilderstern* by Mr. *Price*; 1st Gravemaker by Mr. *Underhill*; the 2d. by Mr. *Dacres*; the *Queen* by Mrs. *Davenport*; *Ophelia* by Mrs. *Saunderson*: No succeeding Tragedy for several years got more reputation or money to the Company than this."‡ Hamlet was one of Betterton's greatest rôles. Pepys, Saturday, 24 August 1661, writes: " Straight to the Opera [the Duke's House] and there saw 'Hamlet, Prince of Denmark,' done with scenes very well, but above all Betterton did the prince's part beyond imagination." Cibber, Steele, Rowe, Anthony Aston write with an admiration that is almost

* The day of the month is unfortunately not known.
† *The Elizabethan Playhouse*, II, p. 138.
‡ *Rosc.us Anglicanus*.

lyric of Betterton's performance. Hamlet was probably this great actor's masterpiece. He played it on Tuesday, 20 September 1709, and though he was then nearly seventy-five years old, the audience saw " the force of action in perfection." Nokes presently succeeded Lovel as Polonius, and Mrs. Ann Shadwell followed Mrs. Davenport as Gertrude. It may be mentioned that the quarto *Hamlet* of 1676 is especially interesting for *This Play being too long to be conveniently Acted, such places as might be least prejudicial to the Plot or Sense, are left out upon the Stage : but that we may no way wrong the incomparable Author, are here inserted according to the Original Copy with this Mark ".*

On Wednesday, 11 September 1661, *Twelfth Night* was revived before a brilliant audience which included the King. It " had mighty success by its well performance." Betterton played Sir Toby; Henry Harris, Aguecheek; Cave Underhill, Feste; Lovel, Malvolio; and Ann Gibbs,* Olivia. " All the Parts being justly acted crown'd the Play." Downes notes that *It was got up on purpose to be acted on Twelfth Night,* and as Pepys saw it on 6 January 1662-3, " acted well, though it be but a silly play, and not related at all to the name or day," this is doubtless the occasion to which our theatrical chronicler refers.

Romeo and Juliet was produced at Lincoln's Inn Fields on Saturday, 1 March 1661-2. Pepys, who was present, liked it even worse than *Twelfth Night,* but one must remember that just after his midday dinner the diarist had had a sharp quarrel with his uncle Thomas, " a close cunning fellow," who was giving trouble about an annuity, and the day before he had been considerably vexed by his boy whom he soundly thrashed for laziness and general insubordination. Moreover, the actors were

* She married Shadwell the poet.

anything but word perfect, and the prompter was continually in request. Nevertheless it was a very strong cast. Henry Harris, a prime favourite with the King and the Duke of York—two excellent judges of acting—and who was being " cried up " by the town even above Betterton, played Romeo, and one cannot believe that this graceful and handsome young fellow, whose dressing-room was the rendezvous of half the wits and gallants in the town, could be ineffective as the ardent Italian amoroso. Mrs. Saunderson was Juliet, and Betterton, Mercutio. The serving men, Sampson and Gregory, fell to the lot of Samuel Sandford and Cave Underhill, each of whom was possessed of a fund of dry caustic humour. Friar Laurence was acted by Richards.

A few years later, a son of the Earl of Berkshire, the Hon. James Howard, a dramatist of some repute in his day,* turned *Romeo and Juliet* into a tragi-comedy, and at the end of the fifth act rescued both lovers, to marry, we may presume, and to live happily ever after.† By a curious arrangement " when the Tragedy was reviv'd again 'twas play'd alternately, tragically one day, and tragicomical another, for several days together." Howard's alteration has not been printed, but it must have been in this version that the character of Count

* His two comedies, *The English Monsieur* (seen by Pepys, 8 December 1666) and *All Mistaken* (Pepys, 20 September 1667), Theatre Royal plays, were very popular. In each of these Hart and Nell Gwyn had original parts. *The English Monsieur* is parodied in *The Rehearsal*. *All Mistaken* was acted before Charles II at Trinity College, Cambridge, in 1667. The comic scenes, sometimes of a Rabelaisian humour, are undeniably amusing.

† Otway incorporated much of *Romeo and Juliet* in his *History and Fall of Caius Marius*, produced at the Duke's House in the autumn of 1679.

Paris' Wife appeared.* This rôle was acted by Mrs. Holden, concerning whom Downes tells an anecdote, which although it " put the House into such a laughter, that London-Bridge at low-water was silent to it " is now unquotable.

In November 1663, Sir Henry Herbert, in his accounts, notes a payment of one pound for a " Revived Play. Mackbethe," and this date is accordingly to be fixed as that of the earliest revival of Shakespeare's great tragedy upon the post-Restoration stage. It must not for a moment be supposed, as is often believed to be the case, that Davenant was by any means the first to interpolate and otherwise tamper with *Macbeth*.† The 1623 Folio, our sole authority for the text, definitely indicates that alterations had crept in even during Shakespeare's own lifetime, or at any rate immediately after his death. Two songs were already introduced from *The Witch*. These Davenant in his version retained, with the addition of a concerted piece by the witches, " Speak, sister, speak," and a second song, " Let's have a dance upon the heath," which both occur in a new scene written to round off Act II, a meeting between Macduff and his wife (a part which has been extensively

* It is impossible satisfactorily to disentangle Downes' narrative. He writes: " There being a Fight and Scuffle in this Play between the House of *Capulet*, and House of *Paris*. . . ." It is mere guess-work to suppose that Mrs. Holden acted Lady Capulet in Shakespeare's tragedy. (Query: In this case could Downes' jest refer to I, 3, l. 71 ?). One must assume that Mrs. Holden played in the Howard version, concerning which, as we know nothing beyond the above, it is idle to speculate.

† The Davenant *Macbeth* was printed in 1673. The student should be warned against the blunders and absurdities of the Introduction to *Macbeth* in the Maidment and Logan *Davenant*, Vol. V. See W. J. Lawrence: " Who wrote the Famous ' Macbeth ' Music ? " *The Elizabethan Playhouse*, I, p. 209.

" written up ") and the weird women, who foretell doom in riddling rhymes much in the same way as they had once prophesied to Banquo and Macbeth. Betterton excelled as Macbeth, whilst " it is related of Mrs. Betterton that though *Lady Macbeth* has been frequently well performed, no actress, not even Mrs. Barry, could in the smallest degree be compared to her." * William Smith played Banquo, but curiously enough Sandford appeared as Banquo's ghost. As Smith was a remarkably handsome, tall, and lusty young fellow, whilst Samuel Sandford is described as " diminutive and mean (being Round-shoulder'd, Meagre-fac'd, Spindle-shank'd, Splay-footed, with a sour Countenance and long lean Arms)†" the contrast must have been of remarkable effect. Macduff was Henry Harris, and his Lady, Mrs. Long.‡ *Macbeth* long remained a stock piece at the Duke's House, rivalling *Hamlet* in popularity. It was, perhaps, the most frequently seen of Shakespeare's tragedies. Davenant's elaborations, the " machines, as flyings for the witches, with all the singing and dancing " were somewhat broadly parodied by Duffett in the burlesque Epilogue to his farce *The Empress of Morocco*,§ produced at the King's House in the spring of 1674.

On Thursday, 10 December 1663, Pepys, calling at Wotton the shoemaker's, hears news " of a rare play to be acted this week of Sir William Davenant's: the story of Henry the Eighth with all his wives." It does not appear that Davenant made an alteration in

---

* C. Dibdin, *Complete History of the English Stage* (8vo, 1800).

† Anthony Aston, *Brief Supplement to Colley Cibber, esq.* (8vo, 1747?).

‡ This famous actress was mistress to the Duke of Richmond.

§ Settle's tragedy was produced at the Duke's House in the winter of 1673. Late in 1673 or in the early months of the following year there seems to have been a special revival of *Macbeth* at the same theatre.

Shakespeare and Fletcher's scenes, and by " of Sir William Davenant's " is meant no more than that the play was to be performed by Davenant's company. The smart touch about " all his wives " is doubtless a mere bit of irresponsible and imaginative gossip. It is just worth while mentioning these details, as some writers have needlessly postulated a version of *Henry VIII* by Davenant.*

In the third week of December, 1663, *Henry VIII* was produced at the Duke's House with such splendour and show that the theatre was repeatedly crowded, and the magnificence of the production became a theatrical tradition. So in *The Rehearsal* (Theatre Royal, 7 December 1672) Bayes speaks of the dance of " the Angels in *Harry* the Eight," and when describing the tableau he has arranged for his drama he cries: " I'll justifie it to be as grand to the eye every whit, I gad, as that great Scene in Harry the Eight, and grander too, I gad; for instead of two Bishops I bring in here four Cardinals." And fourteen years later† in Mrs. Behn's *The Lucky Chance*, Bredwel has a jest about " a broken six-penny Looking-Glass, that shew'd as many Faces as the Scene in *Henry* the Eigth." In this scene of the procession and assisting crowds a great many faces and figures at windows and on balconies were, curiously enough, actually painted upon the " releive " back-cloth and wings. So panoramic an effect, mixed with the actors upon the stage, must have been something extraordinary, but the hint, at any rate, was by no means a complete novelty. In John Webb's designs for the scenery of *The Siege of Rhodes*‡ we have a shutter scene,

* *E.g.* Frederick Hawkins: " ' Henry VIII ' on the Stage." *English Illustrated Magazine*, January 1892.

† Even if this reference is to a recent revival of *Henry VIII* the point remains the same.

‡ *Burlington Magazine*, CXXXIV, Vol. XXV (May 1914).

Act I, scene 1, a view of Rhodes with the Turkish fleet under full sail making towards the city. Act II, scene 1, " The Towne beseiged," is again a shutter which formed the back scene throughout the second act. Here we see an encampment of the Turkish army, with its artillery delivering a cannonade, whilst out in the bay a block-ading force is manœuvring. Act IV, scene 1, shows us Mount Philermos and the plain beneath on which the Turkish battalias are marshalled. Act V, scene 1, a shutter, represents the city being stormed. Troops are advancing in thousands, scaling-ladders are being fixed in position, the Knights are stubbornly defending their walls.

Downes has given us an ample account of the revival of *Henry VIII*. " This Play, by order of *Sir William Davenant*, was all new cloathed in proper habits: The King's was new, and all the Lords, the Cardinals, the Bishops, the Doctors, Proctors, Lawyers, Tipstaves, new Scenes: The Part of the King was so right and justly done by Mr. *Betterton* he being instructed in it by Sir William, who had it from Old Mr. *Lowen*, that had his instructions from Mr. *Shakespear* himself, that I dare and will aver, none can, or ever will come near him in this age, in the performance of that part: Mr. *Harris's* performance of Cardinal *Wolsey** was little inferior to that, he doing it with such just state, port, and mein, that I dare affirm none hitherto has equalled him.

" The Duke of *Buckingham* by Mr. *Smith*; *Norfolk* by Mr. *Nokes*; *Suffolk* by Mr. *Lilliston*; Cardinal *Campeius*

---

* There is a picture by Greenhill of Henry Harris as Cardinal Wolsey from which a fine mezzotint has been engraved. The robes are theatrically effective, but, as might be expected, very inaccurate. In Rowe's *Shakespeare* (1709) the illustration to Henry VIII shows us the King and the Cardinal in traditional attire, whilst the attendant lords wear the costume of Queen Anne's reign, full periwigs, heavy coats, and square-toed shoes.

and *Cranmer* by Mr. *Medburn*; Bishop *Gardiner* by M [r.] *Underhill*; Earl of *Surrey* by Mr. *Young*; Lord *Sands* by Mr. *Price*; Mrs. *Betterton*, Queen *Catherine*: Every Part, by the great care of Sir *William*, being exactly perform'd; it being all new cloath'd and new scenes; it continued acting 15 days together with general applause." The popularity and magnificence, however, of *Henry VIII* were considerably diminished by the production at the King's Theatre early in January 1663-4 of Howard and Dryden's *The Indian Queen* with Ann Marshall as Zempoalla. The pomp of the Tudor court waned before the blazing splendours of Mexico and Peru.

The Rivals, Davenant's adaptation of Shakespeare and Fletcher's *The Two Noble Kinsmen*, which was seen by Pepys at the Duke's House, on Saturday, 10 September 1664, met with striking success. This was probably in no small measure due to the excellent cast, and the diarist notes that there was "good acting in it." Especially does he commend Betterton and his wife and Henry Harris. Downes also singles out Underhill, who played Cunopes, the provost's man, and adds: "all the Women's Parts admirably acted." According to the quarto of 1668, Mrs. Shadwell appeared as Heraclia, Mrs. Davis, Celania; Mrs. Long, Leucippe. It was in this play that Mrs. Davis sang, "My lodging it is on the cold ground," which she performed "so charmingly that not long after it raised her from her bed on the cold ground to a bed royal." But on 11 January 1668, Mrs. Knepp, gossiping with Pepys, told him how Moll Davis "is for certain going away from the Duke's house, the King being in love with her; and a house is taken for her and furnishing; and she hath a ring given her already worth £600." A simple explanation is that Mrs. Betterton originally played Celania, but that this rôle was taken by Moll Davis in a revival of Davenant's play during the winter of 1667, and it was then that she attracted Charles' notice.

It is obvious from even the most superficial consideration of the detailed accounts we are thus able to collect from Pepys and the *Roscius Anglicanus* regarding the production of Shakespeare's plays during the first few years of the actual reign of Charles II that in the Restoration theatre Shakespeare was not only frequently acted, but proved exceptionally popular. We must further take into consideration the indubitable fact that, of several revivals, no record at all has reached us. Nor, unless there exist evidence to that effect, can it be argued from the production of some alteration or sophistication of any one of Shakespeare's plays that the original had not been performed of recent years. For example, it were quite untenable to maintain that because D'Urfey's *The Injured Princess, or the Fatal Wager*, produced at the Theatre Royal in the spring of 1682, is a mere re-writing of *Cymbeline*, *Cymbeline* itself had never been seen by a Restoration audience. We know that *The Taming of the Shrew* was revived at the Theatre Royal in 1663, and yet at the same house a little more than three years later appeared Lacy's adaptation, *Sauny the Scot*. In the summer of 1685 at the Theatre Royal was played D'Urfey's *A Commonwealth of Women*, which is largely borrowed from *The Sea Voyage*. Fletcher's drama was being acted at the same house in 1668, and probably later. In the spring of 1691 *Bussy D'Ambois*, a version of Chapman's tragedy by D'Urfey, was given at the Theatre Royal. Yet Bussy had been one of the favourite rôles of Hart, who had very frequently played it until his retirement some ten years before.

Of all Shakespeare's plays there appears to have been none which was revived more often, and which ever drew more crowded houses than *The Tempest*, or, to speak more precisely, that adaptation of *The Tempest* which has so complicated and curious a theatrical history.

By the regulation of December 1660, *The Tempest* had been assigned as the peculiar property of Davenant's company, and in conjunction with Dryden, whom he called in to assist him, Davenant prepared a version of *The Tempest*, which, after considerable delay, was brought out, as a comedy, at the Duke's House, Lincoln's Inn Fields, on Thursday, 7 November 1667.

It must here be strongly emphasized that in spite of the obstinate insistence of such editors as Dryden has met with and of those other critics who still continue to attribute the alterations almost wholly to Dryden and who, indeed, often ignoring Davenant altogether, speak of Dryden's *Tempest*, it is to Davenant we owe this version of 1667, and Dryden's actual share in the work seems to have been of the smallest. The mistake, so long and steadfastly perpetuated, arose owing to the fact that Davenant died 7 April 1668, and when this version of *The Tempest* was printed quarto 1670, no author's name appeared upon the title-page, but the comedy was introduced by a preface, dated 1 December 1669, and signed John Dryden. Here, Dryden is at some pains to tell us that the character of Hippolito is entirely due to Davenant: " *The Comical parts of the Saylors were also his invention and for the most part his writing.*" Furthermore, upon Davenant's death, the play remained the property of his widow, who, in conjunction with her son, at once assumed control of the theatre.

On or about 30 April 1674, there was produced at Dorset Gardens an opera by Shadwell which was based entirely upon the Davenant-Dryden version of *The*

Tempest. It is thus noticed by Downes :* " *The Tempest,* or *Inchanted Island*;, made into an Opera by Mr. Shadwell: having all new in it; as Scenes, Machines; particularly, one scene painted with myriads of *Ariel* Spirits; and another flying away with a table, furnisht out with fruits, sweet-meats, and all sorts of viands, just when Duke *Trinculo* and his companions were going to dinner; all things perform'd in it so admirably well, that not any succeeding opera got more money." In 1674, Henry Herringman, the same publisher who early in 1670 had issued the Davenant-Dryden version, printed the operatic alteration by Shadwell, again without any notice of authorship on the title-page, but with Dryden's signed preface, the prologue and epilogue of 1667, as they appear in the quarto of 1670. Into this trap all the editors of Dryden have fallen headlong. In every reprint of Dryden's theatre (including Scott) we find the text of the 1674 quarto. Professor Saintsbury, indeed, noticed differences between the two quartos, 1670 and 1674, but unfortunately he took quarto 1674 to be merely a corrected copy of quarto 1670. The apogee of muddledom was reached by H. H. Furness in his untrustworthy edition of *The Tempest*, 1892 (*Variorum Shakespeare*) when, having most ignorantly girded at Dryden on every possible occasion he coolly reprints† as "Dryden's Version" Shadwell's Opera from the quarto of 1674, and ingenuously prefaces it with a few mutilated extracts from Pepys relating to the produc-

* Downes says " In 1673," but his dating is wrong. For a complete and masterly account of the whole difficult question of *The Tempest* see W. J. Lawrence's authoritative *Did Thomas Shadwell write An Opera on " The Tempest,"* to which I am materially indebted. *The Elizabethan Playhouse*, First Series, p. 195.

† Furness announces " I have cut out about twenty or thirty lines "!

tion of November 1667. Furness also supplies us with
some notes upon the sea-terms in Act I, scene 1. It
may be remarked that his notes here are far more
incoherent and unintelligible than he supposes the
nautical expressions to be.

As Mr. W. J. Lawrence has well said: " Based on the
Dryden-D'Avenant comedy of 1667, and comprising all
its features, Shadwell's opera has several distinguishing
characteristics." To discuss these in detail were super-
fluous. " It will suffice to say that the main differentia-
tion of the operatic version lies in the terminal Masque
of *Neptune and Amphitrite.*" In Act II, scene 4, of the
Opera, quarto 1674, occurs a new song, " Arise ye
subterranean winds " the music for which was published
in 1680, in Part II of Pietro Reggio's Songs, under the
title, " A Song in *the Tempest.* The Words by Mr.
Shadwell."

It is exceedingly curious that in the quarto of 1674,
the book of Shadwell's Opera, Herringman should have
printed Dryden's prologue and epilogue of 1667, more
especially as there exist a " Prologue and Epilogue to
the Tempest," which were undoubtedly written by
Shadwell himself for his own production. As these are
preserved in the Egerton MSS.* in the British Museum,
they may, although they have been reprinted by Mr.
W. J. Lawrence, fittingly be given here:

" Prologue

Wee, as the ffathers of the Stage have said,
To treat you here a vast expense have made;
What they have gott from you in chests is laid,
Or is for purchas'd Lands, or houses paid,
You, in this house, all our estate may find,
Wch for your pleasures wholly are design'd.

* No. 2,623.

'Twas foolish, for we might, we must confesse,
Value ourselves much more, and you much lesse;
And like those reverend men, we might have spar'd
And never for our Benefactors car'd;
Still made your Treatment, as they do more Coarse,
As if you did, as fast as they, grow worse:
But we young men, are apt to slight advice,
One day we may decrepid grow and wise:
Then, hoping not to time to get much more,
We'll Save our money, and cry out wee'r poore.
Wee're young, and look yet many yeares to live,
And by your future Bounty hope to thrive;
Then let us laugh, for now no cost wee'l spare
And never think we're poor, while we your favours share,
Without the good old Playes we did advance,
And all ye stages ornament enhance;
To splendid things they follow in, but late:
They ne're invent, but they can imitate:
Had we not for yr. pleasure found new wayes
You still had rusty arras had, and thred-bare playes;
Not scenes nor Woomen, had they had their will,
But some some with grizzl'd Beards had acted Woomen
      still,
Some restive horses, spight of Switch and spurre,
Till others strain against 'em, will not stir.
Envying our Splendid house, and prosp'rous playes,
They scoff at us, and Libell the high wayes.
Tis fitt we, for our faults, rebukes shou'd meet.
The Citty ought to mend those of ye street,
With the best poets' heads our house we grac'd
Wch we in honour to ye Poets plac'd.*

* Cf. Tom D'Urfey's *Collin's Walk Through London* (1690),
Canto IV, where the peripatetic, on visiting Dorset Gardens,
      " . . . saw each box with beauty crown'd
      And pictures deck the structure round,

Too much of the old witt they have, tis true:
But they must look for little of ye new."

" EPILOGUE

When feeble Lovers' appetites decay
They, to provoke, and keep themselves in play,
Must, to their Cost, make ye young Damsells shine;
If Beauty can't provoke, they'l do't by being fine;
That pow'rfull charme, wch cannot be withstood,
Put offe bad faces, and adornes ye good.
Oft an embroider'd Damsel have we seen ⎫
Ugly as Bawd, and finer than a Queen, ⎬
Who by that splendor has victorious been.⎭
She, whose weake Eyes had nere one Victory gott
May conquer with a flaming petticoat;
Witt in a Mistress you have long enjoy'd,
Her beauty's not impair'd but you are cloy'd!
And Since 'tis not Witt's fault that you decay,
You, for yoᵉ want of appetite must pay.
You to provoke yoᵉ Selves must keep her fine,
And she must now at double charges shine.*
Old Sinners thus———
When they feel Age and Impotence approach,
Double the charge of furniture and Coach;

> *Ben, Shakespear,* and the learned rout,
> With noses some and some without."

" These portraits remained *in situ* until the demolition of the
theatre in 1709 " (W. J. Lawrence).

Cf. also the smart reference to Dorset Gardens in Dryden's
Epilogue *Spoken at the opening of the New House* (Theatre Royal,
Drury Lane), 26 March 1674:

> " Though in their House the Poets Heads appear,
> We hope we may presume their Wits are here."

* " Prices of admission were advanced during the run of new
operas, owing to the expense of mounting. Duffett girds at the
practice in the prologue to his *Psyche Debauch'd* (1678) " (W. J.
Lawrence).

When you of Witt and sence were weary growne,
Romantick, riming, fustian Playes were showne,
We then to flying Witches did advance,*

* Compare the anonymous Epilogue to *The Ordinary*. "A
Collection of Poems written upon several Occasions By several
Persons." London, 1673 [8vo], p. 167. The lines are cited by
Mr. G. Thorn-Drury in *Some Seventeenth Century Allusions to
Shakespeare*, p. 17:
   " Now empty shows must want of sense supply,
   Angels shall dance and *Macbeth's* Witches fly."
There had been a revival of the Davenant *Macbeth* at Dorset
Gardens early in 1673. A special feature was made of machines
for the witches, who mounted and flew through the air. In *Notes
and Observations on the Empress of Morocco*, 4to, 1674, the work
of Dryden, Shadwell, and Crowne, the following passage occurs:
" What a beastly pattern of a King whom he intends vertuous,
has he shown in his Muley Labas? Yet he is the only person who
is kept to his Character; for he is a perpetual Fool, and I dare
undertake that if he were Play'd by Nokes, who Acted just such
another Monarch in Mackbeth, it would give new life to the
Play, and do it more good than all its Devils." Mr. Thorn-Drury,
who has drawn my attention to this remarkable passage, queries
if this must not mean that Nokes had attempted to act Macbeth,
and indeed the words admit of no other signification. One may
compare Edmund Smith's *Poem to the memory of Mr. John
Phillips :*
   " So, when Nurse *Nokes* to act young *Ammon* tries
   With shambling legs, long chin, and foolish eyes,
   With dangling hands he strokes th' imperial robe,
   And with a cuckold's air commands the globe:
   The pomp and sound the whole buffoon display'd,
   And *Ammon's* son more mirth than *Gomez* made."
From these lines it would seem that Nokes had (once at least)
appeared as Alexander in *The Rival Queens*. He is called Nurse
Nokes from his famous performance of Lavinia's Nurse in
Otway's *Caius Marius*, produced at the Duke's House in 1679.
Gomez, in Dryden's *The Spanish Friar*, produced at the Duke's
House in the spring of 1681, had been created by Nokes.

And for your pleasures traffic'd into ffrance.*
From thence new acts to please you, we have sought⎫
We have machines to some perfection brought,   ⎬
And above 30 Warbling voyces gott.†   ⎭
Many a God and Goddesse you will heare   ⎫
And we have Singing, Dancing, Devils here   ⎬
Such Devils, and such gods, are very Deare.‡⎭
We, in all ornaments, are lavish growne
And like Improvident Damsells of ye Towne,
For present bravery, all your wealth lay downe,
As if our keepers ever wou'd be kind,   ⎫
The Thought of future wants we never mind,⎬
No pittance is for your Old age design'd.   ⎭
Alone we on yoᵉ Constancy depend,
And hope yoᵉ Love to th' stage will never end.
To please you, we no Art, or cost will spare
To make yr. Mrs. look still young, still faire."

" Shadwell's prologue," says Mr. Lawrence, " prac-
tically dates itself. It is nothing more than a lumbering

* *Circa* 1672-3 Betterton visited Paris by the special command of the king, in order to observe how the English theatre
could be improved in the matter of scenery and decorations.

† " Mostly the boys and men of the Chapel Royal," says Mr.
W. J. Lawrence, who further supplies a most interesting extract
from the Lord Chamberlain's Accounts, 16 May 1674, whereby
instructions were given that all the men and boys belonging to
the Chapel Royal " that sing in ye *Tempest* at his Royall High-
nesse Theatre, doe remaine in towne all the week." On Saturdays,
however, they had to go to Windsor, since the king was in
residence at the Castle, for the Sunday services. They were
allowed " to returne to London on Mundayes if there be occasion
for them."

‡ For the " dancing devils " see *The Tempest* (Shadwell's
version, 4to, 1674), Act II, 3, and for " the gods," the terminal
masque of *Neptune and Amphitrite*.

rejoinder to Dryden's prologue and epilogue for the opening of the new Theatre Royal on 26 March, 1674."

The Davenant-Dryden version of *The Tempest* was produced on Thursday, 7 November 1667, at the Duke's Theatre. Pepys, who was present, found himself among " a great many great ones. The house mighty full; the King and Court there: and the most innocent play that ever I saw; and a curious piece of musique in an echo of half sentences, the echo repeating the former half, while the man goes on to the latter; which is mighty pretty." * All were " mightily pleased with the play." Pepys, who saw the comedy several times, on one occasion was admitted behind the scenes, and " had the pleasure to see the actors in their several dresses, especially the seamen, and monster, which were very droll."

No list of actors was printed with the piece, but we know that Henry Harris played Ferdinand; Edward Angel, " an incomparable Comedian," Stephano;† Cave Underhill, Trincalo.‡ Moll Davis was also in the original

* This is the song sung by Ferdinand, wherein Ariel echoes *Go thy way*, in Act III. It was set by Banister, who with Pelham Humphreys supplied the music for the Davenant-Dryden comedy. For Shadwell's opera new instrumental music was written by Matthew Lock, and new vocal music by Pietro Reggio and J. Hart. The dances were composed by Draghi. In a private letter to myself, Mr. W. Barclay Squire writes: " Excepting Draghi's dances I think we now have the whole of the music for Shadwell's version." In 1690 the Shadwell opera, with various additions, was wholly re-set by Henry Purcell.

† See *An Elegy Upon . . . Mr. Edward Angell*, reprinted in *A Little Ark*, pp. 38-9:
    " Who shall play *Stephano* now? your Tempest's gone
    To raise new Storms i' th' hearts of every one."

‡ This and the Gravedigger in *Hamlet* were, perhaps, the two most famous rôles of this excellent actor, who was nicknamed " Prince Trincalo."

cast, her rôle perhaps being Hippolito, for the " right Heir of the Dukedom of *Mantua* " was assigned to a woman, and " little Mis Davis " in breeches parts had already enraptured the town. After she had left the stage she was succeeded in *The Tempest* by Mrs. Gosnell, who, *teste* Pepys, but ill supplied her place. Betterton himself did not appear in *The Tempest*. The Davenant-Dryden version achieved a veritable triumph, and it was continually being acted to crowded houses, until, curiously enough, it seems to have been entirely absorbed in Shadwell's ornate Opera.

Davenant's innovations kept the stage for well-nigh two centuries, and, however they may be criticized from one standpoint, this fact is proof indisputable of their theatrical effectiveness, which is in itself no mean quality. The Master of the Ship, Stephano, and his mates are intensely amusing, they have a racy humour and zest in no way derivative from Shakespeare ; whilst there is surely no one who cannot but be devoutly thankful to be spared that protracted and intensely dull scene between Alonso, Sebastian, Antonio, and the attendant lords which commences the second act of Shakespeare's original.

In his preface to *The Tempest*, quarto 1670, Dryden explicitly states that the character of Hippolito is entirely due to Davenant. Herman Grimm in his *Fünfzehn Essays* (Berlin, 8vo, 1875), made a futile attempt to show that Hippolito is borrowed from Calderon's *En esta vida todo es verdad, y todo mentira*, whereupon Furness, who obviously has no acquaintance with the Spanish play in question, impertinently belabours Dryden with clumsy abuse. " It is hard to decide whether or not DRYDEN's reputation be additionally damaged by the revelation lately made by an eminent German scholar, that the mutilations, or rather the additions, for which DRYDEN took to himself credit as the author, are wholesale ' conveyances ' from a play of CALDERON."* Even were these assumptions correct, such virulence in wantonly attacking so great a name as Dryden would be singularly indecorous and offensive. When these grandiloquent assertions are wholly incorrect and demonstrably untrue, it is, perhaps, better to refrain from characterizing so inept a tirade in too particular a manner.

Calderon's drama, *En esta vida todo es verdad, y todo mentira*, is a play of strange and beautiful fantasy detailing in exquisite poetry knightly adventure, which, however, to the unimaginative English taste must almost inevitably seem conceited and extravagant, if not altogether too whimsical and grotesquely bizarre. Nevertheless, the whole is informed and irradiated with such grace and lordliness of diction that not even the most regular critic could deny his applause. The drama cannot be earlier than 1637, and it is quoted in a romance printed in 1641, so we are able to date it within the space of a very few years. It was first published as a separate quarto.† The characters are as follows: Focas; Eraclio; Leonido; Astolfo; Ismenia; Lisipo; Federico, Principe; Cintia; Libia; Damas; Luquete, gracioso; Sabañon, gracioso. The plot may be roughly outlined thus‡: Astolfo, the ambassador of Mauricio,

---

* H. H. Furness, *The Tempest* (1892), Preface, pp. viii, ix (*Variorum Shakespeare*). Strunk, in his edition of *All For Love* (Belles-Lettres Series), relying upon the untrustworthy Furness, repeats the error that Davenant derived from Calderon (*Introduction*, p. xxvii).

† I have used the edition of 1671, which is to be found in Vol. VII of a collection, 1637-82.

‡ I have very briefly indicated the complex intrigue of the Second and Third Days, as only the First Day concerns the point in question.

Emperor of Constantinople, after a battle in which Mauricio was slain by Focas, fled to the caverns of Mount Etna carrying with him Eraclio, the infant son of the dead Emperor. Irifile, a maiden beloved by Focas and by him left pregnant on his departure for the war, tried to follow him. In the wild mountain passes she was delivered of a son, Leonido. The mother expired, but the babe being found by Astolfo is brought up with Eraclio far from the haunts of men. Many years after, the First Day (Jornada Prima) commences with the solemn triumph of Focas, who to the sound of many instruments is received in state by Cintia, Queen of Sicily. Presently Libia, daughter of the famous magician Lisippo, appears in great alarm. Among the lonely dells of Etna she has been frightened by the apparition of " a man like a beast." This proves to be Astolfo in search of Eraclio and Leonido. Contrary to his stern precepts they have left their caves to wander abroad. When the long processions and tuneful choirs have passed from the stage, three strange figures, tanned, clad in skins, uncouth and unkempt, make their entrance. The old man is severely blaming the youths for having disobeyed his injunctions, but they excuse themselves, saying that the music and voices irresistibly attracted them from their seclusion. Astolfo replies that in tracking them he has met a woman who will, he declares, ruin them all. Eraclio and Leonido have never seen a woman and Astolfo warns them of impending disaster should they once set eyes upon a fair female form. Soon, however, Eraclio is left alone, and in a few moments Cintia appears. They gaze at each other in wonderment and perplexity. There is also an encounter between Libia and Leonido. Astolfo interrupts, but he is met and recognized by Focas, to whom the old man announces that one of the two savage lads is the Emperor Mauricio's son, but which he refuses to reveal.

Focas threatens Astolfo, and the two youths stoutly defend their foster-father against the royal guards. Much tumult and confusion ensues when suddenly the wizard Lisippo appears. By his incantations he raises a terrific storm and amid the crash of thunder and lightning's blaze the First Day closes.

The Second Day is occupied with the myriad difficulties and entanglements which have arisen owing to the secret Astolfo jealously holds.

In the Third Day Libia proclaims that Eraclio is Mauricio's son. This she has learned from her father, the mage. Leonido wishes to kill Focas sleeping, but he is prevented by Eraclio. Focas awakes and sees the two youths with naked swords, whereupon Leonido asserts he drew to defend the king against Eraclio. This Eraclio denies and during their contention news is brought that Federico, Prince of Calabria, has landed with a hostile force. A battle ensues between the invaders and the army of Focas, who is slain on the field by Eraclio, and the play ends with cries of " Viva Eraclio, Eraclio viva!"*

Divested of all colour, chivalry, poetry, and sentiment, this brief outline, baldly told, cannot but appear too fancifully intricate as well as jejune, yet it must needs suffice for our present purpose. It is enough, indeed, to

---

* It should be noted that Pierre Corneille's tragedy, *Heraclius, Empereur d'Orient*, with " Heraclius, Fils de l'Empereur Maurice, crû Martian Fils de Phocas, Amant d'Eudoxe " and " Martian, Fils de Phocas, crû Léonce Fils de Léontine, Amant de Pulchérie" is wholly different to Calderon's drama. The critics, however, discussed which was the original, and this gave occasion to Voltaire's apt remark : " Le lecteur comparera le Théâtre espagnol avec le français, et il découvrira au premier coup d'oeil quel est l'original. Si après cela il reste des disputes ce ne sera pas contre les personnes éclairées."

show that it can hardly be maintained that such an
incident as the first meeting of Eraclio and Cintia,
easily to be paralleled in folk lore and romance, is
necessarily, or even probably, the source whence
Davenant had his hint of Hippolito and Dorinda. The
scene opens thus:

> "Salen *Cintia* y *Eraclio*.
> *Er.* Ni què se opondra à mís fuerzas?
> Mas què miro! *Cint.* Mas què veo!
> *Er.* Que bello animal! *Cint.* Què fiera
> tan espantosa! *Erac.* Divino
> assombro!
> *Cint.* Horribile presencia!"

It is true that there are in Calderon half a dozen
verses which bear some resemblance to as many lines in
The Tempest ; or, The Enchanted Island, but given the
situation, the coincidence in thought is almost inevitable. If we are to follow Grimm, how vast and nebulous
a field of speculation is opened! One might trace
Eraclio and Leonido back to the Charlemagne cycle and
derive them from the story of *Valentine and Orson*,
written during the reign of Charles VIII and first
printed at Lyons, folio, 1495; and again a weighty
discussion could be set on foot as to the relation of
Calderon's play to *Cymbeline*, for Astolfo is surely very
like Belarius—a rich-marrowed bone for the Shakespearean commentators. To wander wider, is it not
obvious that when the Catechism of the *Book of Common
Prayer* instructs the catechumen " to do my duty in
that state of life unto which it shall please God to call
me," this is a mere translation of Seneca's " dat quidem
operam, ut in hac statione qua positus est, honeste se
et industrie gerat "? But as has been well said: " To
set out to hunt deliberately for literary doubles is to
reduce letters to the level of an acrostic."

There are many contemporary allusions which show that *The Tempest ; or, The Enchanted Island* was most popular with Restoration audiences. Thus, in an anonymous poem, *The Country Club*, 4to, 1679, we have:

"Such noise, such stink, such smoke there was, you'd
    swear
The *Tempest* surely had been acted there.
The cryes of star-board, Lar-board, cheerly boys,
Is but as demy rattles to this noise."

In 1690-1 there was a special revival for which Henry Purcell wrote the music. New and costly spectacular effects were prepared, and for a long while the magnificence and show were the talk of the whole town. In his capital comedy, *The Marriage-Hater Match'd*, produced at the Theatre Royal early in January 1691-2, D'Urfey has the following reference to this sumptuous production:

"Lord *Brainless*. A Player, ha ha ha, why now you Rave, Madam,——Darewel, thou canst witness the contrary of that, thou toldst me her Breeding was such, that she had been familiar with Kings and Queens.

"*Darewell*. Ay my Lord in the Play-house, I told ye she was a High Flyer too, that is, I have seen her upon a Machine in the *Tempest*.

"Lord *Brainless*. In the *Tempest*, why then I suppose I may seek her fortune in the *inchanted Island*."

A performance of *The Tempest* with " all the original Flyings and Musick " is announced in the *Daily Courant*, 13 February 1707-8, " Dorinda by Mrs. *Cross* with the Song of ' Dear pretty Youth.' " " Dear pretty Youth " was first published in *Deliciae Musicae*, Book III (1696, but issued late in 1695), as " A New Song in the *Tempest* Sung by Miss *Cross* to her Lover who is supposed Dead. Set by Mr. *Henry Purcell*."

At Drury Lane, 4 June 1714, Prospero was played by

Powell; Caliban, Johnson; Trincalo, Bullock; Ferdinand, Ryan; Hippolito, Mrs. Mountfort; Dorinda, Mrs. Santlow.

On 2 January 1729, at the same theatre, Mills acted Prospero; Wilks, Ferdinand; Shepherd, Stephano; Harper, Mustacho; Joe Miller, Trincalo; " Jubilee " Norris, Ventoso; Mrs. Cibber, Hippolito; Mrs. Booth, Miranda; Miss Robinson, Ariel, whilst a young nymph of seventeen, Kitty Raftor, who later became Kitty Clive, as Dorinda, charmed a crowded audience.

On 31 January 1746, at Drury Lane, Garrick revived *The Tempest* as by Shakespeare. Luke Sparks was the Prospero; Macklin, Stephano, and Kitty Clive, Ariel. On 19 May following, *The Tempest* was repeated, probably for the benefit of Isaac Sparks, who appeared as Caliban, but the next season the Davenant-Dryden version with Shadwell's alterations again monopolized the stage.

On 26 December of the following year, *The Tempest*, loosely billed as " Not acted 7 years," was produced with Berry as Prospero; Macklin, Trincalo; Isaac Sparks, Caliban; Taswell, a great *farceur*, Sycorax; Peg Woffington, Hippolito; Mrs. Mozeen, Miranda; Kitty Clive, Ariel; and Mrs. Green, Dorinda. The whole concluded with the elaborated Masque of Neptune, Amphitrite, the Sea-gods and Nereids.

On 11 February 1756, at Drury Lane, Garrick put on what is, beyond all doubt, infinitely the worst alteration of *The Tempest* ever perpetrated. This was an operatic version, prepared by himself, into which have been intercalated no less than two and thirty songs and duets. Hippolito and Dorinda disappear, but much matter has been conveyed from *Tyrannic Love*, and we have such numbers as a trio for Trincalo, Stephano, and Ventoso. Beard sang Prospero, and Signora Curioni Miranda. Not impertinently did Theophilus Cibber in *Two Dissertations on the Theatres* write of " *The Tempest* castrated into an opera.* Oh! What an agreeable Lullaby might it have prov'd to our Beaus and Belles to have heard Caliban, Sycorax, and one of the Devils trilling of trios."

On 20 October 1757, Garrick revived Shakespeare's *The Tempest*. It was announced as " Not acted 14 years " and performed seventeen times that season. Mossop sustained Prospero; Miss Pritchard, Miranda; Berry, Caliban; and Woodward is said to have been excellent as Stephano. This was, indeed, the rôle he chose for his last appearance, Drury Lane, 13 January 1777, when Dunstall was Caliban and Quick Trinculo.

At Covent Garden, 27 December 1776, *The Tempest* is billed as " never acted there."

It should be noticed that Bell's acting edition of Shakespeare "regulated from the prompt-books by permission of the managers " (1773-75) supplies an unadulterated, if greatly abridged, text of *The Tempest*, which, according to Boaden, was performed 28 April

---

* Another but equally deplorable opera made out of *The Tempest* was produced at the Edinburgh Theatre in the same year, 1756. The songs only seem to have been preserved, and these are of the most pedestrian order. Milcha, who commences the performance with a doggerel Recitative, has nine songs, and Ariel only two. Curiously enough, Milcha was played by a man, Mr. Sadler.

In 1780 was printed, 8vo, *The Shipwreck, altered from Shakespeare and Dryden, with the original music by Smith, as performed at the Patagonian Theatre, Exeter-Change.* This absurd production opens on " a heath," where assemble the witches borrowed from *Macbeth.* Demons are summoned to wreck the ship and destroy all on board. So contemptible a thing, however, is unworthy of serious consideration. The Patagonian Theatre was situated in Exeter Change, Strand, on a portion of the site of Burleigh House, the town house of the great Lord Treasurer, which was afterwards known as Exeter House. The theatre ceased to exist as such after 1779-80.

1785, " pure and unmixed " at Drury Lane. The masque, however, was omitted. Bensley, " the only Prospero," won great applause, and Miss Phillips as Miranda appeared exquisitely beautiful, whilst " Old Bannister's Caliban contrasted finely with the Ariel of Miss Field." Four years later, however (13 October 1789), Kemble at Drury Lane had restored Hippolito and Dorinda. Mrs. Goodall played the young Duke of Mantua ; Miss Farren, Dorinda ; Mrs. Crouch, Miranda, and Miss Romantzini, Ariel. Strangely enough Kemble places the Shipwreck in Act II. He again altered *The Tempest* for Covent Garden, where his second version was produced 8 December 1806.

On 31 October 1812, at Covent Garden, Young, who attempted Prospero, suffered terribly by comparison with Kemble. But Emery as Caliban, Mathews as Stephano, and Blanchard as Trincalo, proved very great. Mrs. Henry Johnston played Hippolito, and Miss Booth, Dorinda. As Ariel, Miss Bolton " united the elegance of a dancer with the just action and delivery of the more finished actress."

Hippolito and Dorinda did not finally disappear from the theatre until 13 October 1838, upon which night was first seen at Covent Garden, Macready's sumptuous and exceedingly successful production of *The Tempest* " from the text of Shakespeare." Yet the whole dialogue of the first scene was suppressed, and the shipwreck represented as a panoramic spectacle. The critics were divided. *John Bull* pronounced that " poetry was drowned in the vulgar hurly-burly of an Easter piece," whilst Priscilla Horton as Ariel was merely " whisked about by wires and a cog-wheel like . . . the ladies in *Peter Wilkins* " ; but the *Examiner* on the other hand became lyric in its praises of the sprite who " floated in air across the stage, singing or mocking as she floated." It may be surmised that *John Bull* tells the unvarnished truth, and that the mechanism was obvious and pantomimic enough. It is very significant that Hippolito and Dorinda so long maintained their position, and this fact argues that, upon the stage, at any rate, these two characters of Davenant's invention must be found interesting and dramatically effective.

The immense success and continued attraction of Shadwell's opera, *The Tempest ; or, the Inchanted Island*, at the Duke's House inspired Thomas Duffett to burlesque Prospero, Dorinda, Stephano, Ferdinand, and the rest, in *The Mock-Tempest ; or, The Enchanted Castle,* which was produced at the Theatre Royal in the winter of 1674.† It was, Langbaine tells us, " writ on purpose to draw Company from the other Theatre, where was great resort about that time, to see that reviv'd Comedy call'd *The Tempest*, then much in vogue." Thomas Duffett was, we learn from the same authority, " before he became a Poet, a Milliner in the New Exchange." ‡ He has left poems, two comedies, a masque, and three burlesques, the merit of which is vastly underrated. His first play, *The Spanish Rogue*, a rhyming comedy, was produced in the winter of 1673 at the Theatre Royal. William Harris, Marmaduke Watson, Powell senior, Mrs. Boutell, Mrs. Susanna Uphill,‖ Mrs. Corey, and Mrs. Knepp, Pepys' fair

---

* There is a variant of the title: " The New Tempest; or, The Enchanted Castle."

† *Term Catalogue*, Hilary (15 February), 1675.

‡ The New Exchange was a kind of bazaar on the south side of the Strand. It was an immensely popular resort, and there are innumerable references to its shops, its sempstresses and haberdashers. Scene I of the Second Act of Otway's *The Atheist ; or, The Soldier's Fortune* (Duke's House, 1683), is laid in the Exchange, and Mrs. Furnish, an Exchange-Woman, calls her " Very good Gloves or Ribbands, Choice of fine Essences."

‖ Mistress to Sir Robert Howard, who afterwards married her.

friend, were in the cast, the Prologue being spoken by
Mrs. Boutell, and the Epilogue by Mrs. Knepp. It has
some highly diverting scenes, and the intrigue throughout is well-sustained. When printed 4to, 1674, a
dedication placed it " under the protection of the most
perfect beauty and the greatest goodness in the world,"
" Madam Ellen Gwyn."* The device employed by
Mingo in this play and his counterfeiting himself to be
a eunuch may have been derived by Duffett from
Terence's *Eunuchus*.†

About Easter 1674 was performed by the King's
Company, *The Amorous Old-Woman ; or, 'Tis Well if
it Take*, a comedy published in the same year‡ as
" Written by a Person of Honour," but which, on the
authority of Langbaine, is universally ascribed to
Duffett's pen. It has met with little favour from the
critics, but it is a better play than they judge it to be.
The scene lies at Pisa, and Strega " the old Rich de-
formed Lady " was acted by Mrs. Corey. Mrs. Cox,
Mrs. James, and Mrs. Boutell sustained the remaining

---

* Only two other dedications to Nell Gwyn are known, Mrs.
Behn's comedy, *The Feign'd Courtezans*, and Robert Whitcombe's
excessively rare mythological dictionary, *Janua Divorum*, 8vo,
1678. This latter dedication was pointed out to Gordon Goodwin,
the editor of Peter Cunningham's *The Story of Nell Gwyn* (1908),
by Mr. G. Thorn-Drury.

† The *Eunuchus* was largely utilized by Sir Charles Sedley in
his best comedy, *Bellamira ; or, The Mistress*, produced at the
Theatre Royal in 1687. This excellent play is a very frank
satire upon Lady Castlemaine. A more direct adaptation from
Terence by L'Estrange and Echard was performed at Drury
Lane in July 1717, and at the same house twenty years later was
produced *The Eunuch ; or, The Derby Captain*, a farce from
Terence by Thomas Cooke, with Leigh in the title-rôle and
Macklin as Captain Brag (*Thraso*).

‡ *The Term Catalogue*, Easter (26 May), 1674.

female characters, whilst the Prologue was spoken by Mohun. In 1684 *The Amorous Old-Woman* was re-issued with a new title-page as *The Fond Lady*.

Beauties Triumph (4to, 1676), is a masque upon the subject of Paris and the Golden Apple. It was " Presented by the Scholars of Mr. Jeffery Banister and Mr. James Hart At their *New* BOARDING-SCHOOL for Young Ladies and Gentlewomen, kept in that House which was formerly Sir *Arthur Gorges* AT CHELSEY." This occasional piece has fancy but not distinction.

Originally written for presentation at Court before the King, and graced with a prologue by the Earl of Mulgrave, which was spoken by Lady Elizabeth Howard, Elkanah Settle's robustious tragedy, *The Empress of Morocco*, had been produced at the Duke's Theatre, Dorset Gardens, in the autumn of 1673. Settle's heroics " rhyme and rattle " apace and are fluent with " a blund'ring kind of Melody." He has, moreover, considerable skill in managing stage effect and in arranging the conduct of highly spiced melodrama of a transpontine order. Owing to the spectacular magnificence of the scenery, the fine acting of Betterton, Mrs. Betterton, Mrs. Mary Lee, Henry Harris, and William Smith, and even more particularly because of the influence of Rochester, whose whim it was just then to patronize Settle and exalt him as a rival to Dryden, *The Empress of Morocco* had an enormous success with the public. It was published 1673, " With Sculptures. The like never done before. . . . In Quarto. Price, stitcht, 1s," an edition much sought after by collectors on account of the fine old copper-plates. As might have been expected, and as was indeed Rochester's design, Settle's arrogance and inflated coxcombry excessively annoyed the better dramatists, and Dryden in particular was so justly irate that he joined with Shadwell and Crowne in a caustic attack, *Notes and Observations on the Empress*

*of Morocco or some few Erratas to be printed instead of
the Sculptures with the second edition of that Play*, 4to,
1674. In the spring of 1674 also was produced at the
new Theatre Royal (the second Drury Lane) Duffett's
skit, *The Empress of Morocco*. Epistemon told Panta-
gruel that in Hades he saw Cleopatra hawking onions,
whilst Helen was a sluttish chambermaid, and Dido
sold mushrooms. Duffett with some humour meta-
morphoses Settle's heroines and grandees in similar
fashion. Laula, the Queen Mother (Mrs. Betterton),
becomes " an Hostess" acted by Griffin; Mariamne
(Mrs. Mary Lee) " a Scinder VVench," acted by Cardell
Goodman; Morena (Mrs. Johnson) " an Apple-woman,"
acted by Will Harris. The farce commences thus:
" SCENE OPENS and discovers the Court at HOT-
COCKLES.* Muly-Labas† [Coysh] *the Corn-cutter being
taken and about to lay down his Head in* Morena *the
Apple-woman's Lap.*" Instead of Settle's " Villains,
Lord, Priests, Masquers, and Attendants " we find
ourselves in the company of Chimney-sweeps, Strong-
water-men, Draymen, Porters, Tinkers, Gipsies, and
Tapsters. The farce was at the time no doubt sufficiently
effective, although now it is perhaps chiefly interesting
on account of the elaborate epilogue which burlesques
Macbeth. Here we are at once pell-mell amongst the
most fantastic puppetries: " EPILOGUE Being a new
Fancy, after the old and most surprising way of

* " A rustic game in which one player lay face downwards, or
knelt down with his eyes covered, and being struck on the back
by the others in turn, guessed who struck him " (*N.E.D.*). It will
be remembered that one Michaelmas Eve at neighbour Flam-
borough's, Lady Blarney and Miss Carolina Wilhelmina Amelia
Skeggs discovered the Vicar's daughters engaged in " this
primaeval pastime."

† Muley Labas in the tragedy was played by Pepys' friend,
Henry Harris of the Duke's house.

MACBETH Perform'd with new, and costly MACHINES, Which were invented and managed by the most ingenious Operator Mr. *Henry VVright, P.G.Q.*"* Hecate and Three Witches, " According to the Famous Mode of *Macbeth*," commence " The most renowned and melodious Song of *John Dory*† being heard as it were in the Air, sung in parts by Spirits, to raise the expectation, and charm the audience with thoughts sublime and worthy of that Heroick Scene which follows. The scene opens : Thunder and lightning is discover'd, not behind Painted Tiffany to blind and amuse the Senses, but openly, by the most excellent way of Mustard-bowl and Salt-Peter." Then " Three Witches fly over the Pit Riding upon Beesomes " and " *Heccate* descends over the Stage in a Glorious Charriott adorn'd with Pictures of Hell and Devils, and made of a large Wicker Basket." After some discourse in gross parody of *Macbeth* I, 3, " *Enter two Spirits with Brandy burning, which they drink whilst it flames.* Heccate *and the three VVitches sing*

> *To the Tune of, A Boat, a Boat,‡ &c.*
> *A health, a health to Mother* C——
> *From* Moor-fields *fled to* Mill-bank *Castle*
> *She puts off rotten new-rig'd Vessel.*"

* " The whole of this imprint, down to the mystic initials, sounds like a jeer at some grandiloquent announcement made by the rival theatre " (W. J. Lawrence, *The Elizabethan Playhouse*, First Series, p. 219).

† Weber, who in his edition of Beaumont and Fletcher printed this popular song from Thomas Ravenscroft's *Deuteromelia* (1609), states that it is referred to as " an old three-man's song," by R. Carew, *The Survey of Cornwall* (1602).

‡ This is the same tune as the very popular loyal old song, *Here's a Health unto his Majesty, With a fal la la la la !* Cf. Shadwell's *The Miser* (Theatre Royal, January 1672), Act III,

Mother C—— is, of course, the infamous Mrs. Cresswell, and in this strange song other notorious maquerelles of the day are celebrated. Of Mother Gifford* we are told:

> " *She needs must be in spight of fate Rich*
> *Who sells tough Hen for Quail and Partridg :*"

Mother Temple, and Betty Buly " who began the Trade but newly " receive ample mention, but Moseley† is acclaimed as the *doyenne* of these harridans. Hecate then " *speaks to the Audience* ":

" Hail! hail! hail! you less than wits and greater;
Hail Fop in Corner, and the rest now met here,
Though you'l ne're be wits, from your loins shall spread
Diseases that shall reign when you are dead.
        Deed is done!
        VVar's begun!
Great Morocco's *lost and won.*
Bank-side Maulkin thrice has mew'd! no matter:
If puss of t'other house will scratch—have at her!

where Timothy Squeeze says: " We can i'faith, and sing, *a Boat, a Boat*, or *here's a health to his Majesty, with a fa la la la lero.*"

* There are many allusions to all these *ruffiane*, but the following reference in Dryden's *Sir Martin Mar-All*, IV, 1 (produced at the Duke's House, Thursday, 15 August 1667), is peculiarly apposite: " Every Night I fin'd out for a new Maiden-Head, and she has sold it me as often as ever Mother *Temple, Bennet*, or *Gifford*, have put off boil'd Capons for Quails and Partridges."

† Mother Moseley was extensively patronized by Shaftesbury. In Henry Neville Payne's *The Siege of Constantinople*, produced at the Duke's Theatre in the winter of 1674. (4to, 1675) a tragedy which very sharply lashes that crooked politician as the Chancellor, Lorenzo upon his patron designing a frolic, says:
" My Lord, you know your old house, Mother Somelie's,
    You know she always fits you with fresh girls."

T'appease your spirits, and keep our Farce from harm,
Of strong Ingredients we have powerful charm."

The spells are enumerated; Hecate and all the Witches cry, "Huff: no more!" Thereupon "*a Hellish noise is heard within*," and Hecate assures the pit:

" He that wou'd damn this Farce does strive in vain
This charm can never be o'recome by man
Till Whetstones Park remove to Distaff Lane."*

Hecate is called away, and she sings:

"*The Goose and the Gander went over the Green,*
They flew in the Corn that they could not be seen.
        Chorus—*They flew,*" &c.

A trio by the Three Witches concludes this extravaganza:

I
" *Rose-mary's green, Rose-mary's green!*
        derry, derry, down.
When I am King, thou shalt be Queen.
        derry, derry, down.

* Whetstone Park is a narrow roadway, of which the name still remains, between the north side of Lincoln's Inn Fields and the South Side of Holborn. In the reign of Charles II this district was infamous. There are innumerable references, as Dryden, prologue to *The Wild Gallant* when revived; *Mr. Limberham*, Act V (Duke's Theatre, 1679); Shadwell, *The Miser* (Theatre Royal, January 1672); Wycherley, *Love in a Wood*, I, 2 (4to, 1672); Crowne, *The Country Wit*, Act III (Duke's Theatre, 1675), *et saepissime*. Lee, in the Dedication to *The Princess of Cleve* (4to, 1689), speaks of " a Ruffian reeking from *Whetstone's Park*."

Distaff Lane, Cannon Street, is now absorbed in that thoroughfare. The name is preserved in an alley known as Little Distaff Lane. Distaff Lane is mentioned by Stow and in Jonson's *Masque of Christmas*.

2
If I have Gold thou shalt have part.
derry, derry, down.
If I have none thou hast my heart.
derry, derry, down."

A somewhat shambling epilogue in more ordinary fashion, with the appeal "To get good Plays be kind to bad Travesty," concludes the whole entertainment. In this medley Powell acted Hecate; William Harris, Adams, and Lyddal the Three Witches; Cardell Goodman, Thunder, and Nathaniel Kew, Lightning. They were attended by " Spirits, Cats, Musicians."

Somewhere about October 1673, there was produced at the Duke's House the " long expected " opera of *Psyche.** Downes† writes that " *Psyche* came forth in all her ornaments; new scenes, new machines, new cloaths, new French dances: this Opera was splendidly set out, especially in scenes; the charge of which amounted to above 800£. It had a continuance of performance about 8 days together; it prov'd very beneficial to the Company: yet *The Tempest* got them more money."

* There is uncertainty about the exact month. For a full discussion see W. J. Lawrence, *The Elizabethan Playhouse,* First Series, pp. 143-4. *Psyche* was published 4to, 1675, and is announced in *The Term Catalogue,* Hilary, 15 February 1674-5. Shadwell in his preface speaks of the book as having been written sixteen months before. On 22 August 1673, James Vernon, writing a letter from Court to Sir Joseph Williamson at Cologne, incidentally mentions " that the Duke's house are preparing an Opera and great machines. They will have dansers out of France, and St. André comes over with them "—*Letters to Sir Joseph Williamson at Cologne* (Camden Society), i, 179. This reference is undoubtedly to *Psyche.* The passage is cited by Mr. Lawrence.

† Downes' dating, " *February* 1673," is certainly wrong.

Shadwell's libretto * was set to music by Lock and Draghi; St. André arranged the ballet; Stephenson painted the scenery; and Betterton superintended the whole production. After its original run *Psyche* was, of course, given intermittently for some time and proved a huge attraction. But whilst it was in its first flush of success, Duffett hastened to travesty it with a " Mock Opera," and early in 1674 *Psyche Debauch'd*† was produced by the rival company. It is a clever and amusing skit, at times astonishingly akin to more modern pantomime. Several male rôles were, it may be noted, acted by women and *vice versa*. Thus Mrs. Corbett appeared as King Andrew; Nicholas and the rustic Philip, Princes in love with None-so-fair, were acted by Mrs. Knepp and Mr. Charleton; Bruin, the White Bear of Norwich, by William Harris, who seems to have had a most apt talent for farce and extrava-ganza; Apollo, A Wishing-Chair, by Lydall; Jeffrey, Bruin's man, by Coysh; Costard, a Country-man, and Gammer Redstreak his wife, by Powell and the inimit-able Mrs. Corey; Justice Crabb by John Wiltshire whilst of King Andrew's three daughters, Wou'dha-more, Sweet-lips, and None-so-fair, Mrs. Rutter played the eldest, and Joe Haines, the youngest, None-so-fair (Psyche), in which part, from the very first line, when the princess addresses her attendant:

" O, *Glozy*, What a crumptious place is here!"

* It is hardly necessary to say that the book of the opera is merely a version of the *tragédie-ballet*, *Psyché*, by Corneille, Molière, and Quinault, which was produced at the theatre of the Tuileries in January 1671, and at the Palais-Royal on the following 24 July. There were thirty-eight consecutive per-formances.

† Publication was not immediate. *Psyche Debauch'd* was printed quarto, 1678.

he fooled and zanied to his heart's content. The scenes where None-so-fair is carried off by the magic Wishing-Chair (in parody of Psyche and the two Zephyri) to " an Arbour dress'd up with gaudy Play-games for Children," the realms of Bruin, who burlesques Cupid, are exceedingly happy, and at the moment when their sting and savour were poignant and new they must have proved irresistible. In the course of the piece a curious litany is chanted, and amongst other worthies they invoke Pope Joan, Friar Bungay, Wat Tyler, Massaniello, Don Quixote, Moll Cutpurse, Mother Moseley, James Nayler the fanatic, and the astrologer, Lilly. The Inferno of the original opera appropriately enough appears as a common Prison where loud demands of " Garnish, garnish, garnish," are heard.*

The Mock-Tempest ; or, The Enchanted Castle, produced at the Theatre Royal in the winter of 1674, met with great success, and—to quote Mr. W. J. Lawrence— " checked the taste for floridly mounted operas and spectacular extravagances like *The Empress of Morocco.*" It is, indeed, a burlesque full of broad fun, cleverly taking off many a salient point, both of situation and dialogue, in the Shadwell opera. That it did not remain a stock entertainment is, of course, a fate inevitable to parody, especially dramatic parody, which, however smart, is of its nature necessarily and essentially ephemeral and topical. As was to be expected, the more serious dramatists, not knowing whose turn might fall next, looked askance at Duffett's wit, and some ten years later Dryden in his revision of Sir William Soame's

* The *Biographia Dramatica* sententiously says that *Psyche Debauch'd* " met with the contempt it merited." This loose and unsupported statement is entirely negligible. *Psyche Debauch'd* seems to have been at the hour very popular.

Art of Poetry * (1683), ingeniously, but with unfair inference, wrote:

> " The dullest scribblers some admirers found
> And the *Mock Tempest* was a while renown'd:
> But this low stuff the town at last despis'd,
> And scorned the folly that they once had priz'd."†

In 1676‡ was published, " Poems, Songs, Prologues and Epilogues; never before printed. Written by Tho. Duffett; and set by the most eminent Musicians about the Town. In Octavo. Price bound, 1s. Printed for Nicholas Woolfe near *Bread Street* in *Cheapside*." This little book of 120 pages contains much graceful verse. The poems to Francelia are especially charming, in particular, " In cruelty you greater are "; " O wretched state of helpless man "; " Alas how short, how false and vain, Are the uncertain joys of man "; and " Francelia's heart is still the same "; which last was set by Nicholas Staggins. Duffett had a true lyric gift of song, nor are his prologues and epilogues without quality. In 1677, the Dedication to Celia being omitted, the book was re-issued with a fresh title-page: " New Songs and POEMS, A-la-mode both at COVRT and THEATERS, Now Extant. Never before Printed, by P. W. Gent."

* "The | Art | Of | Poetry, | Written in *French* by | The SIEUR *de Boileau*, | Made *English*. | LONDON, | Printed for *R. Bentley*, and *S. Magnes*, in | *Russel-Street* in *Covent Garden*, 1683." 8vo.

† Langbaine writes: " I have heard that when one of his Plays, *viz.*, *The Mock Tempest* was acted in *Dublin*, several Ladies and Persons of the best Quality left the House: such Ribaldry pleasing none but the Rabble." It is quite easy to understand that a burlesque which had achieved an enormous success in London, in Dublin would fall flat.

‡ *Term Catalogue*, Easter (5 May) 1676. The book was licensed by L'Estrange, 30 September 1675.

The first poem in this collection, entitled *Song to the Irish Tune,* which is forty lines in length, may be found (amplified to one hundred and thirty lines) in a broadside " Printed for *P. Brooksley* near the *Hospital-gate* in *West-smithfield.*" It is here termed " Amintor's *Lamentation for* Celia's *Unkindness.* Setting forth the passion of a Young man, who, falling in love with a coy Lady that had no kindness for him pursued his inclinations so far that she was forced to fly beyond Sea to avoid the importunities of his Address whereupon he thus complains:

Both Sexes from this Song may learn, | How in extreams they may discern,
Of what they should beware: | Unkindness and dispair.

To a delicate New Tune; Or. Since *Celias* my foe."

It is difficult to form a just estimate of Duffett. He has till now been generally neglected and ignored, and no detailed study of his work is to be found. It was recently said, and may with advantage again be emphasized, that there is no more ephemeral form of drama than theatrical burlesque. The current jokes, the up-to-date slang, the local and topical allusions, the humour of the stage situations, all depend in the first place upon an intimate knowledge of the play that is being travestied, and the broader the parody the sooner must it lose its essential point. Only exceptional efforts of great genius such as the theatre of Aristophanes or Buckingham's *The Rehearsal* will survive. Again, when we read the printed page of Duffett's quartos we perforce miss half the spirit of his farces, to recapture which in its entirety we must needs have seen Settle's *The Empress of Morocco,* Shadwell's *The Tempest* and *Psyche,* have heard them discussed and criticized in every coffee-house of Covent-Garden and Russell Street, at the Rose Tavern and Wills. Imagination must paint as vividly as may be the candle-lit stage; we must people it with the actors and actresses of old Rowley's prime, with Will Harris, Goodman, Griffin, Mrs. Corey, pretty Mrs. Knepp, and that irresponsible scaramouch Joe Haines. But in spite of all, the music and lilt of their voices; gesture, gag, and grimace, that winged Duffett's lines and woke many a merry laugh, are gone beyond recall. In some sense we may say that only the dry bones of his travesties remain. And yet, even for those who have no very specialized acquaintance with Settle's tragedy and Shadwell's opera, enough is left to vindicate for these burlesques more serious consideration and more particular mention than they have hitherto received. The scenes possess humour, coarse though at times it may be; they have a rollicking vitality; they parody without impertinence, and afford an intimate and undress glimpse of those gallant and picturesque days. It is not asserted that Thomas Duffett is a figure of outstanding importance, but it is maintained that he is a writer of extraordinary interest, accidental though this may be.

    The Tempest has been once again travestied, but not until more than one hundred and seventy years after Duffett's day. In July 1847 an elaborate revival of Shakespeare's play was put on at the Theatre Royal, Liverpool, with James F. Cathcart as Prospero and Miss C. Bell, Ariel.* This inspired Robert Brough, at that time a useful member of the Liverpool stock company, to write a burlesque, which, however, was not performed at the Theatre Royal until about a year later, *circa* August 1848, when Charles Rice was the Caliban. Brough's farce reached London in the winter, and was produced at the Adelphi on Monday, 20 November,

* Curiously enough, there are no details whatsoever of this revival in R. J. Broadbent's *Annals of the Liverpool Stage* (1908).

sharing the bill with *St. Mary's Eve*,* *Slasher and Crasher*, and *The Dance of the Shirt or, The Sempstress' Ball*. According to the fashion of the day it had been furnished with a long and extravagant title: *The Enchanted Isle ; or " Raising the Wind " on the Most Approved Principles : A Drama Without the Smallest Claim to Legitimacy, Consistency, Probability, or Anything Else but Absurdity ; in which will be found Much that is Unaccountably Coincident with Shakespeare's " Tempest."* This farce was printed as " by the Brothers Brough."† It proves, as might be expected, sufficiently topical with parodies of " I dreamed that I dwelt in marble halls," Arline's song in *The Bohemian Girl*, Henry Russell's *The Maniac*, and other fashionable music of the time: it is, moreover, stuffed full of " bare clinches, carwichets, quarter-quibbles and puns " some of which are introduced with great ingenuity and skill, and even though eighty years have flown, it is not unamusing withal. In its day it was immensely popular. *The Times*, 21 November 1848, announced " We may augur a long existence for *The Enchanted Isle*," whilst the critic of the *Illustrated London News* even more enthusiastically declared that " it achieved a triumph. . . . At the fall of the curtain the applause was uproarious." There was indeed a powerful cast. Paul Bedford acted Alonzo; Miss Woolger, Ferdinand, " his son, a fast man, thrown loose upon the waves "; Waye, Gonzalo;

* * *St. Mary's Eve ; A Solway Story*: " An Original Domestic Drama," by William Bayle Bernard, was originally produced at the Adelphi, 10 January 1838. It is a Jacobite story, and the period of the play is 1747. O. Smith acted Barty Sharp, a smuggler, and Madame Céleste, Madeline.
  Slasher and Crasher is a farce by James Maddison Morton It was first performed at the Adelphi, 16 November 1848. It acts one hour. *The Dance of the Shirt* was an occasional piece.
  † Webster's *Acting National Drama*, vol. 14.

O. Smith, great in melodrama, Prospero; Madame Céleste, Ariel, "a Magic Page from Shakespeare's Magic Volume"; Munyard, Caliban; Miss M. Taylor, Miranda; C. J. Smith, Easa di Baccastoppa; Sanders, Smuttifacio. On 28 July 1860 *The Enchanted Isle* was included in the programme at Drury Lane, when five companies united for the benefit of the widow and orphans of Robert Brough, who died at Manchester on 26 June of that year. Fanny Stirling was the Miranda, and she also spoke as prologue an address specially written by Shirley Brooks for the occasion. *The Enchanted Isle* was given by a company of artistic and literary amateurs.

By virtue of that curious arrangement, dated 12 December 1660, which gave Davenant a special monopoly of certain plays such as Denham's *The Sophy*, Massinger's *The Bondman, The Changeling,* Suckling's *Aglaura, The Tamer Tamed, The Maid in the Mill, The Spanish Curate, The Duchess of Malfi,* no less than ten of Shakespeare's works were wholly assigned to the Duke's house: *The Tempest, Pericles, Measure for Measure, Much Ado about Nothing, Romeo and Juliet, Twelfth Night, Henry VIII, King Lear, Macbeth,* and *Hamlet.* All of these, whether in their original form (*Twelfth Night, Henry VIII, Pericles, Hamlet*), or altered by Davenant himself (*The Tempest, Macbeth, Measure for Measure, Much Ado about Nothing**) or by other busy adapters such as James Howard (*Romeo and Juliet*), had a great and remarkable success in the theatre. Strangely enough the only exception seems to have been *King Lear*, concerning which theatrical tradition is entirely and singularly silent, although the *Roscius Anglicanus* records that between 1662 and 1665

---

* *Measure for Measure* and *Much Ado about Nothing* were amalgamated by Davenant into *The Law Against Lovers.*

was produced "*The Tragedy of King* Lear as Mr. *Shakespear* wrote it; before it was altered by Mr. *Tate*." *King Lear* was not seen by that indefatigable playgoer Pepys, and Downes merely chronicles it with Middleton's *A Trick to catch the Old One*,* Brome's *The Sparagus Garden*,† Glapthorne's *Wit in a Constable*,‡ John Cooke's *Green's Tu Quoque; or, The City Gallant*,‖ as old plays which were revived at that time. Of these, Pepys, on Friday, 23 May 1662, saw at "the Opera" *Wit in a Constable*, "the first time that it is acted; but so silly a play I never saw I think in my life." On Thursday, 12 September 1667, he writes: "by that time it was time to go to a play, which I did at the Duke's house, where 'Tu Quoque' was the first time acted, with some

---

* Licensed for printing 7 October 1607, and published, quarto, 1608. There was a second edition in 1616.

† Printed quarto, 1640, as "Acted in the yeare 1635, by the then Company of Revels, at *Salisbury* Court."

‡ Quarto, 1640. Acted at the Cockpit in Drury Lane.

‖ "*Greene's Tu Quoque, or The Cittie Gallant. As it hath beene diuers times acted by the Queenes Maiesties Seruants.* Written by Io. Cooke Gent. Printed at London for *Iohn Trundle*, 1614." This excellent comedy, which Hazlitt considers "very lively and elegant," the work of John Cooke, was dubbed and is universally known as *Greene's Tu Quoque* on account of the inimitable acting of a celebrated comedian, Thomas Greene, who at the Red Bull created Bubble, a silly coxcomb with the tag *tu quoque* always in his mouth. Thomas Heywood, the dramatist, supplied an Address "To the Reader." Other editions were published in 1622 and 1640 (?), and the comedy duly appears in all the issues of Dodsley's *Old Plays*. A text may also be found in the *Tudor Facsimile Texts*. Chetwood speaks of a quarto, 1599, which is probably mythical. Upon the title of the 1614 quarto is a wood-cut of Greene in character. See also the frontispiece to *The Wits, or Sport upon Sport* (1663), an illustration which has been frequently reproduced and is usually misdescribed as the Red Bull Theatre.

alterations of Sir W. Davenant's; but the play is a very silly play methinks; for I, and others that sat by me, Mr. Povy and Mr. Progers, were weary of it; but it will please the citizens." The following Tuesday also, the diarist, his wife, and Mercer going to the Theatre Royal to see *The Scornful Lady*, found the pit empty, "whereupon, for shame, we would not go in, but, against our wills, went all to see 'Tu Quoque' again, where there is pretty store of company, and going with a prejudice the play appeared better to us. . . . But one of the best parts of our sport was a mighty pretty lady that sat behind us, that did laugh so heartily and constantly, that it did me good to hear her." In 1662 Edward Browne, the son of Sir Thomas, saw *Tu Quoque* acted at the King's Arms, Norwich, and in his manuscript account book he has noted that he paid eighteen pence for admission.

Inasmuch as the old prompter has no word of commendation for *King Lear*, whilst he waxes eloquent over *Hamlet, Pericles, The Tempest, Twelfth Night, Henry VIII*, and *Romeo and Juliet*, we may not unfairly infer that Shakespeare's great tragedy, for whatsoever reason it might be, failed either to please the critics or to attract the town. The cast, unfortunately, has not been preserved, but Betterton no doubt sustained the title-rôle.

In the early spring of 1681 there was produced at the Duke's Theatre, Dorset Gardens, an alteration of *King Lear* by Nahum Tate, already known to the literary world as the author of a small volume of *Poems* (8vo, 1677),* and a couple of fairly fortunate dramas, *Brutus*

* Licensed by L'Estrange, 27 November 1676. The book is dedicated to Dr. Walter Needham (1631?-1691), a famous (if unfortunate) physician and anatomist, who, in succession to Dr. Castle, had been appointed physician to Charterhouse, 7 November 1672.

of Alba: or, The Enchanted Lovers and *The Loyal General. Brutus of Alba* was produced at Dorset Gardens in the summer of 1678, and published, quarto, that year with a Dedication to the Earl of Dorset. The story is largely based on the Fourth Book of the *Æneid*, and Tate had, indeed, " *begun and finisht it under the names of* Dido *and* Æneas; *but was wrought by advice of some Friends, to Transform it to the Dress it now wears.*" Æneas accordingly has become " *Brutus*, Prince of the *Dardan* Forces "; Ascanius, " Locrinus, His Son, A Youth "; Dido, the " Queen of *Syracuse* "; Anna, " *Amarante*, Her Confident " ; whilst Creusa is spoken of as Eudemia, and Sychaeus is now Argaces. Soziman, a " Designing Lord," a pointed satire on the treacherous Shaftesbury, is assisted in his villainies by the sorceress Ragusa. The scenes in which this " sullen Dame " and her four attendant witches take part are by no means destitute of fantasy and power, and considerable extracts from these passages were included by Charles Lamb in his *Specimens of English Dramatic Poets* (The Garrick Plays).

The fourth *Æneid* had a particular attraction for Tate, and it was he who furnished the book of Purcell's famous opera *Dido and Æneas,** performed by the pupils

* This opera was revived, 20 November 1895, at the Lyceum Theatre, London, by students of the Royal College of Music, on the occasion of the Purcell Bicentenary. It attracted much attention, and has since that time been several times performed.

In May 1792 there was given at the Haymarket a translation (with music by Stephen Storace) of Metastasio's *Didone Abbandonata*. Madame Mara sang Dido. *Didone Abbandonata* had originally been produced at Naples during the Carnival of 1724. Sarro composed the music. The Romanina (Marianna Bulgarelli) sang Dido, and Niccolini, whose voice was a low contralto, Æneas. This brilliant opera created a furore.

In England there have been some eight or nine dramatic

at Josiah Priest's Chelsea " Boarding-school for Young Gentlewomen." Priest removed from Leicester Fields to Chelsea in 1680, so the opera cannot be earlier than that year, and Mr. W. Barclay Squire, who has examined the question in ample detail, assigns 1688-1690 as the date of this entertainment.* An epilogue, specially written for the occasion by the popular Tom D'Urfey† was spoken by Lady Dorothy Buck. Tate's libretto is not without considerable charm and pathos, and he deserves high meed of praise for his English recitative which Purcell has set to divine music. The connexion between *Brutus of Alba* and *Dido and Æneas*, which has not hitherto been remarked, is very close. Witches appear both in the tragedy and in the opera, and a detailed comparison would evince that striking similarity which might be expected in two dramatic presentations of the same story from the same pen.

The Loyal General, produced at Dorset Gardens in the winter of 1679, is a drama of swift, intensive incident, of treachery, intrigue, and war. Henry Harris acted the King, who concludes the play by his retirement to a hermit's grot; Betterton, the faithful Theocrin; Jevon, Escalus the traitor; Mrs. Mary Lee, Arviola; Mrs. Elizabeth Currer, the amorous Queen; and Bowman, Pisander, her gallant.

Of the plays written by Tate after his success with

pieces dealing with Dido, from *The Tragedie of Dido Queene of Carthage: Played by the Children of her Maiesties Chappell. Written by Christopher Marlowe and Thomas Nash. Gent.* 4to, 1594, to F. C. Burnand's burlesque, *Dido*, produced at the S. James Theatre, London, with Charles Young in the title-rôle, Clara St. Casse as Æneas, and Miss Wyndham as Anna.

* " Purcell's Dramatic Music," *Sammelbände* of the International Music Society, vol. 5.

† Printed in D'Urfey's *New Poems*, 1690.

King Lear, an alteration of *Richard II* is especially interesting. Brought out at the Theatre Royal in the spring of 1681, with an epilogue spoken by the favourite Mrs. Sarah Cook, it had but a very short life, as for political reasons it was " Silenc'd on the Third Day." It may be remembered that well-nigh a century before, in 1601, Queen Elizabeth had complained angrily of some tragedy on the same subject that was " played fourtie times in open streets and houses," bitterly exclaiming to Lambard in her wrath: " I am Richard the Second, knowe yee not that?" Already in 1599 Sir John Hayward, who in his first part of the *Life and Raigne of King Henry the Fourth* had given an account of the deposition of Richard, had been summoned before the Star Chamber, sharply reprimanded, and imprisoned. The first two quartos, 1597 and 1598, of Shakespeare's own play omit the deposition scene, and it is not until the third quarto, 1608, that the " woeful pageant " appears, attention to which is called on the title-page which announces as new in print " additions of the Parliament Sceane and the deposing of King Richard." That the rage of Elizabeth and the apprehensions of the authorities were not without good warrant was shown by an incident connected with the rising of Essex in 1601. On the afternoon immediately preceding the outbreak, a play concerned with the deposition of Richard II was enacted. Moreover, it had been particularly bespoken by Sir Gilly Merrick, one of the conspirators, and the arrangement was made with Augustine Phillips, a member of the company to which Shakespeare belonged. The play in question was performed at the Globe, and perhaps it was Shakespeare's *Richard II.**

* On the other hand the official account of Essex's conspiracy says that " the playe was old," and Camden speaks of it as an " old out-worne " piece. The actors declared they would lose

At a time when party rancour was at its hottest, when the whole country had been convulsed by the illegal Exclusion Bill engineered by " A Name to all succeeding Ages curst," the unprincipled Shaftesbury, who was daily instigating his weak tool, Monmouth, to open insurrection and revolt, the story of Richard II seems to have been an unwise choice—to say the least—to have selected for the public stage. There can be small wonder that the actors were speedily ordered to withdraw a play, which might be supposed necessarily to teem with improper parallels and dangerous allusions political partisans could harmfully snatch at to the inflaming of their prejudice and passions. Nevertheless, Tate was bitterly disappointed that his drama had been thus " stifled," and when it was printed, quarto, the same year as *The History of King Richard the Second acted at the Theatre Royal under the Name of the Sicilian Userper*, he wrote a " Prefatory Epistle in Vindication of the Author, occasioned by the Prohibition of the Play on the Stage." The piece had, indeed, been played twice, but even so at the eleventh hour the author was obliged to change the locale of his scenes from England to Sicily, and ordered to rename his characters so that the connexion with native history might be as far as possible obscured. Accordingly, in his preface, Tate complains that, " *For the two days in which it was Acted the Change of the Scene, Names of Persons, &c., was a great Disadvantage : many things were by this means render'd obscure and incoherent that in their native Dress had appear'd not only proper but gracefull. I call'd my persons* Sicilians *but might as well have made 'em Inhabitants of*

if they revived it, and were promised " forty shillings extraordinary " as a compensation for the pains they were at to produce it. Shakespeare's *Richard II* could hardly be considered " old " or " out-worne " in February 1601.

the Isle of Pines,* *or, World in the* Moon† *for whom an Audience are like to have small Concern.* Richard II accordingly is Oswald; Gaunt, Alcidore; York, Cleon; Bullingbrook, Vortiger; Northumberland, Hermogenes; and the Queen, Aribell. We have a scene with the mobile, a " Shoomaker, Farrier, Weaver, Tanner, Mercer, Brewer, Butcher, Baker, *and infinite others.*"

In spite of his ill hap with *Richard II,* Tate soon tried his hand yet again at a new version of another of Shakespeare's tragedies, and in December 1681, there was produced at the Theatre Royal " The Ingratitude of a Common-wealth or The Fall of *Caius Martius Coriolanus.*" Here Act V is wholly Tate's invention, and although he worked upon somewhat violent and irregular lines, he seems to have done his best to put dramatic movement and effect into the very dull and declamatory original. In his preface he candidly asserts that he chose *Coriolanus* for adaptation because " there appeared in some passages no small resemblance with the busie faction of our own time," and after the

---

* *A New and further Discovery of the Isle of Pines,* by Henry Nevile, 12mo, 1668, was a romance in a letter professing to emanate from Cornelius van Sloetton, a Dutchman. The imaginary island was placed in the centre of the Indian Ocean, and the polygamous hero who was wrecked there, *travaillait si bien* that an ideal commonwealth consisting of twelve thousand English Protestants shortly flourished. This extravagant fiction was attacked in *Das Verdaechtige Pineser Eyland,* Hamburg, 1668, but it was none the less extremely popular, and there is a French version, *Nouvelle Découverte de l'Isle Pinés située au delà de la ligne aequinoctiale. Faite par un Navire Hollandais l'an 1667,* 4to, 1668. This was translated into Italian as *Nuovo scoprimento dell' Isola Pines. . . .* 12mo [1670 ?].

† An allusion to Cyrano de Bergerac's Σεληναρχια, *or the Government of the World in the Moon : Done into English by Tho. St. Serf, Gent.* (16mo, 1659).

rebuff he had experienced over *The Sicilian Usurper*, he was no doubt anxious to invite Court favour by satirizing the turbulent Whigs and their plebeian satellites. The character of Valeria has been considerably elaborated à *la mode*, and she appears as a fantastical talkative lady, a manifest imitation of Jonson's Sempronia.* She also delivers the epilogue. In November 1719 there was brought out at Drury Lane another version of *Coriolanus*, altered by John Dennis as *The Invader of his Country ; or, The Fatal Resentment*, with Booth as Coriolanus and Mrs. Porter, Volumnia. It was acted thrice. Yet a third adaptation, *Coriolanus, or The Roman Matron*, attributed to Thomas Sheridan, was seen at Covent Garden in December 1754, with Sheridan as the hero, Peg Woffington, Veturia, and Mrs. Bellamy, Volumnia. These two favourite actresses, it is interesting to note, had sustained the same characters in James Thomson's cold and correct *Coriolanus*, which was first performed at Covent Garden, 13 January 1749, when " speech-fam'd " Quin played the title-rôle to the vast admiration of the town. Throughout Thomson's tragedy the unity of place is strictly observed, the scene lying in the Volscian camp.

In the autumn of 1684 there was produced at the Theatre Royal *A Duke and No Duke*,† a three act

---

* The great representative of Sempronia was Mrs. Corey. When *Cataline* was revived at the Theatre Royal on Friday, 18 December 1668, her mimicry (at the instigation of Lady Castlemaine) of Lady Harvey caused something like a riot in the house.

† The production is often misdated as 1685. *A Duke and No Duke* was published 1685, " With the several Songs set to Musick, with thorough Basses for the Theorbo or Bass-Viol. Quarto. Price 1s." One of the songs, set by Baptist, was written by Sir George Etherege. The title seems to have been suggested by *A King and No King*.

adaptation by Tate from Sir Aston Cokain's *Trappolin suppos'd a Prince,* itself founded upon a famous Italian mime* *Trappolin Creduto Principe.* Trappolin was acted by Antony Leigh, who "was of the mercurial kind" and in humour "loved to take a full career"; the Duchess of Florence by Mrs. Currer; whilst the epilogue was spoken by Joe Haines. Although in this extravaganza, as the *Biographia Dramatica* sententiously points out, "the whole design is absurd and impossible," yet it proved to have fun and laughter enough—however antic and whimsical—to secure it extraordinary popularity and a long life in the theatre. It was an especial favourite with so good a judge of these matters as Charles II. From time to time, it is true that in after days, Tate's scenes were something revised by later writers, such as Robert Drury, who in 1732 converted them by the addition of a number of new songs into a "farcical ballad opera," in which guise the old play was given with great success at Drury Lane as *The Devil of a Duke; or, Trappolin's Vagaries.* At Covent Garden, too,

---

* *Commedia dell' Arte all' Improviso.* In his prologue, Cokain says of his play:
> "Ingenious Italy hath liked it well.
> Yet it is no translation; for he ne'er
> But twice in Venice did it ever hear."

The Italian Impromptu Comedy, so far from being printed, was but rarely even committed to writing. "The development of the intrigue by dialogue and action," J. A. Symonds explains, "was left to the native wit of the several players." In Cokain's *Trappolin,* many of the stock characters appear: Mattemores, the Spanish Captain; Mago, the wizard; Pucanello; whilst Trappolin is the equivalent of Scaramouch, and Fiametta, his sweetheart, is Colombine.

After the Restoration, Cokain's play was acted with a new prologue written by Duffett. This is printed in his *Poems* (p. 22), 1676; licensed for printing, September 1675.

a comic melodramatic burletta, *The Duke and the Devil*, produced in July 1818, was recognized to be none other than *A Duke or No Duke*, refurbished to suit the taste of the day. Amplified or curtailed as the case might require, Tate's farce held the stage for well nigh one hundred and fifty years, and was still popular in the first quarter of the eighteenth century.

In July-August 1685, was produced at the Queen's Theatre,* Dorset Gardens, *Cuckold's Haven ; or, An Alderman no Conjurer,†* which is an acknowledged alteration by Tate in three acts of *Eastward Hoe,‡* with some conveyance from *The Devil is an Ass*. The play may be dated owing to a reference in the prologue anent Monmouth's abortive rebellion, which had just been quashed :

> " *But now the Monster has her final Rout,*
> *The very dregs of Treason's Tap are out.*"

* Formerly the Duke's.

† Published quarto, 1685. " Cuckold's Haven ; or, An Alderman no Conjurer. A Farce, acted at the Queen's Theatre. Written by N. Tate " (*The Term Catalogues*, Michaelmas [November], 1685). Cuckold's Haven is a point on the Surrey side of the Thames, a little below Rotherhithe Church. It was formerly marked by a high pole, crowned with a mighty pair of horns. See *Industry and Idleness*, Plate V. Hogarth, indeed, is generally said to have derived his idea of these pictures (1747) from *Eastward Hoe*.

‡ Quarto, 1605. " As It was played in the *Black-friers*. By The Children of her Maiesties Revels. *Made* by Geo: Chapman. Ben: Ionson. Ioh: Marston." It was probably produced in the spring of 1605. The history of this piece, which gave great offence at Court, has often been told.

The Devil is an Ass, produced at the Blackfriars in 1616, is an admirable comedy. Says Swinburne: " The wealth of comic matter is only too copious." Pug, " the less devil," who has obtained leave to visit the earth is made an ass of on every

Another interesting allusion to the same event incidentally shows the popularity of *The Tempest*:

" *Our Trinculo and Trapp'lin were undone*
When Lime's *more Farcy Monarchy begun.*"*

Although Professor Parrott has seen fit to criticize
somewhat prejudicially Tate's version of the Jacobean
comedy, *Cuckold's Haven* is nevertheless a merry and
amusing farce, and upon the stage it may well be
conceived to have gone with considerable *brio* and verve.
The piece was for the most part strongly supported.
The lithe and nimble Jevon excelled as Quicksilver;
Anthony Leigh, the most humorous comedian of the
time, had good opportunities for his genius in Security
" a Bawd and Usurer "; Baker acted Golding; Gillo,
Captain Seagull; Joseph Williams, whose only fault—
according to his harshest critic—was that occasionally
" he loved his bottle better than his business," Sir
Petronel Flash; Haines, lawyer Bramble; the inimitable Mrs. Corey, Mrs. Touchstone; Susanna Percival,
Girtred; Mrs. Twiford, Mildred " the sober Daughter ";
Mrs. Price, Security's Wife. Unfortunately the production encountered several drawbacks, the chief being
that, as Tate writes in his Dedication of the printed play,
addressed to Colonel Edmund Ashton, " The Principal
Part (on which the Diversion depended) was, by
Accident, disappointed of Mr. *Nokes's* Performance, for
whom it was design'd and only proper, which caus'd

possible occasion. After the Restoration this play was frequently
acted at the Theatre Royal before the two Companies amalgamated in 1682.

* The sting of this couplet lies in the fact that—as will be
remembered—Trinculo proclaims himself King of the Island,
but his sovereignty only lasts a few hours; and Trappolin's
dukeship was phantasmagorial.

a Retrenchment of whole Scenes in the Action that are in this Copy inserted." This important rôle, Touchstone, was given to Thomas Percival, a useful actor, but of undistinguished mediocrity, and ill able to supply the place of the celebrated Nokes. According to Downes, Percival joined the theatre about 1673-4, a period of considerable changes, when the Duke's company was recruited by Anthony Leigh, Jevon, Gillo, Joseph Williams, Bowman, Mrs. Barry, Mrs. Currer, Charlotte Butler, and other admirable players who supplied the loss of Joseph Price, Lovell, Lilliston, Mrs. Davenport, Mrs. Jennings, Moll Davis, and several more of lesser note. From a list of Percival's characters we may soon gauge that, however industrious, he never rose above a very secondary position. In 1675 he acted Fortinbras in *Hamlet,* and during the winter of the same year Burbon * in Settle's Merovingian tragedy *Love and Revenge,* a wholesale conveyance from William Hemminge's *The Fatal Contract,* quarto, 1653, a drama which had at its original production been received with great favour. There is a little known edition of Hemminge's play, quarto, 1661, and it was again reprinted in 1687 under the title *The Eunuch.* In the spring of 1676 Percival took the small rôle of the Apothecary in D'Urfey's amusing comedy *A Fond Husband ; or, The Plotting Sisters,* which owed the most part of its extraordinary success to the magnificent performance of Anthony Leigh as Fumble, "a superannuated Alderman, that dotes on Black Women: He's very deaf and almost blind; and seeking to cover his imperfection of not

* This reference I owe to Mr. G. Thorn-Drury. We had independently made lists of the characters played by Percival, and he kindly supplied me with five rôles which escaped my notice: Burbon (*Love and Revenge*); Grisolan (*The Duchess of Malfi*); Randall (*The Jovial Crew*); Dr. Quibus (*The Factious Citizen*); Trevile (*Rollo*).

hearing what is said to him, answers quite contrarily."
In August-September 1676 we find Percival as Ordgano,
" Vallet to Don Diego " in Ravenscroft's *The Wrangling
Lovers*;* in the autumn he is Osmin, a Moor, in Mrs.
Behn's *Abdelazer; or The Moor's Revenge*; † in October
Old Monylove in *Tom Essence; or, The Modish Wife*,
attributed by Hazlitt to Ravenscroft, but by other
writers to Thomas Rawlins; in November-December
Carino, Foster-father to Mirtillo, in Settle's *Pastor Fido,
or, The Faithful Shepherd*, an adaptation for the theatre
of Fanshawe's translation from Guarini;‡ and during
the winter of that year Leander in Otway's native and
racy transcript from Molière, *The Cheats of Scapin*. In
March 1677 Percival acted Memnon, an Egyptian Lord,
in Sedley's heroic tragedy *Antony and Cleopatra*, " the
only tragedy," according to Shadwell, " except two
of Johnson's, and one of Shakespeare's, wherein Romans are made to speak and do like Romans "; in
July, Truro, Claudio's servant, in Thomas Porter's *The
French Conjurer*;|| in July-August Darmetas, servant to

* Mrs. Centlivre's *The Wonder, a Woman keeps a Secret* is
indebted to this comedy.
† A very good alteration of *Lust's Dominion; or, The Lascivious Queen*.
‡ The character in the original is Carino, "Vecchio, padre
putativo di Mirtillo." Pastoral plays were fashionable with those
who affected culture, and also popular largely because of the
boundless opportunities for scenic decoration and effect. So
Pepys notes, 13 June 1663, that *The Faithful Shepherdess* was
" much thronged after, and often shown, but it is only for the
scene's sake, which is very fine indeed and worth seeing."
On Tuesday, 25 February 1668, Pepys saw " The Faythful Shepherd," a version from Guarini, played at the Nursery, but he
writes, it was acted " in the meanest manner that I was sick
of it."
|| The plot is founded upon episodes in *Guzman d'Alfarache*.

Sylvanus, in *The Constant Nymph; or, The Rambling Shepherd*, " Written by a Person of Quality," and supported by an extremely strong cast which included Samuel Sandford, Matthew Medbourne, Gillo, Thomas Jevon, Mrs. Mary Lee, Mrs. Barry, Mrs. Norris, Mrs. Anne Quin, and Mrs. Betterton. The scene lies in Arcadia. Percival played Sir Gregory Lovemuch, *The Counterfeit Bridegroom; or, The Defeated Widow* (altered by Mrs. Behn from Middleton's *No Wit, No Help Like a Woman's*) a vacation play of 1677; in the autumn Philippo in Mrs. Behn's excellent comedy *The Rover; or, The Banished Cavalier* (I); Grisolan in a revival of *The Duchess of Malfi*, with Betterton as Bosola, Henry Harris, Ferdinand, and Mrs. Betterton, the Duchess; Isander, a senator in Shadwell's *Timon of Athens*, December 1677 (or perhaps early January 1678). In the summer of 1678 he was Dormilon in Leanerd's *The Counterfeits*.* In the autumn of 1679 Percival appeared as Granius in Otway's *Caius Marius*;† and as Vitellizzo, Chief of the Vitelli, in Lee's *Caesar Borgia*. He also doubled Priam and Calchas in Dryden's *Troilus and Cressida; or, Truth Found too Late.* In the spring of 1680 he was Old Lord Clifford in Crowne's *The Misery of Civil-War*, a palpable adaptation of *King Henry VI* (2nd part), although the prologue says:

" For by his feeble skill, 'tis built alone,
The divine *Shakespear* did not lay one stone."

In a far greater play, Otway's *The Orphan*, brought out that same year, he was the Chaplain. In Lee's *Lucius Junius Brutus*, produced before June 1681, and " acted

* Colley Cibber's *She Wou'd and She Wou'd Not; or, the Kind Impostor* owes much to this comedy.
† A version of *Romeo and Juliet*. Smith acted Marius junior (Romeo), Mrs. Barry, Lavinia (Juliet), and Nokes, in petticoats as the Nurse, made the house rock with laughter.

at the Duke's Theatre for six days; but then prohibited " for political reasons, he appeared as a Fecilian
Priest. In Otway's masterpiece, *Venice Preserv'd*,
February 1682, he was Spinosa, a conspirator; and later
in the spring he played in D'Urfey's capital comedy, *The
Royalist*, Captain Jonas " A Seditious Rascal that
disturbs the People with News and Lyes to Promote his
own Interest." It has with much probability been
suggested that Captain Jonas may be intended for Sir
William Jones, the Attorney-General, a sour, opinion-
ated old Whig, whom Dryden has pilloried for ever as:

> " Bull-fac'd *Jonas*, who coud Statutes draw
> To mean Rebellion, and make Treason Law."*

In 1682, at the amalgamation of the two companies, the
Duke's players removed from Dorset Garden to the
Theatre Royal, which opened under the new union, 16
November. On 4 December *The Duke of Guise*, a tragedy
by Dryden and Lee, was produced. It is obviously
political, and the Whigs did their utmost, but in vain,
to prevent the performance. Pamphlets were written,
and Dryden was obliged to publish *A Vindication of the
Duke of Guise*, 4to, 1683. In the course of his remarks he
has occasion to speak of the playing, and he particularly
mentions the Night Scene (Act IV) between the wizard
Malicorne and his familiar Melanax, " which is one of
the best in the Tragedy though murder'd in the Acting."
Percival was Malicorne and Gillo the demon. At the
retirement of Hart and Mohun, who had excelled in
Brutus and Cassius, *Julius Caesar*, hitherto the special
property of Killigrew's company, became available for
Betterton and the rest. It was accordingly produced in
1683 with Cardell Goodman as Caesar; Betterton,
Brutus; Smith, Cassius; Kynaston, Antony (his old

---

* *Absalom and Achitophel*, The First Part (1681), 581-2.

rôle); Lady Slingsby, Calphurnia; Sarah Cook, Portia.
Percival was cast for Artemidorus the sophist of Cnidos.
In the late winter of that year was revived another play
also that had belonged exclusively to Killigrew, Brome's
charming comedy *A Jovial Crew*, in which Percival
played Randall. In the autumn of 1684 we find him as
Mago, *A Duke and No Duke*, and in the following year
he appeared in place of Nokes, as we have already seen,
as Touchstone in *Cuckold's Haven*. In 1685 also he
played Dr. Quibus in *The Factious Citizen ; or, The
Melancholy Visioner*, with Underhill as Timothy Turbulent; Leigh, Abednego Suckthumb, and Nokes, Cringe,
" a balderdash poet." In July-August 1685 Percival
was Boldsprite, the Ship's Master, in D'Urfey's *A
Commonwealth of Women*,* and in the winter of the same
year he acted Trevile in a revival of *Rollo*.† In January
1686 we find him as Lopez, a Mathematician, in
D'Urfey's *The Banditti ; or, A Ladies Distress*, and
February of the same year at Dorset Garden he played
the Cook in Jevon's admirable farce *The Devil of a Wife*,‡
Jevon himself acted Jobson, and Sue Percival, Nell. In
a slightly altered, but by no means an improved, form as
The Devil to Pay,‖ produced at Drury Lane, 6 August
1731, this farce kept the stage until the first quarter of

---

* An alteration of Fletcher's *The Sea-Voyage*, which was
frequently played at the Theatre Royal during the first decade
after the Restoration.

† Hart had excelled as Rollo; Kynaston played Otto; Mohun,
Aubrey; Burt, La Torch; Mrs. Corey, the Duchess; and Mrs.
Marshall, Edith.

‡ In his preface to *The Banditti*, 4to, 1686, D'Urfey has a
sneer at the success of Jevon's play.

‖ A version by Charles Coffey. As late as December 1852 an
adaptation called *The Basket-Maker's Wife* was produced at
Niblo's Garden, New York.

the nineteenth century. Kitty Clive and Dora Jordan both excelled in the rôle of Jobson's wife.

From his intimate knowledge of the period in question Mr. G. Thorn-Drury has generously furnished me with the following interesting account of Percival, the details of which have hitherto been uncollected: " Thomas Percivall, of the Parish of St. *Martins in the Fields, (that lately belonged to the Play-house*) was indicted, for that he being a person not having God before his Eyes, nor weighing his Duty and Allegiance to our Sovereign Lord and Lady the King and Queen, but endeavouring and intending to deceive the King and People, he did falsely and traiterously clip, cut, file, and diminish the Current Coin of *England*. The Evidence for the King deposed, that when they came to search his Lodgings on the 10th of *September* last, he run away, but was soon stopt, and in his Pocket was found a small Paper of Clippings; and over his Beds-head was found another little Bag of Clippings, which was shewed to the Jury; and a pair of Shears, which were seen to drop from the Prisoner in the Street as he run away; which he did not deny; adding that he found the Shears and the Clippings in a Closet where he lodged, and was going to carry them to Mr. Justice *Bridgmans* when Mr. *Dunn* came upon him; but he was askt why he run away when he saw Mr. *Dunn*; he said, because he was afraid of falling into their hands, which was easily believed; He was found guilty of High Treason." " The Proceedings of the King [*sic*] and Queens Commissions of the *Peace*, and *Oyer* and *Terminer* and *Gaol-Delivery* of *Newgate*, held for the City of *London*, and *County* of Middlesex, at *Justice-Hall* in the *Old Bayly*. On *Thursday, Friday, Saturday, Monday and Tuesday*, being the 12th, 13th, 14th, 16th, and 17th Days of *October* 1693. *And in the Fifth Year* of *Their Majesties Reign*. (fol. p. 4). . . .

Received Sentence of *Death*, 22 . . . Thomas Percival. . ."
(*ibid.*, p. 6). Mr. Thorn-Drury has also supplied me
with the following extracts from Luttrell: " 12 September 1693. On Sunday Mr. Percival belonging to the
playhouse, and yesterday some others, were committed
to Newgate for clipping; tho' 6 were condemned for it
this sessions, and 5 women who formerly pleaded their
bellies, are ordered to be executed." " 14 Oct. 1693.
Thursday the sessions began at the Old Baily's . . .
Percival, the player, found guilty of clipping." " 17
Oct. 1693. This day the sessions ended at the Old
Baily, where 17 received sentence of death; amongst
them . . . Mr. Percival and 6 other clippers." " 24 Oct.
1693. Yesterday 14 malefactors were executed at
Tyburn; 6 of them clippers . . . Percival and Dear, two
clippers, were reprieved." Luttrell is the authority also
for the statement that Mrs. Mountford was told that
her father's life would be spared if she abandoned her
appeal against the acquittal of Lord Mohun.* Percival
got as far as Portsmouth on his way to transportation,
but died and was buried there.

In 1751 Garrick foolishly substituted *Eastward Hoe*
at Drury Lane, on Lord Mayor's Day, 29 October, for
the traditional performance of Ravenscroft's popular
The London Cuckolds. The result of his egregious blunder

---

* Susanna Percival, Thomas Percival's daughter, became
famous as an actress. She married William Mountford, and some
time after his dastardly assassination by Lord Mohun, she
became *en secondes noces* Mrs. Verbruggen. Mountford was
stabbed by Lord Mohun, a fellow of the vilest character, on the
night of 9 December 1691. He lingered until the next day.
Cibber, who has devoted the most brilliant pages of his *Apology*
to an encomium of Mrs. Mountford's genius, writes that she
" was mistress of more variety of humour than I ever knew in
any one woman actress. . . . Nothing, though ever so barren,
if within the bounds of nature could be flat in her hands."

was that in spite of the fine acting of Yates as Touch-stone, Woodward as Quicksilver, "swaggering" Jack Palmer as Sir Petronel Flash, and Kitty Clive as Girtred, the piece was fairly hissed, hooted, and pippin-pelted from the boards, and a second representation could not be so much as attempted.

Old City Manners, a genteel adaptation of *Eastward Hoe* from the pen of Mrs. Lennox, produced at Drury Lane, 9 November 1775, was received with considerable favour. As one might expect, somewhat detrimental changes were made, and the full-flavoured speech of James' day has been finically emasculated. Baddeley of Twelfth-cake fame acted Touchstone; and James Dodd, " the most exquisite coxcomb, the most ridiculous chatterer ever seen," Quicksilver.

Charlotte Lennox (1720-1804) was a miscellaneous writer of some distinction and a not unskilful dramatist. The work by which she is best remembered is *The Female Quixote*, two volumes, 12mo, 1752, an agreeable and ingenious satire upon the romances of De la Cal-prenède and Madeleine de Scudéri. Dr. Johnson thought extravagantly of this lady's talent, and unfortunately his compliments quite turned her head, so that " nobody liked her." Her latter years were saddened by sickness and want, and she died a pensioner on the Royal Literary Fund.

About Easter, 1687, was revived at the Theatre Royal Fletcher's excellent play *The Island Princess*,* with alterations by Tate, which seem quite unnecessary, but are, indeed, of no great moment, being mainly concerned with the phrasing of the dialogue. Kynaston acted the King of Tidore; Gillo the Governor of Ternata; Smith, Armusia; Griffin, Ruy Dias; Sarah Cooke, Quisara the Princess; and Susanna Mountford, Panura.

* Folio, 1647. Acted at Court Christmas, 1621.

Always popular, *The Island Princess* again proved to
have lost no whit of its attraction for the town.   In
January 1669 *The Island Princess** (with alterations)
had been produced at the Theatre Royal, the first
Drury Lane.   The cast was as follows: King of Tidore,
Edward Kynaston;   King of Bakam, Marmaduke
Watson;   Prince of Syana, Grayden;   Governor of
Ternata, William Cartwright; Armusia, Charles Hart;
Ruy Dias, Michael Mohun; Christophero, Richard Bell;
Emanuel, William Beeston;   Soza, Nicholas Burt;
Piniero, Robert Shotterel;   Pedro, William Harris;
Captain, Lyddal;   Quisara, Mrs. Marshall;   Quisana,
Mrs. Corey; Panura, Mrs. Margaret Hughes.   There is
no doubt that the scope for scenic display—an opportunity of which every advantage was taken—suggested
the revival and maintained the popularity of this
romantic drama. On Thursday, 7 January 1668-9, Pepys
saw *The Island Princess*, " the first time I ever saw it;
and it is a pretty good play, many good things being in
it, and a good scene of a town on fire."   On Tuesday,
9 February, at a second visit he liked it " mighty well,
as an excellent play," whilst Friday, 23 April, he writes:
" to the King's playhouse, and saw ' The Generous
Portugalls,' a play that pleases me better and better
every time we see it."   *The Island Princess* is, indeed,
deserving of this warm commendation.

Of *The Island Princess*† " Made into an Opera,"
" All the Musical Entertainments, and the greatest part

* *The Island Princess ; or the Generous Portugal*, 4to, 1669.
† Quarto, 1699.   " Two new Dialogues set by Mr. Jeremiah
Clarke, sung in the last revived Play, called " The Island
Princess, or The generous Portuguese, newly made into an
Opera,' " were given in *Twelve New Songs*, folio, 1699. " The
Prologue, Song-Tunes, Dances, Dialogues, and Epilogue, in the
last New Opera, The Island Princess," were published in *The
Compleat Instructor to the Flute*, 1699.

of the Play New, and Written by Mr. *Motteux*," there is nothing good to report. Produced at the Theatre Royal in December 1698, this " Opera " had a great success owing to the music " charmingly compos'd " by Daniel Purcell and Jeremiah Clarke, together with the fine singing of Leveridge, Pate, and Mrs. Lindsey. It was further helped by the most ornate scenic decoration and a crowd of supers. Having mutilated the original without judgement or mercy Mr. Peter Motteux in his address " To the Reader " coolly announces: " *Tho Mr.* Fletcher's Island Princess *was frequently acted of old, and revived twelve years ago, with some Alterations, the Judicious seem'd satisfy'd, that it wou'd hardly have been relish'd now on the Stage. As I found it not unfit to be made what we here call an Opera, I undertook to revise it, but not as I wou'd have done, had I design'd a correct Play. Let this at once satisfy the Modern Critics and the zealous Admirers of Old Plays; for I neither intended to make it regular, nor to keep in it all that I lik'd in the Original, but only what I thought fit for my Purpose; and the Success has answer'd my Intent, far beyond Expectation.*" Smartly did the author of *The Grove; or, The Rival Muses** (1701) write :

" *Motteux* and *Durfey* are for nothing fit,
But to supply with Songs their want of Wit.
Had not the *Island Princess* been adorn'd
With Tunes, and pompous Scenes, she had been scorn'd.
What was not *Fletcher's*, no more Sense contains,
Than he that wrote the *Jubilee* has Brains ;
Which ne'er had pleas'd the Town, or purchas'd
      Fame,
But that 'twas christ'ned with a modish Name."

* *Poems on Affairs of State*, vol. IV (1707).

Farquhar's *The Constant Couple, or a Trip to the Jubilee,** to which a passing allusion is here made, must be acknowledged to be a tinselly piece of work, although its sham wit and varnish proved effective by candle-light when Wilks or Peg Woffington in breeches played Sir Harry Wildair. The trick has deceived many a bat's-eyed critic in the past, and cozens the unwary even to-day. Inasmuch, however, as *The Constant Couple* no longer holds the boards, the modern has scant excuse for his simplicity.†

* Produced November 1699 at Drury Lane. Quarto, 1700.
Although of more ancient institution the first recorded Jubilee was celebrated by Boniface VIII in 1300. Since 1450 (Nicholas V) the Jubilee has been held every twenty-five years until the present time, with the three exceptions of 1800, 1850, and 1875, when, owing to political disturbances this holy function was omitted. The Jubilee is defined by Moroni as: " Un' indulgenza plenaria e straordinaria concessa dal sommo Pontefice alla Chiesa universale o parzialmente à Roma massima nell' anno Santo." Innocent XII (Antonio Pignatelli), who was elected, 12 July 1691, proclaimed: " il guibileo pel felice governo del pontificato." Of the Sixteenth *Anno Santo*, Gaetano Moroni in his vast *Dizionario di Erudizione Storico-Ecclesiastica* (Venice, 1840), says: " Aperto fu quest' Anno Santo nel 1699 da Innocenzo XII e chiuso nel 1700 da Clemente XI." Innocent XII died 27 September 1700, and Clement XI (Giovanni Francesco Albani) was elected 23 November 1700. This Jubilee and *Anno Santo* were announced by Innocent XII in his bull *Regi saeculorum*, 18 May 1699. The splendid ceremonies attracted to the Eternal City a vast concourse, amongst whom were many strangers of princely rank, and, in particular, a large number of Englishmen of quality, who were making the grand tour.

† Swinburne strongly inveighed against the habit of undiscerning critics who bracket Marlowe's name with Greene and Peele. One may protest with equal warmth against the slovenly custom of placing Farquhar in dramatic connexion with Congreve and Vanbrugh. This confusion is probably due to the

It may be noted that there was a revival of *The Island Princess* (Motteux) at Covent Garden, 10 December 1739. Ryan played Armusia; Johnson, the Governor of Ternata; and the beautiful Mrs. Horton, Quisara.

In 1707 was published " Injur'd Love, or The Cruel Husband, a Tragedy, design'd to be Acted at the Theatre Royal, written by Mr. N. Tate, AUTHOR OF THE TRAGEDY CALL'D KING LEAR."* *Injur'd Love*, which appears never to have been acted, is nothing else than a useless version of *The White Devil*. Webster's great masterpiece had been revived in September 1661 by Killigrew's company at their theatre in Bear Yard, Vere Street, Clare Market, with signal success. It remained a stock piece,† and was frequently acted at

collected edition of Leigh Hunt, who reprinted in one well-known volume (1840) Wycherley, Congreve, Vanbrugh, and Farquhar. But no inference as to merit can thence be drawn. For Farquhar is of another kind and age. He belongs to the period of Colley Cibber and Mrs. Centlivre, nor is he their equal in comedy. He has, it is true, a certain bustle at times, and his best piece, *The Beaux Stratagem*, gives homely pictures of small provincial life with some mildly mirthful touches. But if we compare him with Etherege or Vanbrugh how heavy does his dross appear! As might perhaps be expected superficial critics (no doubt from the old accident of his inclusion in the Leigh Hunt volume) still speak of this third-rate dramatist as the fellow of Wycherley and Congreve.

* " Injured Love; or The Cruel Husband. A Tragedy. Written by Mr. Tate. Quarto. Price 18d." *The Term Catalogues*, Trinity (July), 1707; Easter and Trinity (May and June), 1709.

† Downes gives *The White Devil* among a list of.'' Old Plays '' by various authors, Shakespeare, Jonson, Fletcher, Shirley, Brome, etc., which were acted but now and then; "yet being well performed, were very satisfactory to the Town." Pepys saw *The White Devil* twice, Wednesday, 2 October 1661, and again the following Friday. On both occasions, however, he was very

the Theatre Royal until the retirement of Charles Hart, since which time it has never been presented upon the stage. In 1665 this tragedy was printed, 4to, " Acted (formerly by Her Majesties Servants) at the *Phoenix* in *Drury-Lane,* and AT THIS PRESENT (by His now Majesties) at the THEATRE ROYAL." There is also another edition, 4to, 1672, " As it is Acted at the Theatre Royal By his Majesties Servants."* Unfortunately the cast is not given in either case, and although it were idle to speculate how the rôles might have been allotted one may, perhaps, venture the surmise that Vittoria was played by Mrs. Marshall.

Upon the death of Shadwell Nahum Tate became Laureate, 24 December 1692, an appointment which was duly confirmed at the accession of Queen Anne. With the incoming of the Hanoverian line, however, he seems to have lost this post, as Nicholas Rowe, an aggressive Whig, succeeded him, 1 August 1715. Tate died, 12 August 1715, in difficult and unfortunate circumstances.†

Although, as we have seen, the revival of *King Lear* shortly after the Restoration is not chronicled as having attracted much notice, Nahum Tate's alteration of Shakespeare's tragedy, which was produced in the early spring of 1681 at the Duke's Theatre, Dorset Garden, was received with the greatest enthusiasm. The cast was, indeed, extremely strong, and William Smith, in

late, and his impressions of the play are obviously dictated by ill humour and crossness. On 11 December (Wednesday) 1661, Herbert notes that *Uittoria Corumbana* was acted.

* " *Vittoria Corumbona ;* or, The White Devil. . . . In Quarto. Price, sticht, 1s." *The Term Catalogues,* Michaelmas (20 November), 1671.

† A complete and scholarly study of Nahum Tate is much to be desired. The account given by Canon Leigh Bennett in the *Dictionary of National Biography* is inadequate and unreliable. It cannot be commended.

particular, is traditionally said to have been admirable as Edgar.* Lady Slingsby,† *née* Mary Aldridge, and by her first marriage Mrs. Mary Lee, who played Regan, was a tragedienne of the highest rank, and Anne Shadwell, wife of Shadwell the poet, who acted Goneril, had long proved herself an actress endowed with consummate ability. Strangely enough, however, it does not appear that Betterton's Lear and Mrs. Barry's Cordelia anywhere receive particular mention, although as Tate's version took its place as a stock piece it can hardly be supposed that such great artists were ineffective in these rôles, which is not to say that Betterton's Lear was equal to his Hamlet, Macbeth, and Melantius, or that Mrs. Barry's Cordelia was comparable to her Monimia, Belvidera, and Isabella. All the honours, indeed, seem to have gone to Smith, Lady Slingsby, and Mrs. Shadwell.

Towards the end of his long career Betterton, then over seventy years of age, played the King in a special revival at the Haymarket, 30 October 1706. Verbruggen acted Edgar; Mills, Edmund; Freeman, Gloster; Minns, Kent; Bowen, the Usher; Tom Kent and Will Peer‡ the Two Ruffians; Mrs. Bracegirdle, Cordelia.

---

* After Smith's death in 1695 Edgar was played by George Powell.

† Having retired from the stage some nine years, she died in February 1694, and was buried in old S. Pancras graveyard on 1 March.

‡ William Peer was an actor of such little account that his very existence has been needlessly called in question. But a notice of him may be found in *The Spectator*. He was property-man at the theatre and played such rôles as the Apothecary in Otway's *Caius Marius* (*Romeo and Juliet*); the Presbyterian Parson in D'Urfey's *Love for Money* (Theatre Royal, winter, 1689); Jasper, a valet, in Shadwell's *The Scowerers* (Theatre Royal, December 1690). In Tom Brown's *Letters from the Dead*

" Much," pertinently remarks Davies, " has been said by Downs, by the Tatler, by Cibber, and others, of Betterton's uncommon powers of action and utterance in several of Shakespeare's principal parts, particularly Hamlet, Macbeth, Othello, and Brutus, but no writer has taken notice of his exhibition of Lear; a part of equal consequence, and requiring as perfect skill in the player as any of them. I am almost tempted to believe that this tragedy, notwithstanding that Tate's alterations were approved, was not in an such equal degree of favour, as Hamlet, Othello, and many other of our poet's dramas."

After Betterton's death, Barton Booth, (who had worshipped the veteran almost to idolatry), whilst his triumph as Cato was fresh in all memories, " undertook the representation of Lear, and was much admired in it." His performance is said to have been regal, yet full of passion and fire, and he excelled in the passages of passionate denunciation and wrath. His Edgar was Wilks, who proved particularly fine in the scenes of love and gallantry. " In the challenge of Edmund," moreover, " Wilks was highly spirited with superior elegance of deportment." Miss Santlow, " famed for dance," who afterwards married Booth, was a pleasing Cordelia.

Booth, however, had no mean competitor in a rising young actor, Antony Boheme. On 15 October 1720 *King Lear*, billed as " Never acted there " was produced at Lincoln's Inn Fields. Lear was played by Boheme; Edgar, Ryan; Gloster, Quin; Usher, Jemmy Spiller; Cordelia, Mrs. Seymour; Regan, Mrs. Parker. Boheme soon proved a very serious rival to Booth, and as Lear he was by many preferred to that stately tragedian.

to the Living, we have an epistle from Julian, " late Secretary to the Muses," to Will Pierre of Lincoln's Inn Fields Playhouse. This actual letter was written by Boyer, together with the reply which is dated 5 November 1701.

Macklin said that the young actor " gave a trait of the antique " to his Lear. " In his person he was tall, his features were expressive, with something of the venerable cast which gave force and authority to the various situations and passions of the character; the tones of his voice were equally powerful and harmonious, and his whole action suited to the age and feelings of Lear." Ryan, as Edgar, although not the equal of Wilks, was " manly and feeling," and in his scenes of feigned madness he displayed unsuspected talent. Quin as Gloster was justly celebrated,* and Jemmy Spillor proved an admirable Oswald. Tom Jevon, who originally played this part in 1681, had joined the Duke's company at the age of twenty-one, until which time he practised as a dancing-master, and upon the boards he was famous for his grace and nimbleness. Langbaine especially notes his " activity." He was our first Harlequin, and in low comedy of a fantastic and mercurial kind he won a great reputation. The rôle of the Steward seems to have been unpopular, for Davies tells us: " I have seen it acted by several eminent players, Yates, Shuter, King, Dodd, etc., but the character is so distasteful, and by the comedians falsely supposed to be unimportant, that all of them, of any note, no sooner get into the part but they grow tired and withdraw from it. He generally enters the stage in a careless disengaged manner, humming a tune, as if on purpose to give umbrage to the King by his neglect of him. Vernon was impudently negligent and character-

* Davies in his *Dramatic Miscellanies*, II, pp. 304-5, writes that Quin was succeeded in the rôle of Gloster by " Hulet, a man of great merit in the sock and buskin. At Drury-lane the elder Mills acted Gloster with Booth. Ned Berry, a man of very considerable abilities in a great variety of parts, was Garrick's Gloster for many years." Upon Berry's retirement, Davies himself played Gloster and met with no little applause.

istically provoking in Oswald; however he grew too great for the part, and it is now acted by an inferior player."

After the death of Antony Boheme, Quin was persuaded somewhat against his inclinations to essay Lear. He appeared as the old King for his benefit at Drury Lane on 8 March 1739. Milward acted Edgar; Mills, the Bastard; Theophilus Cibber, Oswald; Mrs. Mills, Cordelia; and Mrs. Furnival, Goneril. Quin, however, is said to have fallen infinitely short of his predecessor, but being so accomplished an artist he was received with deserved applause. His genius would not allow him to be undistinguished, but his sound judgement did not permit him often to repeat so unsuitable a personation.*

The best Edmund during the eighteenth century is considered to have been Thomas Walker,† the original Macheath; "his tread was manly, and his whole behaviour and deportment disengaged and commanding." He was equally admired as the Bastard Faulconbridge in *King John*.

Susannah Maria Cibber,

" Mistress of each soft art, with matchless skill
To turn and wind the passions as she will;
To melt the heart with sympathetic woe,
Awake the sigh, and teach the tear to flow;‡

---

* Quin insisted upon no less than twenty-two rehearsals, but " being at that time young and dissipated, attended only two of them."

† 1698-1744.

‡ *The Rosciad.* Tate Wilkinson used to say, that while he could mimic Garrick, Quin, Mrs. Bellamy, and others, in such a manner as to give a strong idea of their powers, yet Mrs. Cibber's excellence was of that superior kind that he could only retain her in his mind's eye. Davies writes: " Mrs. Cibber, the most pathetic of all actresses, was the only Cordelia of excellence."

was probably the tenderest and most charming Cordelia the stage has ever seen. What she looked like—and she looked exquisitely beautiful—we can judge from the fine mezzotint after Peter van Bleeck, which was published in 1755, and has been often reproduced. The scene represented is that when Cordelia and Aranthe, wandering on the heath, are rescued by Edgar from the two Ruffians, Act III.

On 11 March 1742, at Goodman Fields, David Garrick appeared as Lear for the first time. Mr. and Mrs. Giffard played Edgar and Cordelia. Four years later, 11 June 1746, he made his appearance in this rôle at Covent Garden with Ryan as Edgar, and Mrs. Vincent, Cordelia. Lear appears from the united testimony of his contemporaries to have been the noblest effort of Garrick's genius, and the actor himself seems to have always regarded it as his very highest achievement.* " In Lear," writes Murphy, " Garrick was transformed into a weak old man, still retaining an air of royalty. In the mad scenes his genius was remarkably distinguished. . . . During the whole time he presented a scene of woe and misery, and a total alienation of mind from every idea but that of his unkind daughters." According to Davies: " Garrick rendered the curse so terribly affecting to the audience, that, during his utterance of it, they seemed to shrink from it as from a blast of lightning. His preparation for it was extremely affecting; his throwing away his crutch, kneeling on one knee, clasping his hands together, and lifting his eyes towards heaven, presented a picture worthy the pencil of a Raphael."

* If we may form an opinion, Garrick as an actor was by no means equal to Betterton. Charles Hart was infinitely superior to Betterton, and probably the greatest artist the English stage has ever seen.

On 26 February 1756 *King Lear* was revived at Covent Garden, at which house it was billed as "Not acted 10 years." Spranger Barry played Lear,* with Ryan as Edgar; Luke Sparks, Kent; Ridout, Gloster; Smith, the Bastard; Shuter, the Steward; Miss Nossiter, Cordelia; and Mrs. Hamilton, Regan. Garrick immediately produced Lear at Drury Lane with Mrs. Cibber as Cordelia, and the rivalry between the two theatres divided the town. Epigrams were scattered "thick as autumnal leaves, that strew the brooks In Vallombrosa." Beringer smartly wrote:

> "The town has found out different ways
>   To praise the rival Lears;
> To Barry they give loud huzzas,
>   To Garrick——only tears."

This was capped by:

> "A King—nay, every inch a King:
>   Such Barry doth appear;
> But Garrick's quite a different thing,
>   He's every inch King Lear."

Notwithstanding that Garrick bore away the palm on this particular occasion, Barry's Lear was a performance of the very highest order.

About this time Garrick was suddenly inspired to undo, in some measure, the work of Nahum Tate, and accordingly *King Lear* was announced at Drury Lane as "with restorations from Shakespeare." It is not improbable that he was influenced in this matter by certain pertinent passages in a pamphlet named *An Examen of the Suspicious Husband* (1747), where he read: "Why will you do so great an injury to *Shakespeare* as to perform *Tate's* execrable alteration of him? Read and

---

* Barry had acted Lear in Dublin, May 1755.

consider the two plays seriously and then make the public and the memory of the author some amends by giving us *Lear* in the Original, Fool and all (*Macklin* or *Chapman* will play it well). It can be no mitigation of your fault to plead that *Tate* has seduced you; though you are not the principal, you are accessory to the murder, and will be brought in guilty." Garrick's version probably did not differ materially from *King Lear* as published by Bell " from the Prompt Book of Drury Lane " 1772-3. The tragic catastrophe, which shocked Dr. Johnson so much that he " could hardly ever bring himself to read the scenes again until he undertook to revise them as an editor," could not be risked, and although " it was once in contemplation with Mr. Garrick to restore the part of the fool, which he designed for Woodward, who promised to be very chaste in his colouring, and not to counteract the agonies of Lear: the manager would not hazard so bold an attempt; he feared, with Mr. Colman, that the feelings of Lear would derive no advantage from the buffooneries of the parti-coloured jester."

Colman's version of *King Lear* was produced at Covent Garden 20 February 1768. Powell played the King; Smith, Edgar; Bensley, Edmund; Gibson, Gloster; Cushing, Oswald; Mrs. Yates, Cordelia; Mrs. Stephens, Goneril; Mrs. Du Bellamy, Regan. The attempt was a failure. The love between Edgar and Cordelia is omitted, but the happy ending remains. The Fool, " after the most serious consideration," Colman decided to omit as a character which, " being likely to sink into burlesque in the representation, would not be endured on the modern stage." But the public would only suffer Tate's alteration, and Colman's lukewarm innovations met with scant favour.

At Drury Lane, 8 June 1776, Garrick appeared as Lear for the last time. Two days later, 10 June, he took his farewell of the stage, when he played Don Felix in Mrs. Centlivre's *The Wonder, A Woman keeps a Secret.*

Henderson, who acted Lear at Drury Lane 22 March 1779, proved mediocre in this rôle. Jack Palmer was his Edmund, and Miss Younge, Cordelia.

On 21 January 1788 *King Lear*, billed as "not acted 9 years" was performed at Drury Lane for the benefit of Mrs. Siddons. Kemble appeared as Lear; Mrs. Siddons was Cordelia; Wroughton, Edgar; Barrymore, Edmund; Lamash, Oswald; Mrs. Ward, Regan. Boaden was very impressed by Kemble's majesty and power: "The curse, as he then uttered it, harrowed up the soul; . . . the countenance too, was finely made up, and his grandeur approached the *most* awful impersonation of Michael Angelo." But Kemble's Lear, which seems to have been too classic and statuesque, never ranked with his Coriolanus, his Cato, his Wolsey; whilst Mrs. Siddons was obviously unsuited as Cordelia.

At Covent Garden, 18 May 1808, Charles Kemble for his benefit acted Edgar, and Kemble again played Lear "the first time for eight years." At the same theatre, 27 February 1809, the two brothers repeated these characters. Kemble then insisted upon restoring many of Tate's alterations, which in more recent years had been gradually excised.

During the last illness of George III *King Lear*, as a matter of natural delicacy and tact, had not been performed, but no sooner was the monarch dead than it was revived in the spring of 1820, both at Covent Garden ("Not acted 10 years"), and at Drury Lane. At the former theatre Lucius Junius Booth sustained Lear; Charles Kemble, Edgar; Macready, Edmund; Farley, Oswald; Miss Booth, Cordelia; and Miss Shaw, Aranthe. At Drury Lane, Kean was the Lear with Mrs. W. West as Cordelia; Mrs. Glover, Goneril; and Mrs.

Introduction

Egerton, Regan. Kean had intended to revive the tragic catastrophe, but he was dissuaded by a timorous manager from so daring an innovation. He excised at the moment, however, so far as he could, all that was not Shakespeare's, and early in 1823 he boldly presented the original fifth act. It was " received with silent tears. Every word seemed to come from a breaking heart." Kean's greatness as Lear has been described as " in the highest degree royal, lovable, refined, and powerful."

On 30 March 1829, when Shakespeare's *King Lear* was billed with Young as Lear, and Miss Phillips, Cordelia, we still find Aranthe, acted by Miss Nicol, among the dramatis personae.

It may be noted that " King Lear, A Tragedy in Five Acts by William Shakespeare . . . as now performed at the Theatres Royal, London," is given in Dolby's *British Theatre*, 1824. This, a technical acting edition, has the whole of the stage business, entrances, exits, etc., marked in full detail. There is no mention of Tate, but the love scenes between Edgar and Cordelia, and her attempted seizure by the two Ruffians at Edmund's instigation are retained. Gloster is blinded off stage; the part of Oswald is considerably " written up "; and many of Tate's verbal alterations and other wholly un-Shakespearean passages occur. The catastrophe, how-ever, is tragic and follows the original closely. The King of France and the Fool have not yet been restored, but we find Aranthe, and Edward, the servant who endeavours to prevent the outrage upon Gloster. A printed cast has Kean as Lear; Wallack, Edgar; Younge, Edmund; Browne, Oswald; Miss Boyce, Goneril; Mrs. Knight, Regan; Mrs. W. West, Cordelia; Miss Phillips, Aranthe.

On 25 January 1838, at Covent Garden, Macready revived Shakespeare's *King Lear*. He long hesitated to restore the Fool to the stage, but at last he entrusted this rôle to Priscilla Horton, who interpreted it with the utmost delicacy and charm.   Elton played Edgar; Anderson, Edmund;   Mrs. Clifford, Goneril;   Mrs. Warner, Regan; and Helen Faucit, Cordelia. Since that day Tate has disappeared from the modern theatre. It is true that Macready made cuts and transpositions, but seemingly there was only one actual interpolation—a few lines spoken by Gloster in the scene (Act V) when Edgar leaves him by the tree during the battle.   The original of this speech, which is neither Tate's nor Shakespeare's, Professor Odell was unable to discover. It may be found in the acting edition of *King Lear*, printed in Dolby's *British Theatre*, 1824.

Most critics have passed the severest judgements upon the Restoration adaptations of Shakespeare, and in particular upon Nahum Tate's alteration of *King Lear*. Yet when we review these versions we must take into ample and understanding consideration the conditions under which they were prepared and the reasons why the plays were thus modified.   In the first place it was not through any lack of appreciation of Shakespeare's genius. Without losing themselves in uncritical excesses the dramatists of the reign of Charles II yield to none in their admiration for Shakespeare.   Shadwell speaks of the " inimitable hand of *Shakespeare* ":*   Crowne refers to " The divine *Shakespear* ":† Tate writes:

" Yet he presumes he may be safe to-day
Since *Shakespeare* gave foundation to the play:‡

whilst Dryden in a well-known couplet declares:

" But *Shakespear's* Magick could not copy'd be
Within that Circle none durst walk but he."‖

* Preface to *The History of Timon of Athens*, quarto, 1678.
† Prologue to *The Misery of Civil-War*, quarto, 1680.
‡ Prologue to *The Ingratitude of a Commonwealth ; or, The Fall of Caius Martius Coriolanus*, quarto, 1682.
‖ Prologue to *The Tempest*, quarto, 1670.

Such examples might be infinitely multiplied. But with the Restoration a new dramatic instrument had come into being. The picture stage had replaced the platform stage, and the picture stage necessitated the revision of plays, which were written for another method of presentation, but were now to be interpreted by another theatrical medium. That such revision was generally undertaken in accordance with the taste of the day is not denied, and very often the fashion of two and a half centuries ago seems to us preposterous and absurd. Yet judged by their own criterion and by what their public then demanded, the Restoration dramatists had good warrant for their adaptations. That the Davenant and Dryden *The Tempest*, and Tate's *King Lear* possessed theatrical attractiveness, which is surely in a play a quality of no mean order, is clearly demonstrable from the fact that both of these versions kept the stage until the first quarter of the nineteenth century.* And a drama which lives in the theatre for one hundred and fifty years cannot be ignorantly dismissed with a shrug and a sneer. The reason for such vitality must be seriously pondered and examined.

Nor can we from another point of view afford to cast stones at Shadwell, at Tate, at Crowne, and D'Urfey for their alterations of Shakespeare. Until recent years it was only in few instances and on individual occasions that Shakespeare's plays were given in a coherent and unmutilated form. Even now many productions are chopped and cut, and honeycombed to boot with gags of meanest wit. One has been present at performances of Shakespeare's finest dramas which have been so mammocked and shorn that, without previous know-

---

* An even more striking example, indeed, is Cibber's *Richard III*, which has held its own for over two hundred years. It was certainly acted ten or fifteen years ago; and may still, perhaps, be seen in provincial theatres.

ledge, it would be impossible to follow the connexion of the plot or the sequence of the scenes. The alterations in this case were made by men of neither discernment nor understanding.   The alterations produced in Restoration times were the work of playwrights of practical knowledge and no inconsiderable talent; moreover, in two instances at least, *The Tempest* and *Troilus and Cressida*, they came from the pen of a dramatist of a genius supreme and unsurpassed.

THE
TEMPEST,
OR THE
Enchanted Island.

A

COMEDY.

As it is now Acted at his Highness the Duke of York's

THEATRE.

LONDON,

Printed by *J. M.* for *Henry Herringman* at the *Blew Anchor* in the *Lower-walk* of the *New-Exchange.*

MDCLXX.

PREFACE

TO THE

ENCHANTED ISLAND.

*T*HE *writing of Prefaces to Plays was probably invented by some very ambitious Poet, who never thought he had done enough : perhaps by some Ape of the French Eloquence, who uses to make a Business of a Letter of gallantry, an Examen of a Farce ; and in short, a great pomp and ostentation of words on every trifle. This is certainly the talent of that Nation, and ought not to be invaded by any other. They do that out of Gayety, which would be an imposition upon us.*

We may satisfie our selves with surmounting them in the Sense, and safely leave them those trappings of writing, and flourishes of the Pen, with which they adorn the borders of their Plays, and which are indeed no more than good Landskips to a very indifferent Picture. I must proceed no farther in this argument, lest I run my self beyond my excuse for writing this. Give me leave therefore to tell you, Reader, that I do it not to set a value on any thing I have written in this Play, but out of gratitude to the Memory of Sir William Davenant, *who did me the honour to joyn me with him in the alteration of it.*

It was originally Shakespear's : *a Poet for whom he had particularly a high veneration, and whom he first taught me to admire. The Play, it self had formerly been acted with success in the* Black-Fryers : *and our excellent* Fletcher *had so great a value for it, that he thought fit to make use of the same Design, not much varied, a second time. Those who have seen his* Sea-Voyage, *may easily*

3

discern that it was a Copy of Shakespear's Tempest: *the
Storm, the desart Island, and the Woman who had never
seen a Man, are all sufficient testimonies of it.   But*
Fletcher *was not the only Poet who made use of* Shakespear's *Plot: Sir* John Suckling, *a profess'd admirer of
our Author, has follow'd his footsteps in his* Goblins;
his Regmella *being an open imitation of* Shakespear's
Miranda; *and his Spirits, though counterfeit, yet are
copied from* Ariel. *But Sir* William Davenant, *as he was
a Man of quick and piercing imagination, soon found that
somewhat might be added to the Design of* Shakespear, *of
which neither* Fletcher *nor* Suckling *had ever thought:
and therefore to put the last hand to it, he design'd the
Counterpart to* Shakespear's *Plot, namely, that of a Man
who had never seen a Woman ; that by this means those
two Characters of Innocence and Love might the more
illustrate and commend each other.   This excellent con-
trivance he was pleas'd to communicate to me, and to
desire my assistance in it.   I confess that from the very
first moment it so pleas'd me, that I never writ any thing
with more delight.. I must likewise do him that justice to
acknowledge, that my writing received daily his amend-
ments, and that is the reason why it is not so faulty, as
the rest which I have done without the help or correction
of so judicious a Friend.   The Comical parts of the Saylors
were also his Invention, and for the most part his Writing,
as you will easily discover by the Style.   In the time I writ
with him, I had the opportunity to observe somewhat more
neerly of him, than I had formerly done, when I had only
a bare acquaintance with him :   I found him then of so
quick a Fancy, that nothing was propos'd to him, on
which he could not suddenly produce a thought extreamly
pleasant and surprizing : and those first thoughts of his,
contrary to the old Latine Proverb, were not alwaies the
least happy.   And as his fancy was quick, so likewise
were the products of it remote and new.   He borrowed not*

of any other ; and his imaginations were such as could not easily enter into any other man. His corrections were sober and judicious : and he corrected his own Writings much more severely than those of another man, bestowing twice the time and labour in polishing, which he us'd in invention. It had perhaps been easie enough for me to have arrogated more to my self than was my due in the writing of this Play, and to have pass'd by his name with silence in the publication of it, with the same ingratitude which others have us'd to him, whose Writings he hath not only corrected, as he has done this, but has had a greater inspection over them, and sometimes added whole Scenes together, which may as easily be distinguish'd from the rest, as true Gold from counterfeit by the weight. But besides the unworthiness of the action which deterred me from it (there being nothing so base as to rob the dead of his reputation) I am satisfi'd I could never have receiv'd so much honour in being thought the Author of any Poem how excellent soever, as I shall from the joining my Imperfections with the merit and name of Shakespear *and Sir* William D'avenant.

Decemb. 1   JOHN DRYDEN.
1669.

Dramatis Personæ.

Alonzo Duke of *Savoy,* and Usurper of the Dukedom of *Mantua.*
Ferdinand his Son.
Prospero right Duke of *Millain.*
Antonio his Brother, Usurper of the Dukedom.
Gonzalo a Noble man of *Savoy.*
Hippolito, one that never saw Woman, right Heir of the Dukedom of *Mantua.*
Stephano Master of the Ship.
Mustacho his Mate.
Trincalo Boatswain.
Ventoso a Mariner.
Several Mariners.
A Cabbin-Boy.

Miranda
  and }(Daughters to *Prospero*) that never saw Man.
Dorinda.

Ariel an aiery Spirit, attendant on *Prospero.*
Several Spirits Guards to *Prospero.*
Caliban
Sycorax his Sister} Two Monsters of the Isle.
[*Milcha,* a Spirit.]

6

PROLOGUE to the *Tempest*, or the *Enchanted Island*.

*A*S *when a Tree's cut down the secret root*
 Lives under ground, and thence new Branches shoot ;
So, from old Shakespear's *honour'd dust, this day*
Springs up and buds a new reviving Play.
Shakespear, *who (taught by none) did first impart*
To Fletcher *Wit, to labouring* Johnson *Art.*
He Monarch-like gave those his Subjects law,
And is that Nature which they paint and draw.
Fletcher *reach'd that which on his heights did grow,*
Whilst Johnson *crept and gather'd all below.*
This did his Love, and this his Mirth digest :
One imitates him most, the other best.
If they have since out-writ all other Men,
'Tis with the drops which fell from Shakespear's *Pen.*
The Storm which vanish'd on the Neighb'ring shore,
Was taught by Shakespear's *Tempest first to roar.*
That Innocence and Beauty which did smile
In Fletcher, *grew on this* Enchanted Isle.
But Shakespear's *Magick could not copy'd be,*
Within that Circle none durst walk but he.
I must confess 'twas bold, nor would you now,
That liberty to vulgar Wits allow,
Which works by Magick supernatural things :
But Shakespear's *Pow'r is sacred as a King's.*
Those Legends from old Priest-hood were receiv'd,
And he then writ, as People then believ'd.
But, if for Shakespear *we your grace implore,*
We for our Theatre shall want it more :
Who by our dearth of Youths are forc'd t' employ
One of our Women to present a Boy.

7

The Enchanted Island

And that's a transformation you will say
Exceeding all the Magick in the Play.
Let none expect in the last Act to find,
Her Sex transform'd from Man to Woman-kind.
What e'er she was before the Play began,
All you shall see of her is perfect Man.
Or if your fancy will be farther led,
To find her Woman, it must be abed.

THE
ENCHANTED ISLAND.

Act I.

Enter Mustacho *and* Ventoso.

Vent. WHAT a Sea comes in?

    Must. A hoaming Sea! we shall have foul weather.

Enter Trincalo.

Trinc. The Scud comes against the Wind, 'twill blow hard.

Enter Stephano.

Steph. Bosen!

Trinc. Here, Master what cheer?

Steph. Ill weather! Let's off to Sea.

Must. Let's have Sea-room enough, and then let it blow the Devils head off.

Steph. Boy!

Enter Cabin-Boy.

Boy. Yaw, yaw, here Master.

Steph. Give the Pilot a Dram of the Bottle.

                 [*Exeunt* Stephano *and* Boy.

Enter Mariners and pass over the Stage.

Trinc. Heigh, my hearts, chearly, chearly, my hearts, yare, yare.

Enter Alonzo, Antonio, Gonzalo.

Alon. Good Bosen have a care; where's the Master? Play the Men.

9

Trinc. Pray keep below.

Ant. Where's the Master, Bosen?

Trinc. Do you not hear him? You mar our labour: keep your Cabins, you help the storm.

Gonz. Nay, good Friend be patient.

Trinc. I, when the Sea is: hence; what care these roarers for the name of Duke? To Cabin; silence; trouble us not.

Gonz. Good friend, remember whom thou hast aboard.

Trinc. None that I love more than my self. You are a Counsellour; if you can advise these Elements to silence; use your wisdom: if you cannot, make your self ready in the Cabin for the ill hour. Cheerly good hearts! Out of our way, Sirs.

[*Exeunt* Trincalo *and Mariners.*

Gonz. I have great comfort from this Fellow; me-thinks his complexion is perfect Gallows; stand fast, good Fate, to his Hanging; make the Rope of his Destiny our Cable, for our own does little advantage us: if he be not born to be hang'd we shall be drown'd.

[*Exit.*

Enter Trincalo *and* Stephano.

Trinc. Up aloft Lads. Come, reef both Top-sails.

Steph. Let's weigh, Let's weigh, and off to Sea.

[*Exit* Stephano.

Enter two Mariners and pass over the Stage.

Trinc. Hands down! Man your Main-Capstorm.

Enter Mustacho *and* Ventoso *at the other door.*

Must. Up aloft! And Man your seere-Capstorm.

Vent. My Lads, my hearts of Gold, get in your Capstorm-Bar.

Hoa up, hoa up, &c.   [*Exeunt* Mustacho *and* Ventoso.

Enter Stephano.

Steph. Hold on well! Hold on well! Nip well there; Quarter-Master, get's more Nippers.   [*Exit* Stephano.

Enter two Mariners and pass over again.

Trinc. Turn out, turn out, all hands to Capstorm?
You Dogs, is this a time to sleep?
Heave together Lads.   [Trincalo *whistles.*
                    [*Exeunt* Mustacho *and* Ventoso.

Must. within. Our Viall's broke.

Vent. within. 'Tis but our Vial-block has given way.
Come heave Lads! We are fix'd again. Heave together
Bullyes.

Enter Stephano.

Steph. Cut off the Hamocks! Cut off the Hamocks;
come my Lads: Come *Bullys*, chear up! Heave lustily.
The Anchor's a peek.

Trinc. Is the Anchor a peek?

Steph. Is a weigh! Is a weigh!

Trinc. Up aloft my Lads upon the Fore-Castle! Cut
the Anchor, cut him.

All within. Haul Catt, Haul Catt, *&c.* Haul Catt,
haul: haul, Catt, haul. Below.

Steph. Aft, Aft! And loose the Misen!

Trinc. Get the Misen-tack aboard. Haul Aft Misen-
sheat!

Enter Mustacho.

Must. Loose the main Top sail!

Steph. Furle him again, there's too much Wind.

Trinc. Loose foresail! Haul Aft both sheats!
Trim her right afore the Wind.
Aft! Aft! Lads, and hale up the Misen here

Must. A Mackrel-Gale, Master.

Steph. within. Port hard, port! The Wind grows
scant, bring the Tack aboard, Port is. Star-board, star-
board, a little steady; now steady, keep her thus, no
neerer you cannot come.

Enter Ventoso.

Vent. Some hands down: the Guns are loose.
                              [*Exit* Must.

Trinc. Try the Pump, try the Pump!

[Exit Ventoso.

Enter Mustacho *at the other door.*

Must. O Master! Six foot Water in Hold.

Steph. Clap the Helm hard aboard! Flat, flat, flat in the Fore-sheat there.

Trinc. Over-haul your fore-boling.

Steph. Brace in the Lar-board. *[Exit.*

Trinc. A Curse upon this howling,

[A great cry within.

They are louder than the weather.

[Enter Antonio *and* Gonzalo.

Yet again, what do you here! Shall we give o're, and drown? Ha' you a mind to sink?

Gonz. A pox o' your throat, you bawling, blasphemous, uncharitable Dog.

Trinc. Work you then.

Ant. Hang, Cur, hang, you whorson insolent Noise-maker, we are less afraid to be drown'd than thou art.

Trinc. Brace off the Fore-yard. *[Exit.*

Gonz. I'll warrant him for drowning, though the Ship were no stronger than a Nut-shell, and as leaky as an unstanch'd Wench.

Enter Alonzo *and* Ferdinand.

Ferd. For my self I care not, but your loss brings a thousand Deaths to me.

Alonzo. O name not me, I am grown old, my Son; I now am tedious to the World, and that, by use, is so to me: but, *Ferdinand,* I grieve my subjects loss in thee: Alas! I suffer justly for my Crimes; but why thou shouldest——O Heaven! Hark, farewel my Son! a long farewel! *[A cry within.*

Ferd. Some lucky Plank, when we are lost by Shipwrack, waft hither, and submit it self beneath you. Your Blessing, and I dye contented.

[Embrace and Exeunt.

Enter Trincalo, Mustacho, *and* Ventoso.

Trinc. What must our Mouths be cold then?

Vent. All's lost. To Prayers, to Prayers.

Gonz. The Duke and Prince are gone within to Prayers. Let's assist them.

Must. Nay, we may e'ne pray too; our case is now alike.

Ant. We are meerly cheated of our lives by Drunkards. This wide chopt Rascal: would thou might'st lye drowning
The long washing of ten Tides.

            [Exeunt Trincalo, Mustacho, *and* Ventoso.

Gonz. He'll be hang'd yet, though every drop of Water swears against it; now would I give ten thousand Furlongs of Sea for one Acre of barren ground, Long-heath, Broom-furs, or any thing. The Wills above be done, but I would fain dye a dry death.

            [A confused noise within.

Ant. Mercy upon us! we split, we split.

Gonz. Let's all sink with the Duke, and the young Prince.   *[Exeunt.*

Enter Stephano, Trincalo.

Trinc. The Ship is sinking.   *[A new cry within.*

Steph. Run her ashore!

Trinc. Luffe! luffe! or we are all lost! there's a Rock upon the Star-board Bow.

Steph. She strikes, she strikes! All shift for themselves.   *[Exeunt.*

Enter Prospero *and* Miranda.

Prosp. Miranda! where's your Sister?

Mir. I left her looking from the pointed Rock, at the Walks end, on the huge beat of Waters.

Prosp. It is a dreadful object.

Mir. If by your Art, my dearest Father, you have put them in this roar, allay 'em quickly. Had I been any God of Power, I would have sunk the Sea into the Earth, before it should the Vessel so have swallowed.

Prosp. Collect your self, and tell your piteous heart, There's no harm done.

Mir. O woe the day!

Prosp. There is no harm:
I have done nothing but in care of thee,
My Daughter, and thy pretty Sister:
You both are ignorant of what you are,
Not knowing whence I am, nor that I'm more
Than *Prospero*, Master of a narrow Cell,
And thy unhappy Father.

Mir. I ne're indeavour'd to know more than you were pleas'd to tell me.

Prosp. I should inform thee farther: wipe thou thine Eyes, have comfort; the direful Spectacle of the Wrack, which touch'd the very virtue of compassion in thee, I have with such a pity safely order'd, that not one Creature in the Ship is lost.

Mir. You often, Sir, began to tell me what I am, but then you stopt.

Prosp. The hour's now come;
Obey, and be attentive, Canst thou remember a time before we came into this Cell? I do not think thou canst; for then thou wert not full three years old.

Mir. Certainly I can, Sir.

Prosp. Tell me the Image then of any thing which thou dost keep in thy remembrance still.

Mir. Sir, had I not four or five Women once that tended me?

Prosp. Thou hadst, and more, *Miranda*: what see'st thou else in the dark back-ward, and abyss of Time?
If thou remembrest ought e're thou cam'st here, then, how thou cam'st thou may'st remember too.

Mir. Sir, that I do not.

Prosp. Fifteen Years since, *Miranda*, thy Father was
the Duke of *Millan*, and a Prince of Power.

Mir. Sir, are not you my Father?

Prosp. Thy Mother was all Virtue, and she said,
thou wast my Daughter, and thy Sister too.

Mir. O Heavens! what foul play had we, that we
hither came? or was't a Blessing that we did?

Prosp. Both, both, my Girl.

Mir. How my heart bleeds to think what you have
suffer'd. But, Sir, I pray proceed.

Prosp. My Brother, and thy Uncle, call'd *Antonio*,
To whom I trusted then the manage of
My State, while I was wrap'd with secret Studies:
That false Uncle (do'st thou attend me Child?)

Mir. Sir, most heedfully.

Prosp. Having attain'd the craft of granting Suits,
and of denying them; whom to advance, or lop, for
over-toping, soon was grown the Ivy which did hide
my Princely Trunck, and suckt my verdure out: thou
attend'st not.

Mir. O good Sir, I do.

Prosp. I thus neglecting worldly ends, and bent
To closeness, and the bettering of my Mind,
Wak'd in my false Brother an evil Nature:
He did believe
He was indeed the Duke, because he then
Did execute the outward face of Soveraignty.
Do'st thou still mark me?

Mir. Your story would Cure Deafness.

Prosp. To have no screen between the part he plaid,
And whom he plaid it for; he needs would be
Absolute *Millan*, and confederates
(So dry he was for Sway) with *Savoy's* Duke,
To give him Tribute, and to do him homage.

Mir. False Man!

Prosp. This Duke of *Savoy* being an Enemy,
To me inveterate, strait grants my Brother's Suit,
And on a night Mated to his design, *Antonio* opened the
Gates of *Millan*, and i' th' dead of darkness, hurri'd me
thence with thy young Sister, and thy crying self.

Mir. But wherefore did they not that hour destroy us?

Prosp. They durst not, Girl, in *Millan*, for the love
my People bore me. In short, they hurri'd us away to
Savoy, and thence aboard a Bark at *Nissa's* Port: bore
us some Leagues to Sea, where they prepar'd a rotten
Carkass of a Boat, not rigg'd, no Tackle, Sail, nor Mast;
the very Rats instinctively had quit it: they hoisted
us, to cry to Seas which roar'd to us; to sigh to Winds,
whose pity sighing back again, did seem to do us loving
wrong.

Mir. Alack! what trouble was I then to you?

Prosp. Thou and thy Sister were two Cherubins,
which did preserve me: you both did smile, infus'd with
Fortitude from Heaven.

Mir. How came we ashore?

Prosp. By Providence Divine,
Some food we had, and some fresh Water, which a
Noble man of *Savoy*, called *Gonzalo*, appointed Master
of that black design, gave us; with rich Garments, and
all necessaries, which since have steaded much: and
of his gentleness (knowing I lov'd my Books) he furnisht
me from mine own Library, with Volumes which I prize
above my Dukedom.

Mir. Would I might see that man.

Prosp. Here in this Island we arriv'd, and here have
I your Tutor been. But by my skill I find that my Mid-
Heaven doth depend on a most happy Star, whose
influence if I now court not, but omit, my Fortunes
will ever after droop. Here cease more question, thou
art inclin'd to sleep: 'tis a good dulness, and give it
way; I know thou canst not chuse.   [*She falls asleep.*

Come away my Spirit: I am ready now, approach my
Ariel, Come.

Enter Ariel.

 Ariel. All hail great Master, grave Sir, hail I
  come
To answer thy best pleasure, be it to fly,
To swim, to shoot into the fire, to ride
On the curl'd Clouds; to thy strong bidding, task
Ariel and all his qualities.
 Prosp. Hast thou, Spirit,
Perform'd to point the Tempest that I bad thee?
 Ariel. To every Article.
I boarded the Duke's Ship, now on the Beak,
Now in the Waste, the Deck, in every Cabin,
I flam'd amazement; and sometimes I seem'd
To burn in many places on the Top-Mast,
The Yards and Bore-sprit; I did flame distinctly.
 Prosp. My brave Spirit!
Who was so firm, so constant, that this coil
Did not infect his Reason?
 Ariel. Not a Soul
But felt a Feaver of the Mind, and play'd
Some tricks of desperation; all, but Mariners,
Plung'd in the foaming brine, and quit the Vessel:
The Duke's Son, *Ferdinand*,
With hair upstairing (more like Reeds than Hair)
Was the first Man that leap'd; cry'd, Hell is empty,
And all the Devils are here.
 Prosp. Why that's my Spirit;
But was not this nigh Shore?
 Ariel. Close by, my Master.
 Prosp. But, *Ariel*, are they safe?
 Ariel. Not a hair perisht.
In Troops I have dispers'd them round this Isle.
The Duke's Son I have landed by himself,
Whom I have left warming the air with sighs,

In an odde angle of the Isle, and sitting,
His Arms he folded in this sad knot.
    Prosp. Say how thou hast dispos'd the Mariners
Of the Duke's Ship, and all the rest of the Fleet.
    Ariel. Safely in Harbour
Is the Duke's Ship, in the deep Nook, where once
Thou call'dst me up at Midnight to fetch Dew
From the still vext *Bermoothes*, there she's hid,
The Mariners all under Hatches stow'd,
Whom, with a charm, join'd to their suffer'd labour,
I have left asleep; and for the rest o' th' Fleet
(Which I disperst) they all have met again,
And are upon the *Mediterranean* Float,
Bound sadly home for *Italy*;
Supposing that they saw the Duke's Ship wrackt,
And his great Person perish.
    Prosp. Ariel, thy charge
Exactly is perform'd; but there's more work:
What is the time o' th' day?
    Ariel. Past the Mid-season.
    Prosp. At least two Glasses: the time 'tween six and
      now
Must by us both be spent most preciously.
    Ariel. Is there more toyl? since thou dost give me
      pains,
Let me remember thee what thou hast promis'd,
Which is not yet perform'd me.
    Prosp. How now, *Moodie*?
What is't thou canst demand?
    Ariel. My liberty.
    Prosp. Before the time be out? no more.
    Ariel. I prethee!
Remember I have done thee faithful service,
Told thee no lyes, have made thee no mistakings,
Serv'd without grudge, or grumblings: Thou didst
      promise

To bate me a full year.
 Prosp. Dost thou forget
From what a torment I did free thee?
 Ariel. No.
 Prosp. Thou dost; and think'st it much to tread the
  Ooze
Of the salt deep:
To run against the sharp wind of the North,
To do my business in the Veins of the Earth,
When it is bak'd with Frost.
 Ariel. I do not, Sir.
 Prosp. Thou ly'st, malignant thing! hast thou forgot
The foul Witch *Sycorax,* who with Age and Envy
Was grown into a Hoop? hast thou forgot her?
 Ariel. No, Sir!
 Prosp. Thou hast; where was she born? speak, tell
me.
 Ariel. Sir, in *Argier.*
 Prosp. Oh, was she so! I must
Once every Month recount what thou hast been,
Which thou forgettest. This damn'd Witch *Sycorax*
For mischiefs manifold, and Sorceries too terrible
To enter humane hearing, from *Argier*
Thou know'st was banisht: but for one thing she did,
They would not take her life: is not this true?
 Ariel. I, Sir.
 Prosp. This blew ey'd Hag was hither brought with
  Child,
And here was left by th' Saylors; thou, my Slave,
As thou report'st thy self, wast then her Servant;
And 'cause thou wast a Spirit too delicate
To act her Earthy and abhorr'd Commands,
Refusing her grand Hests, she did confine thee,
By help of her more potent Ministers,
(In her unmitigable rage) into a cloven Pine
Within whose rift imprison'd, thou didst painfully

Remain a dozen Years; within which space she dy'd,
And left thee there; where thou didst vent thy groans,
As fast as Mill-Wheels strike. Then was this Isle,
(Save for two Brats, which she did litter here,
The brutish *Caliban*, and his twin Sister,
Two freckel'd-hag-born Whelps) not honour'd with
A humane shape.
    Ariel. Yes! *Caliban* her Son, and *Sycorax* his Sister.
    Prosp. Dull thing, I say so; he, that *Caliban*,
And she that *Sycorax*, whom I now keep in service.
Thou best knowst
What torment I did find thee in; thy groans
Did make Wolves howl, and penetrate the Breasts
Of ever angry Bears: it was a torment
To lay upon the damn'd, which *Sycorax*
Could ne're again undo: It was my Art,
When I arriv'd, and heard thee, made the Pine
To gape and let thee out.
    Ariel. I thank thee, Master.
    Prosp. If thou more murmurest, I will rend an Oak,
And peg thee in his knotty Entrails,
Till thou hast howld away twelve Winters more.
    Ariel. Pardon, Master,
I will be correspondent to command,
And be a gentle Spirit.
    Prosp. Do so, and after two days I'le discharge thee.
    Ariel. That's my noble Master.
What shall I do? say! what, what shall I do?
    Prosp. Be subject to no sight but mine;
Invisible to every Eye-Ball else: hence with diligence.
My Daughter wakes. Anon thou shalt know more.
                      [*Exit* Ariel.
Thou hast slept well my Child.
    Mir. The sadness of your story put heaviness in me.
    Prosp. Shake it off; come on, I'le now call *Caliban*,
my slave, who never yields us a kind Answer.

Mir. 'Tis a Creature, Sir, I do not love to look on.

Prosp. But as'tis, we cannot miss him; he does make
our Fire, fetch in our wood, and serve in Offices that
profit us: What hoa! Slave! *Caliban!* thou Earth
thou, speak.

Calib. within. There's Wood enough within.

Prosp. Come forth, I say, there's other business for thee.
Come thou Tortoise, when?   [*Enter* Ariel.
Fine Apparition, my quaint *Ariel,*
Hark in thy Ear.

Ariel. My Lord it shall be done.   [*Exit.*

Prosp. Thou poisonous Slave, got by the Devil himself upon thy wicked Dam, come forth.

                    Enter Caliban.

Calib. As wicked Dew, as e're my Mother brush'd
with Raven's Feather from unwholsome Fens, drop on
you both: A South-west blow on you, and blister you
all o're.

Prosp. For this be sure, to night thou shalt have
Cramps, Side-stitches, that shall pen thy breath up;
Urchins shall prick thee till thou bleed'st: thou shalt
be pinch'd as thick as Honey-Combs, each pinch more
stinging than the Bees which made 'em.

Calib. I must eat my Dinner: this Island's mine by
Sycorax my Mother, which thou took'st from me. When
thou cam'st first, thou stroak'st me and mad'st much
of me, would'st give me Water with Berries in't, and
teach me how to name the bigger Light, and how the
less, that burn by day and night; and then I lov'd thee,
and shew'd thee all the qualities of the Isle, the fresh-
Springs, brine-Pits, barren places, and fertil. Curs'd be
I, that I did so: All the Charms of *Sycorax,* Toads,
Beetles, Batts light on thee, for I am all the Subjects
that thou hast. I first was mine own Lord: and here
thou stay'st me in this hard Rock, whiles thou dost keep
me from the rest o'th'Island.

Prosp. Thou most lying Slave, whom stripes may move, not kindness: I have us'd thee (filth that thou art) with humane care, and lodg'd thee in mine own Cell; till thou didst seek to violate the honour of my Children.

Calib. Oh ho, Oh ho, would t' had been done: thou did'st prevent me, I had peopl'd else this Isle with *Calibans.*

Prosp. Abhor'd Slave!
Who ne're would any print of goodness take, being capable of all ill: I pity'd thee, took pains to make thee speak, taught thee each hour one thing or other; when thou didst not, (Savage), know thy own meaning, but would'st gabble, like a thing most brutish, I endow'd thy purposes with words which made them known: But thy wild race (though thou did'st learn) had that in't, which good Natures could not abide to be with: therefore wast thou deservedly pent up into this Rock.

Calib. You taught me Languague, and my profit by it is, that I know to Curse: the red Botch rid you for learning me your languague.

Prosp. Hag-seed hence:
Fetch us in fewel, and be quick
To answer other business: shrugst thou, Malice?
If thou neglectest or dost unwillingly what I Command,
I'le rack thee with old Cramps, fill all thy Bones with
Aches, make thee roar, that Beasts shall tremble
At thy Din.

Calib. No prethee.
I must obey. His Art is of such power,
It would controul my Dam's God, *Setebos,*
And make a Vassal of him.

Prosp. So Slave, hence.

[*Exeunt* Prospero *and* Caliban *severally.*
Enter Dorinda.

Dor. Oh Sister! what have I beheld!
Mir. What is it moves you so?

Dor. From yonder Rock,
As I my Eyes cast down upon the Seas,
The whistling Winds blew rudely on my face,
And the Waves roar'd; at first I thought the War
Had bin between themselves; but straight I spy'd
A huge great Creature.
    Mir. O, you mean the Ship.
    Dor. Is't not a Creature then? it seem'd alive.
    Mir. But what of it?
    Dor. This floating Ram did bear his Horns above;
All ty'd with Ribbands, ruffling in the wind,
Sometimes he nodded down his head a while,
And then the waves did heave him to the Moon,
He clamb'ring to the top of all the Billows,
And then again he curtsy'd down so low,
I could not see him: till at last, all side long
With a great crack his Belly burst in pieces.
    Mir. There all had perisht
Had not my Father's Magick Art reliev'd them.
But, Sister, I have stranger News to tell you;
In this great Creature there were other Creatures,
And shortly we may chance to see that thing,
Which you have heard my Father call, a Man.
    Dor. But what is that? for yet he never told me.
    Mir. I know no more than you: but I have heard
My Father say we Women were made for him.
    Dor. What, that he should eat us, Sister?
    Mir. No sure, you see my Father is a Man, and yet
He does us good. I would he were not old.
    Dor. Methinks indeed it would be finer, if we two
Had two young Fathers.
    Mir. No Sister, no, if they were young, my Father
Said that we must call them Brothers.
    Dor. But pray how does it come that we two are not
Brothers then, and have not beards like him?
    Mir. Now I confess you pose me.

Dor. How did he come to be our Father too?

Mir. I think he found us when we both were little, and grew within the ground.

Dor. Why could he not find more of us? Pray Sister let you and I look up and down one day, to find some little ones for us to play with.

Mir. Agreed; but now we must go in. This is the hour
Wherein my Father's Charm will work,
Which seizes all who are in open Air:
Th' effect of his great Art I long to see,
Which will perform as much as Magick can.

Dor. And I' methinks, more long to see a Man.

[*Exeunt.*

Act II.

Enter Alonzo, Antonio, Gonzalo, *Attendants.*

Gonz. BESEECH your Grace be merry; you have cause, so have we all, of joy for our strange scape: then wisely, good Sir, weigh our sorrow with our comfort.

Alonz. Prithee peace! you cram these words into my ears against my Stomack, how can I rejoyce, when my dear Son perhaps this very moment, is made a meal to some strange Fish?

Ant. Sir, he may live,
I saw him beat the Billows under him, and ride upon their backs; he trod the Water, whose enmity he flung aside, and breasted the most swoln surge that met him, his bold Head 'bove the contentious waves he kept, and oar'd himself with his strong Armes to shore: I do not doubt he came alive to land.

Alonz. No, no, he's gone, and you and I, *Antonio,* were those who caus'd his Death.

Ant. How could we help it?

Alonz. Then, then, we should have helpt it, when
thou betrayedst thy Brother *Prospero,* and *Mantua's*
Infant Sovereign to my Power: And when I, too
ambitious, took by force anothers right;   then lost we
Ferdinand, then forfeited our Navy to this Tempest.

Ant. Indeed we first broke truce with Heav'n;
You to the waves an Infant Prince expos'd,
And on the waves have lost an only Son;
I did usurp my Brother's fertile lands, and now
Am cast upon this desert Isle.

Gonz. These, Sir, 'tis true were Crimes of a black Dye,
But both of you have made amends to Heav'n,
By your late Voyage into *Portugal,*
Where in defense of Christianity,
Your valour has repuls'd the *Moors* of *Spain.*

Alonz. O name it not, *Gonzalo.*
No act but penitence can expiate guilt,
Must we teach Heaven what price to set on Murthers?
What rate on lawless Power, and wild ambition?
Or dare we traffick with the Powers above,
And sell by weight a good deed for a bad?
                              [*Musick within.*

Gonz. Musick!   and in the air!   sure we are shipwrackt on the Dominions of some merry Devil.

Ant. This Isle's inchanted ground, for I have heard
Swift Voices flying by my Ear, and groans
Of lamenting Ghosts.

Alonz. I pull'd a Tree, and Blood pursu'd my hand;
O Heaven! deliver me from this dire place, and all the
after actions of my Life shall mark my Penitence and
my Bounty. Heark!
The sounds approach us.
                    [*A Dialogue within sung in parts.*
   1. *D.* Where does proud Ambition dwell?
   2. In the lowest Rooms of Hell.
   1. Of the damn'd who leads the Host?

2. He who did oppress the most.

1. Who such Troops of damned brings?

2. Most are led by fighting Kings.
Kings who did Crowns unjustly get,
Here on burning Thrones are set.

Chor. Kings who did Crowns, *&c.*

Ant. Do you hear, Sir, how they lay our Crimes before us?

Gonz. Do evil Spirits imitate the good,
In shewing Men their Sins?

Alonz. But in a different way,
Those warn from doing, these upbraid 'em done.

1. Who are the Pillars of Ambitions Court?

2. Grim Deaths and Scarlet Murthers it support.

1. What lyes beneath her Feet?

2. Her footsteps tread,
On Orphans tender Breasts, and Brothers dead.

1. Can Heaven permit such Crimes should be
Rewarded with felicity?

2. Oh no! uneasily their Crowns they wear,
And their own guilt amidst their Guards they fear.
Cares when they wake their minds unquiet keep,
And we in visions lord it o're their sleep.

Chor. Oh no! uneasily their Crowns, *&c.*

Alonz. See where they come in horrid shapes!

Enter the two that sung, in shape of Devils, placing them-
selves at two Corners of the Stage.

Ant. Sure Hell is open to devour us quick.

1. *D.* Say Brother, shall we bear these Mortals hence?

2. First let us shew the shapes of their offence.

1. We'll Muster then their Crimes on either side:
Appear! Appear! Their first begotten, Pride.

Enter Pride.

Pride. Lo! I am here, who led their hearts astray,
And to Ambition did their Minds betray.

Enter Fraud.

Fraud. And guileful Fraud does next appear,
Their wandring steps who led,
When they from Virtue fled,
And in my crooked paths their course did steer.

Enter Rapine.

Rap. From Fraud to Force they soon arrive,
Where Rapine did their actions drive.

Enter Murther.

Mur. There long they cannot stay,
Down the deep precipice they run,
And to secure what they have done,
To murder bend their way.

[*After which they fall into a round encompassing
the Duke, &c., Singing.*

*Around, around, we pace
About this cursed place,
Whilst thus we compass in
These mortals and their sin.*   Dance.

[*All the Spirits vanish.*

Ant. Heav'n has heard me! They are vanish'd.
Alonz. But they have left me all unman'd.
I feel my sinews slacken'd with the fright,
And a cold sweat trills down o're all my Limbs,
As if I were dissolving into Water.
    O *Prospero*! My Crimes 'gainst thee sit heavy on my
heart.
Ant. And mine, 'gainst him and young *Hippolito*.
Gonz. Heav'n have mercy on the penitent!
Alonz. Lead from this cursed ground;
The Seas, in all their rage, are not so dreadful.
This is the Region of despair and death.
Gonz. Shall we not seek some food?
Alonz. Beware all fruit but what the birds have peid,
The shadows of the Trees are poisonous too:

A secret venom slides from every branch.
My conscience doth distract me, O my Son!
Why do I speak of eating or repose,
Before I know thy fortune?   [*Exeunt.*
Enter Ferdinand, *and* Ariel, *invisible, playing and
singing.*

Ariel's *Song.*
*Come unto these yellow sands
And then take hands.
Curtsy'd when you have and kiss'd,
The wild waves whist.*
*Foot it featly here and there, and sweet sprights bear the
Burthen.* [*Burthen dispersedly.*
*Hark! Hark! Bow-waugh; the Watch-dogs bark,
Bow-waugh.*
Ariel. *Hark! Hark! I hear the strain of strutting Chanti-
cleer Cry Cock a doodle do.*

Ferd. Where should this Musick be? I' th' Air, or
    th' Earth?
It sounds no more, and sure it waits upon some God
O' th' Island, sitting on a bank, weeping against the
    Duke
My Father's Wrack. This Musick hover'd o're me
On the Waters allaying both their fury and my passion
With charming Airs; thence I have follow'd it, (or it
Hath drawn me rather) but 'tis gone;
No, it begins again.

Ariel. *Song.*
*Full Fathoms five thy Father lyes,
Of his Bones is Coral made :
Those are Pearls that were his eyes,
Nothing of him that does fade :
But does suffer a Sea-change
Into something rich and strange :*

Sea-Nymphs hourly ring his Knell :
Hark now I hear 'em, Ding dong Bell.

[Burthen, *Ding dong.*

Ferd. The mournful Ditty mentions my drown'd
  Father,
This is no mortal business, nor a sound
Which the Earth owns : I hear it now before me,
However I will on and follow it.

[*Exeunt* Ferdinand *and* Ariel.
Enter Stephano, Mustacho, Ventoso.

Vent. The Runlet of Brandy was a loving Runlet, and
floated after us out of pure pity.

Must. This kind Bottle, like an old acquaintance,
swam after it. And this Scollop-shell is all our Plate
now.

Vent. 'Tis well we have found something since we
landed. I prethee fill a Soop, and let it go round. Where
hast thou laid the Runlet ?

Must. I' th' hollow of an old Tree.

Vent. Fill apace, we cannot live long in this barren
Island, and we may take a soop before Death, as well as
others drink at our Funerals.

Must. This is Prize-Brandy, we steal Custom, and it
costs nothing. Let's have two rounds more.

Vent. Master, what have you sav'd ?

Steph. Just nothing but my self.

Vent. This works comfortably on a cold Stomach.

Steph. Fill's another round.

Vent. Look! *Mustacho* weeps. Hang losses as long
as we have Brandy left. Prithee leave weeping.

Steph. He sheds his Brandy out of his Eyes : he shall
drink no more.

Must. This will be a doleful day with old *Bess.* She
gave me a gilt Nutmeg at parting. That's lost too. But
as you say, hang losses. Prithee fill agen.

Vent. Beshrew thy heart for putting me in mind of

thy Wife; I had not thought of mine else. Nature will shew it self, I must melt. I prithee fill agen, my Wife's a good old Jade, and has but one eye left: but she'll weep out that too, when she hears that I am dead.

Steph. Would you were both hang'd for putting me in thought of mine. But well, if I return not in seven Years to my own Country, she may marry agen: and 'tis from this Island thither at least seven Years swimming.

Must. O at least, having no help of Boat nor Bladders.

Steph. Whoe're she marries, poor Soul, she'll weep a nights when she thinks of *Stephano*.

Vent. But Master, sorrow is dry! here's for you agen.

Steph. A Mariner had e'en as good be a Fish as a Man, but for the comfort we get ashore: O for any old dry Wench now I am wet.

Must. Poor heart! That would soon make you dry agen: but all is barren in this Isle: here we may lye at Hull till the Wind blow Nore and by South, e're we can cry a Sail, a Sail, at sight of a white Apron. And therefore here's another soop to comfort us.

Vent. This Isle's our own, that's our comfort; for the Duke, the Prince, and all their train are perished.

Must. Our Ship is sunk, and we can never get home agen: we must e'en turn Salvages, and the next that catches his Fellow may eat him.

Vent. No, no, let us have a Government; for if we live well and orderly, Heav'n will drive the Shipwracks ashore to make us all rich; therefore let us carry good Consciences, and not eat one another.

Steph. Whoever eats any of my Subjects, I'le break out his Teeth with my Scepter: for I was Master at Sea, and will be Duke on Land. You *Mustacho* have been my Mate, and shall be my Vice-Roy.

Vent. When you are Duke you may chuse your Vice-Roy; but I am a free Subject in a new Plantation, and

will have no Duke without my Voice. And so fill me
the other soop.

Steph. whispering.] *Ventoso*, dost thou hear, I will
advance thee, prithee give me thy voice.

Vent. I'le have no whisperings to corrupt the Election;
and to show that I have no private ends, I declare
aloud, that I will be Vice-Roy; or I'le keep my Voice
for my self.

Must. Stephano, hear me, I will speak for the People,
because they are few, or rather none in the Isle to speak
for themselves. Know then, that to prevent the farther
shedding of Christian Blood, we are all content *Ventoso*
shall be Vice-Roy, upon condition I may be Vice-Roy
over him. Speak good People, are you agreed? What, no
man Answer? Well, you may take their silence for consent.

Vent. You speak for the People, *Mustacho*? I'le
speak for 'em, and declare generally with one voice, one
word and all, that there shall be no Vice-Roy but the
Duke, unless I be he.

Must. You declare for the people, who never saw
your Face! Cold Iron shall decide it.   [*Both draw.*

Steph. Hold, loving Subjects: we will have no Civil
War during our Reign: I do hereby appoint you both
to be my Vice-Roys over the whole Island.

Both. Agreed! Agreed!

Enter Trincalo, *with a great Bottle, half drunk.*

Vent. How! *Trincalo* our brave Bosen!

Must. He reels: can he be drunk with Sea-water?

Trinc. Sings. I shall no more to Sea, to Sea,
          Here I shall dye ashore.
This is a very scurvy Tune to sing at a Man's Funeral;
But here's my Comfort.   [*Drinks.*
Sings. The Master, the Swabber, the Gunner, and I,
          The Surgeon, and his Mate,
      Lov'd *Mall, Meg,* and *Marrian,* and *Margery.*
      But none of us car'd for *Kate.*

For she had a tongue with a tang,
Wou'd cry to a Saylor, go hang:
She lov'd not the savour of Tar nor of Pitch,
Yet a Taylor might scratch her where e'er she
did itch.

This is a scurvy Tune too, but here's my comfort agen.
[Drinks.

Steph. We have got another Subject now; welcome,
welcome into our Dominions!

Trinc. What Subject, or what Dominions? Here's
old Sack boys: the King of good Fellows can be no
subject. I will be Old *Simon* the King.

Must. Hah, old Boy! How didst thou scape?

Trinc. Upon a Butt of Sack, Boys, which the Saylors
threw overboard. But are you alive, hoa! for I will
tipple with no Ghosts till I'm dead. Thy hand *Mustacho*,
and thine *Ventoso*; the storm has done its worst:
Stephano alive too! Give thy Bosen thy hand, Master.

Vent. You must kiss it then, for I must tell you, we
have chosen him Duke in a full Assembly.

Trinc. A Duke! Where? What's he Duke of?

Must. Of this Island, Man. Oh *Trincalo* we are all
made, the Island's empty; all's our own, Boy; and we
will speak to his Grace for thee, that thou may'st be as
great as we are.

Trinc. You great! What the Devil are you?

Vent. We two are Vice-Roys over all the Island; and
when we are weary of Governing thou shalt succeed us.

Trinc. Do you hear, *Ventoso*, I will succeed you in
both your places before you enter into 'em.

Steph. *Trincalo*, sleep and be sober; and make no
more uproars in my Country.

Trinc. Why, what are you, Sir, what are you?

Steph. What I am, I am by free Election, and you
Trincalo are not your self; but we pardon your first fault,
Because it is the first day of our Reign.

Trinc. Umph, were matters carried so swimmingly against me while I was swimming, and saving my self for the good of the people of this Island.

Must. Art thou mad, *Trincalo*, wilt thou disturb a settled Government?

Trinc. I say this Island shall be under *Trincalo*, or it shall be a Common-wealth; and so my Bottle is my Buckler, and so I draw my Sword.   [*Draws.*

Vent. Ah *Trincalo*, I thought thou hadst had more grace,
Than to rebell against thy old Master,
And thy two lawfull Vice-Roys.

Must. Wilt not thou take advice of two that stand
For old Counsellors here, where thou art a meer stranger
To the Laws of the Country.

Trinc. I'll have no Laws.

Vent. Then Civil-War begins
                         [Ventoso, Mustacho *draw.*

Steph. Hold, hold, I'le have no blood-shed:
My subjects are but few: let him make a rebellion
By himself; and a Rebel, I Duke *Stephano* declare him:
Vice-Roys, come away.

Trinc. And Duke *Trincalo* declares, that he will make open War wherever he meets thee or thy Vice-Roys.
              [*Exeunt* Stephano, Mustacho, Ventoso.
         Enter Caliban *with wood upon his Back.*

Trinc. Hah! Who have we here?

Calib. All the infections that the Sun sucks up from Fogs, Fens, Flats, on *Prospero* fall; and make him by inch-meal a Disease: his Spirits hear me, and yet I needs must curse; but they'l not pinch, fright me with Urchin shows, pitch me i' th' mire, nor lead me in the dark out of my way, unless he bid 'em: but for every trifle he sets them on me; sometimes like Baboons they mow and chatter at me, and often bite me; like Hedgehogs then they mount their prickles at me, tumbling before me in my barefoot way. Sometimes I am all wound about with Adders, who with their cloven tongues hiss me to madness. Hah! Yonder stands one of his spirits sent to torment me.

Trinc. What have we here, a Man, or a Fish? This is some Monster of the Isle. Were I in *England,* as once I was, and had him painted; not a Holy day Fool there but would give me Six-pence for the sight of him: well, if I could make him tame, he were a present for an Emperour. Come hither pretty Monster, I'le do thee no harm. Come hither!

Calib. Torment me not;
I'le bring the Wood home faster.

Trinc. He talks none of the wisest: but I'le give him a dram o' th' Bottle, that will clear his understanding. Come on your ways Master Monster, open your Mouth. How now, you perverse Moon-calf! What, I think you cannot tell who is your friend! Open your chops, I say.
[*Pours Wine down his throat.*

Calib. This is a brave God, and bears Cœlestial
  Liquor;
I'le kneel to him.

Trinc. He is a very hopeful Monster. Monster what say'st thou, art thou content to turn civil and sober, as I am? For then thou shalt be my Subject.

Calib. I'le swear upon that Bottle to be true; for the liquor is not Earthly: didst thou not drop from Heaven?

Trinc. Only out of the Moon; I was the Man in her when time was. By this light, a very shallow Monster.

Calib. I'le shew thee every fertile inch i' th' Isle, and kiss thy foot: I prithee be my God, and let me drink.
[*Drinks agen.*

Trinc. Well drawn, Monster, in good faith.

Calib. I'le shew thee the best Springs, I'le pluck thee
    Berries,
I'le fish for thee, and get thee wood enough.
A curse upon the Tyrant whom I serve, I'le bear him
No more sticks, but follow thee.
    Trinc. The poor Monster is loving in his drink.
    Calib. I prithee let me bring thee where Crabs grow,
And I, with my long Nails, will dig thee Pig-nuts,
Shew thee a Jay's Nest, and instruct thee how to snare
The Marmazet; I'le bring thee to cluster'd Filberds;
Wilt thou go with me?
    Trinc. This Monster comes of a good Natur'd Race;
Is there no more of thy Kin in this Island?
    Calib. Divine, here is but one besides my self;
My Lovely Sister, Beautiful and Bright as the full Moon.
    Trinc. Where is she!
    Calib. I left her clambring up a hollow Oak,
And plucking thence the droping Honey-Combs.
Say my King, shall I call her to thee?
    Trinc. She shall swear upon the Bottle too. If she
proves handsom she is mine: Here Monster, Drink agen
for thy good news, thou shalt speak a good word for me.
                  [*Gives him the Bottle.*
    Calib. Farewel, Old Master, farewel, farewel.
    Sings. No more Dams I'le make for Fish,
           Nor fetch in Firing at requiring,
           Nor scrape Trencher, nor wash Dish.
           Ban, ban, *Cackaliban*
           Has a new Master, get a new Man.
           Heigh-day, Freedom, Freedom!
    Trinc. Here's two Subjects got already, the Monster,
and his Sister: Well, Duke *Stephano*, I say, and say
agen, wars will ensue, and so I Drink. [*Drinks.*] From
this Worshipful Monster, and Mistress Monster his
Sister, I'le lay claim to this Island by Alliance. Monster, I say thy Sister shall be my Spouse: Come away

Brother Monster, I'le lead thee to my Butt and Drink
Her Health.   [*Exeunt.*

Enter Prospero *alone.*

Prosp. 'Tis not yet fit to let my Daughters know I
    kept
The Infant Duke of *Mantua* so near them in this Isle,
Whose Father Dying Bequeath'd him to my care,
Till my false Brother (when he design'd t' Usurp
My Dukedom from me) Expos'd him to that fate
He meant for me. By Calculation of his Birth
I saw Death threat'ning him, if, till some time were past,
He should behold the Face of any Woman:
And now the danger's nigh. *Hippolito!*

Enter Hippolito.

Hip. Sir, I attend your pleasure.

Prosp. How I have lov'd thee from thy infancy,
Heav'n knows, and thou thy self canst bear me witness,
Therefore accuse not me for thy restraint.

Hip. Since I knew life, you've kept me in a Rock,
Anf you this day have hurry'd me from thence,
Only to change my Prison, not to free me.
I murmur not, but I may wonder at it.

Prosp. O gentle Youth, Fate waits for thee abroad,
A black Star threatens thee, and Death unseen
Stands ready to devour thee.

Hip. You taught me
Not to fear him in any of his shapes:
Let me meet Death rather than be a Prisoner.

Prosp. 'Tis pity he should seize thy tender Youth.

Hip. Sir, I have heard you say, no Creature liv'd
Within this Isle, but those which Man was Lord of,
Why should then I fear?

Prosp. But here are Creatures which I nam'd not to
    thee,
Who share Man's Sovereignty by Nature's Laws,
And oft depose him from it.

Hip. What are those Creatures, Sir?

Prosp. Those dangerous Enemies of Men call'd women.

Hip. Women! I never heard of them before.
But have I Enemies within this Isle?
And do you keep me from them? Do you think
That I want courage to encounter them?

Prosp. No courage can resist 'em.

Hip. How then have you, Sir,
Liv'd so long unharm'd among them?

Prosp. O they despise Old Age, and spare it for that
reason:
T'is below their Conquest, Their Fury falls
Alone upon the Young.

Hip. Why then the Fury of the Young shall fall on
them again.
Pray turn me loose upon 'em: but, good Sir,
What are Women like?

Prosp. Imagine something between young men and
Angels:
Fatally Beauteous, and have Killing Eyes,
Their Voices Charm beyond the Nightingales;
They're all Enchantment; those who once behold 'em.
Are made their Slaves for ever.

Hip. Then I will wink and fight with 'em.

Prosp. 'Tis but in vain, for when your Eyes are shut,
They through the Lids will shine, and Pierce your Soul:
Absent, they will be present to you.
They'l haunt you in your very Sleep.

Hip. Then I'le revenge it on them when I wake.

Prosp. You are without all possibility of revenge;
They are so Beautiful that you can ne'er attempt,
Nor wish to hurt them.

Hip. Are they so beautiful?

Prosp. Calm Sleep is not so soft, nor Winter Suns,
Nor Summer Shades so pleasant.

Hip. Can they be Fairer than the Plumes of Swans?

Or more Delightful than the Peacocks Feathers?
Or than the gloss upon the necks of Doves?
Or have more various Beauty than the Rain-Bow?
These I have seen, and without danger wondered at.

Prosp. All these are far below 'em: Nature made
Nothing but Woman dangerous and fair:
Therefore if you should chance to see 'em,
Avoid 'em streight, I charge you.

Hip. Well, since you say they are so Dangerous,
I'le so far shun 'em as I may with safety
Of the unblemish'd honour which you taught me.
But let 'em not provoke me, for I'm sure
I shall not then forbear them.

Prosp. Go in and read the Book I gave you last.
To morrow I may bring you better News.

Hip. I shall obey you Sir.   [*Exit* Hippolito.

Prosp. So, so; I hope this Lesson has secur'd him;
For I have been constrain'd to change his Lodging
From yonder Rock where first I bred him up,
And here have brought him home to my own Cell,
Because the Shipwrack happen'd near his Mansion.
I hope he will not stir beyond his limits,
For hitherto he has been all Obedience.
The Planets seem to smile on my designs;
And yet there is one sullen Cloud behind,
I would it were disperst. How, my Daughters!
                    [*Enter* Miranda *and* Dorinda.
I thought I had instructed them enough:
Children, retire; Why do you walk this way?

Mir. It is within our Bounds, Sir.

Prosp. But both take heed, that path is very dangerous.
Remember what I told you.

Dor. Is the man that way, Sir?

Prosp. All that you can imagine ill is there:
The Curled Lyon, and the Rugged Bear
Are not so dreadful as that Man.

Mir. Oh me, why stay we here then?

Dor. I'le keep far enough from his Den, I warrant him.

Mir. But you have told me, Sir, you are a Man;
And yet you are not Dreadful.

Prosp. I Child! But I am a tame Man: Old Men
   are tame
By Nature, but all the Danger lies in a wild
Young Man.

Dor. Do they run wild about the Woods?

Prosp. No, they are wild within Doors, in Chambers,
And in Closets.

Dor. But Father, I would stroak 'em, make 'em gentle,
Then sure they would not hurt me.

Prosp. You must not trust them, Child:
No Woman can come neer'em but she feels
A Pain full nine Months: Well I must in, for new
Affairs require my presence:
Be you, *Miranda*, your Sister's Guardian.

                              [*Exit* Prospero.

Dor. Come, Sister, shall we walk the other way,
The man will catch us else, we have but two Legs,
And he perhaps has four.

Mir. Well, Sister, though he have, yet look about you
And we shall spy him 'ere he comes too near us.

Dor. Come back, that way is towards his Den.

Mir. Let me alone: I'le venture first, for sure he can
Devour but one of us at once.

Dor. How dare you venture?

Mir. We'll find him sitting like a Hare in's Form,
And he shall not see us.

Dor. I, but you know my Father charg'd us both.

Mir. But who shall tell him on't? We'll keep each
Others Counsel.

Dor. I dare not for the world.

Mir. But how shall we hereafter shun him, if we do
not Know him first?

Dor. Nay, I confess, I would fain see him too.
I find it in my Nature,
Because my Father has forbidden me.

Mir. I; there's it, Sister, if he had said nothing I
had been quiet. Go softly, and if you see him first, be
quick and becken me away.

Dor. Well, if he does catch me, I'le humble my self
　　to him,
And ask him Pardon, as I do my Father,
When I have done a Fault.

Mir. And if I can but scape with Life, I had rather
be in pain nine Months, as my Father threatn'd than
lose my Longing.　　　　　　　　　　　　　*[Exeunt.*

The Scene changes, and discovers Hippolito *in a Cave
walking : his face from the Audience*

Hip. Prospero has often said that Nature makes
Nothing in vain : Why then are Women made ?
Are they to suck the Poyson of the Earth,
As gaudy colour'd serpents are ? I'le ask
That question, when next I see him here.

Enter Miranda *and* Dorinda *peeping.*

Dor. O Sister, there it is ; it walks about like one of us.

Mir. I, just so ; and has Legs as we have too.

Hip. It strangely puzzles me : Yet 'tis most likely
Women are some what between men and spirits.

Dor. Heark ! It talks, sure this is not it my Father
　　meant,
For this is just like one of us : Methinks I am not half
So much afraid on't as I was : See, now it turns this way.

Mir. Heav'n, what a goodly thing it is !

Dor. I'le go nearer it.

Mir. O no, 'tis Dangerous, Sister ! I'le go to it.
I would not for the world that you should venture.
My Father charg'd me to secure you from it.

Dor. I warrant you this is a tame Man, dear Sister
He'll not hurt me, I see it by his Looks.

Mir. Indeed he will! But go back, and he shall eat
  me first:
Fye, are you not asham'd to be so much inquisitive?
  Dor. You chide me for't, and wou'd give your self.
  Mir. Come back, or I will tell my Father.
Observe how he begins to stare already.
I'le meet the danger first, and then call you.
  Dor. Nay, Sister, you shall never vanquish me in
  kindness
I'le venture you, no more than you will me.
  Prosp. within. Miranda, Child, where are you!
  Mir. Do you not hear my Father call? Go in.
  Dor. 'Twas you he nam'd, not me: I will but say
My Prayers, And follow you immediately.
  Mir. Well; Sister, you'l repent it.   [*Exit* Miranda.
  Dor. Though I die for't, I must have th' other peep.
  Hip. [*Seeing her.*] What thing is that? Sure 'tis some
  Infant of
The Sun, dress'd in its Father's gayest Beams,
And comes to play with Birds: My Sight is dazl'd,
And yet I find I'm loth to shut my Eyes.
I must go nearer it——but stay a while,
May it not be that Beauteous murderer, Woman,
Which I was charg'd to shun? Speak, what art thou?
Thou shining Vision!
  Dor. Alass! I know not: But I'm told I am a Woman.
Do not hurt me, pray, fair thing.
  Hip. I'd sooner tear my Eyes out, than consent
To do you any harm; though I was told
A Woman was my Enemy.
  Dor. I never knew what it was to be an Enemy.
Nor can I e'er prove so to that which looks
Like you: For though I have been charg'd by him
(Whom yet I never disobey'd) to shun
Your Presence, yet I'd rather dye than lose it:
Therefore, I hope, you will not have the Heart

To hurt me: though I fear you are a man,
That dangerous thing of which I have been warn'd:
Pray tell me what you are?

   Hip. I must confess, I was inform'd I am a Man,
But if I fright you, I shall wish I were some other
      Creature.
I was bid to fear you too.

   Dor. Ay me! Heav'n grant we be not poyson to each
      other!
Alas! can we not meet but we must die?

   Hip. I hope not so!   For when two poysonous
      Creatures,
Both of the same kind meet, yet neither dies.
I've seen two Serpents harmless to each other,
Though they have twin'd into a mutual Knot.
If we have any venome in us, sure,
We cannot be more Poysonous, when we meet,
Than Serpents are. You have a hand like mine,
May I not gently touch it?   [*Takes her hand.*

   Dor. I've touch'd my Father's and my Sisters hands
And felt no pain; but now, alas! there's something,
When I touch yours, which makes me sigh: just so
I've seen two Turtles mourning when they met,
Yet mine's a pleasing grief;   and so methought was
      theirs;
For still they mourn'd, and still they seem'd to murmur too;
And yet they often met.

   Hip. Oh Heavens! I have the same sense too: your
      hand
Methinks goes through me; I feel at my heart,
And find it pleases, though it pains me.

   Prosp. within.] *Dorinda!*

   Dor. My Father calls agen, ah; I must leave you.

   Hip. Alas I'm subject to the same command.

   Dor. This is my first offence against my Father,
Which he, by severing us, too cruelly does punish.

Hip. And this is my first trespass too: but he hath
  more
Offended truth than we have him:
He said our meeting would destructive be,
But I no death but in our parting see.

                              [*Exeunt several ways.*

Act III.

Enter Prospero *and* Miranda.

Prosp. EXCUSE it not, *Miranda*, for to you
        (The Elder, and, I thought the more dis-
   creet)
I gave the conduct of your Sister's actions.
   Mir. Sir, when you call'd me thence, I did not fail.
To mind her of her duty to depart.
   Prosp. How can I think you did remember hers,
When you forgot your own? did you not see
The Man whom I commanded you to shun?
   Mir. I must confess I saw him at a distance.
   Prosp. Did not his Eyes infect and poyson you?
What alteration found you in your self?
   Mir. I only wondred at a sight so new.
   Prosp. But have you no desire once more to see him?
Come, tell me truly what you think of him?
   Mir. As of the gayest thing I ever saw,
So fine, that it appear'd more fit to be
Belov'd than fear'd, and seem'd so near my kind,
That I did think I might have call'd it Sister.
   Prosp. You do not love it?
   Mir. How is 't likely that
I should, except the thing had first lov'd me?
   Prosp. Cherish those thoughts: you have a gen'rous
   soul;
And since I see your Mind not apt to take
The light impressions of a sudden Love,

I will unfold a Secret to your Knowledge.
That Creature which you saw, is of a kind
Which Nature made a prop and guide to yours.

Mir. Why did you then propose him as an object
Of terrour to my Mind? you never us'd
To teach me any thing but God-like Truths,
And what you said I did believe as sacred.

Prosp. I fear'd the pleasing form of this young man
Might unawares possess your tender Breast,
Which for a nobler Guest I had design'd;
For shortly, my *Miranda*, you shall see
Another of his kind, the full blown Flower,
Of which this youth was but the Op'ning-bud.
Go in, and send your Sister to me.

Mir. Heav'n still preserve you, Sir.   [*Exit* Miranda.

Prosp. And make thee fortunate.
Dorinda, now must be examin'd too
Concerning this late interview. I'm sure
Unartful truth lies open in her Mind,
As Crystal streams their sandy bottom show.
I must take care her love grow not too fast,
For Innocence is Love's most fertile soil,
Wherein he soon shoots up and widely spreads,
Nor is that danger which attends *Hippolito* yet over-
    past.

Enter Dorinda.

Prosp. O, come hither, you have seen a Man to day,
Against my strict Command.

Dor. Who I? indeed I saw him but a little, Sir.

Prosp. Come, come, be clear. Your Sister told me all.

Dor. Did she? truly she would have seen him more
    than I,
But that I would not let her.

Prosp. Why so?

Dor. Because, methought, he would have hurt me less
Than he would her. But if I knew you'd not

Be angry with him, I could tell you, Sir,
That he was much to blame.

Prosp. Hah! was he to blame?
Tell me, with that sincerity I taught you,
How you became so bold to see the Man?

Dor. I hope you will forgive me, Sir, because I did
not see him much till he saw me. Sir, he would needs
come in my way, and star'd, and star'd upon my face;
and so I thought I would be reveng'd of him, and
therefore I gaz'd on him as long; but if I e're come neer
a Man again——

Prosp. I told you he was dangerous; but you would
not be warn'd.

Dor. Pray be not angry, Sir, if I tell you, you are
mistaken in him; for he did me no great hurt.

Prosp. But he may do you more harm hereafter.

Dor. No, Sir, I'm as well as e're I was in all my
   life,
But that I cannot eat nor drink for thought of him.
That dangerous man runs ever in my Mind.

Prosp. The way to cure you, is no more to see him.

Dor. Nay pray, Sir, say not so, I promis'd him
To see him once agen; and you know, Sir,
You charg'd me I shou'd never break my Promise.

Prosp. Wou'd you see him who did you so much
   mischief?

Dor. I warrant you I did him as much harm
As he did me, For when I left him, Sir,
He sigh'd so as it griev'd my heart to hear him.

Prosp. Those sighs were poysonous, they infected
   you:
You say they griev'd you to the heart.

Dor. 'Tis true; but yet his looks and words were
gentle.

Prosp. These are the Day-dreams of a Maid in love,
But still I fear the worst.

Dor. O fear not him, Sir,
I know he will not hurt you for my sake;
I'le undertake to tye him to a hair,
And lead him hither as my Pris'ner to you.

    Prosp. Take heed *Dorinda,* you may be deceiv'd;
This Creature is of such a Salvage race,
That no mild usage can reclaim his wildness;
But, like a Lyon's Whelp bred up by hand,
When least you look for't, Nature will present
The Image of his Fathers bloody Paws,
Wherewith he purvey'd for his couching Queen;
And he will leap into his native fury.

    Dor. He cannot change from what I left him, Sir.

    Prosp. You speak of him with too much Passion;
    tell me
(And on your duty tell me true, *Dorinda*)
What past betwixt you and that horrid Creature?

    Dor. How, horrid, Sir! if any else but you
Should call it so, indeed I should be angry.

    Prosp. Go too! you are a foolish Girl; but answer
To what I ask, what thought you when you saw it?

    Dor. At first it star'd upon me and seem'd wild,
And then I trembled; yet it look'd so lovely,
That when I would have fled away, my Feet
Seem'd fasten'd to the ground; then it drew near,
And with amazement askt to touch my hand;
Which, as a ransom for my life, I gave:
But when he had it, with a furious gripe,
He put it to his mouth so eagerly,
I was afraid he would have swallow'd it.

    Prosp. Well, what was his behaviour afterwards?

    Dor. He on a sudden grew so tame and gentle,
That he became more kind to me than you are;
Then, Sir, I grew I know not how, and touching
His hand agen, my heart did beat so strong
As I lackt breath to answer what he ask'd.

Prosp. You 've been too fond, and I should chide you
    for it.

Dor. Then send me to that creature to be pun-
    isht.

Prosp. Poor Child! thy Passion like a lazy Ague
Has seiz'd thy Blood; instead of striving thou
Humour'st and feed'st thy languishing Disease
Thou fight'st the Battels of thy Enemy;
And 'tis one part of what I threatn'd thee,
Not to perceive thy danger.

Dor. Danger, Sir?
If he would hurt me, yet he knows not how.
He hath no Claws, nor Teeth, nor Horns to hurt me;
But looks about him like a Callow-Brid
Just straggl'd from the Nest: pray trust me, Sir,
To go to him agen.

Prosp. Since you will venture,
I charge you bear your self reserv'dly to him,
Let him not dare to touch your naked hand,
But keep at distance from him.

Dor. This is hard.

Prosp. It is the way to make him love you more;
He will despise you if you grow too kind.

Dor. I'le struggle with my heart to follow this;
But if I lose him by it, will you promise
To bring him back again;

Prosp. Fear not, *Dorinda*;
But use him ill and he'l be yours for ever.

Dor. I hope you have not couzen'd me agen.

                     [*Exit* Dorinda.

Prosp. Now my designs are gathering to a head.
My Spirits are obedient to my Charms.
What, *Ariel*! my Servant *Ariel*,
Where art thou?

              Enter Ariel.

Ariel. What wou'd my potent Master? here I am.

Prosp. Thou and thy meaner fellows your last service
Did worthily perform, and I must use you
In such another Work: how goes the day?
  Ariel. On the fourth [hour], my Lord, and on the
    sixth
You said our work should cease.
  Prosp. And so it shall;
And thou shalt have the open Air at freedom.
  Ariel. Thanks my great Lord.
  Prosp. But tell me first, my Spirit,
How fares the Duke, my Brother, and their followers?
  Ariel. Confin'd together, as you gave me order,
In the Lime-Grove which weather-fends your Cell.
Within that Circuit up and down they wander,
But cannot stir one step beyond their compass.
  Prosp. How do they bear their sorrows?
  Ariel. The two Dukes
Appear like Men distracted; their Attendants
Brim-full of sorrow mourning over them;
But chiefly, he you term'd the good *Gonzalo*:
His tears run down his Beard, like Winter-drops
From Eaves of Reeds: your Vision did so work 'em,
That if you now beheld 'em, your affections
Would become tender.
  Prosp. Dost thou think so, Spirit?
  Ariel. Mine would, Sir, were I humane.
  Prosp. And mine shall:
Hast thou, who art but air, a touch, a feeling
Of their Afflictions, and shall not I (a Man
Like them, one who as sharply relish Passions
As they) be kindlier moved than thou art?
Though they have pierc'd me to the quick with in-
    juries,
Yet with my nobler Reason 'gainst my fury,
I will take part; the rarer action is
In Virtue than in Vengeance. Go, my *Ariel*,

Refresh with needful Food their famish'd Bodies.
With shows and cheerful Musick comfort 'em.
    Ariel. Presently, Master.
    Prosp. With a twinckle, *Ariel*.
    Ariel. Before you can say come and go,
And breath twice, and cry so, so.
Each Spirit tripping on his toe,
Shall bring 'em Meat with mop and moe.
Do you love me, Master, I or no?
    Prosp. Dearly, my dainty *Ariel*, but stay, Spirit;
What is become of my Slave *Caliban*,
And *Sycorax* his Sister?
    Ariel. Potent Sir!
They have cast off your Service, and revolted
To the wrack'd Mariners, who have already
Parcell'd your Island into Governments.
    Prosp. No matter, I have now no need of 'em;
But, spirit, now I stay thee on the Wing;
Haste to perform what I have given in charge:
But see they keep within the bounds I set 'em.
    Ariel. I'le keep 'em in with Walls of Adamant,
Invisible as air to mortal Eyes,
But yet unpassable.
    Prosp. Make hast then.   [*Exeunt severally*.
        Enter Alonzo, Antonio, Gonzalo.
    Gonz. I am weary, and can go no farther, Sir,
My old Bones ake, here's a Maze trod indeed,
Through Forth-rights and Meanders, by your Pa-
        tience
I needs must rest.
    Alonz. Old Lord, I cannot blame thee, who am my
        self seiz'd
With a weariness to the dulling of my Spirits:
Sit and rest.   [*They sit*.
Even here I will put off my hope; and keep it
No longer for my Flatterers: he is drown'd

Whom thus we stray to find, and the Sea mocks
Our frustrate Search on Land: Well! let him go.

　　Ant. Do not for one repulse forego the purpose
Which you resolv'd t'effect.

　　Alonz. I'm faint with hunger,
And must despair of food, Heav'n hath incens'd
The Seas and shores against us for our crimes. [*Musick.*
What! Harmony agen, my good Friends, heark!

　　Ant. I fear some other horrid Apparition.
Give us kind Keepers, Heaven I beseech thee!

　　Gonz. 'Tis chearful Musick, this; unlike the first;
And seems as if 'twere meant t' unbend our cares,
And calm your troubled thoughts.

　　　　　　Ariel *invisible SINGS.*
　　Dry those eyes which are o'reflowing,
　　All your storms are over-blowing:
　　While you in this Isle are bideing,
　　You shall feast without providing:
　　Every dainty you can think of,
　　Ev'ry Wine which you would drink of,
　　Shall be yours; all want shall shun you,
　　Ceres *Blessing so is on you.*

　　Alonz. This Voice speaks comfort to us.
　　Ant. Wou'd 'twere come; there is no Musick in a
　　　　Song
To me, my stomack being empty.
　　Gonz. O for a Heavenly Vision of Boyl'd, Bak'd, and
　　　　Roasted!
　　Enter eight fat Spirits, with Cornu-Copia *in their
　　　　　　hands.*
　　Alonz. Are these plump shapes sent to deride our
hunger?
　　Gonz. No, no: it is a Masque of fatten'd Devils,
The Burgo-Masters of the lower Region.
　　　　　　　　　　　　[*Dance and Vanish.*

O for a Collop of that large-haunch'd Devil
Who went out last!

Ant. going to the door. My Lord, the Duke, see yonder.
A Table, as I live, set out and furnisht
With all varieties of Meats and Fruits.

Alonz. 'Tis so indeed, but who dares tast this Feast:
Which Fiends provide, perhaps to poyson us?

Gonz. Why that dare I; if the black Gentleman
Be so ill-natur'd, he may do his pleasure.

Ant. 'Tis certain we must either eat or famish,
I will encounter it, and feed.

Alonz. If both resolve, I will adventure too.

Gonz. Then good my Lord, make haste,
And say no Grace before it, I beseech you,
Because the meat will vanish strait, if, as I fear,
An evil Spirit be our Cook.   [*Exeunt.*
            Enter Trincalo *and* Caliban.

Trinc. Brother Monster, welcome to my private
      Palace.
But where's thy Sister, is she so brave a Lass?

Calib. In all this Isle there are but two more, the
Daughters of the Tyrant *Prospero*; and she is bigger
than 'em both. O here she comes; now thou may'st
judge thy self, my Lord.
            Enter Sycorax.

Trinc. She's monstrous fair indeed. Is this to be my
Spouse? Well, she's Heir of all this Isle (for I will geld
Monster). The *Trincalos*, like other wise Men, have
anciently us'd to Marry for Estate more than for Beauty.

Sycorax. I prithee let me have the gay thing about
thy Neck, and that which dangles at thy Wrist.

      [Sycorax *points to his Bosen's Whistle, and his
            Bottle.*

Trinc. My dear Blobber-lips; this, observe my
Chuck, is a badge of my Sea-Office; my fair Fuss, thou
dost not know it.

Syc. No, my dread Lord.

Trinc. It shall be a Whistle for our first Babe; and when the next Shipwrack puts me again to swimming, I'le dive to get a Coral to it.

Syc. I'le be thy pretty Child, and wear it first.

Trinc. I prithee sweet Babby do not play the wanton, and cry for my Goods e're I'm dead. When thou art my Widow, thou shalt have the Devil and all.

Syc. May I not have the other fine thing?

Trinc. This is a Sucking-Bottle for young *Trincalo*.

Calib. This is a God a mighty Liquor; I did but drink thrice of it, and it hath made me glad e're since.

Syc. He is the bravest God I ever saw.

Calib. You must be kind to him, and he will love you. I prithee speak to her, my Lord, and come neerer her.

Trinc. By this light, I dare not till I have drank: I must fortifie my stomack first.

Syc. I shall have all his fine things when I'm a Widow.   [*Pointing to his Bottle, and Bosen's Whistle.*

Calib. I, but you must be kind and kiss him then.

Trinc. My Brother Monster is a rare Pimp.

Syc. I'le hug thee in my Arms, my Brother's God.

Trinc. Think o' thy Soul, *Trincalo*, thou art a dead Man if this kindness continue.

Calib. And he shall get thee a young *Sycorax*, wilt thou not, my Lord?

Trinc. Indeed I know not how, they do no such thing in my Country.

Syc. I'le shew thee how; thou shalt get me twenty *Sycoraxes*; and I'le get thee twenty *Calibans*.

Trinc. Nay, if they are got, she must do't all her self, that's certain.

Syc. And we will tumble in cool Plashes, and the soft Fens, where we will make us Pillows of Flags and Bull-rushes.

Calib. My Lord, she would be loving to thee, and thou wilt not let her.

Trinc. Ev'ry thing in its Season, Brother Monster; but you must counsel her; fair Maids must not be too forward.

Syc. My Brother's God, I love thee; prithee let me come to thee.

Trinc. Subject Monster, I charge thee keep the Peace between us.

Calib. Shall she not taste of that Immortal Liquor?

Trinc. Umph! That's another question: for if she be thus flipant in her Water, what will she be in her Wine?

Enter Ariel (*invisible*) *and changes the Bottle which stands upon the ground.*

Ariel. There's Water for your Wine.   [*Exit* Ariel.

Trinc. Well! Since it must be so. [*Gives her the Bottle.*] How do you like it now, my Queen that must be?   [*She drinks.*

Syc. Is this your heavenly liquor? I'le bring you to a River of the same.

Trinc. Wilt thou so, Madam Monster? What a mighty Prince shall I be then? I would not change my Dukedom to be great Turk *Trincalo*.

Syc. This is the drink of Frogs.

Trinc. Nay, if the Frogs of this Island drink such, they are the merryest Frogs in Christendom.

Calib. She does not know the virtue of this liquor: I prithee let me drink for her.

Trinc. Well said, Subject Monster. [Caliban *drinks.*

Calib. My Lord, this is meer Water.

Trinc. 'Tis thou hast chang'd the Wine then, and drunk it up, like a debauch'd Fish as thou art. Let me see't, I'll taste it my self. Element! Meer Element! As I live. It was a cold gulp, such as this, which kill'd my famous Predecessor old *Simon* the King.

Calib. How does thy honour ? Prithee be not angry, and I will lick thy shoe.

Trinc. I could find in my heart to turn thee out of my Dominions, for a liquorish Monster.

Calib. O my Lord, I have found it out; this must be done by one of *Prospero's* Spirits.

Trinc. There's nothing but Malice in these Devils, I never lov'd 'em from my Childhood. The Devil take 'em, I would it had bin Holy-water for their sakes.

Syc. Will not thy mightiness revenge our wrongs, on this great Sorcerer? I know thou wilt, for thou art valiant.

Trinc. In my Sack, Madam Monster, as any flesh alive.

Syc. Then I will cleave to thee.

Trinc. Lovingly said, in troth: now cannot I hold out against her. This Wife-like virtue of hers, has overcome me.

Syc. Shall I have thee in my Arms?

Trinc. Thou shalt have Duke *Trincalo* in thy Arms: but prithee be not too boistrous with me at first; do not discourage a young Beginner.   [*They embrace.*

Enter Stephano, Mustacho, Ventoso.

Stand to your Arms, my Spouse, and Subject Monster; the Enemy is come to surprise us in our Quarters. You shall know Rebels that I am Marry'd to a Witch, and we have a thousand Spirits of our Party.

Steph. Hold! I ask a Truce; I and my Vice-Roys (Finding no food, and but a small remainder of Brandy) are come to treat a Peace betwixt us, which may be for the good of both Armies; therefore *Trincalo* disband.

Trinc. Plain *Trincalo*, methinks I might have been a Duke in your Mouth: I'le not accept of your Embassy without my title.

Steph. A title shall break no squares betwixt us:

Vice-Roys, give him his stile of Duke, and treat with him, whilst I walk by in state.

[*Ventoso and* Mustacho *bow whilst* Trincalo
puts on his Cap.

Must. Our Lord and Master, Duke *Stephano,* has sent us in the first place to demand of you, upon what ground you make War against him, having no right to govern here, as being Elected only by your own Voice.

Trinc. To this I answer, that having in the Face of the World Espous'd the lawful Inheritrix of this Island, Queen *Blouze* the First, and having homage done me, by this hectoring Spark her Brother; from these two I claim a lawful Title to this Island.

Must. Who, that Monster? he a Hector?

Calib. Lo! how he mocks me; wilt thou let him, my Lord?

Vent. Lord! Quoth he: the Monster's a very natural.

Syc. Lo! lo! agen; bite him to death I prithee.

Trinc. Vice-Roys! keep good Tongues in your heads I advise you, and proceed to your business, for I have other affairs to dispatch of more importance betwixt Queen Slobber-Chops and my self.

Must. First and foremost, as to your claim that you have answer'd.

Vent. But second and foremost, we demand of you, that if we make a Peace, the Butt also may be comprehended in the Treaty.

Must. Is the Butt safe, Duke *Trincalo?*

Trinc. The Butt is partly safe: but to comprehend it in the Treaty, or indeed to make any Treaty, I cannot, with my honour, without your submission. These two, and the Spirits under me, stand likewise upon their honours.

Calib. Keep the liquor for us, my Lord, and let them drink Brine; for I will not show 'em the quick freshes of the Island.

Steph. I understand, being present, from my Embassadors what your resolution is, and ask an hours time of deliberation, and so I take our leave. But first I desire to be entertain'd, at your Butt, as becomes a Prince, and his Embassadors.

Trinc. That I refuse, till acts of Hostility be ceas'd. These Rogues are rather Spies than Embassadors: I must take heed of my Butt. They come to pry into the secrets of my Dukedom.

Vent. Trincalo you are a barbarous Prince, and so farewel. [*Exeunt* Stephano, Mustacho, Ventoso.

Trinc. Subject Monster! stand you Sentry before my Cellar; my Queen and I will enter and feast our selves within.

Syc. May I not Marry that other King and his two Subjects, to help you a nights?

Trinc. What a careful Spouse have I? Well! If she does Cornute me, the care is taken.
When underneath my Power my Foes have truckl'd,
To be a Prince, who would not be a Cuckold? [*Exeunt.*

Enter Ferdinand, *and* Ariel (*invisible*).

Ferd. How far will this invisible Musician
Conduct my steps? He hovers still about me;
Whether for good or ill I cannot tell;
Nor care I much; for I have been so long
A Slave to chance, that I'm as weary of
Her flatteries as her frowns: but here I am——

Ariel. Here I am.

Ferd. Hah! Art thou so? The Spirit's turn'd an Eccho:
This might seem pleasant, could the burthen of
My Griefs accord with any thing but sighs.
And my last words, like those of dying Men
Need no reply. Fain I would go to shades,
Where few would wish to follow me.

Ariel. Follow me.

Ferd. This evil Spirit grows importunate,
But I'le not take his counsel.
 Ariel. Take his counsel.
 Ferd. It may be the Devil's counsel. I'le never take it.
 Ariel. Take it.
 Ferd. I will discourse no more with thee,
Nor follow one step further.
 Ariel. One step further.
 Ferd. This must have more importance than an
  Eccho.
Some Spirit tempts me to a precipice.
I'll try if it will answer when I sing
My Sorrows to the murmurs of this Brook.

    He Sings.
     Go thy way.
Ariel.   *Go thy way.*
Ferd.   *Why should'st thou stay ?*
Ariel.   *Why should'st thou stay ?*
Ferd. *Where the Winds whistle, and where the streams*
    creep,
  Under yond Willow-tree, fain would I sleep.
    Then let me alone,
    For 'tis time to be gone.
Ariel.   *For 'tis time to be gone.*
Ferd. *What cares or pleasures can be in this Isle?*
  Within this desart place
  There lives no humane race ;
 Fate cannot frown here, nor kind Fortune smile.
Ariel. *Kind Fortune smiles, and she*
  Has yet in store for thee
  Some strange felicity.
  Follow me, follow me,
  And thou shalt see.

 Ferd. I'll take thy word for once ;
Lead on Musician.   *[Exeunt and return.*

Scene changes and discovers Prospero *and* Miranda.

Prosp. Advance the fringed Curtains of thine Eyes,
and say what thou seest yonder.

Mir. Is it a Spirit? Lord! How it looks about! Sir,
I confess it carries a brave form; But 'tis a Spirit.

Prosp. No Girl, it eats and sleeps, and has such senses
as we have. This young Gallant, whom thou see'st,
was in the wrack: were he not somewhat stain'd with
grief (Beauty's worst Cancker) thou might'st call him
a goodly Person: he has lost his Company, and strays
about to find 'em.

Mir. I might call him a thing divine, for nothing
natural I ever saw so noble.

Prosp. It goes on as my Soul prompts it. Spirit, fine
Spirit, I'le free thee within two days for this.

Ferd. She's sure the Mistress, on whom these Airs
attend. Fair Excellence, if, as your form declares, you
are divine, be pleas'd to instruct me how you will be
worship'd; so bright a Beauty cannot sure belong to
humane kind.

Mir. I am, like you, a Mortal, if such you are.

Ferd. My language too! O Heavens! I am the best
of them who speak this Speech, when I'm in my own
Country.

Prosp. How, the best? What wert thou if the Duke
of *Savoy* heard thee?

Ferd. As I am now, who wonders to hear thee speak
of *Savoy*: He does hear me, and that I does I weep;
my self am *Savoy*, whose fatal Eyes (e're since at ebbe)
beheld the Duke my Father wrackt.

Mir. Alack! For pity.

Prosp. At the first sight they have chang'd Eyes:
    dear *Ariel*,
I'll set thee free for this——young Sir, a word.
With hazard of your self you do me wrong.

Mir. Why speaks my Father now so urgently?

This is the third Man that e're I saw, the first
Whom e're I sigh'd for, sweet Heaven move my Father
To be inclin'd my way.

    Ferd. O! If a Virgin! and your affection not gone
      forth,
I'le make you Mistress of *Savoy.*

    Prosp. Soft, Sir! One word more.
They're in each others Power, but this swift
Bus'ness I must uneasie make, lest too
Light winning make the prize light—one word more.
Thou usurp'st the name not due to thee, and hast
Put thy self on this Island as a Spy,
To get the Government from me, the Lord on't.

    Ferd. No, as I am a Man.

    Mir. There's nothing ill can dwell in such a Temple,
If th' Evil Spirit hath so fair a House,
Good things will strive to dwell with it.

    Prosp. No more.   Speak not you for him, he's a
      Traytor.
Come! Thou art my Pris'ner and shalt be in
Bonds. Sea-water shalt thou drink, thy food
Shall be the Fresh-Brook-Muscles, wither'd Roots
And Husks, wherein the Acorn crawl'd; follow.

    Ferd. No, I'll resist such entertainment
Till my Enemy has more power.
               [He draws, and is charm'd from moving.

    Mir. O dear Father! Make not too rash a tryal
Of him, for he is gentle and not fearful.

    Prosp. My Child my Tutor! Put thy Sword up
      Traytor,
Who mak'st a show, but dar'st not strike:
Thy Conscience is possest with guilt. Come from
Thy Ward, for I can here disarm thee with
This Wand, and make thy Weapon drop.

    Mir. Beseech you Father.

    Prosp. Hence: hang not on my Garment.

Mir. Sir, have pity,
I'le be his Surety.
    Prosp. Silence! One word more
Shall make me chide thee, if not hate thee: what?
An Advocate for an Impostor? Sure
Thou think'st there are no more such shapes as his.
To th' most of Men this is a *Caliban*,
And they to him are Angels.
    Mir. My affections are then most humble,
I have no ambition to see a goodlier Man.
    Prosp. Come on, obey:
Thy Nerves are in their Infancy agen, and have
No vigour in them.
    Ferd. So they are:
My Spirits, as in a Dream, are all bound up:
My Father's loss, the weakness which I feel,
The wrack of all my Friends, and this Man's threats,
To whom I am subdu'd, would seem light to me,
Might I but once a day through my Prison
Behold this Maid: all Corners else o' th' Earth
Let liberty make use of: I have space
Enough in such a Prison.
    Prosp. It works: come on:
Thou hast done well, fine *Ariel*: follow me.
Hark what thou shalt more do for me [*Whispers* Ariel.
    Mir. Be of comfort;
My Father's of a better nature, Sir,
Than he appears by Speech: this is unwonted
Which now came from him.
    Prosp. Thou shalt be as free as Mountain Winds:
But then exactly do all points of my Command.
    Ariel. To a Syllable.   [*Exit* Ariel.
    Prosp. to *Mir.* Go in that way, speak not a word for
        him:
I'll separate you.   [*Exit* Miranda.
    Ferd. As soon thou may'st divide the Waters when

Thou strik'st' em, which pursue thy bootless blow,
And meet when 'tis past.

    Prosp. Go practise your Philosophy within;
And if you are the same you speak your self,
Bear your afflictions like a Prince——That Door
Shews you your Lodging.

    Ferd. 'Tis in vain to strive, I must obey.

                         [*Exit* Ferdinand.

    Prosp. This goes as I would wish it.
Now for my second care, *Hippolito*.
I shall not need to chide him for his fault,
His Passion is become his punishment.
Come forth, *Hippolito*.

                Enter Hippolito.

    Hip. entring. 'Tis *Prospero's* Voice.

    Prosp. Hippolito! I know you now expect
I should severely chide you: you have seen
A Woman in contempt of my Commands.

    Hip. But, Sir, you see I am come off unharm'd;
I told you, that you need not doubt my Courage.

    Prosp. You think you have receiv'd no hurt.

    Hip. No, none Sir.
Try me agen, when e're you please I'm ready:
I think I cannot fear an Army of 'em.

    Prosp. How much in vain it is to bridle Nature!

                         [*Aside.*

Well! What was the success of your encounter?

    Hip. Sir, we had none, we yielded both at first,
For I took her to mercy, and she me.

    Prosp. But are you not much chang'd from what you
      were?

    Hip. Methinks I wish and wish! For what I know not,
But still I wish——yet if I had that Woman,
She, I believe, could tell me what I wish for.

    Prosp. What wou'd you do to make that Woman
yours?

Hip. I'd quit the rest o' th' World that I might live
Alone with her, she never should be from me.
We two would sit and look till our Eyes ak'd.

Prosp. You'd soon be weary of her.

Hip. O, Sir never.

Prosp. But you'l grow old and wrinckl'd, as you see
Me now, and then you will not care for her.

Hip. You may do what you please, but, Sir, we two
Can never possibly grow old.

Prosp. You must, *Hippolito.*

Hip. Whether we will or no, Sir, who shall make us?

Prosp. Nature, which made me so.

Hip. But you have told me, [Sir,] her works are
     various;
She made you old, but she has made us young.

Prosp. Time will convince you;
Mean while be sure you tread in honours paths,
That you may merit her: And that you may not want
Fit occasions to employ your Virtue:
In this next Cave there is a Stranger lodg'd,
One of your kind, young, of a noble presence,
And as he says himself, of Princely Birth;
He is my Pris'ner and in deep affliction,
Visit, and comfort him; it will become you.

Hip. It is my duty, Sir.   [*Exit* Hippolito.

Prosp. True, he has seen a Woman, yet he lives,
Perhaps I took the moment of his Birth
Amiss, perhaps my Art it self is false.
On what strange grounds we build our hopes and
     fears!
Mans Life is all a Mist, and in the dark.
Our Fortunes meet us.
If Fate be not, then what can we foresee?
Or how can we avoid it, if it be?
If by Free-will in our own paths we move,
How are we bounded by Decrees above?

Whether we drive, or whether we are driven,
If ill 'tis ours, if good the act of Heaven.

[*Exit* Prospero.

Enter Hippolito *and* Ferdinand.

Scene, a Cave.

Ferd. Your pity, noble Youth, doth much oblige me,
Indeed 'twas sad to lose a Father so.

Hip. Ay, and an only Father too, for sure
You said you had but one.

Ferd. But one Father! he's wondrous simple [*Aside.*

Hip. Are such misfortunes frequent in your World,
Where many Men live?

Ferd. Such we are born to.
But gentle Youth, as you have question'd me,
So give me leave to ask you, what you are?

Hip. Do not you know?

Ferd. How should I?

Hip. I well hop'd I was a Man, but by your ignor-
ance
Of what I am, I fear it is not so.
Well, *Prospero*! this is now the second time
You have deceiv'd me.

Ferd. Sir, there is no doubt
You are a Man: But I would know of whence?

Hip. Why, of this World; I never was in yours.

Ferd. Have you a Father?

Hip. I was told I had one,
And that he was a Man; yet I have been
So much deceived, I dare not tell't you for
A truth: but I have still been kept a Prisoner
For fear of Women.

Ferd. They indeed are dangerous,
For since I came I have beheld one here,
Whose Beauty pierc'd my heart.

Hip. How did she pierce?
You seem not hurt.

Ferd. Alas! the wound was made by her bright Eyes,
And festers by her absence.
But to speak plain to you, Sir I love her.

Hip. Now I suspect that Love's the very thing,
That I feel too! Pray tell me truly, Sir,
Are you not grown unquiet since you saw her?

Ferd. I take no rest.

Hip. Just, just my Disease.
Do you not wish you do not know for what?

Ferd. O no! I know too well for what I wish.

Hip. There, I confess, I differ from you, Sir:
But you desire she may be always with you?

Ferd. I can have no felicity without her.

Hip. Just my condition! Alas, gentle Sir,
I'le pity you, and you shall pity me.

Ferd. I love so much, that if I have her not,
I find I cannot live.

Hip. How! Do you love her?
And would you have her too? That must not be:
For none but I must have her.

Ferd. But perhaps, we do not love the same:
All Beauties are not pleasing alike to all.

Hip. Why are there more fair Women, Sir,
Besides that one I love?

Ferd. That's a strange question. There are many
more
Besides that Beauty which you love.

Hip. I will have all of that kind, if there be a hundred
of 'em.

Ferd. But noble Youth, you know not what you say,

Hip. Sir, they are things I love, I cannot be without
'em:
O, how I rejoyce! More Women!

Ferd. Sir, if you love you must be ty'd to one.

Hip. Ty'd! How ty'd to her?

Ferd. To love none but her.

Hip. But, Sir, I find it is against my Nature.
I must love where I like, and I believe I may like all,
All that are fair: come! Bring me to this Woman,
For I must have her.

Ferd. His simplicity   [*Aside.*
Is such that I can scarce be angry with him.
Perhaps, sweet Youth, when you behold her,
You will find you do not love her.

Hip. I find already I love, because she is another
Woman.

Ferd. You cannot love two Women, both at once.

Hip. Sure 'tis my duty to love all who do
Resemble her whom I've already seen.
I'le have as many as I can, that are
So good, and Angel-like, as she I love.
And will have yours,

Ferd. Pretty Youth, you cannot.

Hip. I can do any thing for that I love.

Ferd. I may, perhaps, by force restrain you from it.

Hip. Why do so if you can. But either promise me
To love no Woman, or you must try your force.

Ferd. I cannot help it, I must love.

Hip. Well you may love, for *Prospero* taught me
Friendship too: you shall love me and other men if
you can find 'em, but all the Angel-women shall be mine.

Ferd. I must break off this Conference, or he [*Aside.*
Will urge me else beyond what I can bear.
Sweet Youth! Some other time we will speak further
Concerning both our loves; at present I
Am indispos'd with weariness and grief,
And would, if you are pleas'd, retire a while.

Hip. Some other time be it; but, Sir, remember
That I both seek and much intreat your friendship,
For next to Women, I find I can love you.

Ferd. I thank you, Sir, I will consider of it.
                                   [*Exit* Ferdinand.

Hip. This Stranger does insult, and comes into
My world to take those Heavenly Beauties from me,
Which I believe I am inspir'd to love:
And yet he said he did desire but one;
He would be poor in love, but I'le be rich.
I now perceive that *Prospero* was cunning;
For when he frighted me from Woman-kind,
Those precious things he for himself design'd.   [*Exit*.

Act IV.

Enter Prospero *and* Miranda.

Prosp. YOUR suit has pity in't, and has prevail'd.
        Within this Cave he lies, and you may see
   him.
But yet take heed; let Prudence be your Guide;
You must not stay, your visit must be short.
                              [*She's going*.
One thing I had forgot; insinuate into his mind
A kindness to that Youth, whom first you saw;
I would have Friendship grow betwixt 'em.
   Mir. You shall be obey'd in all things.
   Prosp. Be earnest to unite their very Souls.
   Mir. I shall endeavour it.
   Prosp. This may secure
Hippolito from that dark danger which
My Art forebodes; for Friendship does provide
A double strength t' oppose th' assaults of Fortune.
                              [*Exit* Prospero.
             Enter Ferdinand.
   Ferd. To be a Pris'ner where I dearly love,
Is but a double tye, a Link of Fortune,
Joyn'd to the Chain of Love: but not to see her,
And yet to be so near her, there's the hardship.
I feel my self as on a Rack, stretch'd out,

And nigh the ground, on which I might have ease,
Yet cannot reach it.

   Mir. Sir! My Lord? Where are you?

   Ferd. Is it your Voice, my Love? Or do I dream?

   Mir. Speak softly, it is I.

   Ferd. O Heavenly Creature!
Ten times more gentle, than your Father's cruel;
How on a sudden all my griefs are vanish'd!

   Mir. I come to help you to support your Griefs.

   Ferd. While I stand gazing thus, and thus have leave
To touch your hand, I do not envy freedom.

   Mir. Hark! Hark! Is't not my Father's Voice I hear?
I fear he calls me back again too soon.

   Ferd. Leave fear to guilty Minds: 'tis scarce a Virtue
When it is paid to Heaven.

   Mir. But there 'tis mixed
With love, and so is mine: yet I may fear;
For I am guilty when I disobey
My Father's will in loving you too much.

   Ferd. But you please Heav'n in disobeying him,
Heav'n bids you succour Captives in distress.

   Mir. How do you bear your Prison?

   Ferd. 'Tis my Palace
While you are here, and love and silence wait
Upon our wishes; do but think we chuse it,
And 'tis what we would chuse.

   Mir. I'm sure what I would.
But how can I be certain that you love me?
Look to't; for I will dye when you are false.
I've heard my Father tell of Maids, who dy'd,
And haunted their false Lovers with their Ghosts.

   Ferd. Your Ghost must take another form to fright
      me,
This shape will be too pleasing: do I love you?
O Heav'n! O Earth! Bear witness to this sound,
If I prove false——

Mir. Oh hold, you shall not swear;
For Heav'n will hate you if you prove forsworn.

Ferd. Did I not love, I could no more endure
This undeserved Captivity, then I
Could wish to gain my Freedom with the loss of you.

Mir. I am a Fool to weep at what I'm glad of:
But I, Sir, have a suit to you, and that,
Shall be the only tryal of your love.

Ferd. Y'ave said enough, never to be deny'd,
Were it my life; for you have far o'rebid
The price of all that humane life is worth.

Mir. Sir, 'tis to love one for my sake,
Who for his own deserves all the respect
Which you can ever pay him.

Ferd. You mean your Father: do not think his
usage
Can make me hate him; when he gave you being,
He then did that which cancell'd all these wrongs.

Mir. I meant not him, for that was a request,
Which if you love I should not need to urge.

Ferd. Is there another whom I ought to love?
And love him for your sake?

Mir. Yes such a one,
Who for his sweetness and his goodly shape,
(If I, who am unskill'd in forms, may judge,)
I think can scarce be equall'd: 'tis a Youth,
A Stranger too as you are.

Ferd. Of such a graceful feature, and must I for your
sake love?

Mir. Yes, Sir, do you scruple to grant the first
request I ever made? He's wholly unacquainted with
the World, and wants your Conversation. You should
have compassion on so meer a stranger.

Ferd. Those need compassion whom you discom-
mend; not whom you praise.

Mir. I only ask this easie tryal of you.

Ferd. Perhaps it might have easier bin if you had
never ask'd it.

Mir. I cannot understand you; and methinks am
  loth
To be more knowing.

Ferd. He has his freedom, and may get access,
When my confinement makes me want that blessing.
I his compassion need, and not he mine.

Mir. If that be all you doubt, trust me for him.
He has a melting heart, and soft to all the Seals
Of kindness; I will undertake for his Compassion.

Ferd. O Heavens! Would I were sure I did not need it.

Mir. Come, you must love him for my sake: you
  shall?

Ferd. Must I for yours, and cannot for my own?
Either you do not love, or think that I do not:
But when you bid me love him, I must hate him.

Mir. Have I so far offended you already,
That he offends you only for my sake?
Yet sure you would not hate him, if you saw
Him as I've done, so full of youth and beauty.

Ferd. O poyson to my hopes!   [*Aside.*
When he did visit me, and I did mention
This Beauteous Creature to him, he did then
Tell me he would have her.

Mir. Alas, what mean you?

Ferd. It is too plain: like most of her frail Sex,
She's false, but has not learnt the art to hide it; [*Aside.*
Nature has done her part, she loves variety.
Why did I think that any Woman could
Be innocent, because she's young? No, no,
Their Nurses teach them Change,
When with two Nipples they divide their Liking.

Mir. I fear I have offended you, and yet
I meant no harm: but if you please to hear me——
                              [*A Noise within.*

Heark, Sir, now I am sure my Father comes,
I know his steps; dear Love retire a while,
I fear I've stay'd too long.
    Ferd. Too long indeed,
And yet not long enough: Oh Jealousie!
Oh Love! How you distract me?   [*Exit* Ferdinand.
    Mir. He appears
Displeas'd with that young Man, I know not why:
But, till I find from whence his hate proceeds,
I must conceal it from my Father's knowledge;
For he will think that guiltless I have caus'd it;
And suffer me no more to see my Love.
                Enter Prospero.
    Prosp. Now I have been indulgent to your wish,
You have seen the Prisoner?
    Mir. Yes.
    Prosp. And he spake to you?
    Mir. He spoke; but he receiv'd short answers from
me.
    Prosp. How like you his converse?
    Mir. At second sight
A Man does not appear so rare a Creature.
    Prosp. Aside. I find she loves him much because she
      hides it.
Love teaches cunning even to Innocence;
And where he gets possession, his first work
Is to dig deep within a heart, and there
Lie hid, and like a Miser in the dark
To feast alone. But tell me, dear *Miranda*,
How does he suffer his imprisonment?
    Mir. I think he seems displeas'd.
    Prosp. O then 'tis plain
His temper is not noble, for the brave
With equal Minds bear good and evil Fortune.
    Mir. O, Sir, but he's pleas'd again so soon
That 'tis not worth your noting.

Prosp. To be soon
Displeas'd and pleas'd so suddenly again,
Does shew him of a various froward nature.
   Mir. The truth is, Sir, he was not vex'd at all,
But only seem'd to be so.
   Prosp. If he be not
And yet seems angry, he is a dissembler,
Which shews the worst of Natures.
   Mir. Truly, Sir,
The Man has faults enough; but in my conscience
That's none of 'em. He can be no dissembler.
   Prosp. Aside. How she excuses him, and yet desires
That I should judge her heart indifferent to him?
Well, since his faults are many, I am glad
You love him not.
   Mir. 'Tis like, Sir, they are many;
But I know none he has: yet let me often
See him, and I shall find 'em all in time.
   Prosp. I'le think on't.
Go in, this is your hour of Orizons.
   Mir. Aside. Forgive me, Truth, for thus disguising thee;
If I can make him think I do not love
The stranger much, he'll let me see him oftner.
                              [*Exit* Miranda.
   Prosp. Stay! Stay——I had forgot to ask her
What she has said of young *Hippolito*:
Oh! Here he comes! And with him my *Dorinda*.
I'le not be seen, let their loves grow in secret.
                              [*Exit* Prospero.
           Enter Hippolito *and* Dorinda.
   Hip. But why are you so sad?
   Dor. But why are you so joyful?
   Hip. I have within me all the various Musick of the
      Woods.
Since last I saw you I have heard brave news!
I'le tell it you, and make you joyful for me.

Dor. Sir, when I saw you first, I through my Eyes
Drew Something in, I know not what it is;
But still it entertains me with such thoughts
As makes me doubtful whether joy becomes me.

Hip. Pray believe me;
As I'm a Man, I'le tell you blessed news.
I have heard there are more Women in the World,
As fair as you are too.

Dor. Is this your news? You see it moves not me.

Hip. And I'le have 'em all.

Dor. What will become of me then?

Hip. I'le have you too.
But are not you acquainted with these Women?

Dor. I never saw but one,

Hip. Is there but one here?
This is a base poor World; I'le go to th' other;
I've heard Men have abundance of 'em there.
But pray where's that one Woman?

Dor. Who, my Sister?

Hip. Is she your Sister? I'm glad o' that: you shall
help me to her, and I'le love you for't.

[Offers to take her hand.

Dor. Away! I will not have you touch my hand.
My Father's counsel which enjoyn'd reservedness,
Was not in vain I see.   [*Aside.*

Hip. What makes you shun me?

Dor. You need not care, you'l have my Sisters hand.

Hip. Why, must not he who touches hers touch
yours?

Dor. You mean to love her too.

Hip. Do not you love her?
Then why should not I do so?

Dor. She is my Sister, and therefore I must love her:
But you cannot love both of us.

Hip. I warrant you I can:
Oh that you had more Sisters!

Dor. You may love her,
But then I'le not love you.
  Hip. O but you must;
One is enough for you, but not for me.
  Dor. My Sister told me she had seen another;
A Man like you, and she lik'd only him;
Therefore if one must be enough for her,
He is that one, and then you cannot have her.
  Hip. If she like him, she may like both of us.
  Dor. But how if I should change and like that Man?
Would you be willing to permit that change?
  Hip. No, for you lik'd me first.
  Dor. So you did me.
  Hip. But I would never have you see that man;
I cannot bear it.
  Dor. I'le see neither of you.
  Hip. Yes, me you may, for we are now acquainted;
But he's the Man of whom your Father warn'd you.
O! He's a terrible, huge, monstrous Creature,
I'm but a Woman to him.
  Dor. I will see him,
Except you'l promise not to see my Sister.
  Hip. Yes for your sake I needs must see your Sister.
  Dor. But she's a terrible, huge Creature too;
If I were not her Sister she would eat me;
Therefore take heed.
  Hip. I heard that she was fair,
And like you.
  Dor. No, indeed, she's like my Father,
With a great Beard; 'twould fright you to look on her,
Therefore that Man and she may go together,
They're fit for no body but one another.
  Hip. Looking in. Yonder he comes with glaring eyes,
    fly! fly!
Before he sees you.
  Dor. Must we part so soon?

Hip. Y'are a lost Woman if you see him.

Dor. I would not willingly be lost, for fear you
Should not find me. I'le avoid him.   [*Exit* Dorinda.

Hip. She fain would have deceived me; but I know
Her Sister must be fair, for she's a Woman.
All of a Kind that I have seen are like
To one another: all the Creatures of
The Rivers and the Woods are so.

Enter Ferdinand.

Ferd. O! Well encounter'd, you are the happy Man!
Y' have got the hearts of both the beauteous Women.

Hip. How! Sir? Pray, are you sure on't?

Ferd. One of 'em charg'd me to love you for her sake.

Hip. Then I must have her.

Ferd. No, not till I am dead.

Hip. How dead? What's that? But whatsoe're it be
I long to have her.

Ferd. Time and my grief may make me dye.

Hip. But for a Friend you should make haste;
I ne're ask'd any thing of you before.

Ferd. I see your Ignorance;
And therefore will instruct you in my meaning.
The Woman, whom I love, saw you and lov'd you.
Now, Sir, if you love her you'l cause my death.

Hip. Be sure I'le do't then.

Ferd. But I am your Friend;
And I request you that you would not love her.

Hip. When Friends request unreasonable things,
Sure th'are to be deny'd: you say she's fair,
And I must love all who are fair; for to tell
You a secret, which I've lately found
Within my self; they all are made for me.

Ferd. That's but a fond conceit: you're made for one,
And one for you.

Hip. You cannot tell me, Sir.
I know I'm made for twenty hundred Women:

(I mean if there so many be i' th' World;)
So that if once I see her I shall love her.
   Ferd. Then do not see her.
   Hip. Yes, Sir, I must see her.
For I wou'd fain have my heart beat again,
Just as it did when I first saw her Sister.
   Ferd. I find I must not let you see her then.
   Hip. How will you hinder me?
   Ferd. By force of Arms.
   Hip. By force of Arms?
My Arms perhaps may be as strong as yours.
   Ferd. He's still so ignorant that I pity him, and fain
                                               [Aside.
Would avoid force: pray, do not see her,
She was mine first;   you have no right to her.
   Hip. I have not yet consider'd what is Right,
But, Sir, I know my inclinations are
To love all Women: and I have been taught
That to dissemble what I think, is base.
In honour then of Truth, I must declare
That I do love, and I will see your Woman.
   Ferd. Wou'd you be willing I should see and love
Your Woman, and endeavour to seduce her
From that affection which she vow'd to you?
   Hip. I wou'd not you should do it;   but if she
Should love you best, I cannot hinder her.
But, Sir, for fear she shou'd, I will provide
Against the worst, and try to get your Woman.
   Ferd. But I pretend no claim at all to yours;
Besides you are more beautiful than I,
And fitter to allure unpractis'd hearts.
Therefore I once more beg you will not see her.
   Hip. I'm glad you let me know I have such
     Beauty.
If that will get me Women, they shall have it
As far as e're 'twill go: I'le never want 'em.

Ferd. Then since you have refused this act of friend-
ship,
Provide your self a Sword; for we must fight.
  Hip. A Sword, what's that?
  Ferd. Why such a thing as this.
  Hip. What should I do with it?
  Ferd. You must stand thus,
And push against me, while I push at you,
Till one of us fall dead.
  Hip. This is brave sport:
But we have no Swords growing in our World.
  Ferd. What shall we do then to decide our quarrel?
  Hip. We'll take the Sword by turns, and fight with it.
  Ferd. Strange ignorance! You must defend your Life,
And so must I: but since you have no Sword
Take this; for in a Corner of my Cave
                                    [*Gives him his Sword.*
I found a rusty one: perhaps 'twas his
Who keeps me Pris'ner here: that I will fit:
When next we meet prepare your self to fight.
  Hip. Make haste then, this shall ne're be yours agen.
I mean to fight with all the men I meet,
And when they're dead, their Women shall be mine.
  Ferd. I see you are unskilful; I desire not
To take your Life: but if you please we'll fight
On these conditions; He who first draws bloud,
Or who can take the others Weapon from him,
Shall be acknowledg'd as the Conquerour,
And both the Women shall be his.
  Hip. Agreed:
And ev'ry day I'le fight for two more with you.
  Ferd. But win these first.
  Hip. I'le warrant you I'le push you.
                                    [*Exeunt severally.*
        Enter Trincalo, Caliban, Sycorax.
  Calib. My Lord, I see 'em coming yonder.

Trinc. Who?

Calib. The starv'd Prince, and his two thirsty Subjects, that would have our Liquor.

Trinc. If thou wert a Monster of parts I would make thee my Master of Ceremonies, to conduct 'em in. The Devil take all Dunces; thou hast lost a brave Employment by not being a Linguist, and for want of behaviour.

Syc. My Lord, shall I go meet 'em? I'le be kind to all of 'em, just as I am to thee.

Trinc. No, that's against the fundamental Laws of my Dukedom: you are in a high place, Spouse, and must give good Example. Here they come, we'll put on the gravity of Statesmen, and be very dull, that we may be held wise.

       Enter Stephano, Ventoso, Mustacho.

Vent. Duke *Trincalo*, we have consider'd.

Trinc. Peace, or War?

Must. Peace, and the Butt.

Steph. I come now as a private person, and promise to live peaceably under your Government.

Trinc. You shall enjoy the benefits of Peace; and the first Fruits of it, amongst all civil Nations, is to be drunk for joy: *Caliban* skink about.

Steph. I long to have a Rowse to her Graces health, and to the *Haunse in Kelder*; or rather *Haddock in Kelder*, for I guess it will be half Fish.   [*Aside.*

Trinc. Subject *Stephano* here's to thee; and let old quarrels be drown'd in this draught.   [*Drinks.*

Steph. Great Magistrate, here's thy Sister's health to thee.   [*Drinks to* Caliban.

Syc. He shall not drink of that immortal liquor, my Lord, let him drink water.

Trinc. O sweet heart, you must not shame your self to day. Gentlemen Subjects, pray bear with her good Huswifry: She wants a little breeding, but she's hearty.

Must. Ventoso here's to thee.   Is it not better to pierce the Butt, than to quarrel and pierce one anothers bellies?

Vent. Let it come Boy.

Trinc. Now wou'd I lay greatness aside, and shake my heels, if I had but Musick.

Calib. O my Lord! My Mother left us in her Will a hundred Spirits to attend us; Devils of all sorts, some great roaring Devils, and some little singing Sprights.

Syc. Shall we call? and thou shalt hear them in the Air.

Trinc. I accept the motion: let us have our Mother-in-Law's Legacy immediately.

Calib. sings.

> We want Musick, we want Mirth,
> Up Dam and cleave the Earth:
> We have now no Lords that wrong us,
> Send thy merry Sprights among us.

> [*Musick heard.*

Trinc. What a merry Tyrant am I, to have my Musick and pay nothing for't? Come, hands, hands, let's lose no time while the Devil's in the Humour,

> [*A Dance.*

Trinc. Enough, enough: now to our Sack agen.

Vent. The Bottle's drunk.

Must. Then the Bottle's a weak shallow Fellow, if it be drunk first.

Trinc. Caliban, give Bottle the belly full agen.

> [*Exit* Caliban.]

Steph. May I ask your Grace a question? Pray is that Hectoring Spark, as you call'd him, flesh or fish?

Trinc. Subject I know not, but he drinks like a Fish.

> *Enter* Caliban.

Steph. O here's the Bottle agen; he has made a good Voyage: come, who begins a Brindis to the Duke?

Trinc. I'le begin it my self: give me the Bottle;
'tis my Prerogative to drink first. *Stephano*, give me thy
hand;   thou hast been a Rebel, but here's to thee:
prithee why should we quarrel?   Shall I swear two
Oaths? By Bottle, and by Butt I love thee: In witness
whereof I drink soundly.   [*Drinks.*

Steph. Your Grace shall find there's no love lost,
For I will pledge you soundly.

Trinc. Thou hast been a false Rebel, but that's all
one; Pledge my Grace faithfully.

Steph. I will pledge your Grace Up se Dutch.

Trinc. But thou shalt not pledge me before I have
drunk agen; would'st thou take the Liquor of Life out
of my hands? I see thou art a piece of a Rebel still,
but here's to thee, now thou shalt have it.

[Stephano *drinks.*

Vent. We loyal Subjects may be choak'd for any
drink we can get.

Trinc. Have patience good people; you are unreasonable, you'd be drunk as soon as I. *Ventoso* you
shall have your time, but you must give place to
Stephano.

Must. Brother *Ventoso*, I am afraid we shall lose
our Places. The Duke grows fond of *Stephano*, and will
declare him Vice-Roy.

Steph. I ha' done my worst at your Graces Bottle.

Trinc. Then the Folks may have it. *Caliban* go to
the Butt, and tell me how it sounds. [*Exit* Caliban.]
Peer *Stephano*, dost thou love me?

Steph. I Love your Grace and all your Princely
Family.

Trinc. 'Tis no matter if thou lov'st me; hang my
Family: thou art my Friend, prithee tell me what thou
think'st of my Princess?

Steph. I look on her as a very Noble Princess.

Trinc. Noble! Indeed she had a Witch to her Mother,

and the Witches are of great Families in *Lapland*; but the Devil was her Father, and I have heard of the Mounsor *De-Viles* in *France*; but look on her Beauty, is she a fit Wife for Duke *Trincalo*? Mark her Behaviour too, she's tippling yonder with the Serving-Men.

Steph. An please your Grace she's somewhat homely; but that's no blemish in a Princess: She is Virtuous.

Trinc. Umph! Virtuous! I am loth to disparage her: but thou art my Friend, can'st thou be close?

Steph. As a stopt Bottle, an 't please your Grace.

Enter Caliban *agen with a Bottle.*

Trinc. Why then I'll tell thee, I found her an hour ago under an Elder Tree, upon a sweet Bed of Nettles, singing Tory, Rory, and Ranthum, Scantum, with her own natural Brother.

Steph. O Jew! Make Love in her own Tribe!

Trinc. But 'tis no matter; to tell thee true, I marry'd her to be a great man and so forth: but make no words on 't, for I care not who knows it; and so here's to thee agen: give me the Bottle, *Caliban*! Did you knock the Butt? How does it sound?

Calib. It sounds as though it had a noise within.

Trinc. I fear the Butt begins to rattle in the Throat, and is departing: give me the Bottle.   [*Drinks.*

Must. A short Life and a merry, I say.

                        [Stephano *whispers* Sycorax.

Syc. But did he tell you so?

Steph. He said you were as ugly as your Mother, and that he Marry'd you only to get Possession of the Island.

Syc. My Mothers Devils fetch him for 't.

Steph. And your Father's too; hem! Skink about his Grace's Health agen. O if you would but cast an Eye of pity upon me——

Syc. I will cast two Eyes of pity on thee, I love thee

more than Haws, or Black-Berries; I have a hoard of
Wildings in the Moss, my Brother knows not of 'em, but
I'le bring thee where they are.

Steph. *Trincalo* was but my Man when time was.

Syc. Wert thou his God, and didst thou give him
Liquor?

Steph. I gave him Brandy, and drunk Sack my self:
wilt thou leave him, and thou shalt be my Princess?

Syc. If thou canst make me glad with this Liquor.

Steph. I warrant thee, we'll ride into the Country
where it grows.

Syc. How wilt thou carry me thither?

Steph. Upon a Hackney-Devil of thy Mothers.

Trinc. What's that you will do? Hah! I hope you
have not betray'd me? How does my Pigs-nye?

[To Sycorax.

Syc. Be gone! Thou shalt not be my Lord; thou
say'st I'm ugly.

Trinc. Did you tell her so—Hah! He's a Rogue, do
not believe him Chuck.

Steph. The foul Words were yours: I will not eat
'em for you.

Trinc. I see if once a Rebel, then ever a Rebel. Did
I receive thee into grace for this? I will correct thee
with my Royal Hand.   [*Strikes* Stephano.

Syc. Dost thou hurt my Love?   [*Flies at* Trincalo.

Trinc. Where are our Guards? Treason, Treason!

[Ventoso, Mustacho, Caliban run betwixt.

Vent. Who took up Arms first, the Prince or the
People?

Trinc. This false Traytor has corrupted the Wife of
my Bosom.   [*Whispers* Mustacho *hastily.*
Mustacho strike on my side, and thou shalt be my Vice-
Roy.

Must. I'm against Rebels! *Ventoso,* obey your Vice-
Roy.

Vent. You a Vice-Roy?

> [*They two Fight off from the rest.*

Steph. Hah! Hector Monster! Do you stand neuter?

Calib. Thou would'st drink my Liquor, I will not help thee.

Syc. 'Twas his doing that I had such a Husband, but I'll claw him.

> [Sycorax *and* Caliban *Fight ;* Sycorax *beating him off the Stage.*

Trinc. The whole Nation is up in Arms, and shall I stand idle?

> [Trincalo *beats off* Stephano *to the door. Exit* Stephano.

I'le not pursue too far,
For fear the Enemy should rally agen and surprise my Butt in the Citadel. Well, I must be rid of my Lady *Trincalo,* she will be in the fashion else; first Cuckold her Husband, and then sue for a Separation, to get Alimony. [*Exit.*

Enter Ferdinand, Hippolito, *with their Swords drawn.*

Ferd. Come, Sir, our Cave affords no choice of place, But the ground's firm and even: are you ready?

Hip. As ready as your self, Sir.

Ferd. You remember on what conditions we must fight?
Who first receives a Wound is to submit.

Hip. Come, come, this loses time; now for the Women, Sir. [*They fight a little,* Ferdinand *hurts him.*

Ferd. Sir, you are wounded.

Hip. No.

Ferd. Believe your blood.

Hip. I feel no hurt, no matter for my blood.

Ferd. Remember our Conditions.

Hip. I'le not leave, till my Sword hits you too.

> [Hippolito *presses* on, Ferdinand *retires and wards.*

Ferd. I'm loth to kill you, you're unskilful, Sir.

Hip. You beat aside my Sword, but let it come
As near as yours, and you shall see my skill.

Ferd. You faint for loss of blood, I see you stagger,
Pray, Sir, retire.

Hip. No! I will ne're go back——
Methinks the Cave turns round, I cannot find—

Ferd. Your Eyes begin to dazle.

Hip. Why do you swim so, and dance about me?
Stand but still till I have made one thrust.

　　　　　　　　　　[Hippolito *thrusts and falls.*

Ferd. O help, help, help!
Unhappy Man! What have I done?

Hip. I'm going to a cold sleep, but when I wake
I'll fight agen. Pray stay for me.　　　[*Swounds.*

Ferd. He's gone! He's gone! O stay sweet lovely
　　Youth!
Help, help!

　　　　　　　　Enter Prospero.

Prosp. What dismal noise is that?

Ferd. O see, Sir, see!
What mischief my unhappy hand has wrought.

Prosp. Alas! How much in vain doth feeble Art
Endeavour to resist the will of Heaven?

　　　　　　　　　　[*Rubs* Hippolito.

He's gone for ever; O thou cruel Son
Of an Inhumane Father! All my designs
Are ruin'd and unravell'd by this blow.
No pleasure now is left me but Revenge.

Ferd. Sir, if you knew my Innocence——

Prosp. Peace, peace,
Can thy excuses give me back his Life?
What *Ariel!* sluggish Spirit, where art thou?

　　　　　　　　Enter Ariel.

Ariel. Here, at thy beck, my Lord.

Prosp. I, now thou com'st,

When Fate is past and not to be recall'd.
Look there, and glut the Malice of thy Nature;
For as thou art thy self, thou canst not be
But glad to see young Virtue nipt i' th' Blossom.
   Ariel. My Lord, the Being high above can witness
I am not glad: we Airy Spirits are not
Of temper so malicious as the Earthy,
But of a Nature more approaching good:
For which we meet in swarms, and often Combat
Betwixt the Confines of the Air and Earth.
   Prosp. Why did'st thou not prevent, at least foretell,
This fatal action then?
   Ariel. Pardon, great Sir,
I meant to do it, but I was forbidden
By the ill Genius of *Hippolito,*
Who came and threatn'd me if I disclos'd it,
To bind me in the bottom of the Sea,
Far from the lightsome Regions of the Air,
(My native Fields) above a hundred Years.
   Prosp. I'll chain thee in the North for thy neglect,
Within the burning Bowels of Mount *Hecla;*
I'll sindge thy airy Wings with sulph'rous Flames,
And choak thy tender Nostrils with blew Smoak:
At ev'ry Hick-up of the belching Mountain
Thou shalt be lifted up to taste fresh Air,
And then fall down agen.
   Ariel. Pardon, dread Lord.
   Prosp. No more of Pardon than just Heav'n intends
    thee,
Shalt thou e're find from me: hence! Flye with speed,
Unbind the Charms which hold this Murtherer's
    Father,
And bring him with my Brother streight before me.
   Ariel. Mercy, my potent Lord, and I'le outfly
Thy thought.   [*Exit* Ariel.
   Ferd. O Heavens! What words are those I heard?

Yet cannot see who spoke 'em: sure the Woman
Whom I lov'd was like this, some aiery Vision.
  Prosp. No, Murd'rer, she's like thee, of mortal mould,
But much too pure to mix with thy black Crimes;
Yet she had faults and must be punish'd for 'em.
Miranda and *Dorinda!* where are ye?
The Will of Heaven's accomplish'd: I have now
No more to fear, and nothing left to hope,
Now you may enter.
              Enter Miranda *and* Dorinda.
  Mir. My Love! Is it permitted me to see
You once again?
  Prosp. You come to look your last;
I will for ever take him from your Eyes.
But, on my Blessing, speak not, nor approach him.
  Dor. Pray, Father is not this my Sisters Man?
He has a noble form; but yet he's not
So excellent as my *Hippolito.*
  Prosp. Alas poor Girl, thou hast no man: look
      yonder;
There's all of him that's left.
  Dor. Why was there ever any more of him?
He lies asleep, Sir, shall I waken him?
                [She kneels by Hippolito, *and jogs him.*
  Ferd. Alas! He's never to be wak'd agen.
  Dor. My Love, my Love! Will you not speak to me?
I fear you have displeas'd him, Sir, and now
He will not answer me; he's dumb and cold too,
But I'le run streight, and make a fire to warm him.
                      [Exit Dorinda *running.*
  Enter Alonzo, Gonzalo, Antonio. Ariel *(invisible).*
  Alonz. Never were Beasts so hunted into toyls,
As we have been pursu'd by dreadful shapes.
But is not that my Son? O *Ferdinand!*
If thou art not a Ghost, let me embrace thee.
  Ferd. My Father! O sinister happiness!

Is it decreed I should recover you
Alive, just in that fatal hour when this
Brave Youth is lost in Death, and by my hand?
    Ant. Heaven! What new wonder's this?
    Gonz. This Isle is full of nothing else.
    Alonz. I thought to dye, and in the Walks above,
Wand'ring by Star-light, to have sought thee out;
But now I should have gone to Heaven in vain,
Whilst thou art here behind.
    Ferd. You must indeed
In vain have gone thither to look for me.
Those who are stain'd with such black crimes as mine,
Come seldom there.
    Prosp. And those who are like him, all foul with guilt,
More seldom upward go. You stare upon me as
You n'ere had seen me; Have fifteen Years
So lost me to your Knowledge, that you retain
No Memory of *Prospero*?
    Gonz. The good old Duke of *Millain*!
    Prosp. I wonder less, that thou *Antonio* know'st me
      not,
Because thou did'st long since forget I was
Thy Brother, else I never had bin here.
    Ant. Shame choaks my words.
    Alonz. And wonder mine.
    Prosp. For you, usurping Prince,   [*To* Alonzo.
Know, by my Art, you Shipwrackt on this Isle,
Where, after I a while had punish'd you,
My Vengeance wou'd have ended; I design'd
To match that Son of yours with this my Daughter.
    Alonz. Pursue it still, I am most willing to't.
    Prosp. So am not I. No Marriages can prosper
Which are with Murd'rers made; look on that Corps,
This, whilst he liv'd, was young *Hippolito*,
That Infant Duke of *Mantua*, Sir, whom you
Expos'd with me; and here I bred him up

Till that Blood-thirsty Man, that *Ferdinand*——
But why do I exclaim on him, when Justice
Calls to unsheath her Sword against his guilt?
   Alonz. What do you mean?
   Prosp. To execute Heav'ns Laws.
Here I am plac'd by Heav'n, here I am Prince,
Though you have dispossess'd me of my *Millain.*
Blood calls for blood; your *Ferdinand* shall die:
And I in bitterness have sent for you
To have the sudden joy of seeing him alive,
And then the greater grief to see him dye.
   Alonz. And think'st thou I or these will tamely stand
To view the Execution?   [*Lays hand upon his Sword.*
   Ferd. Hold, dear Father!
I cannot suffer you t' attempt against
His Life who gave her being whom I love.
   Prosp. Nay then appear my Guards——I thought no
     more
To use their aids; (I'm curs'd because I us'd it)
        [*He stamps, and many Spirits appear.*
But they are now the Ministers of Heaven,
Whilst I revenge this Murder.
   Alonz. Have I for this
Found thee my Son, so soon agen to lose thee!
Antonio, Gonzalo, speak for pity:
He may hear you.
   Ant. I dare not draw that blood
Upon my self, by interceding for him.
   Gonz. You drew this judgment down when you
     usurp'd
That Dukedom which was this dead Prince's right.
   Alonz. Is this a time t' upbraid me with my sins,
When Grief lies heavy on me? Y' are no more
My Friends, but crueller than he, whose Sentence
Has doom'd my Son to Death.
   Ant. You did unworthily t' upbraid him.

Gonz. And you do worse t' endure his crimes.

Ant. *Gonzalo* we'll meet no more as Friends.

Gonz. Agreed *Antonio*: and we agree in discord.

Ferd. to *Mir.* Adieu my fairest Mistress.

Mir. Now I can hold no longer; I must speak.
Though I am loth to disobey you, Sir,
Be not so cruel to the Man I love,
Or be so kind to let me suffer with him.

Ferd. Recall that Pray'r, or I shall wish to live,
Though death be all the mends that I can make.

Prosp. This night I will allow you, *Ferdinand*,
To fit you for your Death, that Cave's your Prison.

Alonz. Ah, *Prospero!* Hear me speak: You are a
Father,
Look on my Age, and look upon his Youth.

Prosp. No more! All you can say is urg'd in vain,
I have no room for pity left within me.
Do you refuse! Help *Ariel* with your Fellows
To drive 'em in: *Alonzo* and his Son
Bestow in yonder Cave, and here *Gonzalo*
Shall with *Antonio* lodge.

   [*Spirits drive 'em in, as they are appointed.*
     Enter Dorinda.

Dor. Sir, I have made a fire, shall he be warm'd?

Prosp. He's dead, and vital warmth will ne'er return.

Dor. Dead, Sir, what's that?

Prosp. His Soul has left his Body.

Dor. When will it come agen?

Prosp. O never, never!
He must be laid in Earth, and there consume.

Dor. He shall not lye in Earth, you do not know
How well he loves me: indeed he'l come agen;
He told me he would go a little while,
But promis'd me he would not tarry long.

Prosp. He's murder'd by the Man who lov'd your Sister.
Now both of you may see what 'tis to break

A Father's Precept; you would needs see Men,
And by that sight are made for ever wretched.
Hippolito is dead, and *Ferdinand* must dye
For murdering him.

    Mir. Have you no pity?

    Prosp. Your disobedience has so much incens'd me,
That I this night can leave no blessing with you.
Help to convey the body to my Couch,
Then leave me to mourn over it alone.

                [They bear off the Body of Hippolito.
       Enter Miranda, *and* Dorinda *again.* Ariel
              behind 'em.

    Ariel. I've bin so chid for my neglect by *Prospero,*
That I must now watch all and be unseen.

    Mir. Sister, I say agen, 'twas long of you
That all this mischief happen'd.

    Dor. Blame not me
For your own fault, your Curiosity
Brought me to see the Man.

    Mir. You safely might
Have seen him and retir'd, but you wou'd needs
Go near him and converse: you may remember
My Father call'd me thence, and I call'd you.

    Dor. That was your envy, Sister, not your love;
You call'd me thence, because you could not be
Alone with him your self; but I am sure
My Man had never gone to Heaven so soon,
But that yours made him go.   *[Crying.*

    Mir. Sister I could not wish that either of 'em
Shou'd go to Heaven without us; but it was
His Fortune, and you must be satisfi'd?

    Dor. I'le not be satisfi'd: my Father says
He'll make your Man as cold as mine is now;
And when he is made cold, my Father will
Not let you strive to make him warm agen.

    Mir. In spight of you mine never shall be cold.

Dor. I'm sure 'twas he that made me miserable;
And I will be reveng'd. Perhaps you think 'tis
Nothing to lose a Man.

Mir. Yes, but there is some difference betwixt
My *Ferdinand*, and your *Hippolito*.

Dor. I, there's your judgment. Your's is the oldest
  Man
I ever saw, except it were my Father.

Mir. Sister, no more: It is not comely in
A Daughter, when she says her Father's old.

Dor. But why do I stay here, whilst my cold Love
Perhaps may want me?
I'le pray my Father to make yours cold too.

Mir. Sister, I'le never sleep with you agen.

Dor. I'le never more meet in a Bed with you,
But lodge on the bare ground, and watch my Love.

Mir. And at the entrance of that Cave I'le lye,
And eccho to each blast of wind a sigh.

  [*Exeunt severally, looking discontentedly on one
    another.*

Ariel. Harsh discord reigns throughout this fatal Isle,
At which good Angels mourn, ill Spirits smile.
Old *Prospero*, by his Daughters rob'd of rest,
Has in displeasure left 'em both unblest.
Unkindly they abjure each others Bed,
To save the Living, and revenge the dead.
Alonzo and his Son are Pris'ners made,
And good *Gonzalo* does their Crimes upbraid.
Antonio and *Gonzalo* disagree,
And wou'd, though in one Cave, at distance be.
The Seamen all that cursed Wine have spent,
Which still renew'd their thirst of Government;
And, wanting Subjects for the food of Pow'r,
Each wou'd to rule alone the rest devour.
The Monsters *Sycorax* and *Caliban*
More monstrous grow by Passions learn'd from Man.

Even I not fram'd of warring Elements,
Partake and suffer in these discontents.
Why shou'd a mortal by Enchantments hold
In Chains a Spirit of ætherial mould?
Accursed Magick we our selves have taught;
And our own Pow'r has our Subjection wrought !

                                                    [*Exit.*

Act V.

Enter Prospero *and* Miranda.

Prosp. YOU beg in vain; I cannot Pardon him,
            He has offended Heaven.
  Mir. Then let Heaven punish him.
  Prosp. It will by me.
  Mir. Grant him at least some respite for my sake.
  Prosp. I by deferring Justice should incense
The Deity against my self and you.
  Mir. Yet I have heard you say, the Powers above
Are slow in punishing; and shou'd not you
Resemble them?
  Prosp. The Powers above may Pardon or Reprieve,
As Sovereign Princes may dispense with Laws,
Which we, as Officers, must Execute.
Our Acts of Grace to Criminals are Treason
To Heavens Prerogative.
  Mir. Do you condemn him for shedding Blood?
  Prosp. Why do you ask that question?
You know I do.
  Mir. Then you must be condemn'd for shedding his,
And he who condemns you, must dye for shedding yours,
And that's the way at last to leave none living.
  Prosp. The Argument is weak, but I want time
To let you see your errours——
Retire, and, if you love him, pray for him. [*He's going.*
  Mir. O stay, Sir, I have yet more Arguments.

Prosp. But none of any weight.

Mir. Have you not said you are his Judge?

Prosp. 'Tis true, I am; what then?

Mir. And can you be his Executioner?
If that be so, then all Men may declare
Their Enemies in fault; and Pow'r without
The Sword of Justice, will presume to punish
What e're it calls a Crime.

Prosp. I cannot force *Gonzalo* or my Brother,
Much less the Father to destroy the Son;
It must be then the Monster *Caliban*,
And he's not here, but *Ariel* strait shall fetch him.

Enter Ariel.

Ariel. My potent Lord, before thou call'st, I come,
To serve thy will.

Prosp. Then Spirit fetch me here my salvage Slave.

Ariel. My Lord, it does not need.

Prosp. Art thou then prone to mischief, wilt thou
be
Thy self the Executioner?

Ariel. Think better of thy aiery Minister,
Who for thy sake, unbid, this night has flown
O're almost all the habitable World.

Prosp. But to what purpose was all thy diligence?

Ariel. When I was chidden by my mighty Lord
For my neglect of young *Hippolito*,
I went to view his Body, and soon found
His Soul was but retir'd, not sally'd out,
And frighted lay at skulk in th' inmost corner
Of his scarce-beating heart.

Prosp. Is he not dead?

Ariel. Hear me my Lord!
I prun'd my Wings, and fitted for a Journey,
From the next Isles of our *Hesperides*
I gather'd Moly first, thence shot my self

To *Palestine*, and watch'd the trickling Balm,
Which caught, I glided to the *British* Isles,
And there the purple Panacea found.
   Prosp. All this to night?
   Ariel. All this, my Lord, I did;
Nor was *Hippolito's* good Angel wanting,
Who climbing up the Circle of the Moon,
While I below got Simples for the Cure,
Went to each Planet which o're-rul'd those Herbs,
And drew it's virtue to increase their pow'r:
Long e're this hour had I been back again,
But that a Storm took me returning back
And flag'd my tender Wings.
   Prosp. Thou shalt have rest my Spirit:
But hast thou search'd the wound?
   Ariel. My Lord I have,
And 'twas in time I did it; for the Soul
Stood almost at life's door, all bare and naked,
Shivering like Boys upon a River's bank,
And loth to tempt the cold air; but I took Her
And stop'd her in, and pour'd into his Mouth
The healing juice of vulnerary Herbs.
   Prosp. Thou art my faithful Servant.
   Ariel. His only danger was his loss of blood
But now he's wak'd, my Lord, and just this hour
He must be dress'd again, as I have done it.
Anoint the Sword which pierc'd him with this Weapon-
   Salve,
And wrap it close from Air till I have time
To visit him again.
   Prosp. It shall be done, be it your task, *Miranda*,
Because your Sister is not present here,
While I go visit your dear *Ferdinand*,
From whom I will a while conceal this News,
That it may be more welcome.

Mir. I obey you,
And with a double duty, Sir: for now
You twice have given me Life.

Prosp. My *Ariel*, follow me.   [*Exeunt severally.*

Hippolito *discovered on a Couch*, Dorinda *by him.*

Dor. How do you find your self?

Hip. I'm somewhat cold;
Can you not draw me nearer to the Sun,
I am too weak to walk?

Dor. My Love, I'le try.

[*She draws the Chair nearer the Audience.*

I thought you never would have walk'd agen;
They told me you were gone away to Heaven;
Have you bin there?

Hip. I know not where I was.

Dor. I will not leave you till you promise me
You will not dye agen.

Hip. Indeed I will not.

Dor. You must not go to Heav'n unless we go
Together; for I've heard my Father say
That we must strive to be each others Guide,
The way to it will else be difficult,
Especially to those who are so Young.
But I much wonder what it is to dye.

Hip. Sure 'tis to Dream, a kind of Breathless Sleep
When once the Soul's gone out.

Dor. What is the Soul?

Hip. A small blew thing that runs about within
us.

Dor. Then I have seen it in a frosty morning
Run smoaking from my Mouth.

Hip. But if my Soul had gone, it should have
walk'd
Upon a Cloud just over you, and peep'd,
And thence I would have call'd you.

Dor. But I should not have heard you, 'tis so far.

Hip. Why then I would have rain'd and snow'd upon
    you,
And thrown down Hail-Stones gently till I hit you,
And made you look at least. But dear *Dorinda*
What is become of him who fought with me?
    Dor. O, I can tell you joyful news of him,
My Father means to make him dye to day,
For what he did to you.
    Hip. That must not be,
My dear *Dorinda*, go and beg your Father
He may not dye, it was my fault he hurt me,
I urg'd him to it first.
    Dor. But if he live, he'll never leave killing you.
    Hip. O no! I just remember when I fell asleep,
I heard him calling me a great way off,
And crying over me as you wou'd do:
Besides we have no cause of quarrel now.
    Dor. Pray how began your difference first?
    Hip. I fought
With him for all the Women in the World.
    Dor. That Hurt you had was justly sent from Heaven,
For wishing to have any more but me.
    Hip. Indeed I think it was; but I repent it,
The fault was only in my Blood, for now
'Tis gone, I find I do not love so many.
    Dor. In confidence of this, I'le beg my Father,
That he may live: I'm glad the naughty Blood,
That made you love so many, is gone out.
    Hip. My Dear, go quickly, least you come too late.
                                                [*Exit* Dorinda.
        Enter Miranda *at the Door, with* Hippolito's
                        Sword wrapt up.
    Hip. Who's this who looks so Fair and Beautiful,
As nothing but *Dorinda* can surpass her?
O! I believe it is that Angel, Woman,
Whom she calls Sister.

Mir. Sir, I am sent hither to dress your Wound,
How do you find your Strength?

Hip. Fair Creature, I am Faint with loss of blood.

Mir. I'm sorry for 't.

Hip. Indeed and so am I,
For if I had that blood, I then should find
A great delight in loving you.

Mir. But, Sir,
I am anothers, and your love is given
Already to my Sister.

Hip. Yet I find
That if you please I can love still a little.

Mir. I cannot be unconstant, nor shou'd you.

Hip. O my wound pains me.

Mir. I am come to ease you.

> [*She unwraps the Sword.*

Hip. Alas! I feel the cold Air come to me,
My wound shoots worse than ever.

> [*She wipes and anoints the Sword.*

Mir. Does it still grieve you?

Hip. Now methinks there's something laid just upon
it.

Mir. Do you find no ease?

Hip. Yes, yes, upon the sudden all the pain
Is leaving me, sweet Heaven how am I eas'd!

> *Enter* Ferdinand *and* Dorinda *to them.*

Ferd. to Dor. Madam, I must confess my life is yours,
I owe it to your generosity.

Dor. I am o'rejoy'd my Father lets you live,
And proud of my good fortune, that he gave
Your life to me,

Mir. How? Gave his life to her!

Hip. Alas! I think she said so; and he said
He ow'd it to her generosity.

Ferd. But is not that your Sister with *Hippolito*?

Dor. So kind already!

Ferd. I came to welcome Life,
And I have met the cruellest of deaths.

Hip. My dear *Dorinda* with another man!

Dor. Sister, what bus'ness have you here?

Mir. You see I dress *Hippolito*.

Dor. Y' are very charitable to a Stranger.

Mir. You are not much behind in Charity,
To beg a Pardon for a Man, whom you
Scarce ever saw before.

Dor. Henceforward let your Surgery alone;
For I had rather he should dye, than you
Should cure his wound.

Mir. And I wish *Ferdinand* had dy'd before
He ow'd his Life to your entreaty.

Ferd. to Hip. Sir, I am glad you are so well recover'd:
You keep your humour still to have all Women.

Hip. Not all, Sir, you except one of the number,
Your new Love there, *Dorinda*.

Mir. Ah *Ferdinand!* Can you become inconstant?
If I must lose you, I had rather death
Should take you from me than you take your self.

Ferd. And if I might have chose, I would have wish'd
That death from *Prospero*, and not this from you.

Dor. I, now I find why I was sent away;
That you might have my Sisters company.

Hip. *Dorinda*, kill me not with your unkindness,
This is too much, first to be false your self,
And then accuse me too.

Ferd. We all accuse
Each other, and each one denys their guilt,
I should be glad it were a mutual errour.
And therefore first to clear my self from fault,
Madam, I beg your pardon, while I say
I only love your Sister.   [*To* Dorinda.

Mir. O blest Word!
I'm sure I love no man but *Ferdinand*.

Dor. Nor I, Heav'n knows, but my *Hippolito.*

Hip. I never knew I lov'd so much, before
I fear'd *Dorinda's* constancy; but now
I am convinc'd that I lov'd none but her,
Because none else can Recompence her loss.

Ferd. 'Twas happy then you had this little tryal.
But how we all so much mistook, I know not.

Mir. I've only this to say in my defence:
My Father sent me hither, to attend
The wounded Stranger.

Dor. And *Hippolito*
Sent me to beg the life of *Ferdinand.*

Ferd. From such small Errours, left at first unheeded.
Have often sprung sad accidents in Love.
But see, our Fathers and our friends are come
To mix their joys with ours.

       Enter Prospero, Alonzo, Antonio, Gonzalo.

Alonz. to Prosp. Let it no more be thought of, your
    purpose
Though it was severe was just. In losing *Ferdinand*
I should have mourn'd, but could not have complain'd.

Prosp. Sir, I am glad kind Heaven decreed it other-
    wise.

Dor. O wonder!
How many goodly Creatures are there here!
How beauteous mankind is!

Hip. O brave new World
That has such People in't!

Alonz. to Ferd. Now all the blessings
Of a glad Father compass thee about,
And make thee happy in thy beauteous choice.

Gonz. I've inward wept, or should have spoke e're
    this.
Look down sweet Heav'n, and on this Couple drop
A blessed Crown, for it is you chalk'd out
The way which brought us hither.

Ant. Though Penitence
Forc'd by necessity can scarce seem real,
Yet dearest Brother I have hope my Blood
May plead for pardon with you: I resign
Dominion, which 'tis true I could not keep,
But Heaven knows too I would not.

Prosp. All past crimes
I bury in the joy of this Blessed day.

Alonz. And that I may not be behind in justice,
To this young Prince I render back his Dukedom,
And as the Duke of *Mantua* thus salute him.

Hip. What is it that you render back, methinks
You give me nothing.

Prosp. You are to be Lord
Of a great People, and o're Towns and Cities.

Hip. And shall these People be all Men and Women?

Gonz. Yes, and shall call you Lord.

Hip. Why then I'le live no longer in a Prison,
But have a whole Cave to my self hereafter.

Prosp. And that your happiness may be com-
     pleat,
I give you my *Dorinda* for your Wife;
She shall be yours for ever, when the Priest
Has made you one.

Hip. How shall he make us one?
Shall I grow to her?

Prosp. By saying holy words
You shall be joyn'd in marriage to each other.

Dor. I warrant you those holy words are charms.
My Father means to conjure us together.

Prosp. to his daughters. My *Ariel* told me, when last
     night you quarrel'd,
You said you would for ever part your Beds;
But what you threaten'd in your anger, Heaven
Has turn'd to Prophecy:
For you, *Miranda*, must with *Ferdinand*,

And you, *Dorinda*, with *Hippolito*
Lye in one Bed hereafter.
    Alonz. And Heav'n make
Those Beds still fruitful in producing Children,
To bless their Parents youth, and Grandsires age.
    Mir. to Dor. If Children come by lying in a Bed,
I wonder you and I had none between us.
    Dor. Sister it was our fault, we meant like fools
To look 'em in the fields, and they it seems
Are only found in Beds.
    Hip. I am o'rejoy'd
That I shall have *Dorinda* in a bed;
We'll lye all night and day together there,
And never rise again.
    Ferd. Aside to him. Hippolito! you yet are ignorant
Of your great Happiness, but there is somewhat
Which for your own and fair *Dorinda's* sake
I must instruct you in.
    Hip. Pray teach me quickly
How Men and Women in your World make love,
I shall soon learn I warrant you.
    Enter Ariel *driving in* Stephano, Trincalo, Mustacho,
                Ventoso, Caliban, Sycorax.
    Prosp. Why that's my dainty *Ariel*, I shall miss
    thee,
But yet thou shalt have freedom.
    Gonz. O look, Sir, look the Master and the Saylors;
The Bosen too——my Prophecy is out,
That if a Gallows were on land, that Man
Could n'ere be drown'd.
    Alonz. to Trinc. Now Blasphemy, what not one Oath
    ashore?
Hast thou no mouth by land? Why star'st thou so?
    Trinc. What more Dukes yet! I must resign my
    Dukedom;
But 'tis no matter, I was almost starv'd in't.

Must. Here's nothing but wild Sallads, without Oyl or Vinegar.

Steph. The Duke and Prince alive! Would I had now our gallant Ship agen, and were her Master, I'd willingly give all my Island for her.

Vent. And I my Vice-Roy-ship.

Trinc. I shall need no Hangman, for I shall e'en hang my self, now my Friend Butt has shed his last drop of Life. Poor Butt is quite departed.

Ant. They talk like mad men.

Prosp. No matter, time will bring 'em to themselves;
And now their Wine is gone they will not quarrel.
Your Ship is safe and tight, and bravely rigg'd,
As when you first set Sail.

Alonz. This news is wonderful.

Ariel. Was it well done, my Lord?

Prosp. Rarely, my diligence.

Gonz. But pray, Sir, what are those mishapen
        Creatures?

Prosp. Their Mother was a Witch, and one so strong
She would controul the Moon, make Flows and Ebbs,
And deal in her Command without her Power.

Syc. O *Setebos*! These be brave Sprights indeed.

Prosp. to Calib. Go Sirrah to my Cell, and as you
        hope
For Pardon, trim it up.

Calib. Most carefully. I will be wise hereafter.
What a dull Fool was I to take those Drunkards
For Gods, when such as these were in the World?

Prosp. Sir, I invite your Highness and your Train
To my poor Cave this night; a part of which
I will imploy in telling you my story.

Alonz. No doubt it must be strangely taking, Sir.

Prosp. When the Morn dawns I'le bring you to your
        Ship,
And promise you calm Seas and happy Gales.

My *Ariel*, that's thy charge: then to the Elements
Be free, and fare thee well.
   Ariel. I'le do it Master.

> Sings. *Where the Bee sucks there suck I,*
> *In a Cowslips Bell, I lye;*
> *There I couch when Owls do cry.*
> *On the Swallows Wing I flye*
> *After Summer merrily.*
> *Merrily, merrily shall I live now*
> *Under the Blossom that hangs on the Bough.*

   Syc. I'll to Sea with thee, and keep thee warm in thy Cabin.
   Trinc. No my dainty Dy-dapper, you have a tender Constitution, and will be sick a Ship-board. You are partly Fish and may swim after me. I wish you a good Voyage.
   Prosp. Now to this Royal Company, my Servant,
Be visible, and entertain them with
A Dance before they part.
   Ariel. I have a gentle Spirit for my Love,
Who twice seven years hath waited for my Freedom,
It shall appear and foot it featly with me.
Milcha, my Love, thy *Ariel* calls thee.
            Enter Milcha.
   Milcha. Here!   *[They dance a Saraband.*
   Prosp. Henceforth this Isle to the afflicted be
A place of Refuge as it was to me:
The Promises of blooming Spring live here,
And all the Blessings of the rip'ning Year:
On my retreat let Heaven and Nature smile,
And ever flourish the *Enchanted Isle.*   *[Exeunt.*

Epilogue.

GALLANTS, by all good signs it does appear,
That Sixty Seven's a very damning year,
For Knaves abroad, and for ill Poets here.

Among the Muses there's a gen'ral rot,
The Rhyming Monsieur and the Spanish Plot;
Defie or Court, all's one, they go to Pot.

The Ghosts of Poets walk within this place,
And haunt us Actors wheresoe're we pass,
In Visions bloodier than King Richard's *was.*

For this poor wretch he has not much to say,
But quietly brings in his part o' th' Play,
And begs the favour to be damn'd to day.

He sends me only like a Sh'riffs Man here
To let you know the Malefactor's neer;
And that he means to die, en Cavalier.

For if you shou'd be gracious to his Pen,
Th' Example will prove ill to other men,
And you'll be troubled with 'em all agen.

THE
MOCK-TEMPEST:
OR THE
Enchanted Caſtle.

ACTED AT THE
Theatre Royal.

Written By T. DUFFETT.

Hic totus volo rideat libellus. Mart.

⚜ ⚜ ⚜ ⚜
⚜ ⚜ ⚜ ⚜
⚜ ⚜ ⚜ ⚜

LONDON,

Printed for *William Cademan* at the *Popes-Head* in the lower
Walk of the *New Exchange* in the *Strand.* 1675

Persons Represented.

Prospero, a Duke, Head-keeper of the Enchanted Castle.
Alonzo, a Duke, his mortal Enemy.
Quakero, son of *Alonzo*.
Gonzalo, a subject of *Alonzos*.
Antonio, his Friend.
Hypolito, Infant Duke of *Mantua*, Innocent and ignorant.
Hectorio, a Pimp.
Miranda ⎫
Dorinda ⎬ the harmless daughters of *Prospero*.
Stephania, a Baud.
Beantosser ⎫
Moustrappa ⎬ Wenches.
Drinkallup ⎭
Ariel, a Spirit waiting on *Prospero*.
A Plenipotentiary.

Wenches, Bridewell-*Keepers*, *Spirits, Devils, Masquers,*
and Prisners.

The Scene in LONDON.

106

The INTRODUCTION, spoken by Mr. *Hains*, and Mrs. *Mackarel*.

Mr. Hains *Enters alone.*

YOU are of late become so mutinous,
   Y'ave forc'd a reverend Bard to quit our House.
Since y'are so soon misled to ruin us,
I'le call a Spirit forth that shall declare,
What all your tricks and secret Virtues are.
What? ho *Ariel*!

Enter Betty Mackarel.

Here's *Betty*——Now rail if you dare:
Speak to 'em *Betty*——ha! asham'd, alass poor Girl,
Whisper me!—Oh I'le tell 'em—Gentlemen! she says,
Y'are grown so wild she could not stay among ye,
And yet her tender heart is loath to wrong ye.
Spare 'em not,
Whom kindness cannot stir, but stripes may move.

   Bet. O Mr. *Hains*! I've often felt their Love.

   Ha. Poh, felt a Pudding that has taken vent,
Their love cools faster, and as soon is spent.
Think of thy high calling *Betty*, now th'art here,
They gaze and wish, but cannot reach thy Sphere,
Though ev'ry one could squeeze thy Orange there.

   Bet. Why this to me, Mr. *Haines* (d'ee conceive me)
     why to me?

   Ha. Ay, why this to *Betty*?
O Virtue, Virtue! vainly art thou sought,
If such as *Betty* must be counted naught:
Examine your Consciences Gentlemen!
When urg'd with heat of love, and hotter Wine,
How have you begg'd, to gain your lewd design:
Betty, dear, dear, dear *Betty*,

I'le spend five Guinnyes on thee, if thou'lst go:
And then they shake their (d'ee conceive me) *Betty* is't
   not so, their yellow Boyes.
   Bet. Fie Mr. *Hains*, y'are very rude (d'ee conceive me.)
   Ha. Then speak your self.
   Bet. Gentlemen! you know what I know.
      If y'are severe, all shall out by this light:
      But if you will be kind, I'le still be right
   Ha. So that's well—make thy Cursy *Betty*.
Now go in Child, I have something to say to these
   Gentlemen in private.   [*Exit* Betty.

PROLOGUE. Spoken by Mr. *Hains*.

SINCE Heroes Ghosts, and Gods have felt your spight:
Your She Familiars, and your dear delight ;
The Devils shall try their power, w'ee to night :
Some do believe that Devils ne'r have been,
Because they think, none can be worse then them :
But Female Sprights by all are felt and seen.
   You see our Study is to please you all :
Lets not by stiff Tom Thimbles *faction fall ;*
Whose censures are meer ign'rance in disguise,
The noyse of envious fools, that would seem wise.
If Bacons *Brazen-head cry——that won't pass,*
Strayt all the little Fops are turn'd to brass,
And Eccho to the braying of that Ass :
Although we take their shapes and sensless sounds,
Lets not be worryd by our own dull Hounds :
Let not their noyse that got your Money there,
Deprave your Judgments, and your pleasure here.
   Ye men of Sense and Wit, resume your Raign.
Th'are honour'd who by noble Foes are slain ;
Such comforts wounded Lovers have who swear,
When their tormenting pains are most severe,
Dam'ee !
It does not vex me to be Clapp'd by her :
Gad she was handsome, though the sport is dear.
But who in your sight at their mercy lyes,
Much like an Eastern *Malefactor dyes,*
Expos'd i'th' Sun to be devour'd by flyes.
   Let Language, Wit and Plot, this Night be safe,
   For all our business is to make you laugh.

THE

New TEMPEST

OR THE

Enchanted Castle.

Act I. Scene 1.

A great noyse heard of beating Doors, and breaking Win-
dowes, crying a Whore, a Whore, &c.
Enter Beantosser, and Moustrappa.

Bean. WHAT a noyse they make!
Mous. A roaring noyse, we shall have
foul weather.
Enter Drinkallup.
Drink. The Dogs have us in the Wind, 'twill go hard.
[*Exeunt Beantosser and* Moustrappa.]
Enter Stephania.
Steph. Hectorio! Hectorio!
All. Hectorio! Hectorio! Hectorio!
Enter Hectorio.
Hect. Here here Mother, what cheer, what cheer.
Steph. Never worse, never worse, barr up the Doors,
barr up the Doors: Oh! Oh!
[*She whistles, Wenches run on and off again.*]
Enter Moustrappa.
All. Barr up the Doors, barr up the Doors.

III

Mous. Let's make all fast enough, and let'm roar the Devils head off.

Steph. Beantosser, Beantosser.

All. Beantosser, Beantosser, Beantosser.

Steph. Why where is this damn'd deaf flunder mouth'd drab?

Enter Beantosser.

Bean. Here here, a pox o' these full mouth'd Fox hounds.

Hect. They hunt devilish hard, I'me affrai'd they'l earth us.

Steph. Give *Hectorio* a dram of the Bottle, the Whey-Blooded Rogue looks as if his heart were melted into his Breeches.   [*Exeunt* Beantosser *and* Hectorio.
Enter Wenches arm'd with Spitts, Forks, Tongs, Chamber-Potts, &c. they pass over the stage.

Steph. Bear up, bear up my brave *Amazons*, y'ave born Ten times as many men in your times: heigh my Girles, stand fast my stout bona Roba's, run, fly, work nimbly, nimbly ye Queans, or all's lost.   [*Exeunt all.*
[*A great noyse again.*

Enter Hectorio, Alonzo, Gonzalo, Quakero.

Alon. Good friend, stand to thy tackling, and play the Man: where's Mother *Stephania.*

Hect. Pry'thee old Goat tye up thy Clack, and move thy hands.

Quak. Friend, friend, look thee, bridle thy unruly member——to wit, thy tongue.

Hect. Work, work, my hearts of Gold.

Quak. Ha, ha, ha, my Father to whom thou spakest so unadvisedly is Duke of that building which do-eth sustain my Lord Mayors Cattle, *Vidicilet*, his Doggs.

Hect. Fill the sweating Tub with Stones, and set it against the Door, quick, quick.

Within.——The Sweating Tub, the Sweating Tub! Stones, Stones!

Quak. He is moreover perpetual Whiffler to the Worshipful company of *Pin-makers*, as I my self am.

Hect. Confound thy Father and thy self.

[*A noyse within.*

What care these Roarers for the worshipful *Pin-makers*? Silence, and to work, or I'le ram thee into a Chamber-pot, and throw thee out at Window.   [*Exeunt all.*

Enter Stephania, Beantosser, Moustrappa *and* Drinkallup.

Steph. Stir, Wenches, stir, bring out all the Jourdans full of Water.

All. The Jourdans, the Jourdans, *&c.*

Beantosser, Drinkallup, *and* Moustrappa *run off several wayes crying the Jourdans.*

[*A great noyse within, all crying a Whore, a Whore, a Whore,* &c.

Steph. Send a Legion of Devils down their yelling throats to pluck their lungs out.——Out ye bauling Curs, ye ill-bred hounds, here are Whores enough for you all, All, if you would behave your selves like civil Gentlemen, and come one after another.

She Whistles, Enter Wenches.

Down, down, down to the Sellar Windows.——

All. The Sellar Windows, the Sellar Windows.

[*The Wenches run down the Trap Door.*

Enter Beantosser, Moustrappa, *and* Drinkallup *hastily one after another.*

Bean. Undone, undone, not one drop of Water in the house.

Mous. With hard labour all their moisture turns into sweat.

Drink. Th'are dryer then hung Beef, and almost as black too.

Bean. Your advice, your advice Mother.

Drink. Dispatch, or w'are ruin'd.——

Steph. Get up in the Windows, you musty Queens,

make water in their Eyes, and burn e'm out, I'me sure y'are hot enough.——

Enter Hectorio.

Hect. Turn out, turn out all hands to the Back-door: is this a time to prate ye spurr-gald jades, ye over-rid Hackneys.——

Mous. O you huffing Son of a Whore.

Drink. You rotten Jack in a box.

Bean. You foul mouth'd Nickumpoop.

Hect. Prate on, prate on, d'ee hear how it Thunders? ——stand still and be damn'd, I'le shift well enough for one.   [*The noyse renew'd.*

[*Exit* Hectorio.

Steph. Turn out, turn out Seditious mutiners, ye or I'le have ye all flead——Out, out!

[*Exeunt* Beantosser, Moustrappa, *and* Drinkallup.
Enter Gonzalo, Alonzo, *and* Quakero.

Gonz. More noyse and terrour then a Tempest at Sea.

Enter Beantosser.

Bean. The green Chamber, the green Chamber.

[Stephania *whistles, the Wenches come up from
· the Trapp-door.*

Steph. Aloft, aloft, to the green Chamber, all to the green Chamber——Aloft, aloft.——

[*Exeunt* Beantosser *and Wenches.*

Alon. My Honour, my Reputation.——

Quak. Yea! Reputation, Reputation!——Woo man, ah! ha!

Steph. Reputation! ye crop-ear'd whelps, Reputation! is not my Reputation dearer to me then your lives, and Souls? Down with the Close stool upon their heads.

You louzy farandinical Sots, Reputation! I have had Lords——Lords! thou whey-bearded Ananias, and then I had a blessing on my endeavours; but this is justly fall'n upon me, for dealing with such zealous Whore-masters, thin-gutted 3*d.* Customers——Out of my sight,

and to work, or by the beards of my renowned Pre-
decessors I'le have you hung out like Wool-sacks to
defend my Walls. See if thou canst preach the Rabble
to Silence, thou canting Hypocritical Abednego.

Quak. Yea, thou babylonish Whore in grain, thou
Harlot of a *London* dye, thou shalt see the strength of
the power of a um——Thou shalt see, I say, look ye
Friends, Brethren and Sisters——Give heedful attention, and a, and I say a um——

> [*A* shout within, and dirt thrown in his mouth.
> [*Exeunt all.*

> *Enter again* Stephania *and* Beantosser.

Bean. We are gone, we are gone, th'are all broke in
the Closet Window,

> *Enter* Hectorio.

Hect. Hell, and Devils, th'are untiling of the House.

> *Enter Wenches.*

Steph. Let off the Bottles of Stepony, they may think
th'are Guns.

Bean. Clap up the middle hatch with the Iron spikes.

Hect. Take down the false Stairs.

> *Enter* Moustrappa.

Mous. Open the Trap-door, that falls into the
Common-shoar.

> *Enter* Drinkallup.

Drink. Hang up the tenter Hooks.——

Steph. Set the great Chest against the stair Door.

> [Stephania *Whistles, Enter Wenches.*

All. To the great Chest, the great Chest.

> [*Exeunt all but* Stephania.

Hect. within. Heave all together, heave Cats, heave.
Heave Cats, heave——cheerily, cheerily.

> *Enter* Alonzo, Gonzalo *and* Quakero.

Alon. Gonz. Quak.——Murther, murther, murther.

Steph. Oh, you obstreperous Woolves, a Rot consume
your Windpipes, y'are louder then the rabble.

Alon. O, this base, this cursed business!

Steph. Cursed bus'ness, thou invincible Fop, thou
Brazen headed Ignoramus——Hast thou a mind to be
limb'd? one word more, and all the Doors shall fly
open : Cursed bus'ness, with a pox to ye. [*She whistles.*
Enter Wenches—And go off again.
Come tag-rag-and-long-tail, Old Satin, Taffaty, and
Velvet, rouze about, charge 'em briskly, showr the Coals
on their pates.——He calls Wenching, base cursed
bus'ness——Oh you rake Hells, sons of unknown
Fathers.
Enter Beantosser.
Bean. Hell take 'em, they clime the Walls like Cats.
Steph. Down with the Tables and Stools upon 'em.
[*Exit* Beantosser.
[*The noyse renew'd.*
Enter Hectorio.
Hect. Sound a Parle, sound a Parle, or they'l break
in upon us——There's no hope left.
Steph. A Parle, thou impudent miscreant! false
hearted Caytiff I'le rather like a noble Roman *Virago*,
make my House my Funeral pile.
Hect. All are resolv'd not to fight a stroak more, sound
a Parle but to gain time.
Steph. To delude the Foe I consent, but never to
yield.   [*She whistles.*
Enter Drinkallup, Beantosser *and* Moustrappa.
Sound a Parle, and hang out the White Flag.
[*A Horn sounds within, and one passes over the
Stage with a Flannel Peticoat on a Stick :
another Horn sounded on the other side.*
Hect. Hark, they answer us.
Steph. Go you *Drinkallup*, and see what they will
demand.   [*Exit* Drinkallup *and returns immediately.*
Drink. Here's a Plenipotentiary desires admittance.
Steph. Let him be blinded, and introduc'd by the
Postern——Casement——Come fellow Souldiers, lets

sit in State, and receive him with undaunted Countenances, as blustring Warriours do, though we are like to dye for fear.

A Guard of Wenches Enter.

Master of our Ceremonies, introduce the Plenipotentiary.   [*A dirty fellow led in between two Wenches.*

Steph. Fellow Souldiers 'tis a Maxim in Warr to treat with our Arms in our hands——(Guard, deliver us your Weapons)——and while we talke of peace to prepare for a Battle; therefore Guard go you and mend the backs of the Chairs.   [*Exeunt Guard.*

Plenipotentiary, be not dismaid with the glittering Splendour of our Court, but boldly deliver what thou hast in Charge.——

Plen. My Master, the many-headed-monster-Multitude, to save the great effusion of Christian Chamberly, will grant you peace on these terms.

Steph. Say on.

Plen. First, they demand the Dominion of the Straights mouth, and all the Mediterranean Sea—— That every Frigot, Fireship, you have, shall strike, furle up their sail, and lye by to the least of their Cock-boats, where-ever they meet, and receive a man aboard to search for prohibited Goods, and permit him to romage fore and aft without resistance.——

Steph. Umph.——My friends, this is very hard.

Plen. Secondly, That all their Vessels shall have and enjoy a free-trade into and out of all your Ports without paying any Custom.——

Steph. The duties of Importation are my greatest Revenue, and must not be parted with.

Bean. But though your People pay for import, we will engage to pay them at going off.

Mous. As we have always done heretofore.

Plen. Lastly, That you re-imburse the charge of the War, pay for the Cure of the wounded, and the recov'ry of those that have surfeited on your rotten Ling and Poys'nous Oyl, and allow Pensions for those that are dismembered——What say ye, Peace, or War?

Steph. War.

All. War, War, War.

Steph. Return for answer, that we will rather dye at their Feet, then submit to such dishonourable Conditions:——Begon:——And so she pray'd me to tell ye.

Plen. Though you refuse peace, I scorn to carry back my present,——there. [*Throwes out a bunch of Carrets.*

Drink. We scorn their Courtesies, and their dry toyes.

Plen. Are ye so fierce? if the Siege continue, you'l Petition for 'em: look for Fire and Sword——And so she pray'd me to tell you.   [*Exit* Plenipotentiary.

Steph. Arm, Arm, give the word, Arm, Arm.

All. Arm, Arm.

Within. Arm, Arm, Arm,   [*Exeunt All.*
                [*The noyse of the assault renew'd.*
    Enter Stephania, Beantosser, *and* Moustrappa.

Steph. Many a brush have I gon through in my time, but never was any so sharp.
                Enter Hectorio.

Hect. S'death, our Ammunition's spent, the dear dear dyet-drink's gone.

Steph. And yet these Canibals, more insatiate then the Sea, are not satisfi'd with our best goods; pull up the Harths, and down with the Chimnies.
            [*Exeunt* Beantosser *and* Moustrappa.

Hect. 'Tis in vain to strive.

Steph. Thou Cow-hearted cormorant, shall we be all lost for thee?

Hect. No, 'tis for thy obstinacy, thou insatiable shee-Woolf.

Steph. Rot your Sheeps blood.

Hect. Confound your brutish heart and bacon, face.

Steph. Nounz, stir about, or I'le beat thy brains out with my Bottle.

Hect. One word more, and by the Lord, *Harry*.

Steph. Thou dar'st not for thy Blood, thou dar'st not.

[*She Whistles.*

Enter all the Wenches.

Steph. For shame let not the Army see our difference, or thy Cowardise.——

Hect. Pull down the House, and bury them in the Ruines: come along boldly, my dear hearts, follow me, I shall find a time.—— [*Exeunt Wenches. Exit* Hectorio.

Steph. To be hang'd——I don't doubt it.

Enter Beantosser.

Bean. O save the Syring and the Pot of Turpentine-pills for my sake.—— [*Exit* Beantosser.

Steph. Save nothing, cut off your Leggs and throw at 'em. Out with the Exchange Womans Trunk of Perfum'd Linnen which the Old Knight us'd to play hey Gamer Cook in——Out, out; save nothing.

[*Exit* Stephania.

Enter Hectorio, *and* Moustrappa.

Hect. Fill the old Justices greazy Night-Cap with the Rosary of Beads the Fryer pawn'd here but last Night, and down with 'em.

Mous. I wish they were all Cannon-bullets for their sakes. [*Exit* Hectorio.

Enter Stephania, *hastily.*

Steph. Hold, hold, if you throw out the Beads, they'l take us for Papishes, and then there's no Mercy; otherwise we may still hope for pity because we are all of one Religion.

Enter Hectorio.

Hect. Set the Led Cistern against the Door; all hands to the Cistern, to the Cistern. [Stephania *whistles.*

Enter all the Wenches.

Steph. My Girles, my Daughters.

Hect. Fellow Souldiers, dear hearts now for the last push.

Steph. All hands to the Cistern, away——[*Exeunt all.*
Enter all, pulling at a Rope.

Hect. Hoa up; hoa up; cheerily, cheerily, pluck all together.——

All. Hoa up! hoa up! hoa up!
Enter Stephania *whistling.*

Steph. Down, down, all hands down, th'are going to spring a Mine.   [*All run down.*
Enter Beantosser, *and* Moustrappa.

Bean. There's a fresh Brigade ef sturdy Blood-hounds come from the Butcher-row.

Mous. The Barr of the Door's broke.——
[*Exeunt* Beantosser *and* Moustrappa.

Steph. Barr it with the Constables staffe that lay here last Night.
Enter Drinkallup.

Drink. O Mother, save your self, save your self.

Steph. Must our mouths be cold then? [*She whistles.*
Enter Hectorio.

Hect. All's lost, all's lost.——   [*Exit* Drinkallup.
Enter Beantosser *and* Moustrappa.

Bean. They break in like a full Sea upon us.

Mous. O Mother, Mother, shift for your self.

Steph. Name not me: the Justices, and Jaylors, are my very good Friends, and Customers.

All. Ah, there's no trust to Friends now.

Steph. If I dye, I dye, but I pity your tender backs, and grieve for the present want all these young Gallants will have of so many excellent Beauties.
[*Exeunt* Hectorio, Beantosser, Moustrappa, *and*
Drinkallup, *and return presently.*

Hect. Yet, yet, you may 'scape perhaps.

Bean. The poor hearts fight as if they were all *Scanderbegs.*

Mous. Yet, shift Mother, in two minutes 'twil be too late.

Steph. No, here will I stay, and like a *Phœnix*, perish in my Nest, the Fates so Decree.

Bean. Then let's among 'em, and dye all together, or break through.——

All. Agreed, agreed.   [*Exeunt all.*
        [*A great noyse of fighting, crying Fire, Murther,*
            &c. *The Rabble, and Wenches enter fighting.*
            It Rains Fire, Apples, Nuts.——A Con-
            stable and Watch enter, and drive all off.

Act I. Scene 2.

The Scene chang'd to Bridewell.
Enter Prospero, *and* Miranda.

Pros. MIRANDA, where's your Sister?
            Mir. I left her on the Dust-Cart-top,
gaping after the huge noyse that went by.——

Pros. It was a dreadful show.

Mir. Oh woe, and alass, ho, ho, ho! I'm glad I did not see it though.

Pros. Hold in thy breath, and tell thy Vertuous Body, there's no harme down, th'are all reserv'd for thine, and thy Sister *Dorindas* private use.

Mir. And shall we have 'em all, a-ha! that will be fine i'fads; but if you don't keep 'em close, pray Father, we shall never have 'em long to our selves pray; for now ev'ry Gentlewoman runs huckstring to Market, the youth are bought up so fast, that poor *Publicans* are allmost starv'd, so they are so.

Pros. Leave that to my Fatherly Care.

Mir. And shall we have 'em all, ha, ha, he! O good dear hau, how the Citizens Wives will curse us.——

Pros. Miranda, you must now leave this Tom-rigging, and learn to behave your self with a grandeur and state, befitting your illustrious Birth and Quality.——Thy Father, *Miranda*, was 50 years ago a man of great power, Duke of my Lord Mayors Dogg-kennel.

Mir. O lo, why Father, Father, are not I *Miranda Whiffe*, sooth, and arn't you *Prospero Whiffe*, sooth, Keeper of *Bridewell*, my Father?

Pros. Thy Mother was all Mettle.——As true as Steel, as right's my Legg, and she said thou wert my Daughter; canst thou remember when thou wert Born, sure thou canst not, for then thou wert but three days old.

Mir. I'fads, I do remember it Father, as well as 'twere but yesterday.

Pros. Then scratch thy tenacious Poll, and tell me what thou findest backward in the misty back and bottomless Pit of time.

Mir. Pray Father had I not Four, or Five Women waiting upon top of me, at my Mothers groaning, pray?

Pros. Thou hadst, and more *Miranda*, for then I had a Tub of humming stuff would make a Cat speak.

Mir. O Gemine! Father how came we hither?

Pros. While I despising mean, and worldly bus'ness, as mis-becoming my grave Place, Quality, did for the bett'ring of my mind, apply my self, to the secret and laudable study of Nine-pins, Shovel-board and Pigeon-holes——do'st thou give ear Infant?

Mir. I do, most Prudent Sir.

Pros. My Brother, to whom I left the manage of my weighty state, having learn'd the mysterious Craft of coupling Doggs, and of untying them; and by strict Observation of their jilting carriage, found the time when *Venus*, Countess, Lady, Beauty, and the rest of my she subjects, were to be oblig'd, by full allowance of their sports, soon grew too Popular, stole the hearts of my currish Vassals, and so became the Ivy-leaf, which cover'd my Princely Issue, and suck'd out all my Juice. Dost observe me Child?

Mir. Yes, forsooth Father, this story would cure Kib'd-heels.

Pros. This Miscreant, so dry he was for sway, betray'd me to *Alonzo*, Duke of Newgate; and in a stormy and dreadfull Night open'd my Kenell Gates, and forc'd me thence with thy young Sister, and thy howling self.

Mir. Father! did they kill us then, pray Father?

Pros. Near the Kenell they dar'd not for the love my dogged Subject bore me.——In short to Newgate we were carry'd,——And thence all in a Cart, without a cov'ring, or a Pad of Straw, to Hyde Park-corner, we were hurri'd there on the stubbed Carkase of a Leafeless Tree, they hoysted us aloft to pipe to winds, whose murm'ring pity whistling back again, did seem to show us cursed kindness.

Mir. O poor Father!——But whereof, how did we 'scape Father?

Pros. Some Friends we had, and some Money, which gaind the assistance of a great man called *Gregoria Dunn,* appointed master of that black design: now luck begins to turn.——But ask no more; I see thou grow'st pinck-ey'd, go in, and let the Nurse lay thee to sleep.

Mir. And shall she give me some Bread and Butter, Father.

Pros. Ay, my Child,——Go in.——[*Exit* Miranda.] So she's fast.——*Ariel*, what ho my *Ariel*?

Enter Ariel *flying down.*

Ari. Hayl most potent Master, I come to serve thy pleasure. Be it to lye, swear, steal, pick pockets, or creep in at Windows——

Pros. How didst thou perform the last task I set thee?

Ari. I gather'd the Rabble together, show'd them the Bawdy House, told e'm they us'd to kill Prentices, and make mutton pyes of 'em——I led them to the Windows, Doors, backward, forward, now to the Sellar, now to the House top——Then I ran and call'd the Constable, who came just as the Rabble broke in, and the defendants were leaping from the Balcony, like Saylers from a sinking Ship. The Duke and his Trayn I clap'd into a Coach.

Pros. Are they all taken and safe?

Ari. All safe in several parts of this thy enchanted Castle of Bridewel, and not a hair of 'em lost.

Pros. 'Twas bravely done my *Ariel*! Whats a Clock?

Ari. Great Tom already has struck ten:
> Now blest are Women that have men,
> To tell fine tale, and warm cold feet,
> While lonely lass lyes gnawing sheet.

Pros. We have much to do e're morning come: follow me, I'le instruct thee within.

> Before the gorgeous Sun upon House top doth Sneer,
> The Laud knows what is to be done, the Laud knows where.   [*Exeunt.*

The End of the First Act.

Act II. Scene 1.

Enter Miranda *and* Dorinda.

Dor. OH Sister Sister, what have I seen pray?

    Mir. Some rare sight I warrant.

Dor. From yonder dust-cart-top, as I star'd upon the noyse, I thought it had been fighting, but at last I saw a huge Creature, for ought I know.

Mir. O whereof you mean the Coach.

Dor. Coach! i'fads, I thought it had been a Fish, I'm sure it was alive, and it ran roaring along, and all the People ran away from it for fear it should eat 'em.

Mir. O lo, O lo Sister, O lo!——ha ha he——

Dor. Why d'ee laugh at one Sister, indeed it had eaten men, for just by our gate it stood still and open'd a great Mouth in the belly of it, and spit 'em out all whole.

Mir. Oh but Sister, whereof I can tell you news pray, my Father told me in that Creature was that thing call'd Husband, and we should see it shortly and have it pray, in a Civil way.

Dor. Husband, what's that?

Mir. Why that's a thing like a man (for ought I know) with a great pair of Hornes upon his head, and my father said 'twas made for Women, look ye.

Dor. What must we ride to water upon't, Sister?

Mir. No, no, it must be our Slave, and give us Golden Cloaths Pray, that other men may lye with us in a Civil way, and then it must Father our Children and keep them.

Dor. And when we are so Old and Ugly, that no body else will lye with us, must it lye with us it self?

Mir. Ay that it must Sister.

Dor. You see my Father gets men to lye with us, is not he a Husband then?

Mir. No, you see he has no Hornes.

Dor. May be he sheds 'em like a Buck, or puts 'em in his pocket like a rich Citizen, because he won't lye with us himself when he can get no body else.

Mir. Fie Sister; no! Fathers and Mothers are kinder and wiser now then they were heretofore look ye; for when they see their Daughters will be modish and kind, they provide 'em Gallants themselves to lye with them.

Dor. But if we must take those our careful Parents get, only for profit, 'tis as bad as marrying.

Mir. They doe it only 'till they get us Husbands to ease them of the trouble.

Dor. O whereof Sister, my Father may spare himself of that trouble, for I am old enough to shift for my self in a civil way, for I was 13. last quarter Sessions, ay and wise enough too.

Mir. So we all think i'vads, but they can get us Coaches and Settlements, whereof if we were left to our selves, we should creep into holes, and get nothing but Bastards.

Dor. If our fathers don't get us Husbands quickly, wee'l make him lye with us himself, shall we Sister?

Mir. Ay ay, that we will, but lets goe in now, He's about something I long to see the end of, come lets not despair, the flesh is strong.

Dor. O for a Husband Sister how I long.

[*Exeunt* Miranda *and* Dorinda.

Act II. Scene 2.

Enter Alonzo, *and* Gonzalo *affrighted.*

Alon. GONZALO Oh——my lodging is inchanted.
Gon. Mine with a Devil and like your Grace is haunted,
Which plays more tricks then e're the witch my Aunt did.
Alon. First doleful groans at both my ears were lugging.
Then whistling voyce like wind in empty muggin.
Gon. Shrieks as of switcheld lass I heard, and anon
Sighs of enchanted ghost like roaring Canon.
Alon. With Princely hoof I knock'd, and noyse did follow,
By which I find O, Heavens! the House is hollow.
My bed of state——
Gon. Of straw you mean——now good my Lord doe not lye.
Alon. Millions of devils mov'd, black, white, and motley,
Six legs a piece, sharp claws.
Gon. Aye mine were so Sir,
Each tooth a needle, and each eye a saucer.
They stole my shooes, and in a hole I found 'em.
The white possest, black Armies did surround 'em.
Feircely the black attaqu'd, and white defended,
Horrour and death in ev'ry Seam attended.

The nimble black like hopping Devils ventur'd,
Mounted the works, and on the half moon enter'd.
But here the white serty'd as thick as sawdust,
And beat them off.
Then march'd up the red listed Reformadoes,
But what they did I dare not tell for fear.

Alon. Sage matrons say, where such kind Foes appear,
The Lord o'th' pasture shall not dye that year.

Gon. Unless he's eaten out——

Alon. On large deal board by prudent vermine chosen,
Two Armies more were fighting for my hosen.
If I but offer composition for my sock,
All leave the field, and to my Carkass flock.
No Fairy pinches half so close, nor no Witch.

Gon. 'Tis worse then nettle, sting of Wasp, or Cowitch.

[Alonzo *pulls a Louse out of his neck.*

Alon. Treason treason, O here's one of the white devils, treason treason, my guard my guard, Oh ho hoe.

Fortune has cheated me of all, pize on her,
I am no Duke now, but a poor Prisoner.

[*A noyse of horrid Instruments.*

Gon. Oh what horrid noyse is this assaults our ears.

Devils rise and Sing.

1 De. *Where be those boyes,*
That make such a noyse,
And won't eat their bread and butter ?

2 De. *Without all doubt.*
Th' are hereabout,
Wee'l teach 'em to make such a Clutter.

3 De. *Who are the ring-leaders, who rules the Roast ?*

4 De. Alonzo *the Duke, and another old Toast.*

1 De. *Wee'l put water in their porridge,*
And straw in their beds,

2 De. *Shooes on their feet, and a Comb in their heads.*

Chorus. *Wee'l put* &c.
      And straw &c.
      Shooes &c.

Alon. O save me, save me, *Gonzalo.*

Gon. I would give him the best member I have, to save my self.

Alon. These great He Devils will hearken to no such Composition.

             The Devils sing again.

1 De. *Rogues that from their Liquor shrink,*
      Shall scorch to death for want of drink.

2 De. *And who with false glass good fellows betray,*

3 De. *And tipple small beer in stead of their wine,*

4 De. *Then bubble their poor weak brothers at play,*
      To the whip and the stocks wee'l confine.

1 De. *So poor, so poor, they still shall remain ;*
      Mirth, or good Wine, they shall ne'r have again,
      Nor never, oh never, be eas'd of their pain.

Chorus. *So poor,* &c.——
      Mirth——
      Nor never——

Gon. Never, oh never, eat Custard again!
      Oh murthering Sentence—Oh, ho, ho!

Alon. Never, never——O Inhumane Correction!
      Oh, they begin again——Oh.——

             The Devils Sing.

1 De. *Who are the pillars of the wenching Trade ?*

2 De. *The zealous professor, and brisk City blade.*

3 De. *The Gallants, and Bullies,*
      Do often grow poor, and bare, and bare.

4 De. *But these Canters, and close City Cullies*
      Are ne'r without Money, or Ware.

1 De. *What Slave permits*
      Such Hypocrites
      In peace to tast of all our sweets ?

2 De. *In the midst of their joyes, they discoveries fear,*

3 De. *And their Wives, if th'ave any, shall make the*
score clear.

4 De. *With Claps, and with Duns, we torment them all*
day,
And at night we take them and their Doxies
away.

Chorus. *With Claps &c.——*
And at night &c.——

Alon. Pox o'the Devil, 'tis too true, they did take our Doxies away.

Gon. Ay, and I would procure 'em a whole Regiment, for my Ransome.

Alon. Alass, they were but Oysters before their meale; besides they were so rotten, they would melt in their mouthes, all their bones were turn'd to gristle: We are kep'd for the standing Dish.

Gon. Nay, then I am safe enough, for I have no more standing Dish, then a post, my hearts no bigger then a Pins-head.

Alon. My poore Boy *Quakero's*, gone too, Oh, ho, ho!

The Devils Sing.

1 De. *Say, say,*
Shall we take up these Rogues, and Carry them
away,
With a tory, rory, Tory, rory, rory, Red-Coats ?

2 De. *Aye, aye.*

3 De. *Aye, aye.*

4 De. *Aye, aye.*

1 De. *Aye, aye.*

Chorus. *With a Tory, rory, Tory, rory, rory, rory.*

2 De. *No, No,*
'Till we show them their Crimes, let e'm stay.
With a Tory, rory, Tory, rory, rantum, scantum.

3 De. *Let 'em stay.*

4 De. *Let 'em stay.*
1 De. *Let 'em stay.*
2 De. *Let 'em stay.*
Chorus. *With a Tory, rory, Tory, rory, rory, rory.*

1 De. *Cabbage is windy, and Mustard is strong,*
    But a Lass with a wide Mouth, and a liquorish
       Tongue.
    Will give thee the Palsie, though never so young.
    Then first let their Pride, let their Pride come
       along.
Chorus. *Cabbage.——*
    But a Lass——
    Will give——
    Then first——

Enter *Pride,* represented by a Painted, gaudy Woman,
    with a Glass in her hand.

She Sings.
Pride. *Lo here, here is Pride, that first left them aside,*
    An honest true Trojan, *and then she dy'd.*

Enter *Fraud,* a female Quaker *Sings.*
Fraud.   *With upright look, and speech sincere,*
    In publick, I a Saint appear.
    But in private I put out the light,
    And I serve for a Whore, or a Baud.
    I have taught them to cheat, Swear, and Fight,
    For by Yea, and by Nay, I am Fraud.

Enter *Rapine,* drest like a Padder, with a Pistole in his
    hand.

Sings.
Rapine.   *Send out a Scout*
    To yonder Hill.
    Stand, and deliver.
    You dogg, must I wait.
    I'm thy fate :

Dispatch, or I'l send thee to Hell.
From Fraud, *they thus proceed to force.*
And then I Rapine, *guide their Course.*

Enter Murther.

A man drest all in Red, with two Bloody Daggers in his
hands, and his Face and Hands stain'd with blood.

Sings.

Murther.   *Wake* Duncan! *would thou couldst.*
    Disguis'd with blood, I lead them on,
        Until to Murther they arrive.
    Then to the Gallows they run.
        Needs must they go, whom the Devils drive.

1 Devil *Sings.*
    Alass poor Mortals.
    They gape like the Earth, in the Dogg-dayes.
    What a rare life the Frogg has ?
        Drawer, Drawer.

2 De. *Anon, Anon.*
1 De. *Give 'em drink, or they'r gone,*
    E'r their torment's began.
    Pour, pour, pour, pour.
    Heark, heark, how it hisses,
        See, see, how it smoaks :
    Who refuses such Liquor as this is,
    May he pine, may he pine, may he pine
        'Till he choakes.

Chorus. *Heark,* &c.

The Devils sing, and Dance round *Alonzo,* and *Gonzalo.*

Chorus. *Around, around.*
    Around, around, around.
    Let's sing, and tear the ground,
    There's no such sport below,
    Where sinfull mortals go.

                    [*Exeunt all the Devils.*

Gon. Oh, oh, are you alive my Lord Duke.

Alon. I cannot tell, Ah, ha,——Feel me, feel me, what a drench they gave us, sure 'twas Spirit of Brimstone. ——I am all in a flame.

Gon. Their design, is to roast us as some do Geese, by putting a hot Iron in their bellies, I begin to drip, they may make a Sop in the Pan already.

Alon. Anon they'l cut off slivers from us, as they did from the whole Ox, in St. *James's* Fair.

Gon. Oh, 'tis intollerable: methinks I hear a great she Devil, call for Groats worth of the Crispe of my Countenance.——They are all for Gristle.

Alon. Another cries Six-peny-worth of the brown, with Gravy, Shalot, and Pepper, Oh there's a Collop gone!

Gon. Shalot, and Pepper, was well thought of, for if I am not well season'd, there's no eating of me.

Alon. Indeed old Lord, you have a kind of Ven'zon haugou.

Gon. How can it be otherwise, my Lord, when I'me roasted with the guts in my belly?

Alon. If *Shat'lin*, or *Locket* had us, what *Olio's*, Raggous, and Pottages, would they make?

Gon. So new a Dish never came from *France*, they would get the Devil and all by us.

Alon. We should out-stink *French* Cheese.

Gon. O help help, here's Raw-head and Bloody bones, the Master Cook of Hell.

> [*A noise of horrid Musick; a Devil arises with a Crown of Fire.*
>
> *Sings.*

Arise, arise, ye Subterranean Feinds,
  Come claw the backs, of guilty hinds:
  And all ye filthy Drabs, and Harlots rise,
  Which use t' infect the Earth with Puddings, and hot
    Pies;

Rise ye who can devouring glasses frame,
By which Wines pass to th' hollow Womb, and Brain ;
Engender Head-akes, make bold elbows shake,
Estates to Pimples, and to desarts turne.
And you whose greedy flames mans very entrals burne,
Ye ramping queans, who ratling Coaches take,
Though y'ave been fluxed 'till Head and Body shake.
Come Clap these Wretches 'till their parts do swell :
Let Nature never make them well.
Cause Leggs, and Arms to pine, cause loss of hair,
Then make them howl with Anguish, and sad groans.
Rise and obey, rise and obey, Raw head and bloody bones.
                                    [*Exit Devils.*

Devils arise with Bellows, and blow *Alonzo*, and *Gonzalo*,
off the Stage.

A Dance.

The End of the Second Act.

Act III. Scene 1.

Enter Stephania, *with a Pitcher*, Beantosser, *and*
Moustrappa, *all drunk.*

Steph. *THERE was a noble Marquess,*
          Took up his Maidens carkass,
          Fast by the Fire side.
A very homely Damsel,
Her lips were soft as Lambs wool,
Or marrow Pasty-fri'd.

This is but a kind of a doleful Tune, to beat Hemp to,
but hang't lets squeeze the Picher, here's to thee my
doughty *Amazon.*

Bean. Right reverend Trot-up-and-down, I'le do thee
reason here Moustrappa.

Steph. Come bouze it about, and a fico for the Justice.
Fortunes a Whore, and will be kind to her Sisters.

Mous. Of the first Five men, we met Three were *Johns,* and Four of those were Cukolds,——Which is a good sign, and so squeez the juice.——

Bean. A strong point of Consolation, let me kiss thee for that, thou pretty, pocky, well favour'd Crack.

Sing.
Steph. *Fill the Dish* Molly,
  And think of a Cully.
  Here's a health to the best.
Give us more Drink, a Surgeon that's jolly.
  And a pox take the rest.
  Molly *fill.*
  We cry still,
  Fill again, and drink round.
'Till we empty the Pitcher, and fill up the Crown.

Bean. Hold, hold, our Sister is grown hollow hearted, and like a jilting Quean, forsakes us in our Tribulation.

Mous. 'Tis ev'n what I look'd for,——The last Dish came as slow, and frothy, as the last words of a declaring *Quaker.*

Bean. When the Spirit sinks down his Throat, and rattles like the departing Water in a leaky Pump.

Steph. Blame her not, you hear she is sound still, ha! wilt thou so?   [*Knocks the Pitcher.*
Why thats very fair,——She sayes, she will do w'ye for a Groat a time, 'till you are not able to stand: I'le be hang'd if the worst Jugg in Town, will do cheaper.

Bean. Look *Moustrappa* Weeps, —— Hang losses, though our Dancing Schooles ruin'd, we have sav'd our Instruments: And as long as Men drink, and Women paint, we shall still jog on.

Steph. There are more of our Dulcimers thump'd ev'ry Night in *Covent-Garden,* then there are Ghittars scrap'd in a Week, in *Madrid;* therefore I say, staunch thou false hearted misbeleiving Jewes-Trump, do not

many industrious Females live well by bidding Gentlemen welcome to Town, singing at their Chamber doors?

Bean. And trucking their *English* small Wares, for
French Toyes.

Mous. O this was a dreadful bout for poor *Moustrappa*.
In robbing me, they pillag'd six Brokers: ruind my
Credit and quite kill'd my old dealer, honest Jack the
Mercer; for just as I had brought his Body to such a
state, that none else would touch him so that I could
set my own rates, they took me from him; the *French*
Farendine, he gave me for a Gown is gone too.——But
let the World rub, when 'tis at worst 'twill mend.

Bean. The devil take thee, for putting me in mind of
my losses: hang me if I can forbear weeping too.

Steph. Then thou art in danger of drowning for the
water's above thy mouth, and there's no passage by the
Nose, for the bridge was down long ago; and so she
prai'd me to tell ye.

Bean. My friend is a brisk *French* Merchant, I knew
him a Taylors Trotter: but from 3 Ounces of Jessimy-
butter, halfe a Pound of Powder, and 6 pair of Jessimy-
Gloves, by cheating the King of his Customes, and his
fellow Subjects of their Money, he's come to his beaten
Farendine Suit ev'ry day: had not this befall'n me, I
had reduc'd him to his first being, and I had hazarded
the saving of his Soul, by the ruine of body, and estate.
——But he is but repreiv'd,——the pox will take him,
for he is a Termagant at laced Mutton.

Steph. Mischeif light on ye both, for minding me of
my losses; there was scarce a Manchild in Town, gentle,
or simple, from Fifteen to Threescore, that did not pay
me Tribute.——When I walk'd the Streets, the Shop-
keepers bow'd, the Prentices wink'd; If five, or six
Gallants stood in the way, Lord what rustling and
cringing was there to Madam *Stephania*?——Aunt, cries
one, how does my little Neece?——The Aunt, and the

Neece, may both be damn'd, for any thing you care to please: me he slips a Guinny. When shall we cut up the Giblet Pye? cryes another.——Go y'are a wag, cry I: there's halfe a Peece. Saies a third, is there never a fresh Runlet tap'd? yes quoth I, but you shall be hang'd e're you lick your lips with it; and so she praid me to tell ye: still something's coming, for every now and then slips in a close thriving Tradesman, look ye Mrs. quoth he, I do not use these things, but the case is thus, I'le be at a word, I want a Wench, give me good sound ware, here's your Money, ready Money: I won't build Sconces, and bilk you, as your Gentlemen Bullies do, let me have weight and measure, one words as good as a thousand. Well quoth I, put your bus'ness into my hand, I'le use a Conscience, aye, and I did too, for as I hope for freedome; sometimes I have hardly got 8*d*. in the Shilling. But such were sure Customers, they never left me for fear of discovery. Oh! I could tell you such stories of Vestry-men, and Burgesses, as would make the Bells ring backwards, i'faith,——Me, and my bus'ness, was the whole talke of the Town, but all was kep'd secret, not a word mention'd, unless 'twer in some Coffee-house, or the Streets.——But now they all forsake me——but 'twill rub out when 'tis dry, and so I squeeze.——

Sing.
Tough Hemp must we beat?
Dry Bread must we eat,
And be bumbled, and jumbl'd, and grumbl'd at too, too, too.
And drink nothing, but Wat, Wat, Water that's cold?
Then Harry, *and* Mary, *be merry and cheery, as long's we can do, do, do.*
And drive away sorrow, untill we are old.
Come bouze it about, and lets squeeze out the Pitcher.
He's a Rogue that stands out, and shall ne'r be the Richer.

   Bean. Heres Ten go downs upon Re. *Moustrappa.*

Mous. Put *rem* to't or I renounce thee.

Bean. Renounce me Puss, not pledge me, thou salt Suburbian Hackney, not pledge me.

Mous. Well Mrs. *Beantosser*, I hant stood three years at Livery, and been hyr'd for 6*d.* a side on Holydaies, by Chimny-Sweepers, and Coblers 'Prentices, I hant so.——

Bean. Who has Mrs. Gillian flirt! Mrs. To and agen, who has?

Mous. I name no body, but touch a gall'd Horse, and he'l wince.

Bean. But I know who has been taken up in the common, and rode so many heats that they got the *French*, fashions that was ev'n your own sweet Monkey face, I scorne to go behind your crooked back to tell you so.

Steph. Fight Dog, fight Bear, still here's the juice of life.

Mous. I never danc'd naked at the *French* house for Mild-Sixpences, goody Lerry-come-twang.

Steph. Out, out, that's old, that's old.

Bean. Nor I never walk'd the Streets at Night, stark naked in a Buckram Suit, trim'd with black Ribons at the Codpeice, Mrs. Gincrack, Mrs. Nimble-go-through.

Steph. No, no, that thou didst not old Tru-peny, that was the Tailors Wife,——but 'tis old too.——

Bean. Who dress'd her self in mans cloathes to commit with another Womans Husband under his natural Wifes nose, not you?

Mous. Who goes ev'ry Night upon Water to see men swim on their backs, and show beastly triks, not *Beantosser*, no?

Bean. Who uses to be drunk at Tavernes tear her friends Wigs, and then give all the Money, she has for a frisk with the Drawer, not Mrs. Betty *Moustrappa*?

Mous. Who storms the Fort in private with a Leathern Gun.

Bean. Go y'are a mean spirited Crack, to be kep'd by a Club of 'Prentices: and so she praid me to tell ye.

Mous. 'Tis better to receive small ware then give broad Gold, as thou doest like a silly Trapes.

Bean. The foul names thy own, and I'le dash it down thy Throat.

Mous. Help, help, murther, she'l murther me.

Steph. Hold, hold, hold, keep the Kings Peace, I say keep the Peace, do you not tremble to use such bug words, if any body should hear you it would bring a scandal on the house, and make 'em think us Whores, Restore her nose *Moustrappa*, and you *Beantosser*, give back her Eye-brows: I say squeeze the juice, and let acts of Hostility cease, I was governaunt at home, and I will be justice of Peace here.

Bean. I will have no Justice.——

Steph. *Beantosser* be orderly, and thou shalt be my Clerk.

Mous. No private bribery to Corrupt Justice, and to show that I desire all things may be done without favour or selfishness, let *Beantosser* be hang'd, and give me her cloathes, and so I squeeze.

Bean. Justice, an't please your Worship, I'le swear the peace against her.

Steph. Bear back, bear back, good People don't press upon the Court.——Constable stand by me, and go fetch the offender before me.

Bean. I command thee to come before my Lord Justice. No——good people will ye ayd and assist me. ——We are resolved to assist Mr. Constable *Beantosser* to the death.——La you there now.

Mous. The Justice is an Ass, the Constable a Sheepshead, and all the good People a Whore, and a Baud: and so she pray'd me to tell ye.

Bean. Grant me a humming Warrant to compel her to come before you volens nolens of her own accord.

Steph. How, how, thou art an evil Counsellor, and a

Traytor; thou seekest to deprive me of my honourable Imployment by force quoth'a, no, some wiser then some: I am a Justice of peace, and must keep the peace. But if I grant a Warrant to compel, I break the Peace. If she comes, she comes, all must be done in a peacefull way: Volens nolens quoth'a.

Bean. Right Worshipfull, 'tis a common way to grant a Warrant.

Steph. Ay, ay, 'tis so common that we Magistrates are all the worse for't, it makes justice so cheap that no People of fashion care for using any.

Bean. An't please your Worship,

Steph. Please me, and please thy self, I say still.

Bean. To accept this small present?

Steph. Hay! more Plots, how darst thou corrupt Justice, thou Treacherous Strumpet! devour the bowels that gave thee Suck? Now do I know she wants Justice, because she would buy it—Clerk, take up the Bribery, and give it to the poor: since my Clerk is absent I will vouchsafe to do it my self.——But did this audacious Tatter-de-mallion declare with her own Corporal voyce, that she would not come before us?

Mous. I did, and I do again send thee word by my self, that thou shalt come before me,——If thou wilt not, I command thee to stay there,——and so I squeeze.

Steph. Does the Rebel send word, her self being present, that she will not appear?——it stands not with our high place to put up such affronts.——Head-Constable, knock her down, and keep the Peace.

[Beantosser *and* Moustrappa *fight.*

Steph. So now the whole Courts in an uproar, fight, 'till the Devil part you.——Hold, hold, fall off, and unite against the common Enemy.

Enter Hectorio, *and* Drinkallup, *drunk and Singing.*

Drink. Francky, *was his name a,*
    And Francky *was his name a ;*

His Beard was black, and his Gills were Red,
And his Bill was all of the same a.
With weapon full sharp, he fought 'till he was dead,
With a Heycock of the game a,
And Francky *was his name a,*
And with weapon &c.

Hect.   Francky's *dead, and gon a,*
    Poor Franchy's *dead, and gon a :*
Thy browes are black, and thy lips are Red,
And thy bellies soft as the down a.
Let me be thy Worm, and at every turn,
I will tickle thy flesh, and bone a.
    Then pri'thee cease they moan a,
    Since Francky's *dead, and gon a.*
    Let me &c.——

Steph. Silence in the Court, to keep a sound Peace, I make you both my High-Constables of *Westminister.*

Bean. ⎫
Mous. ⎭ Agreed, agreed.

Steph. Then by Virtue of my Warrant, which shall be made when we are at leisure, bring those disturbers of the Peace before me.

Bean. Woman, leave thy babbling, and come before the Justice.

Mous. Hectorio, be uncover'd in the Court, and obey the Officers.

Hect. What Court? what Officers?

Bean. Why *Stephania* is Justice of Whorum, and we are both Head-Constables.

Hect. Then Officers, look to your Throats, for there will be above Ten thousand up in Armes to Night. Sings.——*And their bellies soft as the down a.*

Steph. He has confest, and shall be hang'd 'till he's dead. Come thou Rake-hell, villain, dog, where are they, what's their design, who leads 'em on, who brings 'em

off, make his *Mittimus,* before he answers, and send him
to *Tyburn.*

Hect. Old touch and go, why so hasty?——My Lord
Bacchus leads 'em on: my Lady *Venus* brings 'em off:
their design is to rise up in their Beds, at midnight, to
stab all the Women, and behead all the Virgins they
Catch.

Drink. Sings——*With a Hey-cock of the game a.*

Bean. O inhumane *Canibals*!

Mous. Let 'em do their worst, the Women will be
hard enough for 'em, man to man.

Steph. And I believe the Virgins had notice of their
design, for there is not one left in my Liberties: Head-
constables, dispatch this *Westminster* Wedding, I say,
tye 'em up.

Bean. Won't your Worship examine the Woman?

Steph. I say, take her away, shes a Pick-pocket I
know, by her lac'd shooes: besides, heark ye, she's a
Witch, she carries an enchanted Ring about her which
turns Rich men to beggers, and makes an Ass of a
Justice of Peace.

Drink. Gentlemen of the Jury, this Villain is no
honester then he should be, he rob'd me of a dozen of
precious Turpentine guilt Nutmegs, and a Pewter
Squirt.

Hect. Which is flat felony, for that's the Iron work
to her Plough, without which it must stand still, and
her Familiars must starve: and so she prayed me to
tell ye.

Drink. But because the old Rogue is a true friend to
the Chuck-office, I care not much if I save him, therefore you may bring in the Fellony, Man-slaughter.

Hect. Gentlemen, I am a Witness for the King, and
so lets squeeze all round.

Mous. Art thou her Cozen after the flesh?

Drink. No, he is my Husband's Brother, for they tumbl'd both in one Belly.

Bean. Then thy Husband has a whole Legion of Brothers, for halfe the Town have tumbl'd in the same place: and so she pray'd me to tell ye.

Steph. Woman, put me in good Bail, or take her away Jaylor.

Hect. Hold, hold, what Bail dost thou demand?

Steph. Two substantial Citizens, Aldermens fellowes, or common Councel men, but no Cuckolds.

Drink. No Cuckolds, Jaylor take me away,——hold, heark you, If you'l take a Hundred that are Cuckolds, by the help of my friends here they shall be produc'd presently.——Nay don't bob down your heads, I did but try him.

Steph. No, no! no Cuckolds.

Hect. This is flat Tyrany, thou maist as well demand a Tribute of Maiden-heads in the Teens: but Miracles are ceas'd.

Steph. What is this notorious talking Rogue in for?

Mous. For Robbing of the Vestry.

Steph. How Sirrah, who made you a Church-Warden?

Mous. 'Tis but a Vestry matter, and may be agreed at the next Tavern.

Bean. Who will pay Scot and lot, as they say, and serve in all under Offices of trouble, if every Rascal shall usurp that very Office, where they may reward themselves?

Steph. Ay, without Authority, or paying a farthing for't, when 'tis well known substantial House-keepers have given hundreds for't.

Bean. Yes, and thriv'd upon't too, with a blessing on their pious endeavours.

Steph. Head Constables take 'em away to *Limbo.*

Hect. We defie thee, and thy Head-Constables, to mortal battle.

Steph. Then blood will ensue: and so she prai'd me
to tell ye.——Sound a charge, and keep the Peace.
> [*Musick plays, they dance, and* Exeunt.

Act III. Scene 2.

Enter Ariel, *and* Quakero.

Ariel *Sings.*

*F*OLLOW *me, follow me, hey jolly* Robin.
    The Moon shines bright,
    And Women are light,
And most men had rather eat then fight.
    Then leave off your Coging.
And follow me, and follow me hey jolly Robin.

Quak. Four corners on my bed,
    Four beauties there ly spred.
    If any evil come to me,
    O goodness sweet deliver me.

Blessed be thanked, it is now again departed; this
Charme I learn'd in the days of my *Paganis-me*, before
I attain'd to the in-working and the bowel-yernings of
the outgoing of the over-flowings; but now that I am
mounted into the Saddle, and exalted to the House top,
and lifted on the sounding Tub of reformation, I am
above the Fruit-mongers of the hard Streets of stony-
heartedness: and I am above thee Satan——ha it
cometh again.

    Four corners on my bed.

Ariel *Sings.*

Turn thy Stocking, and tye thy Shooe hard.
Thy mouth being wash'd, and wip'd thy beard.
  Come away, come lets be jogging.
    Bo, bo, bo, bo,
  Heark, heark, how the Bettern bellows :
  Now is the time for good fellows.

To it—to it—to it—to it.
  The Citizens Wife.
Leads a merry, merry life,
While her Husband at home does grunt and groan.
Whoo whoo oo oo oo—whoo ooo oo.
Alas poor man he is sick of the yellowes.
  Cuckoe, cuckoe.
Heark, heark, what the little birds tells us.
  Cuckoe, cuckoe, cuckoe.

Quak. Torment me no more thou Hobgoblin, thou *Robin*-goodfellow, thou *Will* with a wisp, thou Spright, thou Fairy, thou, thou nothing, thou something——ha, what should this be, assuredly here hath been some Crouder slain against his consent, or murther'd wrong-fully, or else 'tis the Soul of some profane Singing-man that rejoyceth and gibeth at the death of the Duke my father, Oh! O! O! it comes again.
  Four corners on my bed,
  Four beauties——

      Ariel *Sings.*
Youth, youth of mortal race, give ear,
  Thy Daddies dead, thy Daddies dead.
To Stocks his feet, to Pillory his Ear,
To whip of thong his flesh is ay turned ;
  And tough battoon does thump his bone.
O hone, O hone, O hone, O hone.
    Then little youth Nandy.
    Drink Ale and Brandy.
His knell is hourly rung on his back.
Heark now I hear it, thwick, thwick, thwack,
    Thwick &c.——thwack.

Quak. This dolefull madrigal sayes my Father is in *Limbo*, that is *Mortus est*, that is, he is dead, that is, he is departed, he is gone, he is fled, he is no more; he is, he is, I say, he is, that is, he is not.

His feet Stock-fish, his ears Pilchards, his flesh
   Thornback, and Tough Battoon does thump his bone.
O hone, O hone, O hone, O hone.

Friend *Quakero*, this is no mortal business, though
thou hast done Satan right noteable service in perverting
many, believe him not, I say believe him not : hast thou
forgot how it was resolv'd in a full dispute, where a
friend, ev'n *Guly Penno*, declared that Satan was a lyer,
nay thou hast not forgot, believe him not, yet I will go
to find out and be satisfi'd in the truth of the lye.

   Ariel. *Thwick, thwick, thwick,* &c.   [*Exit* Ariel.

   Quak. Hark, it is there again, it luggeth me by the
Ears, even as a Swine is lugged by a Mastiffe-dog : or
as one of your wicked Idolatrous Misses is led by the
rattling of a guilt Coach, or as, as I say, or as ah ha em,
or as ah a aa.

So much for this time.   [*Exit* Quakero.

The End of the Third Act.

Act IV. Scene 1.

Enter Prospero, *and* Ariel. Prospero *eating a peece of*
Bread and Butter.

Pros. NOW does the charm'd impostume of my Plot
          Swell to a head, and begin to suppurate,
If I can make *Mantua's* Infant Duke,
Switchel my young giglet *Dorinda*.
Sincere *Quakero* to my power bends,
And shall with my discreet *Miranda* yoak,
Or be tormented ever here,
In my enchanted Castle of *Bridewellow*.
Great pity 'tis——for he's a pretty fellow.
Ariel!

   Ari. What says my mighty and most potent Master.

Pros. How do these right puissant Ragamuffins bear their durance?

Ari. The Duke with haughty meen, for lack of food,
Sits cracking Fleas, and sucking of their blood.
With him is good *Gonzale.*

Pros. Is he so, Adsbud.

[*Throwes away his Bread and Butter, in passion.*

Ari. From eyes of Glass the gummy tears that fall
Down Iv'ry beard like Christal vermine crawl.
The rest are picking strawes, and so that's all.

Pros. Where is *Quakero*, that young Princely Sprout?

Ari. Like Lanthorn-jack I led him all about,
And now he's blowing of his nailes without.

Pros. Alass poor Trout.

Ari. I have so gally'd 'em, 'twould make your Graces hair stand on end to see how they look; though your heart more stony was then Coblers wax i'th' dog days, 'twould make it in your mouth dissolve like Culvers dung.

Pros. Do'st thou think so Spirit?

Ari. It makes mine open and shut, open and shut, like a fat Hostesses greazy Pouch, so it does: and then the poor old Gentlewoman and her daughters have almost torne one another to peeces——I pity them.

Pros. And I will——hast thou that art so young a Spirit, so little too——had a touch a feeling of their Case, and shall not I have a relish?——Well, *Ariel* go let a Table be brought to them furnish'd with most sumptuous Cates, but when they try to eat, let two great Babboons be let down with ropes to snatch it away.

Ari. O Sir *Punchanello* did that at the Play-house.

Pros. Did he so——then bend thy ayry ear.

[*Whispers.*

Ari. More toyle——I pry'thee now let me mind thee of thy promise then——where is my Two-penny Custard?

Pros. Ho now moody, doe'st thou murmure?

Ari. No my Lord!

Pros. Thou ly'st, Malignant thing, thou dost.

Ari. I pri'the my Lord, ben't so touchy.

Pros. Hast thou forgot the hairy Woman I freed thee from, who sent thee ev'ry morning down her Gormandizing throat with a Candle and Lanthorn, to tread the Ooze of the salt deep?——At other times she made thee pass up against the strong Northern blasts, when the capacious Bay was bak'd with brandy 'till thou hadst clear'd thy passage to her nose, on whose sulph'rous top thou sat'st Singing like a little Chimny Sweeper, hast thou forgot her?

Ari. No my dread Lord.

Pros. If thou more murmur'st, in some small dimple of her Cheek I'le peg thee, where Twelve Sommers more thou shalt lye stewing like a Maggot in a *Holland* Cheese.

Ari. O pardon great Sir this once, and I will be a good Boy, and never do so more.

Pros. Then do as I commanded, but make hast least the Conjurers of to'ther House steal the Invention—— thou know'st they snatch at all Ingenious tricks.

Ari. I fly most potent Sir.   [*Exit* Ariel *flying.*

Pros. Now for the infant Duke of *Mantua. Hypolito* my Child come forth.

           Enter Hypolito *playing with Nickers.*

Hyp. Anan, anan, forsooth——you Sir, don't you stir the Nickers, I'le play out my game presently.

Pros. Come gentle youth, exalt thy ducal chin, for thou shalt have a Wife my boy.

Hyp. A Wife Sir! what's that, I never saw it?

Pros. No my boy, but they are now so common, young men can hardly walk the streets for them.

Hyp. Don't go away, you Sir, I do but stay for a Wife, and then I'le play out my game——O good Sir, let me have it quickly.

Pros. And so thou shalt, for my daughters sake; if he should know Wives were growing out of fashion, I fear he would not marry, for the stripling has a gentile fancy, I see by the neatness of his cloathes.

Hyp. Will it play at Bullet with me?

Pros. Ay and Cat, and Trap-ball too.

Hyp. What is it like Sir? what is it like?

Pros. 'Tis so inconstant I scarce know what to liken it to, 'tis still unsatisfi'd, restless and wrigling like an Eel.

Hyp. O pray let me have it then; I love Eels mightily.

Pros. But like an Eel 'twill slip from thee.

Hyp. But I'le bite it by the tail then, and shake it 'till it lies still.

Pros. A shrew'd youth! well thou shalt have it, 'tis beautiful as a Colly-flower, but like that too, when 'tis kep'd long, nothing is more unpleasant.

Hyp. O Sir! I won't keep it long.

Pros. A very hopeful Lad!——But it won't part from thee.

Hyp. Then I'le beat it, and kick it, and run away from't.

Pros. Modishly said y'gad, still hopeful——but she'l save thee that trouble, and leave thee as soon any other will keep her; for she's wild and skittish as an unbackt Colt.

Hyp. Is it like a Colt? O Lemine! then I'le ride upon't.

Pros. Alass poor youth! thou wilt soon be tir'd, and thrown off.

Hyp. No Sir, I shall never be weary of Riding; and I'le hold so fast by the Mane and the Tail, that I won't fall off.

Pros. O fie, you must not use it like a Beast.

Hyp. What must I do with it then?

Pros. Why you must eat and drink with it.

Hyp. What is it a Fork, and an Earthern-Pot then?

Pros. No, but she may make Forkes, and crack too many Pots.

Hyp. Then she shall teach me to make Forks.

Pros. Hold there——you must enjoy none but her.

Hyp. Enjoy, ah ha! enjoy! what a word is there? enjoy! O rare!——what is enjoy Sir?

Pros. Why, that is to be happy.

Hyp. Enjoy to be happy, then I'le enjoy all the Wives in the World;——For I love to be happy Sir: enjoy!

Pros. I'le tell you more hereafter; go in and read your Horn-book, that Treatise of Abstruse Philosophy I gave you last.

Hyp. I go forsooth.   [*Exit* Hypolito.

Pros. Now by my best hopes, a shrew'd youth, a very shrew'd youth, and a notable head-peace——I'm glad he's grown so prudent. If all that Marry in this Age of liberty were so Politick, we should see better times.

Enter Hypolito *crying.*

Hyp. O lo! o lo! o lo! Oh, ho, ho, ho!

Pros. What's the matter? what grand intrigue of Fate can reach to the disturbance of thy manly Soul?

Hyp. Manly Soul, quoth a, 'twould disturb any mans Soul: I'me undone Sir, while I was talking with you about a Wife, Tom *Bully* stole away my stones.

Pros. Hah thy stones, what stones?

Hyp. Why my bowling stones. O ho ho, now I can't teach my Wife to play Nickers.

Pros. I'me glad 'tis no worse; O fie, fie my Lord, you must leave off this boyes Play now, and learn to play with Children; go, go in.

Hyp. By never, I'le pay that Rogue Tom *Bully*, when I catch him.   [*Exit* Hypolito.

Pros. Now I must instruct my Daughters.

  Long sleeps and pleasures follow ev'ry Novice:
  But plots and cares, perplex grave men of
   Office.
  Ye Gods!

More blest are men of mean and low condition,
Then *Bridewell*-keeper is, or sage *Magician*.

[*Exit* Prospero.

Act IV. Scene 2.

Enter Miranda, *and* Dorinda.

Dor. OH Sister! I have such a twittering after this Husband,
And my mouth doth so run in a civil way.

Mir. Are you not breeding Teeth Sister?

Dor. Zooks, if I am the King, shall know't.

Mir. 'Vads Sister, ever since my Father told me of it, which is at least six Hours ago, I can't rest Day, nor Night, for ought I know.

Dor. Its hole's hereabout, whereof looky' my Father said that it should get me with Child pray.

Mir. O lo! get you with Child, what's that?

Dor. I can't tell, but I do so shake and laugh when I think of't.

Mir. Heigh ho! whereof Sister you are affraid?——
Let it come to me, vads Sister I won't be affraid.

Dor. Zooks Sister, if my Father should send a hundred to get me with Child in a civil way, I wouldn't be affraid.

Mir. O but Sister, whereof looky', my Father said that a Husband was wild as a Cock-Sparrow or a Curl'd-Lamb, that he did now pray.

Dor. Then I would chirrip to't, and make it hop, and stroak it, and make it wag its tayl and Cry blea, 'till it 'twas as tame as a little Lap-dog, but my Father says they are always gentle at home: and wild abroad.

Mir. Whereof Sister heark ye, now lets leave this idle talk, and play the *Scotch* Morice.

Dor. Then I'le play forward, and backward, for that's the way now.

Mir. No I won't play Boyes play,——I'le tell you what, you should be a School Mistriss, and——

Dor. No Sister, no I'le tell you what? You should be a Citizens Wife pray, and so I should be a Lord looky', and I should come in a Golden-Coach and be your Husbands Customer.

Mir. Ay 'vads that's pretty.

Dor. So I should meet you at the Play-House, and say Madam looky' 'tis a thousand pitties such a glazing Di'mond of beauty should be the Slave of a dull Mechanick Cit. and cry what d'ee lack? Whereof you should cry then, O Lord Sir, you are mistaken Zooks.

Mir. O Lord Sir, you are mistaken Zooks!

Dor. Then I should say Dam'ee Madam! you are a necklace for a Prince, I'le settle Three Pounds a Year upon you, and you shall have a Silver Baby, and a Silver house, and eat nothing but Golden Custards, and Silver-Stew'd-Pruines: then you should say whereof you have got a Wife of your own, my Lord?

Mir. Then you should say whereof you have gotten a wife of your own my Lord.

Dor. Then I should throw my Wig, and say, Oh Madam! if you love me, name her not. She's so dull and musty, the very thought of her will make me swoun, Dam her. But you I doat upon. So then you should let me lye with you in a Civil way.

Mir. O ay, ay, I love that y'vads!

Dor. And then another should lye with you, and another, so at last you should be catch'd in a Baudy-house with your Husbands under 'Prentice looky', and so be brought to *Bridewell* as Mrs. *Tweedlebum* was t'other day.

Mir. No, no, Sister, I wont play so——I'le tell y' what, lets play Truss-fayl, do pray now Sister.

Dor. Come then, I'le lye down first.

Mir. Truss.

Dor. Fayl.

Mir. Send me well upon my Grey Nags taile. O Sister, Sister! here's the Husband thing coming.

Enter Hypolito *reading gravely in a Horn-Book.*

Dor. Looky', looky', O sweet Father its Leggs are twice as long as ours.

Mir. What's that before so trim'd up with yellow Pissabeds, and green Blew Bottles.

Dor. See, see it pulls off half its head.

Mir. Run Sister, run, I'me so affraid 'twill pull your head off too.

Dor. Zooks! I would rather lose a hundred Heads if I had 'em, then stir a foot.

Mir. Oh! it looks angry, I'me so affraid for you Sister.

Dor. Fear not me, if I offend it, I'le ly down and paw it with my Four-feet, as our Shock does when we beat it.

Pros. (Within) Miranda, Miranda!

Dor. O Sister! my Father calls you,——whereof she sayes she won't come for'oth.

Mir. She fibs, she fibs Father,——I wou'd come, but I am not here for'oth——you spiteful pissabed Slut.

Dor. But you are here for'oth.

Mir. I wonder y'are so simple Sister, as if I could not tell where I am better then you——for ought I know.

Dor. I will take Husband first that I will.

Mir. Hussey, am not I the Elder?

Dor. Then you shou'dn't set your Wit against a Child.

Mir. Well then Sister, I'le tell y'what, wee'l play heads or tails, who goes first, that's fair now, e'nt it?

Dor. Ay, and she that don't win shall lose and keep the door.

Mir. Well ther's a good Girle, now toss up.

Dor. A ha! my tails turn'd up, you must watch.

Mir. Good dear Sister have done quickly, prithee do for because you know why Sister.   [*Exit* Miranda.

Hyp. *Prospero* has often told me, Nature makes nothing in vain, why then is this kip kap here——'tis not *aw* nor *e* nor *ee* nor *oo*, nor *l m n o-q-py* you——it strangely puzles me; I'le ask him when I see him next.

Dor. Thing, thing, fine long thing.

Hyp. Bessy come bunny, come buy me some lace Sugarcandy, Cloves and Mace. Sure I am ready for a Wife now, I can read my abstruse Horn *Philosophy*.

Dor. O Rare thing, it talkes just like one of us.

Hyp. Ha——what thing is that? Sure 'tis some Infant of the Park, drest in her Mothers gayest beams of Impudence, and sent down here to play at Hemp and Beetle; but stay, is not this that thing call'd Wife? What art thou, thou fleering thing?

Dor. Alass I am a Woman, and my Father says I must be a Wife in a Civil way, pray thing don't be angry.

Hyp. Angry, no, I'le sooner break my Trapstick; mun if thou art that thing call'd Wife, which troubles poor men so that they can't Wench in quiet——*Prospero* says that I must enjoy thee.

Dor. If thou art that thing call'd Husband which art alwayes sullen and niggardly at home, but merry and expensive abroad, which feedst a Wife with tripe and Cowes heels, and treatest a Mrs. with Woodcock and Teale, and fine things, and at last turnest off a Wife with just enough to buy Bread and Cheese and worsted Farendine, but maintainst thy Miss like a Princess, my Father says thou must get me with Child for ought I know.

Hyp. Get thee with Child, O lo! whats that?

Dor. Whereof I can't tell, but I think you must dig it out of the Parsly-bed.

Hyp. Show me the Parsly-bed then.

Dor. I won't, you ha' got nothing to dig with: you said you must enjoy me, what's that pray?

Hyp. Why *Prospero* says you are like a Colt, and then you should be backt.

Dor. Phoe, I won't play so.

Hyp. Won't you, then look to't, for you are but a Colly-flower, and though y'are so proud to day you'l stink to morrow.

Dor. Zooks this is the silli'st Husband-thing I ever saw: I'le run into the Garden, and teach him more wit in a civil way.

Hyp. Nay if you run from me like an Eel, I'le bite you by the tail.   [*Exeunt running after each other.*

Pros. (Within.) *Miranda! Dorinda!* Daughters, Daughters!

Enter Miranda *hastily.*

Mir. Oh I'me glad my Father comes, for when Fire and Flax are together, none knows how soon mischeif may be done. *Dorinda, Dorinda,* my Fathers coming.

Enter Dorinda *and* Hypolito *hastily.* Hypolito *runs off.*

Dor. O Sister pray lets Dance our new Heroick Song that our Father mayn't know who was here.

They Sing and Dance. Enter Prospero *observing them.*

Mir. *Here comes a lusty Wooer, my dildin, my darling.*
    Here comes a lusty Wooer Lady bright and shining.

Dor. *I Wooe for one of your fair Daughters, my dildin,*
        my darling.
    I Wooe for &c.——Lady bright &c.

Mir. *I'm glad I have one for you my dild, &c.*
    I'm glad &c.——Lady bright, &c.

Dor. *She looks too brown upon me my dild, &c.*
    She looks, &c.——Lady &c.

Pros. Enough, enough, all this won't blind me, come, come, come stand, stand you here, and you there, nay, nay, nay, no whim'pring:

Mir. Indeed, and indeed, pray Father, I did but keep the door.

Pros. Didst thou keep the door for thy younger Sister?

Mir. Yes forsooth, pray Father, that I did.

Pros. Blessing on thy pretty heart, cherish that gentile Motherly humour, thou hast a generous Soul; and since I see thy mind so apt to take the light impression of a modish Love, I will unfold a secret to thee——That Creature, that thou saw'st, is a kind of a Creature which is much like another Creature, that shall be nameless, and that's *Quakero.*

Mir. But Father, pray Father, shall that *Quakero* Creature be my Husband? You said I should have a Husband before she, that you did.

Pros. Shortly my *Miranda* thou shalt see the flower of this bud; this Chit, chit, chit, chit, Cock-sparrow husband may serve thy Sister well enough, thou shalt have a ho-ho-ho-ho-Husband, a Horseman, go in I'le provide for thee.

Mir. Let me have the ho-ho, quickly then pray Father.   [*Going out she returns again.*

Father, Father, I forgot to make my Cursy; b'wy Father.   [*Exit* Miranda.

Pros. Come hither *Dorinda*, why saw you this Husband without my order?

Dor. Who I! truely I didn't saw'd him 'twas he saw'd me.

Pros. Come, come, your Sister told me all.

Dor. Then she fibs for ought I know, for she would ha' seen him first, if I would ha' let her.

Pros. Tell me what past between you?

Dor. Nothing pass'd between us but our great dog Towzer.

Pros. What did he do t'ee? come confess.

Dor. He did nothing, but I am affraid he wou'd if you hadn't come.

Pros. Why, why speak out?

Dor. Because he came towards me with his tail up as stiffe as any thing.

Pros. Ha, I thought as much; wha what did he do then? the truth, I charge you.

Dor. Why he did nothing but walk to his Kennel.

Pros. Walk'd to his Kennel——who?

Dor. Why our great dog Towzer.

Pros. Pho, thou understandst me not, what did the Husband-thing do to thee?

Dor. Why nothing at all, for just as we got to the Parsly-bed, you frighten'd it away.

Pros. I charge you see it no more, 'twill Poyson you, and make you swell as big as a house.

Dor. Not see it, I'le run th'rough Nine Walls, but I'le see it, and have it to, though it make me swell 'till I break in peeces.

Pros. Go get you in, y'are a naughty Girle.

Dor. The World's come to a very fine pass for ought I know, one can't play with a thing an hour or two alone, or be in bed with a man, but one must be naught: I won't endure it much long, that I wont so.

[*Exit* Dorinda.

Pros. So—my wishing Pipe
Has swell'd my hopeing Cistern to a Flood.
Dorind' and *Polito's* agreed, that's good.
Now for *Miranda*, and the youth *Quakero*;
When they are coupl'd too——there ends my
    Care'o.   [*Exit* Prospero.

Act IV. Scene 3.

Enter Alonzo, Gonzalo, *and* Antonio.

Gon. MY hands are so tyr'd with stareing about for meat, that my feet can look no further——I must rest my old bones.

Alon. Old Lord I cannot blame thee, for I am seiz'd

with such a griping, that I cannot rest.——My Courtyers
us'd to tell me I had no humane imperfection; But here
I will put off my hose and keep it no longer for my
Flatterers.   [*Musick as in Air.*

Gon. Ha, these are a sort of doggish greedy Devils,
come to devour the meat e'r 'tis dish'd up.

Anto. Do not for one repulse forgo the great design
you were about to act.

Gon. Oh help, help, something unseen has ty'd my
hands behind me.

Alon. Mine are stollen away too, and 'tis well for
'em, for my mouth is grown so angry for want of meat,
that if they should again appear empty it would devour
them.

Anto. Sure tis the Devils hock-tide, for mine are
bound too.

Musick.

Alon. O heark my fiends,
    I fear we shall behold another horrid sound.

Gon. The Devil takes his time when we are bound.

Alon. He thinks to save his Bacon, feeble feind,
    But with bound hands our hands we will unbind.

Enter Ariel *Singing.*

Song.

Dry your eyes, and cease your howling :
For your Broath is set a Cooling.
While y'are in this Castle staying,
Eat and Drink, ne'r talk of paying.
Wine and Women here are plenty,
You shall tast of ev'ry dainty.
And as soon as you are weary,
Here are Crowds to make you merry.   [*Exit* Ariel.

Alon. I marry this is comfortable.

Anto. No Musick like that which powder'd Beef Sings,
    A consort of Carrets with hey ding a ding.

Gon. Wee'l dye for our meat, then our lives shall maintain.

No butt'ring of Parsnips like long live and raign.

O for a dainty vision of butter'd *Neptunes Tritons*

And *Nereides*.

Two Devils descend, bringing down a Table with meat and drink on it.

Anto. See my Lord a stately Banquet, adzooks!

Gon. First come, first serv'd.

Alon. Happy man catch a Mackarell——But stay is not this meat and drink brought to Poyson us?

Gon. Here may be more Spirit of Sulphur: but hungers sharp, and I will tast in spight of the Devil.

Anto. And I will have a Soop.

Alon. If both resolve, I'le take my part; Devil do thy worst.

[*As they try to eat,* Gonzalo *and* Antonio *are snatch'd up into the Air, and* Alonzo *sinks with the Table out of sight.*

The End of the Fourth Act.

Act V. Scene 1.

Enter Quakero, *and* Ariel.

Quak. I WILL be no longer seduced by Yea and Nay, I defie thee.

Ari. I defie thee.

Quak. Thou art a Torch of Darkness, and a Snuff of the Candle of the Socket, of the Dominion of Darkness.

Ari. O minion of Darkness.

Quak. Thou liest, I am no minion of Darkness, for look thee, a lye is a lye, but the truth is not a lye, and therefore thou art a lyer because thou lyest, as one of us hath he is sweetly in his Scourge-stick of Prophanishness, he is a right precious one, truely, truly.

Ari. You lye, truely.

Quak. Out thou reproacher of friends, thou Bearward of the Bull and Mouth, thou Lambskinner of *Lumbard-street*, thou waspish Woolf of *Westminster*, thou a a, I say thou um ah a, thou-avaunt, begone, fly, vanish, I defie thee, I abhor thee, I renounce thee, yea, I will scare-crow thee, I will top and scourge thee, and I will hum-guig thee, for I see by thy invisible Hornes that thou art the very Devil.

Ari. Thou art the very Devil.

Quak. Out *Dagon, Bell* and the *Dragon,* I knew thee long agone.

Ari. I knew thee long agone.

Quak. What dost thou know of me? Speak, say thy worst, what dost thou know of me?——I may fail, but I cannot fall, for I am a Friend——a Chosen——One of Us.

Ari. A Chosen one of Us.

Quak. None of thy Usses, Satan, none of thy Usses; therefore cease to torment me, for I will not speak one word more.

Ari. One word more.

Quak. Nay but I will not——I will Padlock my lips with Patience, and set the Porter of peaceishness at the Wicket of my Mouth, who shall knock thee down with the Silver head of saving-gableness which is on the long Cane of Conscientious Reproof: So that thou shalt no more enter into the Meeting-House of my heart, look thee——*Obadiah Cod,* one of Us, who now sleep—eth did declare soundly what thou wert, and I find it all as Poor Cod said.

Ari. Alas poor Codshead.

Quak. Mock on, mock on, I will try if thou wilt answer me while I sing my Sorrows to the snapping of my Thumbes: thy gibing is all but nonsense.

Ari. All but nonsense.

Quakero *Sings.* Ariel *answers like an Eccho.*

Quak. How dost do ?
Ari. How dost do ?
Quak. What's that to you ?
Ari. Whats &c.
Quak. Pull out thy whistle, and tune up thy Pipe.
Ari. Pull &c.
Quak. Under yonder hollow Tree, Nan *lyes asleep.*
Ari. Under &c.
Quak. Her thing is her own, and I'le bounce it anon.
Ari. ————and I'le bounce &c.
Quak. What care I for treasure, if Nanny *but smile ?*
Ari. ————if Nanny &c.
Quak. Within this shining place,
  There's not a better Face ;
 Faith now she's down, there I'le get her with Child.
Ari. *Kind* Nanny *smiles, and she*
  Does sigh and snore for thee ;
  O strange Simplicity,
  Follow me, follow me, and thou shalt see.

Quak. Does *Nanny* sigh and snore for me, O Lo!
umph, I ham mollified : *Nanny* snore for me——think
of thy Soul *Quakero,* I say think of thy Soul; if the flesh
prevail, thy Soul is but a dead man.

Ari. Follow me, follow me, and thou shalt see.

Quak. Heark I am called again——this voyce may be
a good Vision——go *Quakero,* I say go——but it may
be a snare, a trick to draw me into derision, go not
Quakero nay, but I will not go——*Nanny* sigh and snore
for me, O dear!

Ari. Follow &c.

Quak. Again——Well I will go and advise with
Friends, but why shouldst thou advise, look thee, thy
intention is good, though the Action may wander, it
matters not, I say, it matters not.——*Nanny* sigh and
snore for me, I will go——yea assuredly I will.

Ari. Follow &c.

Quak. Nay but I will not, it shall not be said *Quakero* followe'd the Devil.——But look thee, go thou before, and I will come after,——if that will do.   [*Exeunt.*

Act V. Scene 2.

Enter Prospero *and* Miranda *at one Door.* Ariel *and* Quakero *at another.* Ariel *goes off immediately.*

Pros. A DVANCE the frizled frouzes of thine Eyes, and glout on yon fair thing.

Mir. O dear sweet Father, is that a ho ho ho a Horseman, Husband?

Pros. It is my Girle, and a yerker too; i'faith were he not tir'd with seeking of his Company, he would play thee such Horse-tricks, would make thee sneer again.

Mir. 'Tis a most crumptious thing; i'vads if you'l let me have it, I'le make no more dirt Pies, nor eat the Chalk you score with, nor spoil your Garden to play with the Carrets before they are ripe——pray sweet honey Father.

Pros. Well I'le leave ye together. But I charge you let him not touch your honour.

Mir. My honour O lo! pray what is that father?

Pros. 'Tis a kind of fluttering Blood, which haunts the head and hinder parts of men, some call it life-Blood, because death often ensues when those tender parts are touch'd: in Women its seat is on the nose, and on the——

Mir. Where else pray tell me, that I may defend it.

Pros. That's the ready way to make it be betrai'd. ——No Child of my bowels, thou shalt never know thy honour from me.

Mir. Now do I long to have this secret of my honour open'd: prythee now, Father tell me where 'tis.

Pros. Why,——I know not what to say——On thy Elbow.

Mir. My Elbow, O lemine! fear it not then, for my honour is so hard with being thump'd and leand upon, that a hundred touches can't hurt it.

Pros. All falls out yet even as my Soul would wish, but I must watch, I don't like this leering *Quakero*, such zealous youthes are very Tyrants in secret.

[*Exit* Prospero.

Quak. Assuredly Satan thou hast told truth, for she is here; But yet thou art a lyer Satan, for she is not here, that is to say, she sleepeth not, I will declare before her umph a ha h.——

Most finest, most delicatest, and most lusciousest Creature, whose face is more delicious then a Pot of Ale with Sugar and Nutmeg, after a long Exercise.

Mir. Ha.

Quak. The favour of whose breath is more comfortable then the hot steam of a Sundays Dinner.

Mir. O Lo!

Quak. Whose Paps are whiter then two Norfolke-dumplins stufft with Plums——and softer then Quaking-puddings.

Mir. Why did you ever feel my Bubbies?

Quak. Nay assuredly, but I hope I shall——

Quak. Whose soft Palmes are pleasanter then a warm cloath to my Sweaty-back, or a hot Trencher to an akeing Belly.

Mir. O rare!

Quak. Whose Legs are smoother then my Chin, on a Saturday-night, and sleeker then thy Elbowes.

Mir. O my honour, my honour, my Father sayes you must not touch my honour pray.

Quak. Nay Sister far, far be it from me to soyl thy honour. Thy nature is more inviteing then a Christn'ing-Bowl of warm red Wine deckt round with Lemon-peel.

Mir. Oh my dear ho, ho, ho, I can no longer forbear.
                                    [*She imbraces him.*

Quak. Ah Sister mine; Now I ham even like unto that little Creature called a Cat, when his back is stroaked, he longeth to play with his tail.

Mir. And what are I like then, tell me what I are like ?

Quak. Why thou are like a pretty little Mouse verily. ——But then I ham two-fold luck thee: first I ham like a Cat, and secondly I am not like a Cat.——First, I ham like a Cat, for when the Cat smells the pretty Mouse, he is restless and eager; Nay, he cannot stand still, but frisketh, and jumpeth, and dance-eth 'till he hath devoured hit;——In like sort, firstly, I ham like a Cat, look thee, for I am inflamed, and eager truely: nay, I am even ravenous after the pretty tender Mouse, as a Bear bereaved of her Whelps. But secondly, I ham not like a Cat, look thee; for that seeketh the destruction, and the nothingness of the Mouse, but I thirsteth for the Propagation, look thee, and the somethingness, yea the fullness of hit——ha, ha, hae.

Mir. And am I like a Mouse i'vads ?

Quak. Unfeignedly.

Mir. Then I'le run into my hole.

Quak. And I will pursue even unto thy very hole, till I have overtaken thee.   [*Exeunt.*

                    Enter Prospero *hastily.*

Pros. Ah how nimble this zealous youth is——*Miranda !*——*Miranda !*

                    Enter Miranda, *and* Quakero.

And you *Quakero*, come back, or I'le throw you over the Balcony, and try if you have as many lives as a Cat.

Mir. Zooks, Father you have spoiled the rarest play of Cat and Mouse.

Pros. Thou shalt be mouz'd my Girle, but every thing in season, *Rome* was not built in a day, go in and trust me.

Mir. Shan't my Puss go with me; come Puss, come little Puss.   [*Exit* Miranda.

Pros. Hypolito my Child!

Enter Hypolito.

Come hither discourse this trusty *Nicodemus*, 'till my return, you must be acquainted with him.

[*Exit* Prospero.

Hyp. Pray Mr. *Nichodemus*, what did your Periwig cost you?

Quak. Ha, ha, ha, he!

Hyp. Ha, ha, he, how much is, ha, ha, he!

Quak. I will be avenged of thee Satan!

Hyp. Sa--tan, my name is *Hypolito*!

Quak. I will no more stir up friends to despise Government, and teach them 'tis a great point of Faith, rather to beleive an ignorant upright Taylor, or a precious enlightened Weaver, then a Book-learned Tythmonger verily.

Hyp. Hey brave Boyes you Rogues Mr. *Nichodemus*, will you play at Nickers you Sir, or Spand-farthing?

Quak. Out thou lew'd scoffer, I ham a Professor.

Hyp. A Professor, what's that?

Quak. That is a friend.

Hyp. And what is a friend?

Quak. Why a friend is one of Us.

Hyp. And what is one of Us.

Quak. Why one of Us is a——I say is a—um a—ha, ha, ha, he.

Hyp. Pray Mr. *Nichodemus*, let me be one of Us, ha, ha, ha, he.

Quak. I would thou wert, I say, I would——thou wert, but thou knowest not the Splendour of the obscurity of the revealed secret, umph--ha, thou understandest not?

Hyp. Yes I understand you well enough, but only I don't know your meaning.

Quak. What Religion art thou of?

Hyp. Religion, why I am a Duke.

Quak. What Faith dost thou profess?

Hyp. Why Faith and Troth, and adznigs, and by this Cheese.

Quak. Ah thou art a beast, and shouldst be chastised; ——therefore provoke me not:——I say provoke me not.

Hyp. Not provoke thee——but I will provoke thee: take that.   [*Kicks him.*

Quak. I ham not provoked.

Hyp. Then have at the again.

Quak. I ham not provoked yet.

Hyp. There, then there.   [*Kicks him.*

Quak. Nay, but I ham not yet provoked.

Hyp. No then I'le wear out my Shooes, but I'le provoke thee; there, there, there, and there.
                                              [*Kicks him.*

Quak. Hold, hold, I say hold, for I ham provoked, and I will chastise thee.

              [*The* Quaker *throwes off his Coat, and beats*
                   Hypolito *'till he lyes as dead.*

Hyp. O murther, murther, I'le fight no more: you pull by the hair Mr. *Nichodemus.*

                   Enter Prospero.

Pros. What dismal noyse is this——ha! *Hypolito* dead, then all my toyl's in vain:——O thou unlucky chit, I wish I'de been betwattl'd, when I had to do with thee.

Quak. Unfeignedly I was provoked, therefore I say have Patience, that is to sayo be pacified.

Pros. Out thou stinking, sneaking Bastard, he's quite dead: If ever thou serv'st me so again, I'le whip thee 'till the Blood drops at thy heels.

Quak. Dead! then by Yea, and Nay, I never saw him in my life.

Pros. O cruel luck! *Ariel*, what ho my Spirit *Ariel*.
Enter Ariel.

Ari. What says my mighty, and most Potent Lord?

Pros. Most potent Lord! most Potent Fiddle-stick!
See thou lazy droan of a Spirit, what mischief here is
done.

Ari. O lo! O lo! O Laud! Ah poor *Polly*, how sadly
his finger's scratch'd; but I'le fly to Mother Damnables,
and fetch some Pilgrim salve to cure it.   [*Exit* Ariel.

Pros. Miranda! Dorinda!
Enter Miranda, *and* Dorinda.

O my Girles, we are all undone, look there *Dorinda*, thy
poor *Polly's* dead.

Mir. O my dear Puss-cat, shall us play Cat and
Mouse?

Pros. Touch him not you Harlotry baggage, why when
I say——come away.

Dor. Alass! What's worse then ill luck?

Enter Alonzo, Gonzalo, *and* Antonio, *as driven in by
Spirits.*

Alon. Never were Hogs so driv'n to *Rumford*, as we
are hunch'd along.

What my Boy *Quakero*, and alive, touch my Flesh.

Quak. My Father after the Flesh, O sorrowfull joy.

Pros. You stare as if you had never seen me: have
so short a time as 50 years made you forget *Prospero*?

Gon. How my good old Neighbour Duke *Prospero*!

Alon. The Devil 'tis: O strange, I thought he had
been hang'd long ago.

Anto. Laud, how a little time will change folkes, I
had quite forgot him, and yet I remember him as well
as if 'twere but yesterday.

Pros. Had I liv'd 'till now where you sent me, I had
been dead 20 years ago——Know 'twas I trappan'd you
to this my enchanted Castle of *Bridewello*, where I yet
govern, and am Lord Paramount. I meant to be friends

with you all, and Marry that strippling to my eldest
Girle; but see what he has done to the Infant Duke of
Mantua.

Gon. Never stir, if it be not honest little Duke *Polly*.

Anto. Alass poor Duke, as towardly a Child as ever
broke bit of bread.

Alon. And what dost thou now intend? we fear thee
not.

Pros. *Quakero* shall be hang'd, and you shall be all
tortur'd; ho within there, prepare the Pillory, the
Whipping-post, the Stocks, and Cat of Nine tailes——
entreat me not, dispatch.

Mir. I can hold no longer, O, ho, ho-ho-ho.

Quak. Ah, ha-ha-ha-e.   [*Enter Devils.*

Pros. Away with them, See it done.

   The Scene of Bridewell. Ariel *flyes down.*

Ari. Stay my most Potent Master, I come from the
sage *Urganda* of *Wildo streeto*, that renowned Enchantress, who has disarm'd all the Knights of the White
Spear and Nut-brown Shield: And that most mighty
Necromancer *Punchanello Alquiffe*, who with one breath
puffs Candle out, and in Rains Fire, makes Sea of
painted Clout to move, and Devils dance: by their ayd
I have compos'd a Suppositorial Ligneous puffe and
blow, which would recal life though Nine days lost, see
here 'tis come.

   Enter Devils with a great pair of Bellows.

Pros. 'Tis joyful newes.

Ari. All must assist in the Ceremony.

Pros. Come then let's about it.

Ari. Help, help Lordlings, and Ladies help
To raise up great Heroick whelp.

   Ariel *Sings.*
   Prospero, Prospero
   Looks feirce as a Hero ;
If Polly *should dye, poor I shall be killed I fearo.*

Chorus. *Then blow the Bellows, blow the Bellows, blow the Bellows blow; blow and puff, blow and puff, puff, puff, and blow, blow, blow.*
>   *Let not his Soul,*
>   *Get out of the hole*
> *And all shall be well I tro, tro, tro, &c.*

Pros. *We conjure thee to wake*
>   *By a Two-peny Cake,*
Alon. *By a Ginger-bread-role,*
Mir. *By a thing with a hole,*
Dor. *Which thou lov'st with thy Soul ;*
Gon. *By a Rattle and Drum,*
Anto. *By a great Sugar-plum,*
Quak. *As big as thy Thumb.*
Chorus. *Polly, Polly, Polly,*
>   *O Polly, Polly, Polly!*
>   *To dye is but folly.*
>   *For shame lye not there,*
>   *While thy Doxie is here.*

All. *How is't.*
Ari. *By th' Mass*
>   *As 'twas.*
All. *Alass.*
Ari. *Prospero, Prospero,*
>   *Looks, &c.*——As before.
Chorus. *Then blow the Bellows, &c.*——As before.

Pros. *We conjure thee agen*
>   *By a hobby Horse fine,*
Mir. *By thy Bullets and Cat-stick,*
Dor. *By thy Rearer and Trap-stick,*
Alon. *By thy stealers and Pickers,*
Gon.   *By thy Marbles and Nickers,*
Anto. *By thy Top and thy Gigg,*
Quak. *By thy Beard, and thy Wigg.*

Chorus. Polly, Polly, &c.——*All as before.*
> [*Then* Hypolito *rises.*

Ari.   Victoria, Victoria! He lives, he lives, he lives.
> [*They Dance confus'dly round him.*

Chorus. *Then let's hugg him, and lugg him, and tugg him, and smugg him : with a hey brave* Polly, *and ho brave* Polly *and take him, and shake him, and wake him, and never forsake him, with a hey brave* Polly, *and ho brave* Polly.

Pros. So, so, so, wellcome to life again, now the man shall have his Mare again, and all friends.

Alon. Thanks *Prospero,* and gentle *Ariel.*

Gon. Thanks *Ariel,* and gentle *Prospero.*

Enter Stephania, Beantosser, Moustrappa, Drinkallup,
> *and* Hectorio.

Steph. Ha, is it so, more Officers then head Constables, you may dismiss the Pris'ners and adjourne the Court.

Bean. What to the old place in *Moor-fields.*

Mous. Ay, ay, and make Proclamation that all good Religious People may take notice of it.

Steph. No, no, wee'l meet here again to morrow. And so she pray'd me to tell ye.

Drink. If any forget the place, that man in black may instruct them, for he's Chaplain to the Society.

Pros. Set open the Gate, you may march off, y'ave had punishment enough for once.
> [*Exeunt Baud, and Whores.*

Now to wipe out the remembrance of all past sorrow, I'le show you the pleasures of my enchanted Castle. ——*Ariel,* see it done, and then be free.

Ari. I'le about it strait.   [*Exit* Ariel.

MUSICK.

The Scene drawn discovers Bridewell *with Prisners in several postures of labour and punishment, then a Baud and Pimp drawn over the Stage in a Cart follow'd by a Rabble ; then arise* Caliban, *and* Sycorax.

Sycorax. *My Lord great* Cac-Cac-Cac-Cac-Calyban.
        For my sweet sake,
        Some pity take
    On beauteous Nimph *in* Caravan:
    And check with seemly snout,
        The Rabble rout.

Calyban. *Sweet* Sycorax, *my* Mopsa *dear,*
        My Dove, my Duck,
        My Honey suck-
    -le which hast neither prick nor peer,
    I'le do't, take tail of Shirt,
        Cleanse Eye from Dirt.

Syc.   *Give all the rest of this fair Crew,*
        A play day too ;
        Let Pillory
        And Stocks agree,
        To set all free:
    Let the Beetle and Whip, be both laid to sleep,
    And Pris'ners Condemn'd, live for want of a slip.

Cal.   *Dear* Dowdy *be jocund, and sleek*
    The dainty fine furrowes of thine Olive Cheek :
        I cannot deny
        My pretty Pigs nye,
        With a Nose like a Rose,
    And a lip as green as a Leek.
    Be calme ye great Parents of the Punch, and the Pad,
    While each Bully and Lass sing and revel like mad.

Chorus. *Be calme, &c.——*
        While each, &c.——

Pimp.   *Compel this roaring rout to fly.*
Baud.   *And wee'l obey you by and by.*
Chorus. *Compel, &c.——*
        And wee'l, &c.——

Rabble. *Give's something to drink, and wee'l go hence,*
        For we meant your honours no offence.

Caly. *Here, here ye dogs, here's Eighteen-pence.*
Syc. *But ere you go, lets have a Dance.*
Chorus. *Here here, &c.——*
        But ere you, &c.——
                    [*They Dance, and Sing this* Chorus.
Be calme ye great Parents of the Punch, and the Pad :
While each Bully and Lass, sing and revel like mad.
            [*Exeunt* Rabble. *The Prisners make a noyse.*

Caly. *Head-keeper, let Correction cease,*
        Let ev'ry back and bum have peace.
Syc. *Do not the noble Crew beguile,*
        They came to sing and dance a while :
        And you of pleasure make a toyle.
Caly. *Be still, be still, ye whips, and ye backs,*
        Obey, obey, my lovely Sycorax.
Chorus. *Be still, &c.——*
        Obey, &c.——

The Head-keeper flyes down and sings.
Head-k. *Her I'le obey whose breath's so strong, one blast*
        Sent from her Lungs would lay my Castle wast ;
          Come down my furies, lash no more,
                But gently poure in
                Salt and Urine,
        To cleanse their crimson Lace from gore :
Whatever they are, or what'ere their transgressions,
        Free all in the Castle, free all ;
Make it as quiet, as at quarter Sessions,
When they make visits to Westminster-*Hall.*
        Here Four Keepers fly down.
        To the Houses you know,
        Round, round, must you go,
And search ev'ry place where their Revels they keep :
But no more 'till I call, shall ye handle the whip.
Chorus. *To the Houses, &c.——*
        Round, &c.——

And search——
But no more——   *[Exeunt Keepers.*
Caly. *Now the Tyrants are gone that made ye affraid :*
  Let each Daughter and Son,
  Make hast to come on ;
  And be merry, be merry, be merry,
  Be merry, as a Maid.
Chorus. *Now the Tyrants, &c.——*
While the *Chorus* is Singing the Prisners are freed, and
make ready for a Dance. The Scene shuts. A dance with
   Bottles in their hands.
Pimp. *Bullies my Lads, your Bottles sound.*
Baud. *And let sweet Eccho from each Lass rebound.*
Chorus. *Bullies, &c.——*
  And let, &c.——
    A Dance.
Chorus. *Drink up all.*
  Drink up all.
  Drink up all.
  ——Up all.
  Drink up all.
The Scene opens, discovers the Sea ;——The Night going
down *Aurora*, and the Sun rising——the Musick sitting
   in an Arch of Chariots.
Caly. See, see black Queen of Night, is sneaking down,
  And under sable Arm, she hides pale Moon.
  And Dame *Aurora*, yonder with eyes grey,
  Shedding Od'rifferous dew, and breaking day.
  Behold the Skies Head-Waggoner, the Sun,
  With Firy steed up yonder Hill does run.
  Miss *Thetis* would from Watry Bed pursue.
  Begone fond Minx, must none have Sun but
   you ?
    Sing.
Caly. *Now your drink, and your Drabs you shall safely*
  enjoy.

Syc.   *No Constables or Watch, shall your quiet destroy.*
Chorus.   *Now, &c.——*
         No Constable, &c.——
Pimp.   *Wee'l closely convey you by a private back door :*
         Your Ale and Stepony wee'l fill on the Score.
Baud.   *Wee'l treat ye great lubbers, as ye sail in the*
         Straits,
         With Trumpets and Cymbals, and loud City
         Waits.
Syc.   *In each room a soft Bed, or a Couch we will lay,*
         To please you all Night, and delight you all day.
Chorus.   *In each room, &c.——*
         To please you, &c.——
         A Dance.

     Ariel *appears in the Air, and Sings.*
             Song.
Where good Ale is, there suck I,
In a Coblers Stall I lye,
While the Watch are passing by ;
Then about the Streets I fly,
After Cullies merrily.
And I merrily, merrily take up my clo'se,
Under the Watch, and the Constables nose.

Pros.   Henceforth may our Enchanted Castle be,
         From Ign'rant Sprights, and sullen Devils free :
         May beautious *Nymphs* like little Lambkins
            play,
         While Swains with am'rous Pipes drive care
            away,
         Our harmless mirth shall still attend you here :
         'Tis mirth that makes you Youthful brisk and
            fair.
         That our Mock-Tempest, then may flourish long,
         Clapp all that would seem beautifull and young.

            FINIS.

EPILOGUE, by *Miranda*.

*G*ENTLEMEN *look'ee now, pray, my Father sayes*
   that I and my Sister must have ye all i'fads :
Whereof I can't tell what to do, I'le swear'o ;
If I take you, I lose my dear Quakero :
His things are precious, and his love is true ;
But there's no trust in ought you say or do :
Yet for ought that I know,
My self could serve you all as well as any ;
But my Father says, pray,
One Dish of meat can never serve so many ;
For though you all agree in one design,
To feed like Schollers on the tender Loyn ;
In this you differ with them, pray ;
One little Chop, and one plain Dish will do.
You must have Sause, warm Plates, fresh hau-gou's too ;
The large Pottage of glitt'ring show and dress,
Must cheat you to the little bit of flesh.
My Father says,
Since with such charge we purchase your Contents,
He thinks 'tis fit we should have Settlements :
For when you have enjoy'd, what that is, I can't tell i'vads ;
   but I beleive you can,——
Y'are dronish, cold and dull as any thing ;
Just like a Bee, when he has lost his sting :
And though with all our tempting sweets we strive,
We ne'r shall catch you more within our Hive.
Then must our sinking joyes ne'r rise again ?
Must we be kind, and show all in vain ?
You lov'd the jilting Mother much and long ;
She's old, the Daughter's active brisk and young :
If you neglect us still, pray,
May all your stony Pride unpiti'd fall ;
And may our harmless Devils take you all.

174

THE

HISTORY

OF

King *LEAR:*

A

TRAGEDY,

Acted at the

DUKE'S THEATRE.

Reviv'd with Alterations.

By N. TATE.

To

My Esteem'd F R I E N D

T H O M A S B O T E L E R, *Esq*;

SIR,

Y OU have a natural Right to this Piece, since by your
Advice I attempted the Revival of it with Alterations.
Nothing but the Pow'r of your Perswasion, and my Zeal
for all the Remains of Shakespear, *cou'd have wrought*
me to so bold an Undertaking. I found that the New-
modelling of this Story, wou'd force me sometimes on the
difficult Task of making the chiefest Persons speak some-
thing like their Characters, on Matter whereof I had no
Ground in my Author. Lear's *real and* Edgar's *pretended*
Madness have so much of extravagant Nature, (*I know*
not how else to express it,) *as cou'd never have started, but*
from our Shakespear's *Creating Fancy. The Images and*
Languages are so odd and surprizing, and yet so agreeable
and proper, that whilst we grant that none but Shakespear
cou'd have form'd such Conceptions ; yet we are satisfied
that they were the only Things in the World that ought
to be said on these Occasions. I found the Whole to
answer your Account of it, a Heap of Jewels, unstrung,
and unpolish'd ; yet so dazling in their Disorder, that I
soon perceiv'd I had seiz'd a Treasure. 'Twas my good
Fortune to light on one Expedient to rectifie what was
wanting in the Regularity and Probability of the Tale,
which was to run through the Whole, as Love *betwixt*
Edgar *and* Cordelia; *that never chang'd Word with each*
other in the Original. This renders Cordelia's *Indifference,*
and her Father's Passion in the first Scene, probable. It
likewise gives Countenance to Edgar's *Disguise, making*
that a generous Design that was before a poor Shift to
save his Life. The Distress of the Story is evidently

heightened by it; and it particularly gave Occasion of a
new Scene, or Two, of more Success (perhaps) than Merit.
This Method necessarily threw me on making the Tale
conclude in a Success to the innocent destrest Persons:
Otherwise I must have incumbered the Stage with dead
Bodies, which Conduct makes many Tragedies conclude
with unseasonable Jests. Yet was I wrack'd with no small
Fears for so bold a Change, 'till I found it well receiv'd
by my Audience; and if this will not satisfy the Reader,
I can produce an Authority that questionless will. Neither
is it of so Trivial an Undertaking to
make a Tragedy end happily, for 'tis   *Mr.* Dryd.
more difficult to save than 'tis to kill: *Pref. to the*
the Dagger and Cup of Poyson are Spanish Fryar.
always in Readiness; but to bring the
Action to the last Extremity, and then by probable
Means to recover All, will require the Art and Judgment
of a Writer, and cost him many a Pang in the Performance.

I have one Thing more to Apologize for, which is that
I have us'd less Quaintness of Expression even in the
newest Parts of this Play. I confess, 'twas Design in
me, partly to comply with my Author's Style, to make the
Scenes of a Piece, and partly to give it some Resemblance
of the Time and Persons here represented. This, Sir, I
submit wholly to you, who are both a Judge and Master
of Style. Nature had exempted you before you went
Abroad from the Morose Suturnine Humour of our Coun-
try, and you brought Home the Refinedness of Travel with-
out the Affectation. Many Faults I see in the following
Pages, and question not but you will discover more; yet
I will presume so far on your Friendship, as to make the
Whole a Present to you, and Subscribe my self,
Your obliged Friend
and humble Servant,
N. Tate.

The Persons.

KING *Lear,*	Mr. *Betterton.*
Gloster,	Mr. *Gillo.*
Kent,	Mr. *Wiltshire.*
Edgar,	Mr. *Smith.*
Bastard,	Mr. *Jo. Williams.*
Cornwall,	Mr. *Norris.*
Albany,	Mr. *Bowman.*
Burgundy,	
Gentleman-Usher,	Mr. *Jevon.*
[*An Old Man, Tenant to Gloster,*]	
[*Physician,*]	
Goneril,	Mrs. *Shadwell.*
Regan,	Lady *Slingsby.*
Cordelia,	Mrs. *Barry.*
[*Arante,*]	

*Guards, Officers, Messengers, [Two Ruffians,]
Attendants.*

179

PROLOGUE.

_SINCE by Mistakes your best Delights are made,
(For e'en your Wives can please in Masquerade,)
'Twere worth our While to'ave drawn you in this Day
By a new Name to our old honest Play ;
But he that did this Evening's Treat prepare
Bluntly resolv'd before-hand to declare
Your Entertainment should be most old Fare.
Yet hopes, since in rich_ Shakespear's _Soil it grew,
'Twill relish yet, with those whose Tasts are true,
And his Ambition is to please a Few.
If then this Heap of Flow'rs shall chance to wear
Fresh Beauty in the Order they now bear,
Even this_ Shakespear's _Praise ; each Rustick knows
'Mongst plenteous Flow'rs a Garland to compose,
Which strung by this course Hand may fairer show,
But 'twas a Power Divine first made 'em grow,
Why shou'd these Scenes lie hid, in which we find
What may at once divert and teach the Mind ;
Morals were always proper for the Stage,
But are ev'n necessary in this Age.
Poets must take the Churches teaching Trade,
Since Priests their Province of Intrigue invade ;
But we the Worst in this Exchange have got,
In vain our Poets preach, whilst Church-men plot._

THE HISTORY

OF

King *LEAR:*

Act I.

Enter Bastard *solus.*

Bast. THOU Nature art my Goddess, to thy Law
My Services are bound; why am I then
Depriv'd of a Son's Right, because I came not
In the dull Road that Custom has prescrib'd?
Why Bastard, wherefore Base, when I can boast
A Mind as gen'rous, and a Shape as true
As honest Madam's Issue? Why are we
Held Base, who in the lusty Stealth of Nature
Take fiercer Qualities than what compound
The scanted Births of the stale Marriage-bed;
Well then, legitimate *Edgar*, to thy Right
Of Law I will oppose a Bastard's Cunning.
Our Father's Love is to the Bastard *Edmund*
As to legitimate *Edgar*; with Success
I've practis'd yet on both their easy Natures:
Here comes the old Man chaf't with th' Information
Which last I forg'd against my Brother *Edgar*,
A Tale so plausible, so boldly utter'd,
And heightned by such lucky Accidents,
That now the slightest Circumstance confirms him,
And Base-born *Edmund* spight of Law inherits.

Enter Kent *and* Gloster.

Glost. Nay, good my Lord, your Charity
O'er shoots it self to plead in his Behalf;
You are your self a Father, and may feel
The Sting of Disobedience from a Son
First-born and best-Belov'd: Oh Villain *Edgar!*

Kent. Be not too rash, all may be Forgery,
And Time yet clear the Duty of your Son.

Glost. Plead with the Seas, and reason down the
    Winds,
Yet shall thou ne'er convince me, I have seen
His foul Designs through all a Father's Fondness:
But be this Light and thou my Witnesses,
That I discard him here from my Possessions,
Divorce him from my Heart, my Blood, and Name.

Bast. It works as I cou'd wish; I'll shew my self.

Glost. Ha! *Edmund!* welcome Boy; O *Kent!* see here
Inverted Nature, *Gloster's* Shame and Glory,
This By-born, the wild sally of my Youth,
Pursues me with all filial Offices,
Whilst *Edgar*, beg'd of Heaven, and born in Honour,
Draws Plagues on my white Head, that urge me still
To curse in Age the Pleasure of my Youth.
Nay, weep not, *Edmund*, for thy Brother's Crimes;
O gen'rous Boy! thou shar'st but half his Blood,
Yet lov'st beyond the Kindness of a Brother:
But I'll reward thy Vertue. Follow me.
My Lord, you wait the King, who comes resolv'd
To quit the Toils of Empire, and divide
His Realms amongst his Daughters; Heaven succeed
    it;
But much I fear the Change.

Kent. I grieve to see him
With such wild Starts of Passion hourly seiz'd,
As render Majesty between itself.

Glost. Alas! 'tis the Infirmity of his Age,

Yet has his Temper even been unfixt,
Chol'rick and sudden ; hark, They approach
[*Exeunt* Gloster *and* Bastard.
Flourish.   Enter Lear, Cornwall, Albany, Burgundy,
Edgar, Goneril, Regan, Cordelia, Edgar *speaking to*
Cordelia *at Entrance.*
Edgar. Cordelia, Royal Fair, turn yet once more,
And e'er successful *Burgundy* receive
The Treasure of thy Beauties from the King,
E'er happy *Burgundy* for ever fold Thee,
Cast back one pitying Look on wretched *Edgar.*
Cord. Alas ! What wou'd the wretched *Edgar* with
The more unfortunate *Cordelia* ?
Who in Obedience to a Father's Will
Flies from her *Edgar's* Arms to *Burgundy's* ?
Lear. Attend my Lords of *Albany* and *Cornwall,*
With Princely *Burgundy.*
Alb. We do, my Liege.
Lear. Give me this Map——Know, Lords, we have
divided
In Three, our Kingdom, having now resolv'd
To disengage from Our long Toil of State,
Conferring All upon your younger Years ;
You *Burgundy, Cornwall* and *Albany,*
Long in our Court have made your amorous sojourn,
And now are to be answer'd.—Tell me, my Daughters,
Which of you loves us most, that we may place
Our largest Bounty with our largest Merit.
Goneril, Our Eldest-born, speak first.
Gon. Sir, I do love you more than Words can utter,
Beyond what can be valu'd Rich, or Rare ;
Nor Liberty, nor Sight, Health, Fame, or Beauty,
Are half so dear, my Life for you were vile,
As much as Child can love the best of Fathers.
Lear. Of all these Bounds, e'en from this Line to this,
With shady Forests, and wide-skirted Meads,

We make thee Lady; to thine and *Albany's* Issue
Be this perpetual.——What says our Second Daughter?
 Reg. My Sister, Sir, in Part, exprest my Love.
For such as Hers, is mine, though more extended;
Sense has no other Joy that I can relish,
I have my All in my dear Liege's Love.
 Lear. Therefore to thee and thine Hereditary
Remain this ample Third of our fair Kingdom.
 Cord. Now comes my Trial, how am I distrest,
            [*Aside*
That must with cold Speech tempt the Chol'rick King
Rather to leave me Dowerless, then condemn me
To loath'd Embraces.
 Lear. Speak now Our last, not least in Our dear Love,
So ends my Task of State,——*Cordelia*, speak?
What canst thou say to win a richer Third
Than what thy Sisters gain'd?
 Cord. Now must my Love, in Words, fall short of
  theirs,
As much as it exceeds in Truth,——Nothing, my Lord.
 Lear. Nothing can come of Nothing, speak agen.
 Cord. Unhappy am I that I can't Dissemble,
Sir, as I ought I love your Majesty,
No more, nor less.
 Lear. Take heed, *Cordelia.*
Thy Fortunes are at stake, think better on't,
And mend thy Speech a little.
 Cord. O my Liege!
You gave me Being, Bred me, dearly love me,
And I return my Duty as I ought;
Obey you, Love you, and most Honour you;
Why have my Sisters Husbands, if they love you All?
Haply when I shall wed, the Lord whose Hand
Shall take my Plight, will carry half my Love;
For I shall never marry like my Sisters,
To love my Father All.

Lear. And goes thy Heart with this?
'Tis said that I am Chol'rick, Judge me, Gods,
Is there not cause? Now Minion, I perceive
The Truth of what has been suggested to us;
Thy Fondness for the Rebel Son of *Gloster*,
False to his Father, as Thou art to my Hopes:
And, oh! take heed, rash Girl, lest we comply
With thy fond Wishes, which thou wilt too late
Repent; for know our Nature cannot brook
A Child so young, and so Ungentle.
    Cord. So Young, my Lord, and True.
    Lear. Thy Truth then be thy Dow'r;
For by the sacred Sun, and solemn Night,
I here disclaim all my paternal Care,
And from this Minute hold thee as a Stranger,
Both to my Blood and Favour.
    Kent. This is Frenzy.
Consider, good my Liege,——
    Lear. Peace, *Kent*;
Come not between a Dragon and his Rage;
I lov'd her most, and in her tender Trust
Design'd to have bestow'd my Age at Ease:
So be my Grave my Peace, as here I give
My Heart from her, and with it all my Wealth:
My Lords of *Cornwall*, and of *Albany*,
I do invest you jointly in full Right
In this fair Third, *Cordelia's* forfeit Dow'r.
Mark me, my Lords, observe our last Resolve,
Our Self, attended with an hundred Knights,
Will make Abode with you in monthly Course;
The Name alone of King remain with me,
Yours be the Execution and Revenues;
This is our final Will; and to confirm it,
This Coronet part between you.
    Kent. Royal *Lear*,
Whom I have ever honour'd as my King,

Lov'd as my Father, as my Master follow'd,
And, as my Patron, thought on in my Prayers,——
   Lear. Away, the Bow is bent, make from the Shaft.
   Kent. No, let it fall and drench within my Heart,
Be *Kent* unmannerly when *Lear* is mad;
Thy youngest Daughter——
   Lear. On thy Life no more.
   Kent. What wilt thou doe, old Man?
   Lear. Out of my Sight.
   Kent. See better first.
   Lear. Now by the God,——
   Kent. Now by the Gods, rash King, thou swear'st in
vain.
   Lear. Ha, Traytour!
   Kent. Do, kill thy Physician *Lear*;
Strike thro' my Throat, yet with my latest Breath
I'll Thunder in thine Ear my just Complaint,
And tell Thee to thy Face that Thou dost ill.
   Lear. Hear me, rash Man; on thy Allegiance hear me;
Since thou hast striv'n to make Us break our Vow,
And prest between our Sentence and our Pow'r,
Which nor our Nature, nor our Place can bear,
We banish thee for ever from our Sight
And Kingdom; if when three Days are expir'd,
Thy hated Trunk be found in our Dominions,
That Moment is thy Death; Away.
   Kent. Why fare thee well, King; since thou art re-
     solv'd,
I take thee at thy Word, and will not stay,
To see Thy Fall: The Gods protect the Maid
That truly thinks, and has most justly said.
Thus to new Climates my old Truth I bear,
Friendship lives hence, and Banishment is here. [*Exit.*
   Lear. Now, *Burgundy*, you see her Price is faln,
Yet if the Fondness of your Passion still
Affects her as she stands, Dow'rless, and lost

In our Esteem, she's your's; take her, or leave her.

 Burg. Pardon me, Royal *Lear,* I but demand
The Dow'r yourself propos'd, and here I take
Cordelia by the Hand, Dutchess of *Burgundy.*

 Lear. Then leave her, Sir, for by a Father's Rage
I tell you all her Wealth. Away.

 Burg. Then, Sir, be pleas'd to charge the Breach
Of our Alliance on your own Will,
Not my Inconstancy.   [*Exeunt.*
     Manent Edgar *and* Cordelia.

 Edg. Has Heaven then weigh'd the Merit of my Love,
Or is't the Raving of my sickly Thought?
Cou'd *Burgundy* forgo so rich a Prize,
And leave her to despairing *Edgar's* Arms?
Have I thy Hand *Cordelia?* Do I clasp it?
The Hand that was this Minute to have join'd
My hated Rival's? Do I kneel before thee,
And offer at thy Feet my panting Heart?
Smile, Princess, and convince me; for as yet
I doubt, and dare not trust the dazling Joy.

 Cord. Some Comfort yet, that 'twas no vicious Blot
That has depriv'd me of a Father's Grace,
But meerly want of that which makes me Rich
In wanting it; a smooth professing Tongue:
O Sisters! I am loth to call your Fault
As it deserves; but use our Father well,
And wrong'd *Cordelia* never shall repine.

 Edg. O heav'nly Maid! that art thyself thy Dow'r,
Richer in Vertue than the Stars in Light,
If *Edgar's* humble Fortunes may be grac't
With thy Acceptance, at thy Feet he lays 'em.
Ha, my *Cordelia!* dost thou turn away?
What have I done t' offend thee?

 Cord. Talk't of Love.

 Edg. Then I've offended oft, *Cordelia* too
Has oft permitted me so to offend.

Cord. When, *Edgar*, I permitted your Addresses,
I was the darling Daughter of a King,
Nor can I now forget my Royal Birth,
And live dependant on my Lover's Fortune;
I cannot to so low a Fate submit;
And therefore study to forget your Passion,
And trouble me upon this Theam no more.

Edg. Thus Majesty takes most State in Distress!
How are we tost on Fortune's fickle Flood!
The Wave that with surprizing Kindness brought
The dear Wreck to my Arms, has snatcht it back,
And left me mourning on the barren Shoar.

Cord. This baseness of th' ignoble *Burgundy*,   [*Aside.*
Draws just Suspicion on the Race of Men;
His Love was Int'rest, so may *Edgar's* be,
And He, but with more Complement, dissemble;
If so, I shall oblige him by denying:
But if his Love be fixt, such constant Flame
As warms our Breasts, if such I find his Passion,
My Heart as grateful to his Truth shall be,
And Cold *Cordelia* prove as kind as He.   [*Exit.*
Enter Bastard *hastily.*

Bast. Brother, I've found you in a lucky Minute,
Fly and be safe, some Villain has incens'd
Our Father against your Life.

Edg. Distrest *Cordelia!* but oh! more Cruel.

Bast. Hear me, Sir, your Life, your Life's in danger.

Edg. A Resolve so sudden,
And of such black Importance!

Bast. 'Twas not sudden,
Some Villain has of long Time laid the Train.

Edg. And yet perhaps 'twas but pretended Coldness,
To try how far my Passion would pursue.

Bast. He hears me not; wake, wake, Sir.

Edg. Say ye, Brother?——
No Tears, good *Edmund*, if thus bring'st me Tidings

To strike me dead, for Charity delay not,
That Present will befit so kind a Hand.
    Bast. Your Danger, Sir, comes on so fast,
That I want Time t' inform you; but retire
Whilst I take Care to turn the pressing Stream.
O Gods! For Heav'n's Sake, Sir.
    Edg. Pardon me, Sir, a serious Thought
Had seiz'd me, but I think you talkt of Danger,
And wisht me to retire; Must all our Vows
End thus?—Friend, I obey you.—O *Cordelia.*

                                    [*Exit.*

    Bast. Ha! ha! fond Man, such credulous Honesty
Lessens the Glory of my Artifice;
His Nature is so far from doing Wrongs,
That he suspects none: If this Letter speed,
And pass for *Edgar's,* as himself wou'd own
The Counterfeit, but for the foul Contents,
Then my Designs are perfect.——Here comes *Gloster.*
                Enter Gloster.
    Glost. Stay, *Edmund,* turn; What Paper were you
reading?
    Bast. A Trifle, Sir.
    Glost. What needed then that terrible Dispatch of it
Into your Pocket? Come, produce it, Sir.
    Bast. A Letter from my Brother, Sir, I had
Just broke the Seal, but knew not the Contents;
Yet, fearing they might prove too blame,
Endeavour'd to conceal it from your Sight.
    Glost. 'Tis *Edgar's* Character.   [*Reads.*
    *This Policy of Fathers is intollerable, that keeps our
    Fortunes from us 'till Age will not suffer us to
    enjoy 'em ; I am weary of the Tyranny : Come
    to me, that of this I may speak more. If our
    Father would sleep 'till I wak't him, you should
    enjoy half his Possessions, and live belov'd of
    your Brother* Edgar.

Sleep 'till I wak't him! you shou'd enjoy
Half his Possessions!——*Edgar* to write this
'Gainst his indulgent Father! Death and Hell!
Fly, *Edmund*, seek him out, wind me into him,
That I may bite the Traytor's Heart, and fold
His bleeding Entrails on my vengeful Arm.

   Bast. Perhaps 'twas writ, my Lord, to prove my
     Vertue.

   Glost. These late Eclipses of the Sun and Moon
Can bode no less; Love cools, and Friendship fails,
In Cities Mutiny, in Countrys Discord,
The Bond of Nature crackt 'twixt Son and Father:
Find out the Villain; do it carefully,
And it shall lose thee Nothing.   [*Exit.*

   Bast. So now my Project's firm; but to make sure
I'll throw in one Proof more and that a bold one;
I'll place old *Gloster* where he shall o're-hear us
Confer of this Design; whilst, to his thinking,
Deluded *Edgar* shall accuse himself.
Be Honesty my Int'rest, and I can
Be Honest too: And what Saint so Divine,
That will successful Villany decline?   [*Exit.*

       Enter Kent *disguis'd.*

   Kent. Now banisht *Kent*, if thou canst pay thy Duty
In this Disguise, where thou dost stand condemn'd,
Thy Master *Lear* shall find thee full of Labours.

       Enter Lear *attended.*

   Lear. In there, and tell our Daughter we are here.
Now, What art thou?

   Kent. A Man, Sir.

   Lear. What dost thou profess, or wou'dst with us?

   Kent. I do profess to be no less than I seem, to serve
him truly that puts me in Trust, to love him that's
honest, to converse with him that's wise and speaks
little, to fight when I can't choose; and to eat no Fish.

   Lear. I say, what art Thou?

Kent. A very honest-hearted Fellow, and as poor as the King.

Lear. Then art thou poor indeed.——What canst thou do?

Kent. I can keep honest Counsel, marr a curious Tale in the Telling, deliver a plain Message bluntly; that which ordinary Men are fit for, I am qualified in; and the best of me is Diligence.

Lear. Follow me; thou shalt serve me.

Enter one of Goneril's *Gentlemen.*

Now, Sir?

Gent. Sir——   [*Exit;* Kent *runs after him.*

Lear. What says the Fellow? Call me the Clatpole back.

Att. My Lord, I know not; but methinks your Highness is entertained with slender Ceremony.

Servant. He says, my Lord, your Daughter is not well.

Lear. Why came not the Slave back when I call'd him?

Serv. My Lord, he answered me i'th' surliest Manner, That he wou'd not.

Re-enter Gentleman *brought in by* Kent.

Lear. I hope our Daughter did not so instruct him. Now, who am I, Sir?

Gent. My Lady's Father.

Lear. My Lord's Knave.——   [*Strikes him.*

Goneril *at the Entrance.*

Gent. I'll not be struck, my Lord.

Kent. Nor tript neither, thou vile Civit-box.

[*Strikes up his Heels.*

Gon. By Day and Night; this is insufferable, I will not bear it.

Lear. Now, Daughter, why that Frontlet on? Speak, do's that Frown become our Presence?

Gon. Sir, this licentious Insolence of your Servants Is most unseemly, hourly they break out

In Quarrels bred by their unbounded Riots,
I had fair hope by making this known to you,
To have had a quick Redress, but find too late
That you protect and countenance their Outrage;
And therefore, Sir, I take this Freedom, which
Necessity makes discreet.

    Lear. Are you our Daughter?

    Gon. Come, Sir, let me entreat you to make use
Of your Discretion, and put off betimes
This Disposition that of late transforms you
From what you rightly are.

    Lear. Does any here know me? Why, this is not *Lear*;
Do's *Lear* walk thus? Speak thus? Where are his Eyes?
Who is it that can tell me who I am?

    Gon. Come, Sir, this Admiration's much o'th' Savour
Of other your new Humours; I beseech you,
To understand my Purposes aright;
As you are old, you shou'd be staid and wise:
Here do you keep an hundred Knights and Squires,
Men so debaucht and bold, that this our Palace
Shews like a riotous Inn, a Tavern, Brothel;
Be then advised by her that else will take
That which she begs, to lessen your Attendance,
Take half away, and see that the Remainder
Be such as may befit your Age, and know
Themselves and You.

    Lear. Darkness and Devils!
Saddle my Horses, call my Train together;
Degenerate Viper, I'll not stay with Thee!
I yet have left a Daughter.——Serpent, Monster!
Lessen my Train, and call 'em riotous?
All Men approv'd, of choice and rarest Parts
That each Particular of Duty know.——
How small, *Cordelia*, was thy Fault? O *Lear*,
Beat at this Gate that let thy Folly in,
And thy dear Judgment out; Go, go, my People.

Going off meets Albany *entring.*

Ingratefull Duke, was this your Will?

   Alb. What, Sir?

   Lear. Death! fifty of my Followers at a Clap!

   Alb. The Matter, Madam?

   Gon. Never afflict yourself to know the Cause,
But give his Dotage Way.

   Lear. Blasts upon thee,
Th' untented Woundings of a Father's Curse
Pierce ev'ry Sense about thee; old fond Eyes,
Lament this Cause again, I'll pluck ye out,
And cast ye with the Waters that ye lose
To temper Clay.——No, *Gorgon*, thou shalt find
That I'll resume the Shape which thou dost think
I have cast off for ever.

   Gon. Mark ye that.

   Lear. Hear Nature!
Dear Goddess hear; and if thou dost intend
To make that Creature Fruitful, change thy Purpose;
Pronounce upon her Womb the Barren Curse,
That from her blasted Body never spring
A Babe to honour her;—But if she must bring forth,
Defeat her Joy with some distorted Birth,
Or monst'rous Form, the Prodigy o' th' Time;
And so perverse of Spirit, that it may live
Her Torment as 'twas born, to fret her Cheeks
With constant Tears, and wrinkle her young Brow.
Turn all her Mother's Pains to Shame and Scorn,
That she may curse her Crime too late, and feel
How sharper than a Serpent's Tooth it is
To have a thankless Child: Away, away. [*Exit cum suis.*

   Gon. Presuming thus upon his numerous Train,
He thinks to play the Tyrant here, and hold
Our Lives at Will.

   Alb. Well, you may bear too far.   [*Exeunt.*

End of the First Act.

Act II.

SCENE, Gloster's *House.*

Enter Bastard.

Bast. THE Duke comes here to Night, I'll take the
Advantage
Of his Arrival to compleat my Project:
Brother, a Word, come forth; 'tis I your Friend,
Enter Edgar.
My Father watches for you, fly this Place,
Intelligence is giv'n where you're hid;
Take the Advantage of the Night; bethink ye,
Have you not spoke against the Duke of *Cornwal*
Something might shew you a Favourer of
Duke *Albany's* Party?
   Edg. Nothing; why ask you?
   Bast. Because he's coming here to Night in haste,
And *Regan* with him——Heark! the Guards; Away.
   Edg. Let 'em come on, I'll stay and clear myself.
   Bast. Your Innocence at Leisure may be heard,
But *Gloster's* storming Rage as yet is deaf,
And you may perish e'er allow'd the Hearing
                        [Exit Edgar.
Gloster comes yonder: Now to my feign'd Scuffle—
Yield, come before my Father! Lights here, Lights!
Some Blood drawn on me wou'd beget Opinion
                       [Stabs his Arm.
Of our more fierce Encounter.—I have seen
Drunkards do more than this in Sport.
Enter Gloster *and Servants.*
   Glost. Now, *Edmund,* where's the Traytour?
   Bast. That Name, Sir,
Strikes Horrour through me; but my Brother, Sir,
Stood here i'th' Dark.

Glost. Thou bleed'st! pursue the Villain,
And bring him Piece-meal to me.

   Bast. Sir, he's fled.

   Glost. Let him fly far, this Kingdom shall not hide
      him:
The Noble Duke, my Patron comes to Night;
By his Authority I will proclaim
Rewards for him that brings him to the Stake,
And Death for the Concealer.
Then of my Lands, loyal and natural Boy,
I'll work the Means to make thee capable.   [*Exeunt.*

   Enter Kent (*disguis'd still*) *and* Goneril's *Gentleman,*
                     severally.

   Gent. Good-morrow, Friend, belongst thou to this
House?

   Kent. Ask them will answer thee.

   Gent. Where may we set our Horses?

   Kent. I'th' Mire.

   Gent. I am in haste, prethee an' thou lov'st me, tell me.

   Kent. I love thee not.

   Gent. Why then I care not for thee.

   Kent. An' I had thee in *Lipsbury* Pinfold, I'd make
thee care for me.

   Gent. What do'st thou mean, I know thee not?

   Kent. But, Minion, I know thee.

   Gent. What dost thou know me for?

   Kent. For a base, proud, beggarly, white-liver'd,
Glass-gazing, superserviceable, finical Rogue; One that
wou'd be a Pimp in Way of good Service, and art
nothing but a Composition of Knave, Beggar, Coward,
Pandar.——

   Gent. What a monst'rous Fellow art thou to rail at
One that is neither known of thee, nor knows thee?

   Kent. Impudent Slave! not know me, who but two
Days since tript up thy Heels before the King: Draw,
Miscreant, or I'll make the Moon shine through thee.

Gent. What means the Fellow;——Why, prethee, prethee; I tell thee I have nothing to do with thee.

Kent. I know your Rogueship's Office; you come with Letters against the King, taking my young Lady *Vanity's* Part against her Royal Father: Draw, Rascal.

Gent. Murther, Murther, help.

Kent. Dost thou scream Peacock, strike Puppet, stand dappar Slave.

Gent. Help Hea'! Murther, help.

[Exit. Kent after him.

Flourish.   Enter Duke of Cornwal, Regan, *attended;* Gloster, Bastard.

Glost. All Welcome to your Graces, you do me Honour.

Duke. Gloster, W'ave heard with Sorrow that your Life
Has been attempted by your impious Son;
But *Edmund* here has paid you strictest Duty.

Glost. He did betray his Practice, and receiv'd
The Hurt you see, striving to apprehend him.

Duke. Is he pursu'd?

Glost. He is, my Lord.

Reg. Use our Authority to apprehend
The Traytour, and do Justice on his Head;
For you, *Edmund,* that have so signaliz'd
Your Vertue, you from henceforth shall be ours;
Natures of such firm Trust we much shall need,
A charming Youth, and worth my further Thought.

[Aside.

Duke. Lay Comforts, noble *Gloster,* to your Breast,
As we to ours. This Night be spent in Revels:
We chuse you, *Gloster,* for our Host to Night,
A troublesome Expression of our Love.
On, to the Sports before us.——Who are these?

Enter the Gentleman pursu'd by Kent.

Glost. Now, what's the Matter?

Duke. Keep Peace upon your Lives, he dies that
    strikes.
Whence, and what are ye?
    Att. Sir, they are Messengers, the one from your
Sister, the other from the King.
    Duke. Your Difference? Speak.
    Gent. I'm scarce in Breath, my Lord.
    Kent. No Marvel, you have so bestir'd your Valour.
Nature disclaims the Dastard; a Taylor made him.
    Duke. Speak yet, how grew your Quarrel?
    Gent. Sir, this old Ruffian here, whose Life I spar'd,
In Pity to his Beard.——
    Kent. Thou Essence Bottle!
In Pity to my Beard——Your Leave my Lord,
And I will tread the Muss-cat into Mortar.
    Duke. Know'st thou our Presence?
    Kent. Yes, Sir, but Anger has a Privilege.
    Duke. Why art thou angry?
    Kent. That such a Slave as this shou'd wear a Sword
And have no Courage? Office, and no Honesty;
Not Frost and Fire hold more Antipathy
Then I and such a Knave.
    Glost. Why dost thou call him Knave?
    Kent. His Countenance likes me not.
    Duke. No more perhaps does Mine, nor His, or Hers.
    Kent. Plain-Dealing is my Trade, and to be plain, Sir,
I have seen better Faces in my Time,
Then stands on any Shoulders now before me.
    Reg. This is some Fellow, that having once been
    prais'd
For Bluntness, since affects a sawcy Rudeness;
But I have known one of these surly Knaves,
That in his Plainness harbour'd more Design
Then twenty cringing complementing Minions.
    Duke. What's the Offence you gave him?
    Gent. Never any, Sir;

It pleas'd the King, his Master, lately
To strike me on a slender Misconstruction,
Whilst watching his Advantage, this old Lurcher,
Tript me behind, for which the King extoll'd him;
And, flusht with the Honour of this bold Exploit,
Drew on me here agen.

 Duke. Bring forth the Stocks, we'll teach you.

 Kent. Sir, I'm too old to learn;
Call not the Stocks for me, I serve the King;
On whose Employment I was sent to you;
You'll shew too small Respect, and too bold Malice
Against the Person of my Royal Master,
Stocking his Messenger.

 Duke. Bring forth the Stocks, as I have Life and
  Honour,
There shall he sit 'till Noon.

 Reg. 'Till Noon, my Lord! 'Till Night, and all Night
too.

 Kent. Why Madam, if I were your Father's Dog
You wou'd not use me so.

 Reg. Sir, being his Knave, I will.

 Glost. Let me beseech your Graces to forbear him;
His Fault is much, and the good King his Master
Will check him for't, but needs must take it ill
To be thus slighted in his Messenger.

 Duke. We'll answer that;
Our Sister may receive it worse, to have
Her Gentleman assaulted: To our Business lead. [*Exit.*

 Glost. I am sorry for thee, Friend, 'tis the Duke's
  Pleasure,
Whose Disposition will not be controll'd,
But I'll entreat for thee.

 Kent. Pray do not, Sir——
I have watcht and travell'd hard,
Some Time I shall sleep out, the rest I'll whistle:
Fare-well t'ye, Sir.   [*Exit* Gloster.

All weary, and o'er-watcht,
I feel the drowzy Guest steal on me; take
Advantage heavy Eyes on this kind Slumber,
Not to behold this vile and shamefull Lodging. [*Sleeps.*
                    Enter Edgar.
    Edg. I heard myself proclaim'd,
And by the friendly Hollow of a Tree,
Escape the Hunt, no Port is free, no Place
Where Guards and most unusual Vigilance
Do not attend to take me.——How easie now
'Twere to defeat the Malice of my Trale,
And leave the Griefs on my Sword's reeking Point;
But Love detains me from Death's peaceful Call,
Still whispering me, *Cordelia's* in Distress;
Unkind as she is, I cannot see her wretched,
But must be neer to wait upon her Fortune.
Who knows but the white Minute yet may come,
When *Edgar* may do Service to *Cordelia.*
That charming Hope still ties me to the Oar
Of Painfull Life, and makes me too, submit
To th' humblest Shifts to keep that Life a-Foot;
My Face I will besmear, and knit my Locks,
The Country gives me Proof and President
Of Bedlam Beggars, who, with roaring Voices
Strike in their numm'd and mortify'd bare Arms
Pins, Iron-spikes, Thorns, Sprigs of Rosemary,
And thus from Sheep-coats, Villages, and Mills,
Sometimes with Prayers, sometimes with Lunatick Bans,
Enforce their Charity, poor *Tyrligod,* poor *Tom,*
That's something yet, *Edgar* I am no more.   [*Exit.*
        Kent *in the Stocks still; Enter* Lear *attended.*
    Lear. 'Tis strange that they should so depart from
        Home,
And not send back our Messenger.
    Kent. Hail, noble Master.
    Lear. How! Mak'st thou this Shame thy Pastime?

What's he that has so much mistook thy Place,
To set thee here?

Kent. It is both He and She, Sir, your Son and Daughter.

Lear. No.

Kent. Yes.

Lear. No, I say.

Kent. I say, yea.

Lear. By *Jupiter* I swear no.

Kent. By *Juno* I swear, I swear ay.

Lear. They durst not do't;
They cou'd not, wou'd not do't; 'tis worse than Murder,
To do upon Respect such violent Out-rage.
Resolve me with all modest Haste, which Way
Thou mayst deserve, or they impose this Usage?

Kent. My Lord, when at their Home
I did commend your Highness Letters to them,
'Ere I was Ris'n arriv'd another Post,
Steer'd in his Haste, breathless and panting forth
From *Goneril*, his Mistress, Salutations,
Whose Message being deliver'd, they took Horse,
Commanding me to follow, and attend
The Leisure of their Answer; which I did;
But meeting that other Messenger,
Whose Welcome I perceiv'd had poison'd mine;
Being the very Fellow that of late
Had shewn such Rudeness to your Highness, I
Having more Man than Wit about me, drew;
On which he rais'd the House with Coward's Cries:
This was the Trespass which your Son and Daughter
Thought worth the Shame you see it suffer here.

Lear. Oh! how this Spleen swells upward to my Heart,
And heaves for Passage.——Down climbing Rage;
Thy Element's below; where is this Daughter?

Kent. Within, Sir, at a Masque.

Enter Gloster.

Lear. Now *Gloster*——Ha!
Deny to speak with me; th'are sick, th'are weary,
They have travell'd hard to Night;—mere Fetches;
Bring me a better Answer.
    Glost. My dear Lord,
You know the fiery Quality of the Duke.——
    Lear. Vengeance, Death, Plague, Confusion;
Fiery! what Quality,——Why *Gloster, Gloster*,
I'd speak with the Duke of *Cornwal*, and his Wife.
    Glost. I have inform'd 'em so.
    Lear. Inform'd 'em! dost thou understand me, Man,
I tell thee, *Gloster*,——
    Glost. I, my good Lord.
    Lear. The King wou'd speak with *Cornwal*, the dear
    Father
Wou'd with his Daughter speak, commands her Service.
Are they inform'd of this! My Breath and Blood!
Fiery! the fiery Duke! tell the hot Duke——
No, but not yet, may be he is not well,
Infirmity does still neglect all Office;
I beg his Pardon, and I'll chide my Rashness
That took the indispos'd and sickly Fit
For the sound Man:——But wherefore sits he there?
Death on my State, this Act convinces me
That this Retiredness of the Duke and her
Is plain Contempt; give me my Servant forth;
Go tell the Duke and 's Wife I'd speak with 'em;
Now, instantly, bid 'em come forth and hear me;
Or at their Chamber Door I'll beat the Drum,
'Till it cry sleep to Death.——
          Enter Cornwal *and* Regan.
Oh! Are you come?
    Duke. Health to the King.
    Reg. I am glad to see your Highness.
    Lear. Regan, I think you are, I know what Cause

I have to think so; shou'd'st thou not be glad
I wou'd divorce me from thy Mother's Tomb?
Beloved *Regan*, thou wilt shake to hear
What I shall utter: Thou cou'd'st ne'er h'thought it,
Thy Sister's naught, O *Regan*, she has ty'd
                  [Kent *here set at liberty.*
Ingratitude like a keen Vulture here,
I scarce can speak to thee.
   Reg. I pray you, Sir, take Patience; I have Hope
That you know less to value her Desert,
Than she to slack her Duty.
   Lear. Ha! How's that?
   Reg. I cannot think my Sister in the least
Would fail in her Respects; but if perchance
She has restrain'd the Riots of your Followers,
'Tis on such Grounds, and to such wholesome Ends,
As clear her from all Blame.
   Lear. My Curses on her.
   Reg. O Sir, you're old,
And shou'd content you to be rul'd and led,
By some Descretion that discerns your State
Better than yourself; therefore, Sir,
Return to our Sister, and say you have wrong'd her.
   Lear. Ha! Ask her Forgiveness?
No, no, 'twas my Mistake, thou didst not mean so
Dear Daughter, I confess that I am old;
Age is unnecessary, but thou art good,
And wilt dispense with my Infirmity.
   Reg. Good Sir, no more of these unsightly Passions;
Return back to our Sister.
   Lear. Never, *Regan*,
She has abated me of Half my Train,
Look'd black upon me, stabb'd me with her Tongue;
All the stor'd Vengeances of Heav'n fall
On her Ingratefull Head; strike her young Bones
Ye taking Ayrs with Lameness.

Reg. O the blest Gods! Thus will you wish on me,
When the rash Mood——
　　Lear. No, *Regan*, Thou shalt never have my Curse,
Thy tender Nature cannot give thee o're
To such Impiety; Thou better know'st
The Offices of Nature, Bond of Child-hood,
And Dues of Gratitude; thou bear'st in Mind
The Half o'th' Kingdom, which our Love conferr'd
On thee and thine.
　　Reg. Good Sir, to th' Purpose.
　　Lear. Who put my Man i'th' Stocks?
　　Duke. What Trumpet's that?
　　Reg. I know't, my Sister's, this confirms her Let-
ters.
Sir, is your Lady come?
　　　　　Enter Goneril's *Gentleman.*
　　Lear. More Torture still:
This is a Slave, whose easie borrow'd Pride
Dwells in the fickle Grace of her he follows;
A Fashion-fop, that spends the Day in dressing,
And all to bear his Ladie's flatt'ring Message,
That can deliver with a Grace her Lie,
And with as bold a Face bring back a greater.
Out, Varlet, from my Sight.
　　Duke. What means your Grace?
　　Lear. Who stockt my Servant? *Regan*, I have hope
Thou didst not know it.
　　　　　Enter Goneril.
Who comes here? Oh Heav'ns!
If you do love old Men; if your sweet sway,
Allow Obedience; if yourselves are Old,
Make it your Cause, send down and take my Part?
Why, *Gorgon*, dost thou come to hunt me here?
Art not asham'd to look upon this Beard?
Darkness upon my Eyes, they play me false,
O *Regan*, wilt thou take her by the Hand?

Gon. Why not by th' Hand, Sir? How have I
offended?
All's not Offence that Indiscretion finds,
And Dotage terms so.

Lear. Heart, thou art too tough.

Reg. I pray you, Sir, being old, confess you are so,
If 'till the Expiration of your Month,
You will return and sojourn with our Sister,
Dismissing half your Train, come then to me;
I am now from Home, and out of that Provision
That shall be needful for your Entertainment.

Lear. Return with her, and fifty Knights dismisst,
No, rather I'll forswear all Roofs, and chuse
To be Companion to the Midnight Wolf.
My naked Head expos'd to th' merc'less Air,
Than have my smallest Wants supply'd by her.

Gon. At your Choice, Sir.

Lear. Now, I prithee Daughter, do not make me mad;
I will not trouble thee, my Child, farewell.
We'll meet no more, no more see one another;
Let Shame come when it will, I do not call it,
I do not bid the Thunder-bearer strike,
Nor tell Tales of thee to avenging Heav'n;
Mend when thou canst, be better at thy Leisure,
I can be patient, I can stay with *Regan,*
I, and my hundred Knights.

Regan. Your Pardon, Sir,
I lookt not for you yet, nor am provided
For your fit Welcome.

Lear. Is this well spoken now?

Reg. My Sister treats you fair; what! fifty Followers?
Is it not well? What should you need of more?

Gon. Why might not you, my Lord, receive Attendance
From those whom she calls Servants, or from mine?

Reg. Why not, my Lord? If then they chance to
slack you,

We cou'd controll 'em.—If you come to me,
For now I see the Danger, I entreat you
To bring but Five and Twenty; to no more
Will I give Place.
    Lear. Hold now, my Temper, stand this Bolt un-
      mov'd,
And I am Thunder-Proof;
The wicked, when compar'd with the more Wicked,
Seem beautiful, and not to be the Worst,
Stands in some Rank of Praise; now, *Goneril,*
Thou art Innocent agen, I'll go with thee;
Thy Fifty yet do's double Five and Twenty,
And thou art twice her Love.
    Gon. Hear me, my Lord.
What need you Five and Twenty, Ten, or Five,
To follow in a House, where twice so many
Have a Command t'attend you?
    Reg. What need one?
    Lear. Blood! Fire! here——Leaprosies and bluest
    Plagues!
Room, room for Hell to belch her Horrors up
And drench the *Circes* in a Stream of Fire;
Hark, how th' Infernals eccho to my Rage
Their Whips and Snakes.——
    Reg. How leud a Thing is Passion!
    Gon. So Old and Stomachful.
                [Lightning and Thunder.
    Lear. Heav'ns drop your Patience down;
You see me here, ye Gods, a poor old Man,
As full of Grief as Age, wretched in both——
I'll bear no more: No, you unnatural Haggs,
I will have such Revenges on you both,
That all the World shall——I will do such Things,
What they are yet I know not, but they shall be
The Terrors of the Earth; you think I'll weep,
                   [Thunder again.

This Heart shall break into a thousand Pieces
Before I'll weep.——O Gods! I shall go mad.   [*Exit.*
    Duke. 'Tis a wild Night, come out o' th' Storm.
                                                      [*Exeunt.*
        End of the Second Act.

Act III.

SCENE, *A Desert Heath.*
Enter Lear *and* Kent *in the Storm.*

Lear. BLOW Winds, and burst your Cheeks, rage
        louder yet,
Fantastick Lightning singe, singe my white Head;
Spout Cataracts, and Hurricanos fall,
'Till you have drown'd the Towns and Palaces
Of proud ingratefull Man.
    Kent. Not all my best Intreaties can perswade him
Into some needfull Shelter, or to 'bide
This poor slight Cov'ring on his aged Head,
Expos'd to this wild War of Earth and Heav'n.
    Lear. Rumble thy fill, fight Whirlwind, Rain and Fire;
Not Fire, Wind, Rain, or Thunder are my Daughters:
I tax not you, ye Elements, with Unkindness;
I never gave you Kingdoms, call'd you Children;
You owe me no Obedience, then let fall
Your horrible Pleasure, here I stand your Slave,
A poor, infirm, weak, and despis'd old Man;
Yet will I call you servile Ministers,
That have with two Pernicious Daughters join'd,
Their high-engender'd Battle against a Head
So Old and White as mine; Oh! oh! 'tis Foul.
    Kent. Hard by, Sir, is a Hovel, that will lend
Some Shelter from this Tempest.
    Lear. I will forget my Nature, what! so kind a Father?
I, there's the Point.

Kent. Consider, good my Liege.　Things that love
　　Night,
Love not such Nights as this; these wrathfull Skies
Frighten the very Wanderers o' th' Dark,
And make 'em keep their Caves; such drenching Rain,
Such Sheets of Fire, such Claps of horrid Thunder,
Such Groans of roaring Winds have ne're been known.
　　Lear. Let the great Gods,
That keep the dreadful Pudder o're our Heads,
Find out their Enemies now.　Tremble thou Wretch,
That hast within thee undiscover'd Crimes!
Hide, that bloody Hand,————————
Thou perjur'd Villain, holy Hypocrite,
That drink'st the Widows Tears, sigh now, and cry
These dreadful Summoners Grace, I am a Man
More sin'd against, than sinning.
　　Kent. Good Sir, to th' Hovell.
　　Lear. My Wit begins to burn,
Come on my Boy, how dost my Boy?　Art cold?
I'm cold my Self; shew this Straw, my Fellow,
The Art of our Necessity is strange,
And can make vile Things precious; my poor Knave,
Cold as I am at Heart, I've one Place there
　　　　　　　　　　　　　　　[Loud. *Storm.*
That's sorry yet for Thee.　　　　　　　　[*Exit.*
　　　　　Gloster's *Palace. Enter* Bastard.
　　Bast. The Storm is in our louder Rev'lings drown'd.
Thus wou'd I Reign, cou'd I but mount a Throne.
The Riots of these proud imperial Sisters
Already have impos'd the galling Yoke
Of Taxes, and hard Impossitions, on
The drudging Peasant's Neck, who bellow out
Their loud Complaints in vain—Triumphant Queens!
With what Assurance do they treat the Crowd.
O for a Tast of such Majestick Beauty,
Which none but my hot Veins are fit t' engage;

Nor are my Wishes desp'rate, for even now,
During the Banquet, I observ'd their Glances
Shot thick at me; and, as they left the Room,
Each cast, by stealth, a kind inviting Smile,
The happy Earnest————ha!
    Two Servants, from several Entrances, deliver him each
              a Letter, and Exeunt.
Where Merit is so Transparent, not to behold it [*Reads.*
Were Blindness, and not to reward it Ingratitude.
                           Goneril.

Enough! Blind and Ingratefull should I be
Not to obey the Summons of this Oracle.
Now for a Second Letter.   [*Opens the other.*
If Modesty be not your Enemy, doubt not to   [*Reads.*
Find me your Friend.
                           Regan.

Excellent *Sybil!* O my glowing Blood!
I am already sick of Expectation,
And pant for the Possession.——Here *Gloster* comes
With Business on his Brow; be husht my Joys.
                [*Enter* Gloster.]
    Glost. I come to seek thee, *Edmund,* to impart a
Business of Importance; I knew thy loyal Heart is
toucht to see the Cruelty of these ingratefull Daughters
against our royal Master
    Bast. Most Savage and Unnatural.
    Glost. This Change in the State sits uneasie. The
Commons repine aloud at their female Tyrants, already
they cry out for the Re-Instalment of their good old
King, whose Injuries, I fear, will inflame 'em into
Mutiny.
    Bast. 'Tis to be hop'd, not fear'd.
    Glost. Thou hast it Boy, 'tis to be hop'd indeed;
On me they cast their Eyes, and hourly court me
To lead 'em on; and whilst this Head is mine,
I'm Theirs. A little covert Craft, my Boy,

And then for open Action; 'twill be Employment
Worthy such honest daring Souls as thine.
Thou, *Edmund*, art my trusty Emissary,
Haste on the Spur, at the first Break of Day,
　　　　　　　　　　　　　[Gives him Letters.
With these Dispatches to the Duke of *Combray*;
You know what mortal Feuds have always flam'd
Between this Duke of *Cornwal's* Family, and his;
Full Twenty Thousand Mountaineers
Th' inveterate Prince will send to our Assistance.
Dispatch; commend us to his Grace, and prosper.
　　Bast. Yes, credulous old Man,　　　　　　*[Aside.*
I will commend you to his Grace,
His Grace the Duke of *Cornwal*————instantly
To shew him these Contents in thy own Character,
And seal'd with thy own Signet; then forthwith
The Chol'rick Duke gives Sentence on thy Life;
And to my Hand thy vast Revenues,
To glut my Pleasure that 'till now has starv'd.
Gloster *going off is met by* Cordelia *ent'ring [with* Arante.]
　　　　　Bastard *observing at a Distance.*
　　Cord. Turn, *Gloster*, Turn, by the sacred Pow'rs
I do conjure you, give my Griefs a Hearing;
You must, you shall, nay, I am sure you will,
For you were always styl'd the Just and Good.
　　Glost. What wou'd thou, Princess? rise, and speak
　　　　thy Griefs.
　　Cord. Nay, you shall promise to redress 'em too,
Or here I'll kneel for ever; I entreat
Thy Succour for a Father, and a King,
An injur'd Father, and an injur'd King.
　　Bast. O charming Sorrow! How her Tears adorn
　　　　her,
Like Dew on Flow'rs, but she is Virtuous,
And I must quench this hopeless Fire i' th' kindling.
　　Glost. Consider, Princess,

For whom thou beg'st, 'tis for the King that wrong'd
    thee.

    Cord. O name not that; he did not, cou'd not wrong
    me.

Nay, muse not, *Gloster*, for it is too likely
This injur'd King e'er this, is past your Aid,
And gone Distracted with his savage Wrongs.

    Bast. I'll gaze no more,—and yet my Eyes are
    charm'd.

    Cord. Or, what if it be worse?

As 'tis too probable, this furious Night
Has pierc'd his tender Body, the bleak Winds,
And cold Rain chill'd, or Lightning struck him dead;
If it be so, your Promise is discharg'd,
And I have only one poor Boon to beg,
That you'd convey me to his breathless Trunk,
With my torn Robes to wrap his hoary Head,
With my torn Hair to bind his Hands and Feet,
Then with a Show'r of Tears
To wash his Clay-smear'd Cheeks, and Die beside him.

    Glost. Rise, fair *Cordelia*, thou hast Piety
Enough t'attone for both thy Sisters Crimes.
I have already plotted to restore
My injur'd Master, and thy Vertue tells me
We shall succeed, and suddenly.   [*Exit.*

    Cord. Dispatch, *Arante,*
Provide me a Disguise, we'll instantly
Go seek the King, and bring him some Relief.

    Ar. How, Madam! Are you Ignorant
Of what your impious Sisters have decreed?
Immediate Death for any that relieve him.

    Cord. I cannot dread the Furies in this Case.

    Ar. In such a Night as this? Consider Madam,
For many Miles about there's scarce a Bush
To shelter in.

    Cord. Therefore no shelter for the King,

And more our Charity to find him out:
What have not Women dar'd for vicious Love?
And we'll be shining Proofs that they can dare
For Piety as much. Blow Winds, and Light'nings fall,
Bold in my Virgin Innocence, I'll fly
My Royal Father to relieve, or die. [*Exit* [*with* Arante.]
   Bast. Provide me a Disguise, we'll instantly
Go seek the King;——ha! ha! A lucky Change,
That Vertue which I fear'd would be my Hind'rance,
Has prov'd the Bond to my Design;
I'll bribe two Ruffians shall at Distance follow,
And seise 'em in some desert Place; and there
Whilst one retains her, t'other shall return
T'inform me where she's lodg'd; I'll be Disguis'd too,
Whilst they are poching for me, I'll to the Duke
With these Dispatches, then to th' Field,
Where, like the vig'rous *Jove*, I will enjoy
This *Semele* in a Storm, 'twill deaf her Cries
Like Drums in Battle, lest her Groans should pierce
My pittying Ear, and make the amorous Fight less fierce.
                        [*Exit.*

  Storm still. The Field Scene. Enter Lear *and* Kent.
  Kent. Here is the Place my Lord; good my Lord
    enter;
The Tyranny of this open Night's too rough
For Nature to endure.
  Lear. Let me alone.
  Kent. Good my Lord; enter.
  Lear. Wilt break my Heart?
  Kent. Beseech you, Sir.
  Lear. Thou think'st 'tis much that this contentious
    Storm
Invades us to the Skin; so 'tis to thee;
But where the greater Malady is fixt,
The lesser is scarce felt: The Tempest in my Mind
Does from my Senses take all feeling else,

Save what beats there. Filial Ingratitude!
Is it not as this Mouth should tear this Hand
For lifting Food to't?——But I'll punish home.
No, I will no more; in such a Night
To shut me out——Pour on, I will endure
In such a Night as this: O *Regan, Goneril!*
Your old kind Father, whose frank Heart gave All;
O that Way madness lies; let me shun that;
No more of that.

 Kent. See, my Lord, here's the Entrance.
 Lear. Well, I'll go in
And pass it all, I'll pray, and then I'll sleep:
Poor naked Wretches, wheresoe're you are,
That 'bide the pelting of this pittiless Storm,
How shall your houseless Heads and unfed Sides
Sustain this Shock? Your raggedness defend you
From Seasons such as these.
O! I have ta'en too little Care of this,
Take Physick, Pomp,
Expose thy self to feel what Wretches feel,
That thou may'st cast the Superflux to them,
And shew the Heav'ns more just.
    Edgar *in the Hovell.*
Five Fathom and a half, poor *Tom.*
 Kent. What art thou that dost grumble there i' th'
  Straw?
Come forth.
   [*Enter* Edgar *disguis'd as a madman.*]
 Edg. Away! The foul Fiend follows me—Through
the sharp Haw-Thorn blows the cold Wind.——Mum,
go to the Bed and warm thee.——Ha! What do I see?
By all my Griefs the poor old King bareheaded,
And drencht in this fowl Storm, professing *Syren,*
Are all your Protestations come to this?
 Lear. Tell me, Fellow, did'st thou give all to thy
Daughters?

Edg. Who gives any Thing to poor *Tom*, whom the foul Fiend has led through Fire, and through Flame, through Bushes, and Bogs; that has laid Knives under his Pillow, and Halters in his Pue; that has made him proud of Heart to ride on a Bay-trotting Horse over four inch'd Bridges, to course his own Shadow for a Traitor. —— Bless thy five Wits.   *Tom's* a cold. [*Shivers.*]   Bless thee from Whirl-Winds, Star-blasting, and Taking: Do poor *Tom* some Charity, whom the foul Fiend vexes.—Sa, sa; there I could have him now, and there, and there agen.

Lear. Have his Daughters brought him to this pass? Cou'dst thou save Nothing? Didst thou give them All?

Kent. He has no Daughters, Sir.

Lear. Death, Traytor, nothing cou'd have subdu'd
   Nature
To such a Lowness but his unkind Daughters.

Edg. Pillicock sat upon Pillicock Hill; Hallo, hallo,
   hallo.

Lear. Is it the Fashion that discarded Fathers
Should have such little Mercy on their Flesh?
Judicious Punishment, 'twas his Flesh begot
Those Pelican Daughters.

Edg. Take heed of the fowl Fiend; obey thy Parents, keep thy Word justly; swear not; commit not with Man's sworn Spouse; set not thy sweet Heart on proud Array; *Tom's* a cold.

Lear. What hast thou been?

Edg. A serving Man proud of Heart, that curl'd my Hair, us'd Perfume and Washes; that serv'd the Lust of my Mistresses Heart, and did the Act of Darkness with her; swore as many Oaths as I spoke Words; and broke 'em all in the sweet Face of Heaven: Let not the Paint, nor the Patch, nor the Rushing of Silks betray thy poor Heart to Women; keep thy Foot out of Brothels, thy Hand out of Plackets, thy Pen from Creditors Books, and defie the foul Fiend.—Still through the Haw-Thorn blows the cold Wind.——Sess, Suum, Mun, Nonny, Dolphin, my Boy!—Hist, the Boy the Boy! Sesey! Soft, let him trot by.

Lear. Death! thou wert better in thy Grave, then thus to answer with thy uncover'd Body, this Extremity of the Sky. And yet consider him well, and Man's no more than this; thou art indebted to the Worm for no Silk, to the Beast for no Hide, to the Cat for no Perfume. ——Ha! here's two of us are Sophisticated; thou art the Thing itself, unaccomodated Man is no more than such a poor bare fork'd Animal as thou art.
Off, off, ye vain Disguises, empty Lendings,
I'll be my Original Self, quick, quick, Uncase me.

Kent. Defend his Wits, good Heaven!

Lear. One Point I had forgot; what's your Name?

Edg. Poor *Tom*, that eats the swiming Frog, the Wall-Newt and the Water Newt; that in the Fury of his Heart, when the foul Fiend rages, eats Cow-Dung for Sallets, swallows the old Rat, and the Ditch-Dog, that drinks the green Mantle of the standing Pool, that's whipt from Tithing to Tithing, that has three Suits to his Back, Six Shirts to his Body.

      Horse to ride, and Weapon to wear,
      But Rats and Mice, and such small Deer,
      Have been *Tom's* Food for seven long Year.
Beware, my Follower; Peace, Smulkin, Peace, thou foul Fiend.

Lear. One Word more, but be sure true Councel; tell me, is a Madman a Gentleman, or a Yeoman?

Kent. I fear'd 'twou'd come to this; his Wits are gone.

Edg. Fraterreto calls me, and tells me, *Nero*, is an Angler in the Lake of Darkness. Pray, *Innocent*, and beware the foul Fiend.

Lear. Right, ha! ha! Was it not Pleasant to have a Thousand with red hot Spits come hizzing in upon 'em.

Edg. My Tears begin to take his Part so much
They marr my Counterfeiting.   [*Aside.*

Lear. The little Dogs and all, Trey, Blanch, and
Sweet-Heart, see they bark at me.

Edg. Tom will throw his Head at 'em; avaunt, ye
Curs.

> Be thy Mouth, or black, or white,
> Tooth that poysons if it bite;
> Mastiff, Grey-Hound, Mungrell, Grim,
> Hound, or Spanniel, Brach, or dym;
> Bob-Tail, Tight, or Trundle-Tail,
> *Tom* will make 'em weep and wail;
> For with throwing thus my Head,
> Dogs leap the Hatch, and all are fled.

Ud, de, de, de, See, see, see, Come, march to Wakes,
and Fairs, and Market-Towns.——Poor *Tom*, thy Horn
is dry.

Lear. You, Sir, I entertain you for One of my Hundred, only I do not like the Fashion of your Garments;
you'll say they're *Persian*, but no Matter, let 'em be
chang'd.

Enter Gloster.

Edg. This is the foul *Flibertigibet*; he begins at Cur-
few, and walks at first Cock, he gives the Web, and the
Pin; knits the Elflock; squints the Eye, and makes the
Hair-Lip;   mildews the white Wheat, and hurts the
poor Creature of the Earth.

> *Swithin* footed Thrice the Cold,
> He met the Night-Mare and her Nine-Fold,
>   'Twas there he did appoint her;
> He bid her alight, and her Troth plight,
>   And arroynt the Witch arroynt her.

Glost. What, has your Grace no better Company?

Edg. The Prince of Darkness is a Gentleman; *Modo*
he is call'd, and *Mahu.*

Glost. Go with me, Sir, hard by I have a Tenant.

My Duty cannot suffer me to obey in all your Daughters hard Commands, who have enjoyn'd me to make fast my Doors, and let this tyrannous Night take hold upon you. Yet have I ventur'd to come to seek you out, and bring you where both Fire and Food is ready.

Kent. Good my Lord take his Offer.

Lear. First let me talk with this Philosopher;
Say, *Stagirite*, what is the Cause of Thunder.

Glost. Beseech you, Sir, go with me.

Lear. I'll take a Word with this same learned *Theban.* What is your study?

Edg. How to prevent the Fiend, and to kill Vermin.

Lear. Let me ask you a Word in private.

Kent. His Wits are quite unsettled; good Sir, let's force him hence.

Glost. Can'st blame him? His Daughters seeks his Death; this Bedlam but disturbs him the more. Fellow, be gone.

Edg. Child *Rowland* to the dark Tow'r came,
His Word, was still, Fi, Fo, and Fum,
I smell the Blood of a *British* Man.——Oh! Torture!
                                                    [*Exit.*

Glost. Now, I prethee Friend, let's take him in our
Arms, and carry him where he shall meet both Welcome,
        and Protection.
Good Sir, along with us.

Lear. You say right, let 'em Anatomize *Regan*, for what breeds about her Heart; is there any Cause in Nature for these hard Hearts?

Kent. I beseech your Grace.

Lear. Hist!——Make no Noise, make no Noise——so so; we'll to Supper i' th' Morning.   [*Exeunt.*

            Enter Cordelia *and* Arante.

Ar. Dear Madam, rest ye here, our Search is vain,
Look, here's a Shed; beseech ye, enter here.

Cord. Prethee go thy self, seek thy own Ease,
Where the Mind's free, the Body's delicate;
This Tempest but diverts me from the Thought
Of what would hurt me more.
Enter two Ruffians.

  1. *Ruff.* We have dogg'd 'em far enough, this Place is
    private;
I'll keep 'em Prisoners here within this Hovel,
Whilst you return and bring Lord *Edmund* hither;
But help me first to House 'em.
  2. *Ruff.* Nothing but this, dear Devil,   [*Shows Gold.*
Shou'd have drawn me through all this Tempest;
But to our Work.
[*They seize* Cordelia *and* Arante, *who shriek out.*
Soft Madam, we are Friends; dispatch, I say.
  Cord. Help, Murder, help; Gods! Some kind Thun-
    derbolt
To strike me dead.
Enter Edgar.

  Edg. What Cry was that?——Ha, Women seiz'd by
    Ruffians?
Is this a Place and Time for Villany?
Avaunt, ye Bloud-Hounds.
[*Drives 'em with his Quarter Staff.*
  Both. The Devil, the Devil!   [*Run off.*
  Edg. O speak, what are ye that appear to be
O' th' tender Sex, and yet unguarded wander
Through the dread Mazes of this dreadful Night,
Where (tho' at full) the clouded Moon scarce darts
Imperfect Glimmerings?
  Cord. First say, what art thou?
Our Guardian Angel, that wer't pleas'd t'assume
That horrid Shape to fright the Ravishers?
We'll kneel to thee.
  Edg. O my tumultuous Blood!
By all my trembling Veins, *Cordelia's* Voice!

'Tis she herself!——My Senses sure confirm
To my wild Garb, and I am mad indeed.　　　*[Aside.*

　Cord. What e'er thou art, befriend a wretched Virgin,
And, if thou canst, direct our weary Search.

　Edg. Who relieves poor *Tom*, that sleeps on the
Nettle, with the Hedge Pig for his Pillow.

　　　Whilst *Smug* ply'd the Bellows
　　　She truckt with her Fellows,
　　　　The Freckle-Fac't Mab
　　　　Was a Blouze, and a Drab,
Yet *Swithin* made *Oberon* jealous.——Oh! Torture.

　Ar. Alack! Madam, a poor wand'ring Lunatick.

　Cord. And yet his Language seem'd but now well
　　temper'd.
Speak, Friend, to one more wretched than thy self;
And if thou hast one Interval of Sense,
Inform us, if thou canst, where we may find
A poor old Man, who through this heath has stray'd
The tedious Night.—Speak, sawest thou such a one?

　Edg. The King her Father, whom she's come to seek;
Through all the Terrors of this Night: O Gods! *[Aside.*
That such amazing Piety, such Tenderness
Shou'd yet to me be Cruel.
Yes, Fair One, such a one was lately here,
And is convey'd by some that came to seek him,
To a Neighb'ring Cottage; but distinctly where,
I know not.

　Cord. Blessings on 'em;
Let's find him out, *Arante*, for thou seest
We are in Heavens Protection.　　　*[Going off.*

　Edg. O *Cordelia*!

　Cord. Ha!——Thou know'st my Name.

　Edg. As you did once know *Edgar's.*

　Cord. *Edgar*!

　Edg. The poor Remains of *Edgar*, what your Scorn
Has left him.

　Cord. Do we wake, *Arante*?

Edg. My Father seeks my Life, which I preserv'd,
In hopes of some blest Minute to oblidge
Distrest *Cordelia*, and the Gods have giv'n it;
That Thought alone prevail'd with me to take
This Frantick Dress, to make the Earth my Bed,
With these bare Limbs all Change of Seasons bide,
Noons scorching Heat, and Midnights piercing Cold,
To feed on Offals, and to drink with Herds,
To combat with the Winds, and be the Sport
Of Clowns, or what's more wretched yet, their Pity.
  Ar. Was ever Tale so full of Misery!
  Edg. But such a Fall as this I grant was due
To my aspiring Love, for 'twas presumptuous,
Though not presumtuously pursu'd;
For well you know I wore my Flames conceal'd,
And silent as the Lamps that burn in Tombs
'Till you perceiv'd my Grief, with modest Grace
Drew forth the Secret, and then seal'd my Pardon.
  Cord. You had your Pardon, nor can you challenge
    more.
  Edg. What do I challenge more?
Such Vanity agrees not with these Rags;
When in my prosp'rous State, rich *Gloster's* Heir,
You silenc'd my Pretences, and enjoyn'd me
To trouble you upon that Theam no more;
Then what Reception must Loves Language find
From these bare Limbs and Beggar's humble Weeds?
  Cord. Such as a Voice of Pardon to a Wretch con-
    demn'd;
Such as the Shouts
Of succ'ring Forces to a Town besieg'd.
  Edg. Ah! What new Method now of Cruelty!
  Cord. Come to my Arms, thou dearest, best of Men,
And take the kindest Vows that e'er were spoke
By a protesting Maid.
  Edg. Is't possible?
  Cord. By the dear Vital Stream that bathes my Heart,

These hallowed Rags of thine, and naked Virtue,
These abject Tassels, these fantastick Shreds,
(Ridiculous ev'n to the meanest Clown)
To me are dearer than the richest Pomp
Of purple Monarchs.
    Edg. Generous charming Maid,
The Gods alone that made, can rate thy Worth!
This most amazing Excellence shall be
Fame's Triumph in succeeding Ages, when
Thy bright Example shall adorn the Scene,
And teach the World Perfection.
    Cord. Cold and weary,
We'll rest a while, *Arante*, on that Straw,
Then forward to find out the poor old King.
    Edg. Look, I have Flint and Steel, the Implements
Of wand'ring Lunaticks; I'll strike a Light,
And make a Fire beneath this Shed, to dry
Thy Storm drencht Garments, 'ere thou lie to rest thee;
Then fierce and wakeful as th' *Hesperian* Dragon,
I'll watch beside thee to protect thy Sleep;
Mean while the Stars shall dart their kindest Beams,
And Angels visit my *Cordelia's* Dreams.   [*Exeunt.*

SCENE, *the Palace.*
Enter Cornwall, Regan, Bastard, *Servants.*   Cornwall
with Gloster's *Letters.*
    Duke. I will have my Revenge e're I depart his House
Regan, see here, a Plot upon our State;
'Tis *Gloster's* Character, that has betray'd
His double Trust of Subject, and of Host.
    Reg. Then double be our Vengeance, this confirms
Th' Intelligence that we now receiv'd,
That he has been this Night to seek the King;
But who, Sir, was the kind Discoverer?
    Duke. Our *Eagle,* quick to spy, and fierce to seize;
Our trusty *Edmund.*

Reg. 'Twas a noble Service;
O *Cornwal*, take him to thy deepest Trust,
And wear him as a Jewel at thy Heart.
  Bast. Think, Sir, how hard a Fortune I sustain,
That makes me thus repent of serving you;   [*Weeps.*
O that this Treason had not been, or I
Not the Discoverer.
  Duke. Edmund, thou shall find
A Father in our Love, and from this Minute
We call thee Earl of *Gloster*; but there yet
Remains another Justice to be done,
And that's to punish this discarded Traytor;
But lest thy tender Nature should relent
At his just Sufferings, nor brook the Sight,
We wish thee to withdraw.
  Reg. The *Grotto*, Sir, within the lower Grove
Has Privacy to suit a Mourner's Thought.
                              [*To* Edmund *aside.*
  Bast. And there I may expect a Comforter,
Ha, Madam?
  Reg. What may happen, Sir, I know not,
But 'twas a Friend's Advice.   [*Exit* Bastard.
  Duke. Bring in the Traytor.
                    Gloster *brought in.*
Bind fast his Arms.
  Glost. What mean your Graces?
You are my Guests, pray do me no foul Play.
  Duke. Bind him, I say, hard, harder yet.
  Reg. Now, Traytor, thou shalt find——
  Duke. Speak, Rebel, where hast thou sent the King?
Whom, spight of our Decree, thou saw'st last Night.
  Glost. I'm ty'd to th' Stake, and must stand the
    Course.
  Reg. Say where, and why thou hast conceal'd him?
  Glost. Because I wou'd not see thy cruel Hands
Tear out his poor old Eyes, nor thy fierce Sister

Carve his anointed Flesh; but I shall see
The swift wing'd Vengeance overtake such Children.

    Duke. See't thou shalt never, Slaves perform your Work,
Out with those treacherous Eyes; dispatch, I say,
If thou seest Vengeance.——

    Glost. He that will think to live 'till he be old,
Give me some Help.——O cruel! oh! ye Gods.
                  [*They put out his Eyes.*

    Serv. Hold, hold, my Lord, I bar your Cruelty,
I cannot love your safety, and give Way
To such a barbarous Practise.

    Duke. Ha? my Villain.

    Serv. I have been your Servant from my Infancy,
But better Service have I never done you
Than with this Boldness.——

    Duke. Take thy Death, Slave.

    Serv. Nay, then revenge whilst yet my Bloud is warm.
                          [*Fight.*

    Reg. Help here.——Are you not hurt, my Lord?

    Glost. Edmund, enkindle all the Sparks of Nature
To quit this horrid Act.

    Reg. Out treacherous Villain,
Thou call'st on him that hates thee, it was he
That broacht thy Treason, shew'd us thy Dispatches;
There,——read, and save the *Cambrian* Prince a Labour.
If thy Eyes fail thee, call for Spectacles.

    Glost. O my Folly!
Then *Edgar,* was abus'd, kind Gods, forgive me that.

    Reg. How is't, my Lord?

    Duke. Turn out that Eye-less Villain, let him smell
His Way to *Cambray,* throw this Slave upon a Dunghil.
Regan, I bleed a pace, give me your Arm.   [*Exeunt.*

    Glost. All Dark, and Comfortless!
Where are those various Objects, that, but now,
Employ'd my busie Eyes? Where those Eyes?

Dead are their piercing Rays that lately shot
O'er flow'ry Vales to distant Sunny Hills,
And drew with Joy the vast Horizon in.
These groping Hands are now my only Guides,
And Feeling all my Sight.
O Misery! What Words can sound my Grief?
Shut from the Living whilst amongst the Living;
Dark as the Grave amidst the bustling World.
At once from Business, and from Pleasure bar'd:
No more to view the Beauty of the Spring,
Nor see the Face of Kindred, or of Friend;
Yet still one Way th' extreamest Fate affords,
And ev'n the Blind can find the Way to Death
Must I then tamely die, and unreveng'd?
So *Lear* may fall: No, with these bleeding Rings
I will present me to the pitying Croud,
And with the Rhetorick of these dropping Veins
Enflame 'em to revenge their King and me;
Then when the glorious Mischief is on Wing,
This Lumber from some Precipice I'll throw,
And dash it on the ragged Flint below;
Whence my freed Soul to her bright Sphear shall fly,⎫
Through boundless Orbs, eternal Regions spy,   ⎬
And, like the Sun, be All one glorious Eye.   [*Exit.*⎭

End of the Third Act.

Act IV.

A Grotto.

Edmund *and* Regan *amorously Seated, listening to*
Musick.

Bast. WHY were those Beauties made another's
right,
Which none can prize like me? Charming Queen,
Take my blooming Youth, for ever fold me

In those soft Arms, lull me in endless Sleep,
That I may dream of Pleasures too transporting
For Life to bear.
    Reg. Live, live, my *Gloster*,
And feel no Death, but that of swooning Joy?
I yield the Blisses on no harder Terms
Than that thou continue to be happy.
    Bast. This Jealousy is yet more kind, is't possible
That I should wander from a Paradise
To feed on sickly Weeds? Such Sweets live here
That Constancy will be no Vertue in me:
And yet must I forthwith go meet her Sister,   [*Aside.*
To whom, I must protest as much,——
Suppose it be the same; why, best of all,
And I have then my Lesson already conn'd.
    Reg. Wear this Remembrance of me.——I dare now
                      [*Gives him a Ring.*
Absent my self no longer from the Duke,
Whose Wound grows Dangerous, I hope Mortal.
    Bast. And let this happy Image of your *Gloster*,
            [*Pulling out a Picture, drops a Note.*
Lodge in that Breast where all his Treasure lies. [*Exit.*
    Reg. To this brave Youth a Woman's blooming
    Beauties
Are due; my Fool usurps my Bed——What's here?
Confusion on my Eyes.   [*Reads.*
    Where Merit is transparent, not to behold it were
    Blindness ; and not to reward it, Ingratitude.
                          Goneril.

Vexatious Accident! Yet fortunate too,
My Jealousie's confirmed, and I am taught
To cast for my Defence——   [*Enter an Officer.*
Now, what mean those Shouts? And that thy hasty
    Entrance?
    Off. A most surprizing and a sudden Change;
The Peasants are all up in Mutiny,

And only want a Chief to lead 'em on
To storm your Palace.
　Reg. On what Provocation?
　Off. At last Day's publick Festival, to which
The Yeomen from all Quarters had repair'd,
Old *Gloster*, whom you late depriv'd of Sight,
(His Veins yet streaming fresh,) presents himself,
Proclaims your Cruelty, and their Oppression,
With the King's Injuries; which so enrag'd 'em,
That now that Mutiny, which long had crept,
Takes Wing, and threatens your best Pow'rs.
　Reg. White-liver'd Slave!
Our Forces rais'd, and led by valiant *Edmund*,
Shall drive this Monster of Rebellion back
To her dark Cell; young *Gloster's* Arm allays
The Storm, his Father's feeble Breath did raise.　[*Exit.*

　　　The Field SCENE, *Enter* Edgar.
　Edg. The lowest and most abject Thing of Fortune
Stands still in Hope, and is secure from Fear;
The lamentable Change is from the Best,
The worst returns to better.——Who comes here?
　　　Enter Gloster, *led by an old Man.*
My Father poorly led! depriv'd of Sight!
The precious Stones torn from their bleeding Rings!
Something I heard of this inhumane Deed,
But disbeliev'd it, as an Act too horrid
For the hot Hell of a curst Woman's Fury;
When will the Measure of my Woes be full?
　Glost. Revenge, thou art on foot, Success attend
　　thee.
Well have I sold my Eyes, if the Event
Prove happy for the injur'd King.
　Old M. O, my good Lord, I have been your Tenant,
and your Father's Tenant these Fourscore Years.
　Glost. Away, get thee away, good Friend be gone,

Thy Comforts can do me no good at all,
Thee they may hurt.

 Old M. You cannot see your Way.

 Glost. I have no Way, and therefore want no Eyes,
I stumbled when I saw: O dear Son *Edgar*,
The Food of thy abused Father's Wrath,
Might I but live to see thee in my Touch,
I'd say, I had Eyes agen.

 Edg. Alas, he's sensible that I was wrong'd,
And shou'd I own myself, his tender Heart
Would break betwixt the Extreams of Grief and Joy.

 Old M. How now, who's there?

 Edg. A Charity for poor *Tom.* Play fair, and defy the
  foul Fiend.

O Gods! And must I still pursue this Trade, [*Aside.*
Trifling beneath such Loads of Misery?

 Old M. 'Tis poor mad *Tom.*

 Glost. In the late Storm, I such a Fellow saw,
Which made me think a Man a Worm,
Where is the Lunatick?

 Old M. Here, my Lord.

 Glost. Get thee now away, if for my Sake
Thou wilt o're-take us hence a Mile, or two,
I' th' Way tow'rd *Dover,* do't for ancient Love,
And bring some Cov'ring for this naked Wretch,
Whom I'll intreat to lead me.

 Old M. Alack, my Lord, he's Mad.

 Glost. 'Tis the Time's Plague when Mad-Men lead the
  Blind.

Do as I bid thee.

 Old M. I'll bring him the best 'Parrel that I have,
Come on't what will.   [*Exit.*

 Glost. Sirrah, naked Fellow.

 Edg. Poor *Tom's* a cold;——I cannot fool it longer,
And yet I must.——Bless thy sweet Eyes, they bleed;
Believe't poor *Tom* ev'n weeps his Blind to see 'em.

Glost. Know'st thou the Way to *Dover*?

Edg. Both Stile and Gate, Horse Way and Foot-Path;
poor Tom has been scar'd out of his good Wits; bless
every true Man's Son from the foul Fiend.

Glost. Here take this Purse; that I am wretched
Makes thee the happier, Heav'n deal so still.
Thus let the griping Userers Hoard be scatter'd,
So Distribution shall undo Excess
And each Man have enough. Dost thou know *Dover*?

Edg. I, Master.

Glost. There's a Cliff, whose high and bending Head
Looks dreadfully down on the roaring Deep;
Bring me but to the very Brink of it,
And I'll repair the Poverty thou bear'st
With something rich about me, from that Place
I shall no leading need.

Edg. Give me thy Arm: Poor *Tom* shall guide
thee.

Glost. Soft, for I hear the Tread of Passengers.

Enter Kent *and* Cordelia.

Cord. Ah me! your Fear's too true, it was the King;
I spoke but now with some that met him
As mad as the vex'd Sea singing aloud,
Crown'd with rank Femiter, and Furrow Weeds,
With Berries, Burdocks, Violets, Dazies, Poppies,
And all the idle Flowers that grow
In our sustaining Corn; conduct me to him,
And Heav'n so prosper thee.

Kent. I will, good Lady.
Ha, *Gloster* here!——Turn, poor dark Man, and hear
A Friend's Condolement, who at Sight of thine
Forgets his own Distress, thy old true *Kent*.

Glost. How, *Kent*? From whence return'd?

Kent. I have not since my Banishment been absent,
But in Disguise follow'd th' abandon'd King:
'Twas me thou saw'st with him in the late Storm.

Glost. Let me embrace thee, had I Eyes, I now
Should weep for Joy; but let this trickling Blood
Suffice instead of Tears.

Cord. O Misery!
To whom shall I complain, or in what Language?
Forgive, O wretched Man, the Piety
That brought thee to this Pass, 'twas I that caus'd it;
I cast me at thy Feet and beg of thee
To crush these weeping Eyes to equal Darkness,
If that will give thee any Recompence.

Edg. Was ever Season so distrest as this?   [*Aside.*

Glost. I think *Cordelia's* Voice! rise pious Princess,
And take a dark Man's Blessing.

Cord. O, my *Edgar*!
My Vertue's now grown guilty, works the Bane
Of those that do befriend me, Heav'n forsakes me,
And when you look that Way, it is but just
That you shou'd hate me too.

Edg. O wave this cutting Speech, and spare to Wound
A Heart that's on the Rack.

Glost. No longer cloud thee, *Kent* in that Disguise,
There's Business for thee, and of noblest Weight;
Our injur'd Country is at length in Arms,
Urg'd by the King's inhumane Wrongs and Mine,
And only want a Chief to lead 'em on.
That Task be thine.

Edg. Brave *Britains*, then there's Life in't yet. [*Aside.*

Kent. Then have we one Cast for our Fortune yet.
Come, Princess, I'll bestow you with the King,
Then on the Spur to head these Forces.
Farewel, good *Gloster*, to our conduct trust.

Glost. And be your Cause as prosp'rous as 'tis just.
                                        [*Exit.*

Goneril's *Palace. Enter* Goneril, *Attendants.*

Gon. It was great Ignorance, *Gloster's* Eyes being out,
To let him live, where he arrives he moves

All Hearts against us; *Edmund* I think is gone,
In Pity to his Misery, to dispatch him.
 Gent. No, Madam, he's return'd on speedy Summons
Back to your Sister.
 Gon. Ha! I like not that,
Such speed must have the Wings of Love; where's
  Albany?
 Gent. Madam, within, but never Man so chang'd;
I told him of the Uproar of the Peasants,
He smil'd at it, when I inform'd him
Of *Gloster's* Treason.——
 Gon. Trouble him no farther,
It is his coward Spirit; back to our Sister,
Hasten her Musters, and let her know
I have giv'n the Distaff into my Husband's Hands.
That done, with special Care deliver these Dispatches
In private to young *Gloster*.
Enter a Messenger.
 Mess. O Madam, most unseasonable News,
The Duke of *Cornwall's* dead of his late Wound,
Whose Loss your Sister has in Part supply'd,
Making brave *Edmund* General of her Forces.
 Gon. One Way I like this well;
But being a Widow, and my *Gloster* with her,
May blast the promis'd Harvest of our Love.
A Word more, Sir,——add Speed to your Journey,
And if you chance to meet with that blind Traitor,
Preferment falls on him that cuts him off. [*Exeunt.*

The Field SCENE, Gloster *and* Edgar.
 Glost. When shall we come to th' Top of that same
  Hill?
 Edg. We climb it now, mark how we labour.
 Glost. Methinks the Ground is even.
 Edg. Horrible Steep; heark, do you hear the Sea?
 Glost. No truly.

Edg. Why then your other Senses grow imperfect
By your Eyes Anguish.
Glost. So may it be indeed.
Methinks thy Voice is alter'd, and thou speak'st
In better Phrase and Matter than thou didst.
Edg. You are much deceiv'd, in nothing am I alter'd
But in my Garments.
Glost. Methinks y'are better spoken.
Edg. Come on, Sir, here's the Place, how fearfull
And dizzy 'tis to cast one's Eyes so low.
The Crows and Choughs that Wing the mid-Way Air
Shew scarce so big as Beetles; half Way down
Hangs one that gathers Sampire, dreadfull Trade!
The Fisher-Men that walk upon the Beach
Appear like Mice; and yon tall Anch'ring Barque
Seems lessen'd to her Cock, her Cock a Buoy,
Almost too small for Sight; the murmuring Surge
Cannot be heard so high; I'll look no more
Lest my Brain turn, and the Disorder make me
Tumble down head-long.
Glost. Set me where you stand.
Edg. You are now within a Foot of th'extream
    Verge.
For all beneath the Moon I wou'd not now
Leap forward.
Glost. Let go my Hand;
Here, Friend, is another Purse, in it a Jewel
Well worth a poor Man's Taking; get thee farther,
Bid me farewel, and let me hear thee going.
Edg. Fare you well, Sir.——That I do trifle thus
With this his Despair, is with Design to cure it.
Glost. Thus, mighty Gods, this World I do renounce,
And in your Sight shake my Afflictions off;
If I cou'd bear 'em longer, and not fall
To quarrel with your great opposeless Wills,
My Snuff and feebler Part of Nature shou'd

Burn itself out; if *Edgar* liv'd, O, bless him.
Now, Fellow, fare thee well.
   Edg. Gone, Sir, Farewell.
And yet I know not how Conceit may rob
The Treasury of Life, had he been where he thought,
By this had Thought been past.——Alive, or Dead?
Hoa, Sir, Friend; hear you, Sir, speak.——
Thus might he pass indeed,——yet he revives.
What are you, Sir?
   Glost. Away, and let me die.
   Edg. Hadst thou been ought but Gosmore Feathers,
     Air,
Falling so many Fathom down,
Thou hadst shiver'd like an Egg; but thou dost breathe,
Hast heavy Substance, bleed'st? Not speak! Art sound?
Thy Life's a Miracle.
   Glost. But have I faln, or no?
   Edg. From the dread Summet of this chalky Bourn:
Look up, an Height, the shrill tun'd Lark so high
Cannot be seen, or heard; do but look up.
   Glost. Alack, I have no Eyes.
Is Wretchedness depriv'd that Benefit
To End it self by Death?
   Edg. Give me your Arm.
Up; so, how is't? Feel you your Legs? You stand.
   Glost. Too well, too well.
   Edg. Upon the Brow o' th' Cliff, what Thing was that
Which parted from you?
   Glost. A poor unfortunate Beggar.
   Edg. As I stood here below, methought his Eyes
Were two full Moons, wide Nostrils breathing Fire.
It was some Fiend, therefore thou happy Father,
Think that th' all powerfull Gods, who made them
     Honours
Of Mens Impossibilities, have preserv'd thee.
   Glost. 'Tis wonderfull; henceforth I'll bear Affliction

'Till it expire; the Goblin which you speak of,
I took for a Man; oft-times t'would say,
The Fiend, the Fiend: He led me to that Place.

Edg. Bear free and patient Thoughts? But who comes
here?

Enter Lear, *a Coronet of Flowers on his Head ;*
Wreaths, and Garlands about him.

Lear. No, no; they cannot touch me for coyning;
I am the King himself.

Edg. O piercing Sight.

Lear. Nature's above Art in that Respect; there's
your Press-Money: That Fellow handles his Bow like a
Cow-Keeper:——Draw me a Clothier's Yard. A Mouse,
a Mouse, peace, hoa! There's my Gauntlet; I'll prove
it on a Giant: Bring up the brown Bills: O well flown
Bird; i' th' White, i' th' White.——Heugh! Give the
Word.

Edg. Sweet *Marjorum.*

Lear. Pass.

Glost. I know that Voice.

Lear. Ha! *Goneril* with a white Beard! They flatter'd me like a Dog, and told me I had white Hairs on
my Chin, before the black ones were there; to say ay
and no to every Thing that I said: Ay and no too was
no good Divinity. When the Rain came once to wet me,
and the Winds to make me chatter; when the Thunder
wou'd not peace at my bidding. There I found 'em,
there I smelt 'em out; go too, they are not Men of their
Words; they told me I was a King; 'tis a Lye, I am not
Ague proof.

Glost. That Voice I well remember, is't not the King's?

Lear. I, every Inch a King, when I do Stare
See how the Subject quakes.
I pardon that Man's Life, what was the Cause?
Adultery? Thou shalt not Die. Die for Adultery!
The Wren goes to't, and the small gilded Flie

Engenders in my Sight: Let Copulation Thrive,
For *Gloster's* Bastard Son was kinder to his Father
Than were my Daughters got i' th' lawfull Bed.
To't Luxury, pell mell, for I lack Souldiers.

　Glost. Not all my Sorrows past so deep have toucht
　　me,
As the sad Accents: Sight were now a Torment——

　Lear. Behold that simp'ring Lady, she that starts
At Pleasures Name, and thinks her Ear profan'd
With the least wanton Word; wou'd you believe it,
The Fitcher, nor the pamper'd Steed goes to't
With such a riotous Appetite: Down from the Waste
they are *Centaurs*, though Women all above; but to the
Girdle do the Gods inherit, beneath is all the Fiends;
there's Hell, there's Darkness, the sulphurous un-
fathom'd.—Fie! Fie! Pah!——An Ounce of *Civet*, good
Apothecary, to sweeten my Imagination.——There's
Money for thee.

　Glost. Let me kiss that Hand.

　Lear. Let me wipe it first; it smells of Mortality.

　Glost. Speak, Sir, do you know me?

　Lear. I remember thy Eyes well enough: Nay, do
thy worst, blind *Cupid*, I'll not love.——Read me this
Challenge, mark but the penning of it.

　Glost. Were all the Letters Suns, I cou'd not see.

　Edg. I wou'd not take this from Report; wretched
　　Cordelia!
What will thy Virtue do when thou shalt find
This fresh Affliction added to the Tale
Of thy unparallell'd Griefs.

　Lear. Read.

　Glost. What! with this Case of Eyes?

　Lear. O ho! Are you there with me? No Eyes in
your Head, and no Money in your Purse? Yet you see
how this World goes.

　Glost. I see it feelingly.

Lear. What! Art mad! A Man may see how this World goes with no Eyes. Look with thy Ears; see how yon Justice rails on that simple Thief; shake 'em together, and the first that Drops, be it Thief, or Justice, is a Villain.——Thou hast seen a Farmer's Dog bark at a Beggar.

Glost. Ay, Sir.

Lear. And the Man ran from the Curr; there thou might'st behold the great Image of Authority, a Dog's obey'd in Office. Thou Rascal, Beadle, hold up thy bloody Hand, why dost thou lash that Strumpet? Thou hotly lust'st to enjoy her in that Kind for which thou whipst her; do, do, the Judge that sentenc'd her has been before-hand with thee.

Glost. How stiff is my vile Sense, that yields not yet?

Lear. I tell thee the Usurer hangs the Couz'ner,—— through tatter'd Robes small Vices do appear; Robes, and Fur-Gowns hide all: Place Sins with Gold; why there 'tis for thee, my Friend, make much of it; it has the Power to seal the Accuser's Lips. Get thee glass Eyes, and like a scurvy Politician, seem to see the Things thou dost not. Pull, pull off my Boots; hard, harder; so, so.

Glost. O Matter and Impertinency mixt?
Reason in Madness.

Lear. If thou wilt weep my Fortunes, take my Eyes,
I know thee well enough, thy Name is *Gloster*.
Thou must be patient, we come crying hither
Thou know'st, the first Time that we taste the Air
We wail and cry,——I'll preach to thee, Mark.

Edg. Break lab'ring Heart.

Lear. When we are born we cry that we are come
To this great Stage of Fools.——

Enter Two or Three Gentlemen.

Gent. O! here he is; lay Hand upon him, Sir:
Your dearest Daughter sends——

Lear. No Rescue? What! A Prisoner? I am even the natural Fool of Fortune: Use me well, you shall have Ransome.——Let me have Surgeons? O! I am cut to th' Brains.

Gent. You shall have any Thing.

Lear. No Seconds? All my self? I will die bravely like a smug Bridegroom, flusht and pamper'd as a Priest's Whore. I am a King, my Masters, know ye that?

Gent. You are a Royal One, and we Obey you?

Lear. It were an excellent Stratagem to shoe a Troop of Horse with Felt, I'll put in proof.——no Noise, no Noise.——Now will we steal upon these Sons-in-Law, and then——Kill, kill, kill, kill! [*Exit Running.*

Glost. A Sight most moving in the meanest Wretch, Past speaking in a King. Now, good Sir, what are you?

Edg. A most poor Man made tame to Fortune's
  Strokes,
And prone to pity by experienc'd Sorrows; give me your
  Hand.

Glost. You ever gentle Gods take my Breath from me, And let not my ill Genius tempt me more To Die before you please.

Enter Goneril's *Gentleman-Usher.*

Gent. A proclaim'd Prize, O most happily met, That Eye-less Head of thine was first fram'd Flesh To raise my Fortunes; thou old unhappy Traytor, The Sword is out that must destroy thee.

Glost. Now let thy friendly Hand put Strength enough
  to't.

Gent. Wherefore bold Peasant, Dar'st thou support a publisht Traytor? Hence, Lest I destroy thee too. Let go his Arm.

Edg. 'Chill not let go, Zir, without 'vurther 'Casion.

Gent. Let go, Slave, or thou Dyest.

Edg. Good Gentlemen go your Gate, and let poor Volk pass; and Chu'd ha' bin' Zwagger'd out of my

Life, it wou'd not a bin zo long as 'tis by a Vort-Night.
——Nay, an' thou com'st near th' old Man, I'st try
whether your Costard, or my Ballow be th' harder.

Gent. Out Dunghil.

Edg. Chill pick your Teeth, Zir; come, no Matter vor
your Voines.

Gent. Slave, thou hast slain me; oh, untimely Death!

Edg. I know thee well, a serviceable Villain,
As duteous to the Vices of thy Mistress,
As Lust cou'd wish.

Glost. What! Is he dead?

Edg. Sit you, Sir, and rest you.
This is a Letter Carrier, and may have
Some Papers of Intelligence, that may stand
Our Party in good stead to know.——What's here?
      [*Takes a Letter out of his Pocket; opens, and reads.*
To *Edmund* Earl of *Gloster*.

> *Let our Mutual Loves be remembred, you have many*
> *Opportunities to Cut him off. If he return the*
> *Conqueror, then I am still a Prisoner, and his*
> *Bed my Goal; from the loath'd Warmth of*
> *which deliver me, and supply the Place for your*
> *Labour.*   Goneril.

A Plot upon her Husband's Life,
And the Exchange my Brother!——Here i' th' Sands
I'll rake thee up, thou Messenger of Lust,
Griev'd only that thou hadst no other Deaths-Man.
In Time and Place convenient I'll produce
These Letters to the Sight of th' injur'd Duke,
As best shall serve our Purpose; come, your Hand.
Far off methinks I hear the beaten Drum,
Come, Sir, I will bestow you with a Friend.   [*Exeunt.*

A Chamber. Lear *a sleep on a Couch;* Cordelia, [Physician]
            and Attendants standing by him.

Cord. His Sleep is sound, and may have good Effect

To cure his jarring Senses, and repair
This Breach of Nature.

    Phys. We have employ'd the utmost Pow'r of Art,
And this deep Rest will perfect our Design.

    Cord. O *Regan, Goneril!* Inhumane Sisters,
Had he not been your Father, these white Hairs
Had challeng'd sure some Pity? Was this a Face
To be expos'd against the jarring Winds?
My Enemy's Dog, though he had bit me, shou'd
Have stood that Night against my Fire.—He wakes,
    speak to him.

    Gent. Madam, do you, 'tis fittest.

    Cord. How do's my royal Lord? How fairs your
    Majesty?

    Lear. You do me Wrong to take me out o' th' Grave.
Ha! Is this too a World of Cruelty?
I know my Privilege, think not that I will
Be us'd like a wretched Mortal? No,
No more of that.

    Cord. Speak to me, Sir, whom am I?

    Lear. You are a Soul in Bliss, but I am bound
Upon a Wheel of Fire, which my own Tears
Do scald like Molten Lead.

    Cord. Sir, do you know me?

    Lear. You are a Spirit, I know; where did you die?

    Cord. Still, still, far wide.

    Phys. Madam he's scarce awake; he'll soon grow
    more compos'd.

    Lear. Where have I been? Where am I? Fair Day-
    Light!
I am mightily abus'd, I shou'd even die with Pity
To see another thus. I will not swear
These are my Hands.

    Cord. O look upon me, Sir,
And hold your Hands in Blessing over me; nay,
You must not kneel.

Lear. Pray do not mock me.
I am a very foolish fond old Man,
Fourscore and upward; and to deal plainly with you,
I fear I am not in my perfect Mind.
    Cord. Nay, then farewel to Patience: Witness for me
Ye mighty Pow'rs, I ne're complain'd 'till now!
    Lear. Methinks I shou'd know you, and know this
        Man,
Yet I am doubtfull, for I am mainly ignorant
What Place this is, and all the Skill I have
Remembers not these Garments; nor do I know
Where I did sleep last Night.——Pray do not mock me,
For, as I am a Man, I think that Lady
To be my Child *Cordelia.*
    Cord. O my dear, dear Father!
    Lear. Be your Tears wet? Yes faith; pray do not
        weep,
I know I have giv'n thee Cause, and am so humbled
With Crosses since, that I cou'd ask
Forgiveness of thee, were it possible
That thou cou'dst grant it; but I'm well assur'd
Thou can'st not; therefore I do stand thy Justice;
If thou hast Poyson for me I will drink it,
Bless thee, and die.
    Cord. O pity, Sir, a bleeding Heart, and cease
This killing Language.
    Lear. Tell me, Friends, where am I?
    Gent. In your own Kingdom, Sir.
    Lear. Do not abuse me.
    Gent. Be comforted, good Madam, for the Violence
Of his Distemper's past; we'll lead him in,
Nor trouble him, 'till he is better settled.
Wil't please you, Sir, walk into freer Air?
    Lear. You must bear with me, I am Old and Foolish.
                    [*They lead him off.*
    Cord. The Gods restore you.——Heark, I hear afar

The beaten Drum, Old *Kent's* a Man of's Word.
O for an Arm
Like the fierce Thunderer's, when th' Earth-born Sons
Storm'd Heav'n, to fight this injur'd Father's Battle!
That I cou'd shift my Sex, and die me deep
In his Opposer's Blood! But as I may,
With Women's Weapons, Piety and Pray'rs,
I'll aid his Cause.——You never erring Gods
Fight on his Side, and Thunder on his Foes
Such Tempests as his poor ag'd Head sustain'd,
Your Image suffers when a Monarch bleeds.
'Tis your own Cause, for that your Succors bring,
Revenge your selves, and right an injur'd King.

End of the Fourth Act.

Act V.

SCENE, *A Camp.*
Enter Goneril *and Attendants.*

Gon. OUR Sister's Pow'rs already are arriv'd,
And She herself has promis'd to prevent
The Night with her Approach: Have you provided
The Banquet I bespoke for her Reception
At my Tent?
  Att. So, please your Grace, we have.
  Gon. But thou, my Poysner, must prepare the Bowl
That Crowns this Banquet, when our Mirth is High,
The Trumpets sounding, and the Flutes replying,
Then is the Time to give this fatal Draught
To this Imperious Sister; if then our Arms succeed,
Edmund, more dear then Victory, is mine.
But if Defeat, or Death it self attend me,
'Twill charm my Ghost to think I've left behind me,
No happy Rival. Heark, she comes.
                              [*Trumpet. Exeunt.*

Enter Bastard *in his Tent.*

Bast. To both these Sisters have I sworn my Love,
Each jealous of the other, as the Stung
Are of the Adder; neither can be held
If both remain alive; where shall I fix?
Cornwall is dead, and *Regan's* empty Bed
Seems cast by Fortune for me, but already
I have enjoy'd her, and bright *Goneril*
With equal Charms brings dear Variety,
And yet untasted Beauty: I will use
Her Husband's Countenance for the Battail, then
Usurp at once his Bed and Throne.   [*Enter Officers.*
My trusty Scouts y'are well return'd; have ye de-
        scry'd
The Strength and Posture of the Enemy?
    Off. We have, and were surpriz'd to find
The banish'd *Kent* return'd, and at their Head;
Your Brother *Edgar* on the Rear; old *Gloster*
(A moving Spectacle) led through their Ranks,
Whose pow'rfull Tongue, and more prevailing Wrongs,
Have so enrag'd their rustick Spirits, that with
Th' approaching Dawn we must expect their Battle.
    Bast. You bring a welcome Hearing; each to his
        Charge.
Line well your Ranks, and stand on your Award,
To Night repose you, i'th' Morn we'll give
The Sun a Sight that shall be worth his rising.
                                        [*Exeunt.*

SCENE *A Valley near the Camp.*
Enter Edgar *and* Gloster.

Edg. Here, Sir, take you the Shadow of this Tree
For your good Host; pray that the Right may thrive:
If ever I return to you again
I'll bring you Comfort.   [*Exit.*
    Glost. Thanks, friendly Sir;
The Fortune your good Cause deserves betide you.

An Alarm ; after which Gloster *speaks.*

The Fight grows hot; the whole War's now at work,
And the goar'd Battle bleeds in every Vein.
Whilst Drums and Trumpets drown loud Slaughters
        Roar;
Where's *Gloster* now that us'd to head the Fray,
And scour the Ranks where deadliest Danger lay?
Here, like a Shepherd, in a lonely Shade,
Idle, unarm'd, and listning to the Fight;
Yet the disabled Courser, maim'd and blind,
When to the Stall he hears the ratling War,
Foaming with Rage, tears up the batter'd Ground,
And tugs for Liberty.
No more of Shelter, thou blind Worm, but forth
To th' open Field, the War may come this Way,
And crush thee into Rest.——Here lay thee down,
And tear the Earth, that Work befits a Mole.
O dark Despair! When, *Edgar*, wilt thou come
To pardon, and dismiss me to the Grave?

                          [*A Retreat sounded.*

Heark! A Retreat, the King has lost, or Won.

                Re-enter Edgar, *bloody.*

  Edg. Away, old Man, give me your Hand, away!
King *Lear* has lost; he and his Daughter tane,
And this, ye Gods, is all that I can save
Of this most precious Wreck; give me your Hand.
  Glost. No farther, Sir, a Man may rot, even here.
  Edg. What! In ill Thoughts again? Men must endure
Their going hence, ev'n as their coming hither.
  Glost. And that's true too.   [*Exeunt.*
Flourish. Enter in Conquest, Albany, Goneril, Regan,
        Bastard.——Lear, Kent, Cordelia, *Prisoners.*
  Alb. It is enough to have Conquer'd, Cruelty
Shou'd ne're survive the Fight. Captain o' th'Guards,
Treat well your royal Prisoners 'till you have
Our farther Orders, as you hold our Pleasure.

Gon. Heark! Sir, not as you hold our Husband's
    Pleasure.   [*To the Captain aside.*
But as you hold your Life, dispatch your Pris'ners.
Our Empire can have no sure Settlement
But in their Death, the Earth that covers them
Binds fast our Throne. Let me hear they are dead.
    Capt. I shall obey your Orders.
    Bast. Sir, I approve it safest to pronounce
Sentence of Death upon this wretched King,
Whose Age has Charms in it, his Title more,
To draw the Commons once more to his Side,
'Twere best prevent——
    Alb. Sir, by your Favour,
I hold you but a Subject of this War,
Not as a Brother.
    Reg. That's as we list to Grace him.
Have you forgot that He did lead our Pow'rs;
Bore the Commission of our Place and Person?
And that Authority may well stand up,
And call it self your Brother.
    Gon. Not so hot,
In his own Merits he exalts himself
More than in your Addition.
                 Enter Edgar *disguis'd.*
    Alb. What art thou?
    Edg. Pardon me, Sir, that I presume to stop
A Prince and Conquerour, yet e'er you Triumph,
Give Ear to what a Stranger can deliver
Of what concerns you more than Triumph can.
I do impeach your General there of Treason,
Lord *Edmund*, that usurps the Name of *Gloster*,
Of foulest Practice 'gainst your Life and Honour;
This Charge is true, and wretched though I seem,
I can produce a Champion that will prove
In single Combat what I do avouch:
If *Edmund* dares but trust his Cause and Sword.

Bast. What will not *Edmund* dare! My Lord, I beg
The Favour that you'd instantly appoint
The Place where I may meet this Challenger,
Whom I will sacrifice to my wrong'd Fame;
Remember, Sir, that injur'd Honour's nice,
And cannot brook delay.

Alb. Anon, before our Tent, i' th' Army's View,
There let the Herald cry.

Edg. I thank your Highness in my Champion's Name,
He'll wait your Trumpet's Call.

Alb. Lead.   [*Exeunt.*

Manent Lear, Kent, Cordelia, *guarded.*

Lear. O *Kent, Cordelia!*
You are the onely Pair that I e'er wrong'd,
And the just Gods have made you Witnesses
Of my Disgrace, the very Shame of Fortune,
To see me chain'd and shackled at these Years!
Yet were you but Spectatours of my Woes,
Not Fellow-Sufferers, all were well!

Cord. This Language, Sir, adds yet to our Affliction.

Lear. Thou, *Kent,* didst head the Troops that fought
my Battel,
Expos'd thy Life and Fortunes for a Master
That had (as I remember) banisht thee.

Kent. Pardon me, Sir, that once I broke your Orders;
Banish'd by you, I kept me here disguis'd
To watch your Fortunes, and protect your Person;
You know you entertain'd a rough blunt Fellow,
One *Cajus,* and you thought he did you Service.

Lear. My trusty *Cajus,* I have lost him too! [*Weeps.*
'Twas a rough Honesty.

Kent. I was that *Cajus,*
Disguis'd in that course Dress, to follow you.

Lear. My *Cajus* too! Wer't thou my trusty *Cajus?*
Enough, enough.——

Cord. Ah me, he faints! his Blood forsakes his Cheek,
Help, *Kent.*——

Lear. No, no, they shall not see us weep,
We'll see them rot first.—Guards, lead away to Prison;
Come *Kent, Cordelia*, come;
We two will sit alone, like Birds i'th' Cage,
When thou dost ask me Blessing, I'll kneel down
And ask of Thee Forgiveness; thus we'll live,
And Pray, and Sing, and tell old Tales, and laugh
At gilded Butter-Flies, hear Sycophants
Talk of Court News, and we'll talk with them too,
Who loses and who wins, who's in, who's out,
And take upon us the Mystery of Things
As if we were Heav'ns Spies.

Cord. Upon such Sacrifices
The Gods themselves throw Incense.

Lear. Have I caught ye?
He that parts us must bring a Brand from Heav'n:
Together we'll out-toil the Spight of Hell,
And die the Wonders of the World; away.
                                       [*Exeunt guarded.*

Flourish. Enter before the Tents, Albany, Goneril, Regan,
     Guards and Attendants ; Goneril *speaking apart to the
     Captain of the Guards entring.*

Gon. Here's Gold for thee, thou know'st our late
     Command
Upon your Pris'ners Lives; about it streight, and at
Our Ev'ning Banquet let it raise our Mirth,
To hear that they are dead.

Capt. I shall not fail your Orders.   [*Exit.*
          Albany, Goneril, Regan, *take their Seats.*

Alb. Now, *Gloster*, trust to thy single Vertue, for thy
     Souldiers
All levied in my Name, have in my Name
Took their Discharge; now let our Trumpets speak,
And Herald read out this.   [*Herald reads.*

If any Man of Quality, within the Lists of the
Army, will maintain upon Edmund, *suppos'd*
Earl of Gloster, *that he is a manifold Traitor,*
let him appear by the third Sound of the Trum-
pet; he is bold in his Defence.——*Agen, agen.*
               [*Trumpets answers from within.*
          Enter Edgar *arm'd.*

Alb. Lord *Edgar!*
Bast. Ha! My Brother!
This is the onely Combatant that I cou'd fear?
For in my Breast Guilt Duels on his Side,
But, Conscience, what have I to do with thee?
Awe thou thy dull Legitimate Slaves, but I
Was born a Libertine, and so I keep me.
  Edg. My Noble Prince, a Word;——e'er we engage
Into your Highness's Hands I give this Paper,
It will the Truth of my Impeachment prove,
What ever be my Fortune in the Fight.
  Alb. We shall peruse it.
  Edg. Now *Edmund*, draw thy Sword,
That if my Speech has wrong'd a noble Heart,
Thy Arm may doe thee Justice: Here i'th' Presence
Of this high Prince, these Queens, and this crown'd List,
I brand thee with the spotted Name of Traytour.
False to thy Gods, thy Father, and thy Brother,
And what is more, thy Friend, false to this Prince:
If then thou shar'st a Spark of *Gloster's* Virtue,
Acquit thy self; or if thou shar'st his Courage,
Meet this Defiance bravely.
  Bast. And dares *Edgar*,
The beaten routed *Edgar*, brave his Conquerour?
From all thy Troops and Thee I forc't the Field,
Thou hast lost the gen'ral Stake, and art thou now
Come with thy petty single Stock to play
This after Game?
  Edg. Half-blooded Man,

Thy Father's Sin first, then his Punishment;
The dark and vicious Place where he begot thee
Cost him his Eyes; from thy licentious Mother
Thou draw'st thy Villany; but for thy Part,
Of *Gloster's* Blood, I hold thee worth my Sword.

   Bast. Thou bear'st thee on thy Mother's Piety,
Which I despise; thy Mother being chaste
Thou art assur'd thou art but *Gloster's* Son;
But mine, disdaining Constancy, leaves me
To hope that I am sprung from nobler Blood,
And possibly a King might be my Sire:
But be my Birth's uncertain Chance as 'twill,
Who 'twas that had the Hit to Father me
I know not; 'tis enough that I am I:
Of this one Thing I'm certain,——that I have
A daring Soul, and so have at thy Heart.
Sound Trumpets.   [*Fight,* Bastard *falls.*

   Gon. and Reg. Save him, save him.

   Gon. This was Practice, *Gloster,*
Thou won'st the Field, and was not bound to fight
A vanquisht Enemy. Thou art not conquer'd,
But couz'ned and betray'd.

   Alb. Shut your Mouth, Lady,
Or with this Paper I shall stop it.——Hold, Madam,
Thou worse than any Name, read thy own Evil;
No Tearing, Lady, I perceive you know it.

   Gon. Say, if I do, who shall arraign me for't?
The Laws are mine, not thine.

   Alb. Most monst'rous! Ha! Thou know'st it too?

   Bast. Ask me not what I know,
I have not Breath to answer idle Questions.

   Alb. I am resolv'd——your Right, brave Sir, has
    conquer'd.   [*To* Edgar.
Along with me, I must consult your Father.
          [*Exit* Albany *and* Edgar.

   Reg. Help every Hand to save a noble Life;

My half o'th' Kingdom for a Man of Skill
To stop this precious Stream.
　　Bast. Away ye Empericks,
Torment me not with your vain Offices;
The Sword has pierc'd too far; *Legitimacy*
At last has got it.
　　Reg. The Pride of Nature dies.
　　Gon. Away, the Minutes are too precious,
Disturb us not with thy impertinent Sorrow.
　　Reg. Art thou my Rival then profest?
　　Gon. Why, was our Love a Secret? Cou'd there
　　　be
Beauty like mine, and Gallantry like his,
And not a mutual Love? Just Nature then
Had err'd. Behold that Copy of Perfection,
That Youth whose Story will have no foul Page,
But where it says he stoopt to *Regan's* Arms:
Which yet was but Compliance, not Affection;
A Charity to begging, ruin'd Beauty!
　　Reg. Who begg'd when *Goneril* writ that? Expose it.
　　　　　　　　　　　　　　[*Throws her a Letter.*
And let it be your Army's Mirth, as 'twas
This charming Youth's and mine, when in the Bow'r
He breath'd the warmest Ecstasies of Love;
Then panting on my Breast, cry'd, matchless *Regan!*
That *Goneril* and thou shou'd e'er be kin!
　　Gon. Die, *Circe,* for thy Charms are at an End,
Expire before my Face, and let me see
How well that boasted Beauty will become
Congealing Blood, and Death's convulsive Pangs:
Die and be husht, for at my Tent last Night
Thou drank'st thy Bane, amidst thy rev'ling Bowls:
Ha! Dost thou Smile? Is then thy Death thy Sport?
Or has the trusty Potion made thee mad?
　　Reg. Thou com'st as short of me in thy Revenge,
As in my *Gloster's* Love; my Jealousie

Inspir'd me to prevent thy feeble Malice,
And Poison thee at thy own Banquet.

Gon. Ha!

Bast. No more, my Queen's, of this untimely Strife,
You both deserv'd my Love, and both possest it.
Come, Soldiers, bear me in; and let
Your Royal Presence grace my last Minutes;
Now, *Edgar*, thy proud Conquest I forgive;
Who wou'd not choose, like me, to yield his Breath
T' have Rival Queens contend for him in Death?

[*Exit.*

SCENE, *A Prison.*
Lear *asleep, with his Head on* Cordelia's *Lap.*

Cord. What Toils, thou wretched King, hast thou en-
dur'd
To make thee draw, in Chains, a Sleep so sound?
Thy better Angel charm thy ravisht Mind
With fancy'd Freedom; Peace is us'd to lodge
On Cottage Straw. Thou hast the Beggar's Bed,
Therefore shoud'st have the Beggar's careless Thought.
And now, my *Edgar*, I remember thee,
What Fate has seiz'd thee in this general Wreck
I know not, but I know thou must be wretched,
Because *Cordelia* holds thee dear.
O Gods! A sudden Gloom o'er-whelms me, and the
Image
Of Death o'er-spreads the Place.—Ha! Who are these?
Enter Captain *and* Officers *with Cords.*

Capt. Now, Sirs, dispatch, already you are paid
In Part, the Best of your Reward's to come.

Lear. Charge, charge upon their Flank, their last Wing
haults.
Push, push the Battel, and the Day's our own.
Their Ranks are broke, down with *Albany.*
Who holds my Hands?——O thou deceiving Sleep,
I was this very Minute on the Chace;

And now a Prisoner here.——What mean the Slaves?
You will not murder me?

    Cord. Help, Earth and Heaven!
For your Soul's Sake, dear Sirs, and for the Gods.

    Offi. No Tears, good Lady, no pleading against Gold
    and Preferment.
Come, Sirs, make ready your Cords.

    Cord. You, Sir, I'll seize,
You have a humane Form, and if no Prayer's
Can touch your Soul to spare a poor King's Life,
If there be any Thing that you hold dear,
By that I beg you to dispatch me first.

    Capt. Comply with her Request; dispatch her first.

    Lear. Off Hell-Hounds, by the Gods I charge you
    spare her;
'Tis my *Cordelia*, my true pious Daughter;
No pity?——Nay, then take an old Man's Vengeance.
    Snatches a Partizan, and strikes down Two of them;
        the Rest quit Cordelia, *and turn upon him.*
              Enter Edgar *and* Albany.

    Edg. Death! Hell! Ye Vultures, hold your impious
    Hands,
Or take a speedier Death than you wou'd give.

    Capt. By whose Command?

    Edg. Behold the Duke, your Lord.

    Alb. Guards, seize those Instruments of Cruelty.

    Cord. My *Edgar*, O!

    Edg. My dear *Cordelia*! Lucky was the Minute
Of our Approach, the Gods have weigh'd our Suff'rings;
W' are past the Fire, and now must shine to Ages.

    Gent. Look here, my Lord, see where the generous
    King
Has slain two of 'em.

    Lear. Did I not, Fellow?
I've seen the Day, with my good biting Faulchion
I cou'd have made 'em skip: I am Old now,

And these vile Crosses spoil me; Out of Breath.
Fie, oh! quite out of Breath, and spent.

    Alb. Bring in old *Kent*; and, *Edgar*, guide you
      hither
Your Father, whom you said was near,   [*Exit* Edgar.
He may be an Ear-Witness as the least
Of our Proceedings.   [Kent *brought in here.*

    Lear. Who are you?
My Eyes are none o'th Best, I'll tell you streight;
Oh *Albany*! Well, Sir, we are your Captives,
And you are come to see Death pass upon us.
Why this Delay.——Or is't your Highness's Pleasure
To give us first the Torture? Say ye so?
Why here's old *Kent* and I, as tough a Pair
As e'er bore Tyrants Stroke.——But my *Cordelia*,
My poor *Cordelia* here, O pity.——

    Alb. Take off their Chains.——Thou injur'd Majesty,
The Wheel of Fortune now has made her Circle,
And Blessings yet stand 'twixt thy Grave and thee.

    Lear. Com'st thou inhumane Lord, to sooth us back
To a Fool's Paradice of Hope, to make
Our Doom more wretched? Go to, we are too well
Acquainted with Misfortune to be gull'd
With Lying Hope; no, we will hope no more.

    Alb. I have a Tale, t'unfold so full of Wonder
As cannot meet an easy Faith;
But by that Royal injur'd Head 'tis true.

    Kent. What wou'd your Highness?

    Alb. Know, the noble *Edgar*
Impeacht Lord *Edmund*, since the Fight, of Treason,
And dar'd him for the Proof to single Combat,
In which the Gods confirm'd his Charge by Conquest;
I left ev'n now the Traytor wounded Mortally!

    Lear. And whether tends this Story?

    Alb. 'Ere they fought
Lord *Edgar* gave into my Hands this Paper,

A blacker Scrowl of Treason, and of Lust,
Than can be found in the Records of Hell;
There, sacred Sir, behold the Character
Of *Goneril*, the worst of Daughters, but
More vicious Wife.

Cord. Cou'd there be yet Addition to their Guilt?
What will not they that wrong a Father do?

Alb. Since then my Injuries, *Lear*, fall in with thine,
I have resolv'd the same Redress for both.

Kent. What says my Lord?

Cord. Speak, for methought I heard
The charming Voice of a descending God.

Alb. The Troops, by *Edmund* rais'd, I have disbanded;
Those that remain are under my Command.
What Comfort may be brought to chear your Age,
And heal your savage Wrongs, shall be apply'd,
For to your Majesty we do resign
Your Kingdom, save what Part your self conferr'd
On us in Marriage.

Kent. Hear you that, my Liege?

Cord. Then there are Gods, and Vertue is their Care.

Lear. Is't Possible?
Let the Spheres stop their Course, the Sun make Hault,
The Winds be husht, the Seas and Fountains rest;
All Nature pause, and listen to the Change.
Where is my *Kent*, my *Cajus?*

Kent. Here, my Liege.

Lear. Why I have News that will recal thy Youth;
Ha! Didst thou hear't, or did th' inspiring Gods
Whisper to me alone? Old *Lear* shall be
A King again.

Kent. The Prince, that like a God has Pow'r, has said it.

Lear. *Cordelia* then shall be a Queen, mark that:
Cordelia shall be a Queen; Winds catch the Sound,
And bear it on your rosie Wings to Heav'n.
Cordelia is a Queen.

Re-enter Edgar *with* Gloster.

Alb. Look, Sir, where pious *Edgar* comes,
Leading his Eye-less Father. O my Liege!
His wond'rous Story will deserve your Leisure;
What he has done and suffer'd for your Sake,
What for the fair *Cordelia's*.

Glost. Where's my Liege? Conduct me to his Knees,
    to hail
His second Birth of Empire; my dear *Edgar*
Has, with himself, reveal'd the King's blest Restaura-
tion

Lear. My poor dark *Gloster*.

Glost. O let me kiss that once more sceptred Hand!

Lear. Hold, thou mistak'st the Majesty, kneel here;
Cordelia has our Pow'r, *Cordelia's* Queen.
Speak, is not that the noble Suff'ring *Edgar*?

Glost. My pious Son, more dear than my lost Eyes.

Lear. I wrong'd him too, but here's the fair Amends.

Edg. Your Leave, my Liege, for an unwelcome Mes-
sage.
Edmund (but that's a Trifle) is expir'd;
What more will touch you, your imperious Daughters,
Goneril and haughty *Regan*, both are dead,
Each by the other poison'd at a Banquet;
This, Dying, they confest.

Cord. O fatal Period of ill govern'd Life!

Lear. Ingratefull as they were, my Heart feels yet
A Pang of Nature for their wretched Fall;——
But, *Edgar*, I defer thy Joys too long:
Thou serv'dst distrest *Cordelia*; take her Crown'd;
Th' imperial Grace fresh blooming on her Brow;
Nay, *Gloster*, thou hast here a Father's Right,
Thy helping Hand t'heap Blessings on their Heads.

Kent. Old *Kent* throws in his hearty Wishes too.

Edg. The Gods and you too largely Recompence
What I have done; the Gift strikes Merit dumb.

Cord. Nor do I blush to own my Self o'er-paid
For all my Suff'rings past.

    Glost. Now, gentle Gods, give *Gloster* his Discharge.

    Lear. No, *Gloster*, thou hast Business yet for Life;
Thou, *Kent*, and I, retir'd to some cool Cell
Will gently pass our short Reserves of Time
In calm Reflections on our Fortunes past,
Cheer'd with Relation of the prosperous Reign
Of this celestial Pair; thus our Remains
Shall in an even Course of Thoughts be past,
Enjoy the present Hour, nor fear the last.

    Edg. Our drooping Country now erects her Head,
Peace spreads her balmy Wings, and Plenty blooms.
Divine *Cordelia*, all the Gods can witness
How much thy Love to Empire I prefer!
Thy bright Example shall convince the World
(Whatever Storms of Fortune are decreed)
That Truth and Vertue shall at last succeed.

                                  [Exeunt Omnes.

EPILOGUE, spoken by Mrs. *Barry*.

INCONSTANCY, the reigning Sin o'th' Age,
Will scarce endure true Lovers on the Stage,
You hardly ev'n in Plays with such dispense,
And Poets kill 'em in their own Defence.
Yet One bold Proof I was resolv'd to give,
That I cou'd three Hours Constancy Out-live.
You fear, perhaps, whilst on the Stage w'are made
Such Saints, we shall indeed take up the Trade ;
Sometimes we threaten,—but our Vertue may
For Truth I fear with your Pit-Valour weigh :
For (not to flatter either) I much doubt ⎫
When we are off the Stage, and you are out, ⎬
We are not quite so Coy, nor you so Stout. ⎭
We talk of Nunneries,——but to be sincere ⎫
Whoever lives to see us Cloyster'd there, ⎬
May hope to meet our Critiques at Tangier. ⎭
For Shame give over this inglorious Trade
Of worrying Poets, and go maule th' Alcade.
Well—since y'are all for blust'ring in the Pit, ⎫
The Play's Reviver humbly do's admit ⎬
Your abs'lute Pow'r to damn his Part of it. ⎭
But still so many Master-Touches shine
Of that vast Hand that first laid this Design,
That in great Shakespear's *Right, He's bold to say,* ⎫
If you like nothing you have seen to Day, ⎬
The Play your Judgment damns, not you the Play. ⎭

FINIS.

$\mathcal{N}otes$

THE TEMPEST

P. 3, *an imposition*. A task imposed on us.

P. 3, *Sense*. 4to, 1670, has *Scene*.

P. 3, *his Sea-Voyage*. *The Sea-Voyage*, acted at the Globe, was licensed by Sir Henry Herbert, 22 June, 1622. It was first printed in the folio of 1647. After the Restoration it was revived 25 September, 1667, at the Theatre Royal, when Mrs. Knepp acted Aminta. It seems to have been frequently played at this time as a counter-attraction to *The Tempest* at the rival theatre.

In July-August, 1685, there was produced at the Theatre Royal, *A Commonwealth of Women*, an alteration of Fletcher's play by Thomas D'Urfey. This proved very successful, and was seen at intervals for more than half a century. At Drury Lane, 21 April, 1746, Macklin, Peg Woffington, and Kitty Clive appeared in D'Urfey's romantic drama.

P. 4, *his Goblins*. *The Goblins*, acted at the Blackfriars, was printed 8vo, 1646. It was revived at the Theatre Royal, 24 January, 1667. " The Goblins are Tamoren and his friends, who, having been defeated in a battle, retreat to a wood, turn thieves, and disguise themselves as Devils " (Genest). The character of Reginella (not Regmella as Dryden calls her) has considerable charm, but the course of action of the play on the whole is utterly bewildering and confused.

P. 9, *A hoaming Sea*. Hoaming=very rough. Mr. Thorn-Drury has supplied me with the following quotation for this rare word:

> " When a strong sudden Flow and Hoaming Seas
> Our trembling Fleet with uncouth Furies seize."

The First Book of Virgil's Æneis, " Made English " by Luke Milbourne, 4to, 1688. " Hoaming " also occurs in Echard's translation of the *Rudens* (1694): " Now 'tis such a hoaming Sea, we've little hopes o' Sport."

It has been stated in foolish ignorance that hoaming is an error for "*combing* in the form of *coaming,* or else for foaming"!

P. 9, *Scud.* The light feathery portions of cloud blown off the main clouds are technically known as scud. The sentence is obscure.

P. 9, *Yaw, yaw.* A corruption of yare, yare=eager; ready; prepared; from A.-S. geáro. Cf. *Measure for Measure,* IV, 2: "You shall find me yare." Ray gives it as a Suffolk word, and the "hear, hear" of Lowestoft boatmen of to-day is probably a disguised "yare, yare."

P. 10, *reef both Top-sails.* This is to reduce the area of the sail by taking a sort of tuck in them (like the tuck in a shirt sleeve) by means of reef points.

P. 10, *Capstorm.* A rare form of capstan. *N.E.D.* quotes this passage.

P. 10, *seere-Capstorm.* The stern or aftermost capstan. The order directs that more men should be put on to work it round and round. It may be noted that Furness, in his Variorum *Tempest* (1892), when citing this passage can give no explanation of Seere-Capstorm and, superficially relying upon some idle information, is content to say: "There is no such thing as a 'Seere-Capstorm' and there has never been such a thing"! Moreover, in his Preface (ix) he has: "SHAKESPEARE'S seamanship . . . is beyond criticism. . . . Turn to DRYDEN, where, amidst a wild and incoherent mass of nautical nonsense, orders are issued which, if obeyed, would drive the ship straight to destruction on the rocks." This is simply untrue. The fact is Furness has not troubled to inquire into the technical points, and in his ignorance blunders into the nonsense of which he impudently accuses Dryden.

P. 10, *Nippers.* "A piece of braided cordage used to prevent a cable from slipping." *N.E.D.* cites this passage.

P. 11, *Viall.* The first issue of 1670 and T. Johnson's edition, Hague 1710, here misprint "Vall." This error was corrected in the second issue of 1670. *Viall* or *Vial-block*="a large single-sheaved block through which the messenger passed when the anchor was weighed by the fore or jeer capstan" (Smyth, *Sailor's Word-book,* 1867). *N.E.D.* cites this passage.

P. 11, *a peek.* "The anchor is apeek when the cable has been sufficiently hove in to bring the ship over it " (Admiral Smyth, *Sailor's Word-book*, 1867).

P. 11, *Cut the Anchor*. A misprint for " Cat the Anchor."

P. 11, *Haul Catt*. " *Cat* is . . . a . . . strong tackle, or complication of pullies, to hook and draw the anchor . . . up to the cat head " (Falconer, *Dict. Marine*, 1789).

P. 11, *Haul Aft Misen-sheat*. The sheet is the rope at the bottom corner of a sail to haul it round in a different direction.

P. 11, *A Mackrel-Gale*. A strong breeze such as mackerel are caught in. Cf. Dryden, *The Hind and the Panther*, III, 456 :
" The wind was fair, but blew a *mackrel* gale."

P. 12, *Over-haul your fore-boling*. A " fore bowline " is a rope on a sail, and to " over haul " it you let it go loose and slack on the sail.

P. 12, *Brace off the Fore-yard*. To brace off the fore-yard the fore brace (the rope at each end of the fore-yard) is slackened to let the yard go round more to the other side, so that when eased the yard would swing round to catch the wind on whichever side it was most convenient.

P. 13, *Luffe*. When a ship is sailing sideways in a slanting direction, the wind being in the wrong quarter, and it is needful to use the wind as much as possible, the ship goes to one side and is in more or less danger. When getting too much over it is necessary to luff, that is the ship must be brought round with the rudder to catch the wind full behind her, to drive her along evenly although she will not be going in the exact direction required.

P. 22, *Abhor'd Slave !* It may be noticed that in the First Folio Shakespeare, 1623, this speech, which Dryden assigns to Prospero, is given (improperly as I am convinced) to Miranda. Theobald well says : " I am persuaded the author never design'd this speech for Miranda," and Capell supports him. Several modern editors justly follow Theobald.

P. 22, *red Botch*. An inflamed ulcer.

P. 27, *trills*. To trill is to flow in a slender stream, but more constantly and continuously than to trickle. *N.E.D.* cites this passage.

P. 27, *peid*. Pecked. This rare word, which is omitted by *N.E.D.*, is found in some compound dialect forms. Wood pie

(Somerset) = the green woodpecker. Wood pie (Staffordshire, Hants) = woodpecker. Shadwell's version of *The Tempest* has " peck'd " in this passage.

P. 30, *Salvages*. This obsolete form of savage is found in Gower, and persisted for several centuries. Thus in Tate and Brady's version (1696) of the *Psalms*, VII, 2, we have:

" Lest, like a salvage Lion he
My helpless Soul devour."

P. 32, *Old Simon the King*. Simon Wadloe, landlord of the Old Devil Tavern, Temple Bar, which was frequented and made famous by Ben Jonson, was the original of this popular old song. *Old Simon the King* was the favourite air of Squire Western in *Tom Jones* (Book IV, Chapter 5).

P. 49, *Forth-rights*. A forth-right is a straight path or direct course.

P. 50, *eight fat Spirits*. In *The Rehearsal*, produced at the Theatre Royal, 7 December, 1671, Buckingham has a jest on these Spirits, when Bayes (Actus III, scæna 5) cries to his soldiers: " Udzookers, you dance worse than the Angels in *Harry* the Eight, or the fat Spirits in *The Tempest*, I gad."

P. 51, *going to the door*. This is one of the four permanent doors of the Restoration theatre, which stood (each with its balcony above) two and two, upper and lower, on either side of the stage.

P. 51, *Bosen's Whistle*. " A silver whistle, suspended from the neck by a lanyard, is the modern boatswain's badge of office, and it is familiarly termed his *call* " (Anon., *Shakespeare a Seaman. S. James Magazine*, July, 1862).

P. 52, *Plashes*. Puddles or marshy pools; standing water.

P. 53, *she would be loving*. This is the scene referred to by Congreve in *The Way of the World* (produced at Lincoln's Inn Fields, March, 1700), Act I, when Fainall says of Sir Wilful: " When he's drunk he's as loving as the Monster in *The Tempest*, and much after the same manner." Sycorax (not Caliban) is the Monster to whom allusion is made.

P. 55, *natural*. A loony; a half-witted fool. Cf. Bishop Beveridge's *Works* (2nd edition, folio, 1729) *Sermon CXLV* " Of Prayer " (*c.* 1680), vol. II, p. 350: " We are still mere naturals, no better than fools and madmen."

P. 77, *skink about.* Serve drink round; pour out liquor. *N.E.D.* cites this passage. Cf. Shirley's *The Lady of Pleasure,* licensed 15 October, 1635; 4to, 1637; IV, 2: " A drawer is my Ganymede, he shall skink brisk nectar to us."

P. 77, *Hanse in Kelder.* Literally Jack-in-the-Cellar, *i.e.,* the unborn babe in the womb. Cf. Dryden's *Amboyna* (1673), IV, 1, where Harman senior remarks at Towerson and Ysabinda's wedding: " You *Englishmen . . .* cannot stay for Ceremonies; a good honest *Dutchman* would have been plying the Glass all this while, and drunk to the hopes of *Hans in Kelder* till ' twas Bedtime.' "

P. 78. [*Exit* Caliban. I have supplied this exit, and also Caliban's exit at " tell me how it sounds." Both these are unmarked in the former editions, 1670, 1700, and 1710.

P. 78, *Brindis.* Italian, *brindisi* and *brindesi*; " a drinking a health to one " (Florio). *N.E.D.* does not notice this rare word, but includes another form, " Brendice," which Dryden has used in his tragedy *Amboyna : or, The Cruelties of the Dutch to the English Merchants* (1673), I, 1: " I go to fill a Brendice to my Noble Captain's Health."

P. 79, *Up se Dutch.* Up se = Op zijn, in the fashion or manner of. Cf. *The Alchemist,* IV, 6:
> " I doe not like the dulnesse of your eye:
> It hath a heavy cast, 'tis upsee Dutch."

P. 81, *Pigs-nye.* Pet; darling. The word is from baby talk. Cf. Massinger's *The Picture* (licensed 8 June, 1629), 4to, 1630, II, 1:
> " If thou art,
> As I believe, the pigzney of his heart."

P. 92, *Moly.* A fabulous herb of magic power, having a black root and white blossom, and known by this name among the gods, which was given by Hermes to Ulysses, as a counter-charm to the enchantments of Circe (*Odyssey,* X, 302–344). Cf. *Comus* (1634):
> " And yet more med'cinal is it then that Moly
> That Hermes once to wise Ulysses gave."

P. 93, *vulnerary.* Healing; curative.

P. 95, *Hippolito's Sword.* There is an error here. Miranda should have brought Ferdinand's sword. Ariel had said:

" Anoint the Sword which pierc'd him with this Weapon-Salve,
And wrap it close from Air till I have time
To visit him again."

Weapon-salve was supposed to cure a wounded person by being
applied to the sword by which the hurt had been inflicted. It
was first discovered by Paracelsus. Cf. Davenant's *The Unfortunate Lovers*, 4to, 1649, II, 1:

> " Our medicine we apply,
> Like the weapon-salve, not to ourselves but him
> Who was the sword that made the wound."

Also Mrs. Behn's *The Young King*, 4to, 1683, V, 5:

> " That Balm it was, that like the Weapon-salve
> Heals at a Distance——."

P. 102, *Saraband*. A slow and stately Spanish dance.

P. 103, *The Rhyming Monsieur and the Spanish Plot*. By the
winter of 1667 the vogue of the heroic drama written in couplets
was already very great, and in spite of parodies and criticism
rhyme long continued to hold its own on the stage. Howard
and Dryden's *The Indian Queen*, produced at the Theatre Royal
in January 1663-4, and Dryden's sequel *The Indian Emperor*,
produced at the same house in the spring of 1665, both had an
unprecedented success. In the Prologue to *Aureng-Zebe* (Theatre
Royal, 1675), Dryden confesses that he

> " Grows weary of his long-lived Mistris Rhyme."

None the less *Aureng-Zebe* drew thronging audiences, as also
did Crowne's *The Destruction of Jerusalem*, a rhyming tragedy in
two parts, produced at the Theatre Royal in the spring of 1677.
In the Prologue to *Secret Love* (Theatre Royal, 2 March, 1667),
Dryden insists that he has observed in this play:

> " The Unities of Action, Place, and Time;
> The Scenes unbroken; and a mingled chime
> Of *Johnsons* Humour with *Corneilles* rhyme."

Spanish influence had been very strong in the English drama
before the closing of the theatres in 1642. Fletcher in particular
is indebted to Spanish literature. But immediately after the
Restoration, and for at least half a century following, the
Spanish playwrights were even more largely drawn upon by
English authors. In some cases, it is true, Spanish comedies
filtered into England by way of France. But Charles II himself

suggested *Los Empeños de Seis Horas* to Sir Samuel Tuke as
" an excellent design " for an English play, and he also handed
Moreto's *No puede ser* to Crowne.   Tuke's *The Adventures of
Five Hours,* produced at the Duke's House, 8 January, 1663,
won an instant triumph, " and the house, by its frequent
plaudits, did show their sufficient approbation."   " It took
successively 13 days together, no other Play intervening,"
and was constantly in the bills.

In the original Prologue to *The Wild Gallant,* as produced at
the Vere Street Theatre, 5 February, 1662-3, Dryden introduces
two Astrologers to foretell the fate of the new play, and after
some prognostication the second Astrologer says:
> " But yet the greatest Mischief does remain,
> The twelfth Apartment bears the Lord of Spain;
> Whence I conclude, it is your Author's Lot,
> To be indanger'd by a Spanish plot."

The reference is probably to the success of Tuke's *The Adventures
of Five Hours* at the rival house.   It may be that in spite of his
assertion later in the Prologue, " This Play is English, and the
growth your own," Dryden drew something for *The Wild
Gallant* from the Spanish theatre.

THE MOCK-TEMPEST

P. 105, *Hic totus volo.*   Martial, XI, 15, 3.

P. 107, *Mr. Hains and Mrs. Mackarel.*   Joseph Haines, the
famous low comedian and incomparable dancer, is mentioned
by Pepys, 7 March, 1667-8, as having then lately joined the
Theatre Royal.   He was, says Aston, " more remarkable for the
witty, tho' wicked, Pranks he play'd, and for his Prologues and
Epilogues, than for Acting."   He died in 1701.

Betty Mackarel was a notorious bona-roba of the day.   She
began life as an orange-wench in the King's house.   There is a
reference to Betty Mackarel in the Epilogue to Duffett's farce,
The Empress of Morocco, produced at the King's House in the
spring of 1674, when Heccate says: " Where's Mack'rel back
and Jilting-*Sue* ?"   There is a pun here as mackerel-back is
obsolescent slang for " long-backed."   Jilting Sue is Sue Flavel,

a well-known prostitute of the day. Mr. G. Thorn-Drury has further furnished me with the following allusions to Mrs. Mackarel: Philips' *Don Quixote*, 1687, p. 184: "*Camilla . . . could not but wonder to hear so young a Questrel as she discourse with all the Experience of an *Orange-Moll*, or a *Betty-Mackarel*." *Ibid.*, p. 412: "Teresa's a Woman of extraordinary Parts, and were it not that she's a little Jealous, I would not change her for the Gyantess *Betty-Makarela*, who as my Master says, was one of the most diligent Women of her Time." Also *Poems on Affairs of State*, vol. III (1704), "To Mr. Julian," p. 143:

"May *Betty Mackrel* cease to be a Whore,
And Villain *Frank* kiss *Mazarin* no more."

One may parallel the indecent jest about the Orange with a similar passage in *The Country Wife*, III, 2.

P. 108, *I'le still be right.* Cf. The Duke of Buckingham's alteration of *The Chances*, 4to, 1682, IV, 2: "What's here, musick and women? would I had one of em. [*One of 'em looks out of the window*]. That's a whore; I know her by her smile. . . . [*Another looks out.*] Ah rogue! she's right too, I'm sure on't."

P. 109. *Tom Thimble.* Tom Thimble is a comic character in *The Rehearsal*, produced at the Theatre Royal, 7 December, 1671.

P. 109, *Bacon's Brazen-head.* The old legend of Friar Bacon, who made an enchanted head of brass which was to speak thrice. The Friar, however, was overcome with sleep and Miles, his servant, failed to awake him. Meanwhile the head at intervals uttered these cryptic words: "Time is; Time was; Time is past." With the last sentence it fell to pieces. Story tells that other famous occultists, Pope Silvester II, Robert Grosseteste, and Albertus Magnus, made similar heads of brass that prophesied.

P. 111, *A great noyse heard of beating Doors. The Mock-Tempest*, which on the half-title is called *The New Tempest*, opens with a formidable attack by the mobile upon a brothel. On Shrove Tuesday in each year, as also during Eastertide, it was customary for the apprentices of the metropolis to avail themselves of their holidays by assembling in large numbers and making organized assaults upon notorious houses of ill fame, which they sacked and even demolished. In Middleton's *Inner Temple Masque* (4to, 1619), we have:

" Stand forth, Shrove Tuesday, one a' the silenc'st bricklayers;
'Tis in your charge to pull down bawdy-houses."
And in Marmion's *Holland's Leaguer*, acted at Salisbury Court,
December, 1631, Act IV, 3, which scene is the exterior of the
Leaguer:

" Good sir, let's think on some revenge! call up
The gentlemen 'prentices and make a Shrove Tuesday."
Holland's Leaguer was a celebrated brothel, which stood where
is now Holland Street, Blackfriars. The fourth act of the play
passes chiefly before this house, which is sometimes called a
castle or fort. The first scene of *The Mock-Tempest* may be
compared with Marmion.

Pepys, 24 March (Easter Tuesday), 1667-8, gives a long
account of " the tumult at the other end of the town, about
Moore-fields, among the 'prentices, taking the liberty of these
holydays to pull down bawdy-houses." There was a dangerous
riot and the military had to be called out under the command
of Lord Craven. When several of the 'prentices were imprisoned
in the Clerkenwell Bridewell " the rest did come and break open
the prison and release them," giving out that they were for
pulling down the bawdy-houses " which is one of the greatest
grievances of the nation." When this was reported to Charles he
said: " Why, why do they go to them, then?" Which certainly
seems an extremely pertinent query, although Pepys thought it
" a very poor, cold, insipid, answer." The following morning
Pepys found the Duke of York and all with him " full of the
talk of the 'prentices, who are not yet [put] down, though the
guards and the militia of the town have been in armes all this
night and the night before. . . . Some blood hath been spilt,
but a great many houses pulled down; and, among others, the
Duke of York was mighty merry at that of Damaris Page's, the
great bawd of the seamen; . . . it was said how these idle fellows
have had the confidence to say that they did ill in contenting
themselves in pulling down the little bawdy-houses, and did
not go and pull down the great bawdy-house at White Hall."
Eight of the ringleaders in these riots were captured and condemned to death. On 9 May, four were drawn, hanged, and quar-
tered at Tyburn, two of their heads being fixed upon London
Bridge (*The London Gazette*, No. 259). See also " The Tryals

of such persons as under the notion of London Apprentices were tumultuously assembled in Moore Fields, under colour of pulling down bawdy-houses," 4to, 1668. A number of lampoons appeared, and Evelyn, 2 April, remarks: " Amongst other libertine libels there was one now printed, and thrown about, a bold petition of the poore whores to Lady Castelmaine," and Pepys, four days later, writes: " I do hear that my Lady Castelmaine is horribly vexed at the late libell, the petition of the poor whores about the town, whose houses were pulled down the other day. I have got one of them, but it is not very witty, but devilish severe against her and the King; and I wonder how it durst be printed and spread abroad." This pasquil is entitled: " The Poor-Whores Petition to the Most Splendid, Illustrious, Serene, and Eminent Lady of Pleasure, the Countess of *Castlemayne*, etc. *The Humble Petition of the Undone Company of poore distressed Whores, Bawds, Pimps, and Panders, etc.*" It is " Signed by Us *Madam Cresswell* and *Damaris Page*, in behalf of our Sisters and Fellow-Sufferers (in this day of our Calamity) . . . this present 25th day of *March*, 1668." A very few days after appeared " The Gracious ANSWER of the most Illustrious *Lady* of *Pleasure*, the *Countess* of *Castlem*. . . To the Poor-Whores Petition." This commences: " Right Trusty and Well-beloved Madam *Cresswell* and *Damaris Page* with the rest of the suffering Sisterhood . . ." and concludes " CASTLEM. . . . *Given at our Closset in King street, Westminster*, Die Veneris, April 24 1668." These two remarkable documents may be seen in full in Steinman's *Memoir of Barbara, Duchess of Cleveland*, 1871, pp. 100-111.

P. 112, *flunder mouth'd*. Flounder-mouth'd: having a large gaping mouth like a flounder. The phrase is not uncommon. Cf. Cowley, *The Cutter of Colman Street* (1663), IV, 6: " She . . . rails at me like a Flounder-mouth'd Fish-woman."

P. 112, *Sweating Tub*. A patient suffering from the *lues venerea* was disciplined by long and severe sweating in a heated tub, which, combined with strict abstinence, was formerly considered an excellent remedy for the disease. Cf. *Measure for Measure*, III, 2: " Troth, sir, she has eaten up all her beef, and she is herself in the tub." Also *Timon of Athens*, IV, 3, 83-87.

P. 113, *Whiffler*. Minsheu, *Dictionary* (1617), describes whiffler as a club- or staff-bearer. The word is originally from *whiffle,* a fife or small flute. Whifflers were those who preceded armies or processions, as fifers or pipers. In process of time whiffler came to mean anyone who went before in a procession or marshalled it. Sometimes the whifflers carried white wands of office. In *Westward Ho* (4to, 1607), V, 4, "torchmen and whifflers" are spoken of as going in ceremonious procession.

P. 114, *farandinical.* Of the nature of farandine; hence second-rate, worthless. *N.E.D.* cites this passage. Farandine was a cloth made partly of silk, and partly of wool or hair.

P. 114, *Ananias.* A generic name for a Puritan in allusion to Ananias, the deacon of Amsterdam, in *The Alchemist.*

P. 115, *Abednego.* A name much favoured by fanatics from the story of Shadrach, Meshach, and Abednego (*Daniel*, iii).

P. 115, *Stepony.* A kind of wine made from raisins with lemon-juice and sugar added. Cf. Etherege, *The Comical Revenge* (4to, 1664), V, 4: "Do you not Understand the Mystery of *Stiponie Jenny?*"

P. 116, *tag-rag-and-long-tail.* All and sundry; used especially of the lower classes and the mobile. Cf. D'Urfey's *Pills to Purge Melancholy* (1719), IV, 113: "To make a Match with Tag-rag, and Long-Tail." The phrase is oftener " Tag, rag, and bobtail," as Pepys, 6 March, 1659-60: " Well, they all went down into the dining-room, where it was full of tag, rag, and bobtail, dancing, singing, and drinking, of which I was ashamed."

P. 118, *Ling.* " The best Sort of Salt Fish "—Mrs. Glasse's *Cookery* (1747). Cf. Pepys, 20 March, 1666-7: " had a good dinner of ling and herring pie, very good meat, best of the kind that ever I had."

P. 118. *dyet-drink.* A drink prescribed for medicinal purposes. Cf. Etherege, *The Comical Revenge* (4to, 1664), IV, 6, where Betty says that Dufoy's illness was known by the discovery of " a Bottle of Diet-Drink he brought and hid behind the stairs."

P. 119, *my Bottle.* A goodly-sized case-bottle was considered part of the essential equipment of a procuress. Cf. Shadwell's *The Miser*, produced at the Theatre Royal, January, 1672, Act I, where Goldingham numbers amongst his unredeemed pledges " a Bauds Silver Aqua-Vitae Bottle." An ancient sybil of this profession, with her rundlet of Nancy, figures prominently in the sixth picture of Hogarth's *The Harlot's Progress,* and one may remember Foote's Mrs. Cole (a satire on Mother Douglas) with her modest demand for mint-water—but on occasion quaffing French drams supernaculum—and her parting instructions to Sir George's man: "Richard, you may as well give me the bottle into the chair for fear I should be taken ill on the road."

P. 119, *the Syring and the Pot of Turpentine-pills.* Cf. *The Chances* (folio, 1647), III, 3, where the Landlady says of Don John:

> "He's ne'er without a noise of syringes
> In's pocket (those proclaim him,) birding-pills."

A noise=a company, a quantity. Birding=wenching: this term is still in use among the vulgar. Also cf. Shadwell's *The Virtuoso* (Duke's Theatre, spring, 1676), Act I: "Then says another with great Gallantry, pulling out his Box of Pills, *Dam-me,* Tom, *I am not in a condition; here's my Turpentine for my Third Clap:* when you would think he was not old enough to be able to get one."

P. 120, *Butcher-row.* A very narrow street at the back of the Strand, so called from the butchers' shambles on the south side. Nat Lee died (1692) at the Bear and Harrow, a noted eating-house in this street.

There was also a Butcher-row immediately outside Aldgate.

P. 120, *Scanderbegs.* Scanderbeg is a common term for a militant warrior or conqueror from George Castriota (1404-67), a famous Albanian hero, who was for more than a quarter of a century the principal obstacle to the unlimited extension of the Ottoman Empire. He was at first a commander under Amurath II, and owing to his success he was raised to the rank of Sanjak with the title Iscander Bey (Lord Alexander). In 1443 he renounced Moslemism, and won several battles against the Turks. At the instigation of Pius II he headed a crusade, and defeated Mohammed II and a vast army at Croia.

P. 122, *Shovel-board and Pigeon-holes.* Shovel-board was a game in which a coin, a counter, or some other disk was driven by a smart blow with the hand along a highly polished board or table marked with transverse lines. Cf. Shadwell's *The Miser* (1672), III, 1: "He has already lost his Edward Shillings that he kept for Shovel-board." Among the Herbert documents is a License for the "use of one Shovelbord" (*Dramatic Records* edited by T. Q. Adams (1917), p. 131).

Pigeon-holes: "A game like our modern bagatelle, where there was a machine with arches for the balls to run through resembling the cavities made for pigeons in a dove-house"; Halliwell. Cf. *Poor Robin's Almanack*, 1699:

> " The boys are by themselves at sholes
>   At nine-pins or at pigeon-holes."

P. 123, *Kib'd-heels*. A kibe is a chilblain upon the heel. Cf. *Hamlet*, V, 1: " The toe of the peasant comes so near the heel of the courtier, he galls his kibe."

P. 123, *Gregoria Dunn*. Edward Dun succeeded Richard Brandon as common hangman. Brandon, who is generally considered to have been the executioner of Charles I, died 20 June, 1649. He and his father, Gregory, two notorious characters, were known as old Gregory and young Gregory, whence Gregory became a generic name applied to an executioner. In "The Players Petition to the Long Parliament After being long Silenc'd, that they might Play again, 1642" (Jordan's *Royal Arbor of Loyal Poesie*, 1664), we have:

> " The Cheap-side Cross shall be new guilt, new painted
> *Gregory* be made a Sheriff, and *Tyburn* sainted."

Dun probably died in 1678. The first printed notice of his successor, John Ketch, appears 2 December, 1678.

P. 123, *pinck-ey'd*. pink =to blink; to half-close the eyes (*Dutch*; pinken, to shut the eyes, wink). Cf. *Roxburgh Ballads* (1681), V, 86:

> " When our senses are drown'd, and our eyes they do pink."

P. 124, *lonely lass*. Cf. Ben's Ballad of Buxom Joan, *Love for Love* (30 April, 1695, Lincoln's Inn Fields), Act III:

> " For now the time was ended,
>   When she no more intended
>   To lick her lips at men, sir,
>   And gnaw the sheets in vain, sir,
>   And lie o'nights alone."

P. 125, *i'vads*. Or i'fads=In faith. A rustic expression. *N.E.D.* quotes this passage. Cf. *The Country Wife* (4to, 1675), IV, 2, where Mrs. Pinchwife says: " But yet evads I'll try, so

I will." Also D'Urfey, *Pills to Purge Melancholy* (1719), II, 342:
" Ivads no—I an't such a Baby neither."

P. 126, *switcheld*. To switchel is a cant word meaning to have sexual intercourse.

P. 127, *half moon. Demilune.* " An outwork resembling a bastion with a crescent-shaped gorge, constructed to protect a bastion or curtain."

P. 127, *Serty'd*. Made a sortie; dashed out. *N.E.D.*, not before 1871.

P. 127, *Reformadoes*. A reformado is an officer left without a command owing to the " reforming or disbanding " of his company, but retaining his rank and seniority, and receiving full or half pay. Hence it may also signify a volunteer serving in the army (or navy) without a commission but with the rank of an officer.

P. 127, *pize on her*. Pize, which was vulgarly used in various imprecatory expressions, is a word of uncertain origin. It has been well suggested that it may be an arbitrary substitute for Pest or Pox, which latter came into common speech *circa* 1600. Pize is a favourite word with old Bellair in Etherege's *The Man of Mode* (Duke's Theatre, winter of 1676); also cf. Shadwell's *The Squire of Alsatia* (Theatre Royal, spring of 1688), Act I, where the rustic Belfond senior says: " Ah, sweet rogues! While in the countrey a pies take them! there's such a stir with Pish, fie, nay, Mr. *Timothy*."

P. 128, *Canters*. A fanatic who used religious cant, and so in the seventeenth century an apposite nickname of the Puritans. Evelyn in his *Diary*, 4 June, 1652, writes: " On Whit Sunday I went to the church (which is a very fair one) and heard one of the canters, who dismissed the assembly rudely, and without any blessing."

P. 128, *bubble*. Cheat. Cf. *The Country Wife* (4to, 1675), III, 2, when Horner says of Sparkish: " he is to be bubbled of his mistress as of his money."

P. 130, *and then she dy'd*. A proverbial expression as in Dryden's *The Wild Gallant* (4to, 1669), I, 2: " *Bibber*. Has he used you, *Frances*? put so much more into his bill for lodging. *Loveby*. Honest *Will*, and so he died; I thank thee."

P. 130, *by Yea and by Nay*. " Yea and Nay " was a phrase

often derisively applied to the Puritans of every kidney in allusion to the Scriptural injunction, *S. Matthew*, v, 33-7, which these fanatics feigned exactly to follow. Timothy Thin-beard, a rascally Puritan, in Heywood's *If you Know Not Me, You Know Nobody*, Part II (4to, 1606), is continually asseverating " By yea and nay." Cf. The Prologue (spoken by Smith) to Mrs. Behn's *The False Count* (Duke's Theatre, autumn, 1682):

> " But shou'd the Torys now . . .
> Resolve to hiss, as late did Popish Crew,
> By Yea and Nay, she'll throw herself on you,
> The grand Inquest of Whigs, to whom she's true."

P. 132, *St. James Fair*. St. James' Fair, in Westminster, was held in the open space near St. James' Palace, and afterwards in St. James' Market. It was opened on the Eve of St. James, 24 July, and lasted a fortnight. Prohibited by the Parliament in 1651, it was revived at the Restoration, but fell into disuse before the close of the reign of Charles II. Pepys visited the Fair, 26 July, 1660.

P. 132, *Crispe*. The crackling of roast pork. *N.E.D.* quotes this passage.

P. 132, *haugou*. Haut-goût, a relish or savoury.

P. 132, *Shat'lin*. Chatelin's. There are innumerable references to this famous ordinary. Cf. Pepys, 13 March, 1667-8: " At noon all of us to Chatelin's, the French house in Covent Garden, to dinner."

P. 132, *Locket*. This fashionable ordinary stood on the site of Drummond's Bank, Charing Cross. It was named from Adam Locket, the landlord, who died in 1688. In 1702, an Edward Locket, probably a son, was proprietor. The reputation of the house was on the wane during the latter years of Anne, and in the reign of George I its vogue came entirely to an end. There are frequent references in almost every writer of the period. Cf. a prologue which appears in *Covent Garden Drollery* (1672) and was later spoken before D'Urfey's *The Fool Turn'd Critick* (Theatre Royal, spring, 1678):

> " Next these we welcome such as briskly dine
> At *Locket's* at *Gifford's* or with *Shatiline*."

P. 133, *Lamb's wool*. There is a play upon words here. Lamb's-Wool Ale is hot ale mixed with the pulp of roasted apples, sugared and well spiced. Lamb's-wool is historically famous on account of that impious wretch, Lord Howard of Esrick, who, having been lodged in the Tower on a charge connected with the so-called Popish Plot, to prove his innocence took the Sacrament according to the Protestant rite of the Book of Common Prayer. It is said, however, that on this occasion, instead of wine lamb's-wool was profanely used in the administration. Cf. Dryden's pointed jibe—*Absalom and Achitophel* (November, 1681), I, 575-6:

> " And Canting *Nadab* let Oblivion damn,
> Who made new Porridge for the Paschal Lamb."

Cf. also *Absalon's IX Worthies* (a broadside):

> " Then prophane *Nadab*, that hates all sacred things,
> And on that score abominateth Kings;
> With *Mahomet* wine he damneth, with intent
> To erect his Paschal-lamb's-wool Sacrament."

In D'Urfey's capital comedy *The Royalist*, produced at the Duke's house in the spring of 1682 (published 4to, 1682), V, 1, the First Committeeman says: " Nor you never gave 'em the Sacrament in Lambswool and Plumb-Cake to be secret did you?" A ballad on the Rye House Plot, *The Conspiracy ; or, The Discovery of the Fanatic Plot*, sings:

> " Next valiant and noble Lord *Howard*
> That formerly dealt in lamb's wool;
> Who knowing what it is to be towered,
> By impeaching may fill the jails full."

P. 133, *fico*. faire la figue: dar la higa. Cf. Pistol's " a fico for the phrase !" (*Merry Wives of Windsor*, I, 3).

P. 134, *Crack*. A whore. Cf. Farquhar, *Love and a Bottle* (1698), V, 2: " You imagine I have got your whore, cousin, your crack." Grose, *Dict. Vulgar Tongue*, gives the word, and it is also cited by the *Lexicon Balatronicum* (1811). It was, in fact, in common use for wellnigh two centuries.

P. 135, *Farendine*. A cloth made partly of silk, and partly of wool or hair. Cf. Wycherley's *Love in a Wood* (4to, 1672), III, 1: " Was he not the man that give me my first Farrendon gown ?"

P. 135, *Jessimy-butter*. Jessimy=jasmine. Jessimy-butter was a toilet-cream made with jasmine. Cf. Edward Phillips,

The New World of English Words (4th edition, folio, 1678),
" with the flowers whereof Jesemin Butter is made."

Jessimy-Gloves are gloves perfumed with jasmine. Cf. Pepys,
26 October, 1666: " I did give each of them a pair of Jesimy
plain gloves." Scented gloves were introduced into England by
the Earl of Oxford on his return from Italy, in the fifteenth
year of Queen Elizabeth, during whose reign and for a century
and a half later they were very fashionable. In Etherege's *The
Man of Mode* (Duke's Theatre, 1676) Sir Fopling Flutter's
gloves are " Orangerii," and going to the theatre he was " almost
poison'd with a pair of Cordivant Gloves " worn by his neighbour.
Thereupon, Mrs. Loveit sympathizingly exclaims: " Oh! filthy
Cordivant, how I hate the Smell!" In Dryden's *The Kind
Keeper* (Duke's Theatre, 1679), Mrs. Tricksy remarked to
Limberham: " I have been looking over the last Present of
Orange Gloves you made me: and methinks I do not like the
Scent—O Lord, Mr. *Woodall*, did you bring those you wear
from *Paris*?" " Mine are *Roman*, Madam," replied Woodall,
to which the lady answered, " The Scent I love, of all the
World."

P. 135, *laced Mutton*. A cant term for a prostitute. Cf.
Marlowe's *Doctor Faustus* (4to, 1604), where, in the scene with
the Seven Deadly Sins, Lechery says: " I am one that loves an
inch of raw mutton better than an ell of fried Stockfish." Also
Middleton and Dekker, *The Roaring Girle, or Moll Cut-Purse*
(4to, 1611), a Fortune play, Act III, where Mistress Openwork
says of her husband: " It cannot sink into me that he feeds
upon stale mutton abroad, having better and fresher at home."

P. 135, *and so she praid me to tell ye*. A cant phrase of the day,
used somewhat meaninglessly to round off a sentence.

P. 135, *Aunt*. A slang word for a bawd. It is of frequent
occurrence, and is to be found in Grose's *Dictionary of the Vulgar
Tongue* (1785).

P. 137, *Suburbian Hackney*. In the days of Elizabeth and for
more than a century and a half after her reign the suburbs
(especially the Bankside, Turnbull Street in Clerkenwell, and
Shoreditch), were notorious for their houses of ill-fame. In
Heywood's *The Rape of Lucrece* (4to, 1608), the merry lord,
Valerius, sings " a song of all the pretty Suburbians," II, 3.

Cf. *Measure for Measure*, I, 2, where Pompey says to Mrs. Overdone, " All houses of resort in the suburbs of Vienna must be plucked down."

Hackney=a prostitute of the lowest order. Cotgrave (1611), *Bringuenaudée*—a common hackney. Cf. Mrs. Behn's *The City Heiress* (1682), IV, 1: " Some common Hackney of the Suburbs."

P. 137, *the French*. Morbus Gallicus, so termed almost immediately upon its appearance in Europe. One of the earliest works issued from the Aldine Press in 1497 was the *Libellus de Epidemia quam vulgo morbum Gallicum vocant*, written by Nicolao Leoniceno.

P. 137, *danc'd naked at the French house*. The French house here mentioned was a notorious bordello of the day. Wycherley places the second scene of Act I, *Love in a Wood* (4to, 1672), at " The French House." This may be the same house as that to which Duffett here alludes. Again, in *The Gentleman Dancing-Master* (4to, 1673), the second scene of Act I lies at " The French House," which is invaded by Mrs. Flirt and Mrs. Flounce, " two common Women of the Town."

danc'd naked. Cf. Pepys, 30 May, 1668: " And here I first understood by their talk the meaning of the company that lately were called Ballers; Harris telling how it was by a meeting of some young blades, when he was among them, and my Lady Bennet and her ladies; and their there dancing naked, and all the roguish things in the world." Harris was Henry Harris, the famous actor of the Duke's House. " Lady " Bennet was a procuress well-known in her day. There are frequent references. She is described in *The Tatler* (84) as " the celebrated Madam Bennet," and it was to her that Wycherley addressed his ironical dedication of *The Plain Dealer* (4to, 1676). It may be remembered that in " The Rake's Progress," III, Hogarth shows us the interior of a brothel. Of this picture Mr. Clerk writes: " In the front, a woman is undressing, in order to exhibit some indecent postures—(a filthy practice by which she obtained a precarious maintenance)."

P. 137, *Mild-sixpences*. Cf. *The London Chaunticleers*, " A Witty Comedy, Full of Various and Delightful Mirth. Anon. 4to, 1659." " He has got my box of mill'd sixpences and Harry groates." This is the earliest quotation given by the *N.E.D.* under "milled." Henry Noel Humphreys, *The Coinage of the British Empire* (4to, 1854), records: "In 1663 the first issue of the improved milled coinage took place."

P. 137, *Lerry-come-twang.* Lerry is a mocking nonce diminutive of "Leery poope," itself a corruption of "Liripoop= Liripipe" in the sense of a fool, an idiot. Cf. Fletcher's *The Pilgrim* (acted at Court 1621; folio 1647), Act II, where testy old Alphonso says of Juletta, with whom he is angered:
"And keep me this young lirry-poop within doors."

P. 138, *bug words.* Bug-bear words; words that terrify and alarm. Cf. *Sir Martin Mar-all* (Dryden and Newcastle), produced at the Duke's House, Thursday, 15 August, 1667, I: "I . . . have nothing to hope for now but Death." *Warner*: "Death is a Bug-word, things are not brought to that Extremity."

P. 139, *Tatter-de-mallion.* This word first appears about 1611, since when its use is common.

P. 141, *Mittimus.* A warrant of commitment to prison. Cf. Dryden's *The Wild Gallant* (4to, 1669), IV, i, where Justice Trice says: "Hang him, rogue; make his mittimus immediately."

P. 141, *Westminster wedding.* A Westminster wedding is a slang phrase for "a whore and a rogue married together." *A New Dictionary . . . of the Canting Crew.* B. E. Gent (early eighteenth century). Cf. the lampoon *A* Westminster *Wedding: Or, The Town-Mouth; alias, the Recorder of* London *and his Lady*, February 17, 1679. *Poems on State Affairs*, III (1704), p. 193. Judge Jeffreys was the Recorder of London, and a few months before his election, in May, he married Lady Jones, a "brisk young widow" who is said by scandal to have borne a child shortly after the wedding. Jeffreys' first wife died in February, 1679.

P. 143, *Coging.* Wheedling; cajoling. As in T. Jordan's *The Cheaters Cheated*:
"Citizens are full of slight,
They will cog and flatter."
Also (more especially of dice) tricking; cheating.

P. 144, *yellowes*. Jealousy. Cf. Dekker's *Satiromastix* (4to, 1602), II, 1:

> " But all thy thoughts are yellow, thy sweet bloud
> Rebels, th'art jealous Wat."

Also Ford's *The Fancies, Chast and Noble* (4to, 1638), II, 2:

> "*Troylo*. Yet is this bachelor-miracle not free
> From the epidemical headache.
>
> *Livio*. The yellows?
>
> *Troy*. Huge jealous fits."

The idea here is emphasized in the refrain of the song *Cuckoe, cuckoe.*

P. 144, *Crouder*. A fiddler. Cf. Fuller, *Worthies*, II, 306; " Sung but by some blind Crowder." Crouder is a favourite word with Duffett. Cf. *Psyche Debauch'd* (4to, 1678), Act I: "*Enter a Countrey* Crouder *followed by a Milk-maid with her Payl dressed up as on May-day.*" And later the line: " No Crouder e'r will Fiddle us."

P. 144, *Nandy*. It must be borne in mind that Quakero represents Ferdinand.

P. 145, *Thorn back*. The common ray or skate, as having several rows of short sharp spines arranged along the back and tail.

P. 145, *Guly Penno*. William Penn, 1644-1718.

P. 146, *gally'd*. To galley is to play a trick upon; a slang term. Grose, *A Classical Dictionary of the Vulgar Tongue* (1785).

P. 146, *Culvers*. Culver is a pigeon, a dove. The wood-pigeon is still so called in the South and West of England. Cf. *The Ring and the Book*, xii, 479:

> " The lark, the thrush, the culver too."

P. 146, *a touch a feeling of their Case*. An indecent jest is here intended. Cf. *The Chances*, folio, 1647, IV, 3:

> "*Duke*. [*To the* Bawd.] What are you?
>
> *Petruchio*. Bawd to this piece of pie-meat.
>
> *Bawd*.   A poor gentlewoman
> That lies in town about law business
> And't like your worships.
>
> *Petru*.   You shall have law, believe it.
>
> *Bawd*. I'll show your mastership my case.

Petru.   By no means;

I had rather see a custard.

Bawd.   My dead husband

Left it even thus, sir.

John.   Bless mine eyes from blasting!

I never was so frighted with a case."

P. 146, *the Play-house.* Mr. W. J. Lawrence is of opinion that these references are to the " business " with the banquet in Shadwell's *Tempest* (III, 3), at the Duke's House. The two Spirits who there descend and fly away with the table of meat and fruits were no doubt dressed in some fantastic ape-like shapes with long tails. They are alluded to by Alonzo and Gonzalo as " Devils " and " Fiends." Punchanello would then be the rival manager (of the Duke's Theatre). Mr. Lawrence writes in a private letter to myself: " I feel sure *The Tempest* had never been given anywhere by puppets, unless, indeed, Punch had indulged in some burlesque of the Shadwell production. But this would have taken the wind out of Duffett's sails, and for that reason hardly seems probable."

P. 147, *Nickers.* Marbles generally made of baked clay. Cf. Mrs. Behn's *The Round-heads ; or, The Good Old Cause* (4to, 1682), IV, 4: " The fine Gentleman . . . gave me these two fine Pieces of Gold . . . and I'm resolv'd to lay it all out in a Sword, not a penny in Nickers."

P. 148, *Bullet.* Old French *boulete*, bowls. The game was also so called (locally) in Scotland.

P. 148, *Cat and Trap-ball.* Tip-cat. Trap-ball: " a game in which a ball placed upon one end (slightly hollowed) of a trap is thrown into the air by the batsman striking the other end with his bat with which he then hits the ball away " (*N.E.D.*). Cf. Shadwell's *The Sullen Lovers*, produced at the Duke's House, Saturday, 2 May, 1668, Act III, where the clerk says: " Master *Dash* and I came to play a match at trap-ball," and Sir Positive (a caricature of Sir Robert Howard) replies: " Have you the confidence to talk of trap-ball before me? . . . Why, I was so eminent at it when I was a schoolboy, that I was called *Trap Positive* all over the school." Cf. also Pepys, 8 May, 1668: " Lord! to see how this play of Sir Positive At-all, in abuse of Sir Robert Howard do take . . . every body . . . telling more stories of him. . . . The Duke of York himself said that of his playing at trap-ball is true." Act IV, Sir Positive declares: " I . . . play at cat, stool-ball, scotch hop, and trap-ball."

P. 148, *Lemine*. A childish corruption of *Gemini*, a mild exclamation or petty oath in use principally among the vulgar. Cf. Otway's *The Soldier's Fortune* (Duke's House, 1680), II, 1: " Gemini! what would become of me?" Also Ravenscroft's *The London Cuckolds* (Duke's House, 1681), II, 3: " *Peggy*. O Leminy! not in a week, Aunt; and does my Nuncle own all this Town? "

P. 150, *Scotch Morice*. The morris, originally a grotesque dance performed by fancy characters (generally Friar Tuck, Maid Marian, etc., from the Robin Hood legend), came to mean any fantastic or novel round.

P. 151, *Truss-fayl*. Truss-a-fail, a romping game. Cf. W. Hawkins, *Apollo Shroving* (1627), V, iv: " The waues . . . play at trusse and at leap frogge on one anothers back." Also John Cleveland, *The Model of new Religion* (c. 1658), *Works*, 1687 (p. 245):
" Or do the Iuncto leap at truss-a-fail?
Three Tenents clap while five hang on the tail?"

P. 152, *Pissabeds*. A common country name for Dandelions. French, *pissenlit*. Cf. Heywood's *Loves Mistris* (1636), V:
" Garlands . . . of Blew bottles and yellow pissabeds
That grew amongst the Wheate."
Blue-bottle: a rustic name for the blue corn-flowers.

P. 152, *Shock*. These were fashionable dogs for ladies. According to Sir Jasper Fidget (*The Country Wife*) one of Horner's occupations was to be " visiting our wives, . . . picking fleas out of their shocks for 'em."

P. 153, *Kip Kap*. A term of contempt for a young babyish person. Flemish, *kippe* = a young calf. This rare word is not in the *N.E.D.*

P. 153, *fleering*. To fleer is to grin and look amorously or sillily. Cf. Burton's *Anatomy of Melancholy* (1621), I, ii, iii, xi: " How popular and curteous, how they grinne and fleire vpon euery man they meet."

P. 153, *mun*. Man, used in the vocative. A vulgarism, which came to be a merely meaningless interjection. It was addressed to females as well as to males. Cf. Congreve's *Love for Love*, produced at the New Theatre, Little Lincoln's-Inn Fields, 30 April, 1695, Act II, where Miss Prue says to Mrs. Frail: " Smell, cousin ; . . . It's better than lavender, Mun ?"

P. 153, *a Mrs.* A mistress.

P. 157, *hock-tide.* Monday and Tuesday after Dominica in Albis (Low Sunday). In pre-Reformation times money was collected for church and parish purposes with many festive and sportive customs, some of which survived until the nineteenth century. One of the earlier customs (to which reference is made here) was the seizing and binding (by women on Monday and by men on Tuesday) of persons of the opposite sex, who paid a small coin to be released. In later days chains or ropes were stretched across the street to stop passers-by for the same purpose.

P. 159, *top and scourge.* As in Shirley's *The Gamester* (1633), III, 2 :

" I'll send my nephew ; he shall top and top him
And scourge him like a top too."

P. 159, *humguig.* Mr. G. Thorn-Drury has furnished me with the following note on this rare word : " A guig or gig (*ut infra*) is a top ; and the humming-top of my childhood was worked by a string. There is no reason why a whip-top shouldn't be so made that it might be whipped till it hummed." Accordingly to humguig is to whip a top until it spins humming ; and derivatively, to lash lustily. Humguig (perhaps only here) is omitted in the *N.E.D.*

P. 161, *glout.* To stare at ; to make eyes at. Cf. the Prologue, written by Otway, spoken by Mrs. Barry, to Mrs. Behn's *The City Heiress* (Duke's Theatre, 1682) :

" Ye go to Church to glout and ogle there."

Also Orrery's *Guzman* (1679), IV : " Guzman glouts at her, sighs, and folds his arms." The more usual meaning of " to glout " is to frown or to scowl and this is the only explanation given by the *N.E.D.*

P. 162, *long Exercise.* Exercise was the puritanical term for private worship. Cf. 1663, *Flagellum ; or, O. Cromwell* (1672), 21 : " The Family was called together to prayers ; at which Exercise . . . they continued long." Also Mrs. Behn, *The Round-Heads*

(4to, 1682), II, 1: " his Prayers; from which long-winded Exercise I have of late withdrawn my self." And Otway, *The Atheist*, produced in the autumn of 1683, V, 1: " My Lover *Gratian* sighs, and turns up his Eyes like a godly Brother at Exercise."

P. 164, *Nicodemus*. A generic name for a fanatic.

P. 164, *enlightened Weaver*. Cf. *King Henry IV*, Part I, ii, 4, where Falstaff says: " I would I were a weaver; I could sing psalms or anything." Davies, *Dramatic Miscellanies* (1784), I, p. 235, writes: " It is a common expression this day, in Scotland, to say ' psalm-singing weavers.' " The Protestants who came from Flanders and brought with them the woollen manufactory, were much given to singing hymns whilst at their work. In *Epicœne*, III, 2, the Parson has a bad cold, " got . . . with sitting up late, and singing catches with cloth-workers."

P. 164, *Spand-farthing*. Span-farthing, or span-counter: A game in which the object of one player was to throw his farthings (or counters) so close to those of his opponent that the distance could be spanned by the hand. Cf. *Northward Ho*, Dekker and Webster (4to, 1607), I: " You shall find me playing at span-counter " (a pun is intended). Also Swift's *Modern Education* (1720): " His chief solace is to steal down and play at span-farthing with the page or young black-a-moor."

P. 166, *Pilgrim-salve*. " An old ointment made chiefly of swine's grease and isinglass " (Halliwell). Cf. *Rosemary and Bayes* (1672), " Cutaneous pustules for which the pilgrim's salve will be necessary."

P. 167, *Urganda of Wildo streeto*. Urganda is a prominent figure in the Amadis cycle of romance. It should be noticed that the Urganda of the original *Amadis de Gaul* is a true fairy, like the Lady of the Lake; but the Urganda of the additional books of *Amadis*, of *Esplandian*, and *Lisuarte of Greece* is a fell enchantress resembling Lucan's Erichtho, " grata Deis Erebi." So Urganda came to be a generic name for any foul and ugly hag.

Great Wild Street, Lincoln's Inn, led from the Drury Lane end of Great Queen Street to Sardinia Street. In Restoration days and later it was much frequented by prostitutes. Pope (*aetat.* 20) in a letter, 18 March, 1708, to Henry Cromwell says: " In the town it is ten to one, but a young fellow may find his strayed heart again with some Wild Street or Drury Lane damsel."

Duffett's allusion, which would be full of point to the audience, is doubtless to some well-known bawd or bona roba who resided in Wild Street at that time.

P. 167, *Punchanello Alquiffe.* Mr. W. J. Lawrence writes of this passage: " Perhaps the Dorset Garden manager was called Punchanello because he was turning his actors into flying puppets—after the puppet method of the hour." Mr. Lawrence has furnished me with the very pertinent lines from Rochester's prologue to Fane's *Love in the Dark* (4to, 1675):

" Players turned puppets now at your desire
   In their mouths nonsense in their tails a wire,
   They fly through crowds of clouts and showers of fire."

The date of Fane's play is doubtful, and Mr. Lawrence points out that the reference " may be to *Psyche,* a predecessor of *The Tempest.*" I am inclined to think that the allusion is *The Tempest.*

P. 168, *Rearer.* A battledore.

P. 168, *By thy stealers and Pickers.* Cf. *Hamlet,* III, ii, where to Rosencrantz, " My lord, you once did love me," Hamlet replies: " So I do still, by these pickers and stealers." " Pickers and stealers " is a slang term for the hand and fingers. It is derived from the Catechism in the Book of Common Prayer. The catechumen in his duty to his neighbour is taught " to keep his hands from picking and stealing."

P. 168, *thy Top and thy Gigg.* A gigg is a whipping-top. Cf. Brome, *The New Academy* (8vo, 1658), IV, 1: " I broke and did away all my storehouse of tops, gigs, balls, cat and catsticks."

P. 169, *a Baud and Pimp . . . in a Cart.* Bawds and pandars were drawn through the streets in a cart surrounded by the mobile beating basins and performing rough music. See " the Comical Passages of an Italian Bridewell," *The Honest Whore,* II (4to, 1630), V, 2. Mistress Horseleech, the procuress in this play, is said to have been " five times carted."

P. 171, *Pad.* Pad = a path or highway; hence a highwayman, a robber. Cf. foot-pad. *Don Juan* (1823), XI, 11:

" These freeborn sounds proceeded from four pads
   In ambush laid,   . "

P. 173, *Cullies.* Cully was originally slang or rogues' cant for one who is cheated and fleeced. It is a very common term in the seventeenth and eighteenth centuries. Cf. Sedley's *Bellamira* (4to, 1687), I, 1: " I'll . . . shew her I am not such a cully as she takes me for."

KING LEAR

P. 177, *Thomas Boteler.* Thomas Butler, of the family of the Duke of Ormond.

P. 178, *Spanish Fryar.* Dryden's admirable comedy, *The Spanish Fryar,* was published 4to, 1681.

P. 179, *The Persons.* A manuscript hand (*circa* 1697-8) has attached to the British Museum copy of Tate's *King Lear* the following cast: Lear, Powell; Kent, Underhill; Edgar, Verbruggen; Bastard, Husbands; Gentleman-Usher, Bright; Goneril, Mrs. Lee; Regan, Mrs. Bowman; Cordelia, Mrs. Bracegirdle. In the original cast it may be noted that Lady Slingsby (*née* Mary Aldridge) was our first titled actress. Anne Shadwell was the wife of the poet.

I have added to the Persons: An Old Man, Tenant to Gloster: Physician: Arante: Two Ruffians. These are not listed by the original editions.

P. 191, *Clatpole.* This form used by Tate is the reading of the Shakespearean quartos. Tate's *King Lear,* 12mo, 1729, has " Clodpole." Johnson and Dyce in their editions of Shakespeare prefer " clodpoll." Clatpole = blockhead.

P. 195, *Lipsbury Pinfold.* The Shakespearean commentators tell us " It is not yet come to knowledge where that Lipsbury is." Nares says it is a coined name. Pinfold = a boxing ring. Dyce notes that a pinfold is also a pound.

P. 195, *glass-gazing.* A glass-gazer is one who wastes his time in admiring his reflection in a mirror.

P. 197, *Muss-cat.* Musk-cat; a fop drenched with perfumes.

P. 198, *Lurcher.* A swindler, a rogue.

P. 207, *Pudder.* Tate has the reading of the Shakespearean folios, for which some recent editors have substituted " pother."

P. 208, [*Enter* Gloster]. I have inserted this entrance, which the old editions do not mark.

P. 209, [with *Arante*]. The old editions do not mark Arante's entrance and exit in this scene.

P. 211, *Semele*. Semele, beloved of Jupiter, demanded that he should appear to her in his full glory. He did so, but she was overwhelmed by the thunder and blasted by the fiery lightnings. As she expired, the god rescued Bacchus, their unborn son.

P. 212, [*Enter* Edgar *disguis'd*.] I have supplied this entrance of Edgar.

P. 212, *bareheaded*. The quartos 1681 and 1699 misprint " beheaded."

P. 213, *Star-blasting, and Taking*. Star-blasting, coming under the baneful influence of an evil planet.

Taking, being bewitched or enchanted.

P. 214, *Wall-Newt and the Water Newt*. The Wall-Newt is the lizard; the Water Newt the tadpole. The Tate quarto, 1681, prints " Wall-Nut " and " Water-Nut." The Shakespeare folios read " wall-Neut " and " water-Neut," whence this error.

P. 215, *Lym*. A large dog of the spaniel kind. A hunting dog so called from the leam (leash) in which he is held. Tate mistakenly read " Hym."

P. 215, *Tight*. Tyke. Tate read " Hight." About much of Edgar's mad language he does not seem to have been very clear.

P. 215, *knits the Elflock*. The elflock was a tangled lock of hair fantastically supposed to have been dishevelled by Queen Mab. It was unlucky to comb it straight. Cf. *Romeo and Juliet*, I, 4, 89:

" This is that very Mab,
That plats the manes of horses in the night;
And bakes the elf-locks in foul sluttish hairs,
Which once untangled much misfortune bodes."

P. 216, *Stagirite*. Philosopher. Aristotle the Stagirite was born at Stageira, a sea-port in the district of Chalcidice.

P. 227, *rank Femiter*. Tate follows the Shakespearean quartos which read " Femiter." The more usual form is Fumiter. There are five species of Fumitories in England, all of them weeds which infest cultivated grounds and hedge-rows.

P. 227, *Burdocks*. The burdock is a coarse weedy plant

common on waste ground. Its prickly flower-head is called a bur, and it has large leaves like those of the dock.

P. 232, *i' th' White*. The white is the mark fixed in the centre of the butts, the archers' aim. Shakespeare has " clout," a word of precisely the same signification.

P. 233, *Fitcher*. Or Fitchew, also fitchet, and fytchock. The pole-cat, which is very lecherous. Hence frequently used for a whore. Cf. *The Scornful Lady*, V, 1, where Loveless senior, after mocking the wanton Abigail, cries : " Farewell, fytchock."

P. 236, *Costard or my Ballow*. A costard is a large kind of apple; hence, slang, the head.

Ballow is defined by Grose (*Provincial Glossary*) as a North-country word for a pole.

P. 236, *vor your Voines*. Voines = foins, pushes or thrusts with a sword.

P. 254, *Tangier*. Tangier, the dowry of Catharine of Braganza, was first given up to the English fleet by the Portuguese, 30 January, 1662; and Lord Peterborough was then left governor, with a garrison. The fortress and harbour were improved at great expense. At length the House of Commons became disinclined to support an army there, and in 1683 the king sent Lord Dartmouth to bring home the troops and destroy the works. Hereupon the importance of the position vanished, and it fell into the hands of the Moors. Many views of Tangier during the English occupation were taken and engraved by Hollar.